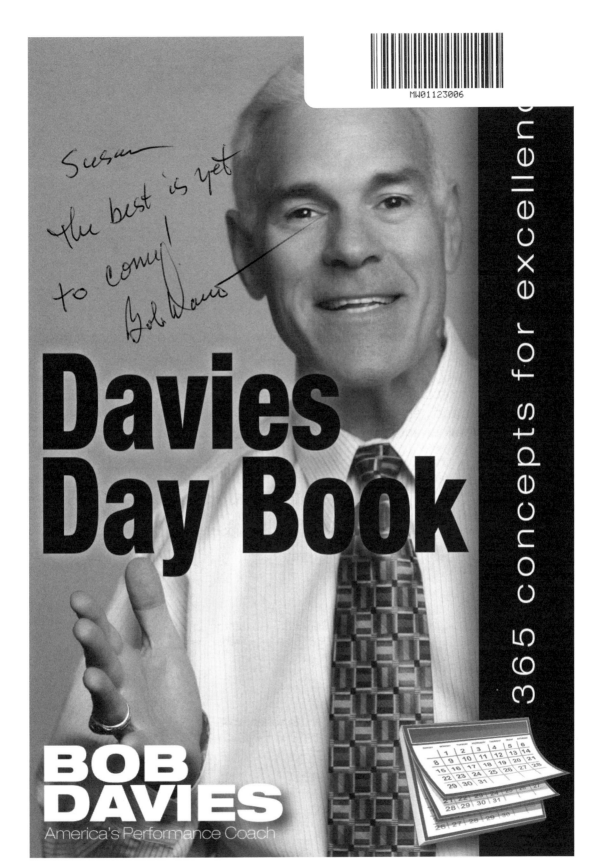

Susan
the best is yet
to come!
Bob Davies

Davies Day Book

365 concepts for excellence

BOB
DAVIES
America's Performance Coach

Motivated Publishing
STUDIOS

Davies Day Book

By: Bob Davies

Published by: Bob Davies

www.bobdavies.com

Email: info@bobdavies.com

ISBN: 978-0-9664666-1-4 (softcover)
ISBN: 978-0-9664666-2-1 (hardcover)

Printed in the USA

First Edition, October 2014
[Ed - Dec-12-14 POD]
[Ed - Jun-25-15 7x10 format]

Interior layout by: MPS
Cover design by: MPS
Project Management by: Rod Schulhauser

Table of Contents

Preface

First Things First

Disclaimer: You are participating with this food plan voluntarily and you assume the risks and rewards. You acknowledge that it is recommended that you show this food plan to your physician to ensure that it doesn't negatively interact with any medications you may be taking.

Finding the Range:

Give yourself 100 pounds for your first 5 feet of height. For each inch taller men add 7 pounds per inch of height and women add 5 pounds. For a 5'10 man the normal range would be in the 170s. Don't worry about how you respond to that number. It's just a reference.

What you'll need:

1. A digital weight scale.
2. A digital food scale
3. A method of finding your body fat % and BMI—An Omron. (Google this and you can find an inexpensive Omron on-line.)
4. Buy your food. Women have 4 ounces of protein, everything else is the same.

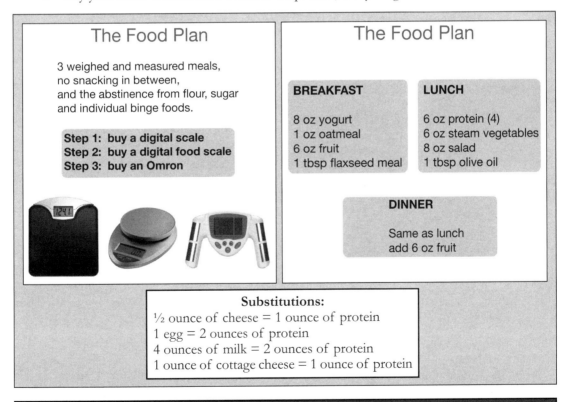

The Food Plan

3 weighed and measured meals,
no snacking in between,
and the abstinence from flour, sugar
and individual binge foods.

Step 1: buy a digital scale
Step 2: buy a digital food scale
Step 3: buy an Omron

The Food Plan

BREAKFAST

8 oz yogurt
1 oz oatmeal
6 oz fruit
1 tbsp flaxseed meal

LUNCH

6 oz protein (4)
6 oz steam vegetables
8 oz salad
1 tbsp olive oil

DINNER

Same as lunch
add 6 oz fruit

Substitutions:
½ ounce of cheese = 1 ounce of protein
1 egg = 2 ounces of protein
4 ounces of milk = 2 ounces of protein
1 ounce of cottage cheese = 1 ounce of protein

Reminder:
This is a commitment to excellence and a self-development program. The food plan is simply one of the tools that we use in our journey to be our best possible selves. You can participate with this program and not be on the food plan. The only prerequisite for participation is a desire to improve and learn.

Introduction

Welcome to our program of excellence. In a short period of time you will experience increased happiness and well-being. Aristotle claimed that happiness was the result of an active life governed by reason. Steven Covey said, "I am not the product of my circumstances. I am the product of my decisions." I say, "You have far more capacity to create the circumstances and events in your life than you are aware of. Your thinking creates your reality."

This is a book for constant improvement. This is a book for you, the reader, who is inspired to be the best version of you that you can be. This book is a tool and a part of a curriculum for living. It is designed to be a part of your routine. It's a routine that makes your lifestyle an asset, not a liability.

This first began as a support tool for my weight management program. However, with the discovery of TOFI, thin on the outside, fat on the inside, it became important for everyone to be paying attention to their physiology, their nutrition, their emotions, their feelings and thoughts regardless of outward appearances. So this goes far beyond a weight management program. This is about self-mastery.

The tools of the program are as follows:

1. Read one page, one concept every day.
2. Meditate 5-10 minutes every day.
3. Follow the food plan every day.
4. Attend the support and reinforcement live teleconference calls.

This is our program. This is your program. It is designed to take into account the leading concepts of how humans learn, constant short reinforcement over a long period of time. Every day of every year you will experience the same concept for that day. If you are using the food plan you will most likely be at your normal weight range within three months and then the journey will continue with the ongoing personal development to keep what you have, excellence of mind, spirit and body.

You will be amazed almost immediately. You will know a new freedom and a new happiness. You will comprehend the word serenity and you will see how your experience can benefit others. Unsupportive feelings will disappear. Your whole attitude on life will change. You will intuitively have the wisdom to handle situations that used to perplex you.

This is your program. It is designed to be repeated one day at a time, one week at a time and one year at a time. If you are participating with health as a goal then you will most likely reach your natural weight range within three months. Then the journey is ongoing personal development to keep what you have, excellence of mind, spirit and body.

You will start refreshed every year with each day bringing you the same concept that you experienced a year ago for that day but you will have "new eyes." That's how it will be every day, every year.

I welcome you to the journey. Others will see what you have and want it for themselves. They will join you. They will start with you on the day they join. You don't need to read the previous days regardless of when you personally join. You don't need to read ahead. Just read the current day, every day. Don't dwell on any particular day's concept. If you get confused you can bring it up on the conference call. You will experience great joy by allowing your exposure to these concepts to be seeded over time.

I'm excited about participating on this journey with you. Congratulations on caring enough to take action.

KOKO, keep on keeping on.

Bob Davies

JANUARY

Davies
Day Book

365 concepts for excellence

January 1

New Year's Resolutions—Why Bother?

NEW YEAR'S RESOLUTIONS

1. lose weight
2. exercise
3. drink more water
4. quit smoking
5. earlier to bed
6. drink less
7. pay off credit cards
8. phone mom
9. remember birthdays
10. save money

Only 45% of Americans bother to make New Year's Resolutions. More than half of us say why bother, I never keep them and I'll just feel guilty and like a failure anyway. For those who do losing weight and getting organized are the top two. Here are a few suggestions to help you have this year's resolutions stick.

Answer the question, "why bother." Why do you want to achieve these goals? What are the benefits for you after you have accomplished your goals? What is the pain if you don't? Make a list of the benefits you will have from your accomplishments and the worst that can happen if you don't? Now make a choice.

Challenge:

Identify the why bother to reach your goals. Make a list of the benefits you will have from the accomplishments.

Tapping in Meditation:

I am a spiritual and mental magnet attracting to myself all things which are good, bless and prosper me. I am healthy and prosperous. My purpose today is to be in action towards reaching my goals.

Journal Notes:

Day/Year	
Day/Year	
Day/Year	
Day/Year	
Day/Year	

January 2

Turn New Year's Resolutions into Reality—NIT-WIT

First, identify what you want, what you will need to do to have what you want and what you will need to do this week.

Next, before you commit, identify what the "NOT IF IT TAKES" (NIT) criteria. What are you not willing to do to reach your goals? Be clear about this. I'm willing to commit to reaching my goals by doing the activities necessary but not if it takes eliminating flour and sugar completely, or not if it takes working out on the weekends, or not if it takes prospecting in the evenings etc. Now you are in a position to make specific commitments for this week and to be held accountable to accomplish them.

The other approach is to have a WHATEVER IT TAKES (WIT) commitment. Someone who doesn't differentiate between the two is considered to be a NIT-WIT!

Do this without judgment. Make careful weekly commitments and have someone else hold you accountable to do what you say you will do.

Challenge:
Carefully negotiate what you will commit to do and then execute. It's only seven days!

Tapping in Meditation:
I take great pride in taking action as I reach my goals. I take action and I do reach my goals. My purpose today is to _____.

Journal Notes:

Day/Year	
Day/Year	
Day/Year	
Day/Year	
Day/Year	

January 3
How to Make Commitments—4 Phase Strategy

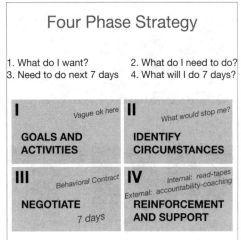

Four Phase Strategy

1. What do I want?
2. What do I need to do?
3. Need to do next 7 days
4. What will I do 7 days?

I — *Vague ok here*

GOALS AND ACTIVITIES

II — *What would stop me?*

IDENTIFY CIRCUMSTANCES

III — *Behavioral Contract*

NEGOTIATE — *7 days*

IV — *Internal: read-tapes* *External: accountability-coaching*

REINFORCEMENT AND SUPPORT

Start by asking these 4 questions; what am I building, what do I need to do to have what I want, what do I need to do this week and what will I do this week?

What are you building, why bother, how much is enough? Once you are clear then you need to go from being vague and general into being specific. What are the activities that you will need to do to reach your goals? What are the activities you will need to execute over the next seven days? Since our focus is a calendar week, what are the actions you need to complete by this Sunday?

Now for the actual commitment. What will you do by the end of this week? Before you make this commitment, make sure that you carefully consider your circumstances; your time concerns, your preferences, likes and dislikes. Once you make your commitment then you agree that the option of not executing does not exist, so be very careful.

Finally, add accountability to each commitment with a penalty for non-performance.

Challenge:
Make a list of what actions you will take this week and ask someone else to hold you accountable. (Use behavioral contracting on www.bobdaviescoaching.com)

Tapping in Meditation:
When I make a commitment I do what I said I will do. I am careful with what I say I will do. My purpose today is to make a commitment and take the action necessary.

Journal Notes:

Day/Year	
Day/Year	
Day/Year	
Day/Year	
Day/Year	

Make a Decision

I was waiting to pick up a friend at the airport. That day I had one of those experiences that changes people's lives. It happened just two feet away from me. I noticed a man, carrying two bags, coming towards me. He stopped next to me to greet his family.

First he dropped his bags and came closer to his younger son, about 6 years old. They gave each other a warm, loving hug. The father then looked in his son's eyes and said, "I missed you so much, it's good to see you son." The boy smiled and said "me too, Dad."

The man then walked over to his older son, about 9 years old. "Oh, you are quite the young man, I love you very much," and cupped his face. They had a tender hug as well.

Afterwards the father said, "Hi baby girl" to his baby daughter. She was squiring excitedly in her mother's arm and watching her father nonstop. The man gently took his daughter, quickly kissed her face all over and then held her close to his chest. The little girl laid her head on his shoulder in pure joy.

After several moments the man looked at his wife and said, "I've saved the best for last" and embraced her with the most passionate kiss. They stared at each other beaming with smiles. They reminded me of newlyweds.

Suddenly, I heard myself asking, "Wow, how long have you been married?" "Been together 14 years and married for 12 of those" he said. I couldn't help to ask, "How long have you been away?" He replied with a joyous smile, "Two whole days!"

I was stunned. I had imagined that he must have been gone for several weeks. I could only say, "I hope my marriage is still that passionate after 12 years."

The man looked straight into my eyes and told me something that changed my life. "Don't hope, friend, decide!"

Challenge:
Make a decision that your New Year's Resolutions will stick. Take the actions.

Tapping in Meditation:
My purpose today is to be surrounded by love. Divine love surrounds me, enfolds, me and enwraps me and I move forward in peace.

Journal Notes:

Day/Year	
Day/Year	
Day/Year	
Day/Year	

January 5

Be Precise with Precision Probing

As a society we have very sloppy communication. When it comes to operating our nervous system, staying focused and remaining in action we need to be very specific. Here are a series of questions that will be helpful not only to you in your planning for your weekly commitments, but also to the person or program holding you accountable.

Precision probing is a way of asking questions. It's easy. Use this format: _____ specifically.

- Who specifically?
- What specifically?
- When specifically?
- Where specifically?
- How much specifically?

For comparisons, more, better, less, improve, use compared to what?

Challenge the universal qualifiers, All, Every, Never.

I commit to working out this week. When specifically will you work out? How long specifically? Everyday?

I will make more prospecting calls this week. More, compared to what? How many specifically? When specifically?

Challenge:
Memorize precision probing and make it a part of your weekly planning.

Tapping in Meditation:
I have clarity, joy and excitement in my life at all times. I am joyous, well prepared and happy at all times. My purpose today is to impact people with the clarity of my specific communication, and I do positively impact people.

Journal Notes:

Day/Year	
Day/Year	
Day/Year	
Day/Year	
Day/Year	

January 6

Be Realistic. Don't Go From Zero to Hero.

Many of my one on one coaching conversations have started like this; "I'm going to call all of the people in my Verizon data base to set an appointment for their 401K roll-overs.

There are two things that immediately catch my attention. First, the universal qualifier of ALL. Is that what this person really means? This commitment is for a seven day time frame. What if they have over 1000 in their database? So I'll test for reality. How many did you call last week? The usual answer is ZERO! How about the week before that? Same answer. Maybe I'll suggest a target such as calling 50 Verizon employees this week. Would that be ok?

If they say yes they were not at stake about calling all of their clients and it wasn't a realistic commitment.

Challenge:
Make sure you are testing for reality in the commitments that you make or if you're working with another person test for reality before accepting a commitment.

Tapping in Meditation:
My purpose today is to be committed. I make a plan and I do it because I said I would. I live my life as my commitments. I do what I said I would do on time or before. I make a plan and I do it because I said I would.

Journal Notes:

Day/Year	
Day/Year	
Day/Year	
Day/Year	
Day/Year	

January 7

Use the 6 Ps

There is an old navy phrase referred to as the 6 Ps. Precise Previous Planning Prevents Poor Performance.

I love the military. Although I never had the privilege to serve my background as an athlete and college football coach, plus my being a skydiver many times brings forth the question were you in the military?

No I wasn't but I certainly appreciate their practice of precise planning, precise measurement and accountability. This is one of the cornerstones of our program that will result in health, business and personal excellence.

Challenge:

Every Sunday make a precise plan for what you want to accomplish next week. Start by evaluating last week, then commit for the next seven days.

Tapping in Meditation:

My purpose today is to take great pride and I am precisely prepared. I am consistently a top performer. I am persistent. I am a self-starter. I am highly motivated.

Journal Notes:

Day/Year	
Day/Year	
Day/Year	
Day/Year	
Day/Year	

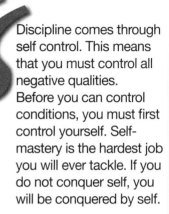

January 8

What I can Control—I Must Control

I can control my lifestyle. I can control my preparation. I can control my measurement and tracking. I can control my attitude. I can control my effort. What I can control, I must control.

Challenge:

Take control of what I can control, my attitude, my lifestyle, my preparation and my effort.

Tapping in Meditation:

My purpose today is to be safe and sound and I am. Everything works together for me today and I move forward in peace. Because I am well prepared I stay on purpose the entire day.

> Discipline comes through self control. This means that you must control all negative qualities. Before you can control conditions, you must first control yourself. Self-mastery is the hardest job you will ever tackle. If you do not conquer self, you will be conquered by self.
>
> **—Napolean Hill** (Think and Grow Rich)

Journal Notes:

Day/Year	
Day/Year	
Day/Year	
Day/Year	
Day/Year	

January 9

Definition of Elite Performance

Years ago I was speaking for Re/Max of Canada who at the time was the countries number 1 real estate company. They paraded across the stage their number one producer, a gentleman who did 16 million when the average was 1 million.

That is not why I would have recognized and awarded that person. Comparing people is not relevant. No two people have the same set of circumstances, obstacles or challenges. To say he is the top producer compared to the average is meaningless. What about the part time producer, the single parent with two school children, who said she would do 3 million and she did 3 million?

I would have brought her up on stage with the same amount of recognition because what I'm recognizing is one of our 4 core principles, "I do what I say I will do."

The 16 million dollar producer had a higher commitment level then the 3 million dollar producer. However, here is what they had in common. Regardless of how high or how low your commitment level is, I would consider you an elite performance if you do what you said you would do and had reasonable results from your efforts.

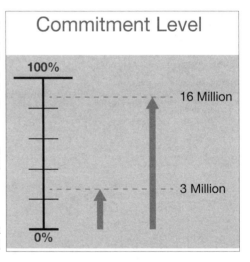

That's my definition of elite performance. Can you live with that? Be careful about what you commit to and make sure that you do what you said you would do.

Challenge:
Make a careful commitment today and for this week and make sure that you do what you said you would do.

Tapping in Meditation:
My purpose today is that I do what I say I will do on time or before. I take great joy in honoring my word.

Journal Notes:

Day/Year	
Day/Year	
Day/Year	
Day/Year	
Day/Year	

January 10

Minimum Level Objectives and Stretch Targets.

There is a traditional management myth that states if you shoot for the moon and fall short then you are better off than if you shot lower and fall short. Absolute and utter nonsense. Look at what is accepted and even expected here, falling short. Shoot for the minimum level that you give your word you will do and falling short doesn't exist.

No, this doesn't limit you or have you play small. It has you play realistically. You still have your stretch targets, the objective that you are striving for, but you are being held accountable to achieve the minimum level you have committed to and falling short of that level does not exist.

You can't predict the circumstances, changing priorities or obstacles that will surprise you today and this week. You will be glad that you differentiated a minimum level objective so you can handle everything and still do what you said you would do.

Challenge:
Hold yourself back a bit to a more realistic commitment. The key is to have small successes over time.

Tapping in Meditation:
My purpose today is to touch hearts by my doing. It's not the things I get but the hearts I touch that will determine my success in life.

Journal Notes:

Day/Year	
Day/Year	
Day/Year	
Day/Year	
Day/Year	

January 11

The 14 Principles of Life by Buddha

1. The greatest enemy of a human is himself.
2. The greatest human failing is arrogance.
3. The greatest human stupidity is being untruthful.
4. The greatest human sadness is the feeling of jealousy.
5. The greatest mistake of a man is not to be true to the best one knows.
6. The greatest human sin is being untruthful to himself and others.
7. The most piteous human characteristic is feeling inferior.
8. The most commendable human characteristic is determination.
9. The greatest destroyer of a human is desperation.
10. The greatest possession of a human is good health.
11. The greatest debt for a human is the debt of his moral duty to others.
12. The greatest gift a human can give to himself and others is tolerance and forgiveness.
13. The greatest human weaknesses are lamentation and lack of wisdom.
14. The greatest source of serenity and peace is the love for giving and helping.

Challenge:

Neither believe nor disbelieve, verify! Which of these 14 principles speaks to you? Live that one in particular just for today.

Tapping in Meditation:

My purpose today is to be peace and love. I am peace and love. I give freely to others.

Journal Notes:

Day/Year	
Day/Year	
Day/Year	
Day/Year	
Day/Year	

January 12

Avoid Pain and Seek Comfort—Learned Helplessness

Everyone shares the same basic genetic coding. Our DNA has not changed over the last 100,000 years. All of us are motivated by this principle, "Avoid Pain and Seek Comfort."

This is not an option. This is an instinct. This instinct does not require your awareness, your understanding or your willingness to comply. It is an instinct that mandates compliance.

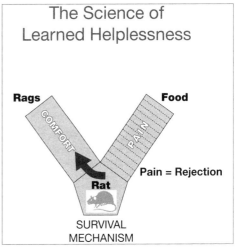

Scientists put a rat in a v-shaped structure. They placed food at the end of the alley way to the right and rags at the end of the left. When they placed a hungry rat at the base it immediately ran to the right to get the food. This demonstrated that the rat was capable of and willing to do what it needed to do to reach its goal.

Next they placed a metal grid on the floor to the right and added a shock to the grid. When they placed the rat back into the box the rat once again started to go over the right alley way to reach the food. However, it received a tremendous shock and instinctively ran away to the left and the comfort of the rags.

A rich memory was formed. On the following trial the metal grid was left on the floor but the shock was removed. Upon placing the rat in the structure it immediately ran to the left. The memory of the strong shock was so deeply embedded on one trial that they rat would not go to the right over that grid again. It didn't matter that the threat was removed. When reality is in conflict with perception, perception will always win. The truth is not relevant. This is called learned helplessness.

Challenge:
Where do you have "learned helplessness?" Where do you believe that you can't do something and you hold that as true? Challenge the lies you tell yourself.

Tapping in Meditation:
My purpose today is to be of service to others and move boldly forward though my perception of fears and I do.

Journal Notes:

Day/Year	
Day/Year	
Day/Year	
Day/Year	
Day/Year	

January 13
Instincts Trump Intentions—Behavioral Contracting

Promise:
> I will go to the gym four times this week.

Penalty for Non Performance:
> I will anonymously donate $100 to the opposite political party of my choice, if Democrat give to the Republican party and vice versa.

Inspect and Verify:
> I can produce the debited amount in my bank statements.

Imagine that I puff air into your eyes. What will your eye lids do? They will blink. Now this time I want you to intend not to blink. You know the air puff is coming so don't blink. I puff the air into your eyes and what do they do? That's right, they blink. Instincts trump intentions. This genetically coded trait saves lives. The non-conscious mind is 400 times faster than the conscious. Instincts bypass the outer cortex and do not require our conscious mind (slow) to function. The instinct that is most prevailing in humans is the following"

"All human performance is the avoidance of the highest level of perceived pain and the seeking of comfort."

This does not require your compliance or awareness. You can't fight this with willpower. You can only tap into it. You need to make sure that you manipulate this to work for you.

Here's how, use a behavioral contract. A behavioral contract is a specific declaration (what you commit to do) plus accountability with someone else holding you accountable to do what you say you will do.

The accountability portion is the leveraging of pain. Agree to a painful consequence if you don't do what you commit to do. Make it a painful consequence like a fine or something else very unpleasant. Now your brain will continue to do what it instinctively is genetically coded to do; recognize the highest level of perceived pain and compel your avoidance. How do you avoid the pain of a $100 penalty if you don't go to the gym 4 times this week? By going to the gym 4 times!

Challenge:
You are almost midway through the first month of the year. What is one small activity that you can do this week and you know that you would not ordinarily do? Put that into a behavioral contract. Specifically state the action you will do by this Sunday and then place a painful penalty if you don't do it. Have someone else check in with you at the end of the week to either enforce the penalty or verify that you did what you said you would do.

Tapping in Meditation:
My purpose today is to find the joy and share it with others. Live fully and be my word.

Journal Notes:

Day/Year	
Day/Year	
Day/Year	
Day/Year	
Day/Year	

January 14

My Mini Bar Story and Behavioral Contracting

It was back in the 1980s. I had left coaching college football and was out on my own as a motivational speaker. I was travelling from Los Angeles to Newark for a speaking engagement. All I had to eat is what they served me on the plane, a small box of raisins and a small bagel. They were so small that I thought people would think I was exaggerating so I kept them and took this picture.

When I finally arrived to my hotel I was starving. The highest level of perceived pain was my hunger. Remember, all human performance is the avoidance of pain and the seeking of comfort. Hence my full attention went to the solution of my pain, the mini bar.

I went to the mini bar and started to binge. I ate the entire bag of cookies, two bags of potato chips, a complete jar of peanuts, seven individual candy bars, a box of Cracker Jacks, and a square of marsh mellows and Rice Crispies. I ate everything in the mini bar and then I had a Diet Coke! I just ate over 5,000 calories. I just binged!

Then I had a moment of surrender. I said I was a fraud. I was unsuccessful, I was overweight, I wasn't in a relationship yet I was still teaching success principles, I was a fraud. I realized that as a football coach I had taught the athletes at Cal State Fullerton how to be their best and go beyond their own self-imposed limitations, but I hadn't yet learned to apply this to myself. I needed to do more research.

I completed this research and on my next trip I had a different dynamic. I told 5 people that if I went into the mini bar I would give them each $250. That's $1,250 total.

On my next trip again after a long flight I go into my hotel room and human instincts take hold again. I am starving. My attention goes to solve the highest level of pain, the hunger. As I walk over to the mini bar my brain continues to do what it is designed to do, make sure I am avoiding the highest level of perceived pain, the $1,250 and I step away from the mini bar. It was easy. I went from believing that I couldn't do something to having it be a non-issue. I tapped into the human instinct of avoiding the highest level of perceived pain and it was EASY!

Challenge:
What do you believe that you can't do? Don't buy it. Use a behavioral contract to take one small action towards the accomplishment of your goal.

Tapping in Meditation:
My purpose today is to do violence to my limiting beliefs and I do.

Journal Notes:

Day/Year	
Day/Year	
Day/Year	
Day/Year	

January 15

Surrender

The
Power
of
Surrender

I thought this was a myth until I read it in a scientific journal, "How do they catch monkeys in Africa?" There is a story that says in Africa (and India), the natives use a technique to catch monkeys. They hollow out one end of a coconut and they put peanuts in there (I've also heard sugar, bananas... but it's the same concept). The monkey puts his hand in the coconut and when he makes a fist to grab the peanuts, he's trapped. The natives will pull a string attached to the other end of the coconut and capture the monkey.

Motivational speakers use this story all the time to inspire people to "let go" of their old perceptions—since in truth, the monkey was never trapped. All he had to do was let go of the peanuts.

When I binged at the mini bar I have a moment of surrender. This was the first time that I didn't go victim and blame other people for my problems.

Challenge:

Where do you need to surrender? Where do you need to let go of old beliefs and attachments? Where are you harboring resentments, anger? Who do you need to forgive?

Tapping in Meditation:

My purpose today is to be peaceful and surrender to the infinite wisdom of the universe. I am my best when I let go of attachments to dysfunctional beliefs and behaviors and I do. I am peaceful.

Journal Notes:

Day/Year	
Day/Year	
Day/Year	
Day/Year	
Day/Year	

January 16

Limited Perception

Look at the nearest wall. Albert Einstein says that there is more space then there is matter in that wall or in anything that we perceive as being solid. All matter is simply made up of protons, neutrons and electrons in constant circulation around a nucleus. This rotation is at such a speed that humans with our limited perception see it and touch it as a solid.

You look at the head of a pin and see it as clear and empty. You believe what your senses tell you that there is nothing on the head of the pin. You would live your life as if that is true. However, when scientists magnify the head of a pin thousands of times beyond the limits of human perception they see the true reality. Magnified they see a human hair, blood cells, and the most common cold virus the Rhinovirus.

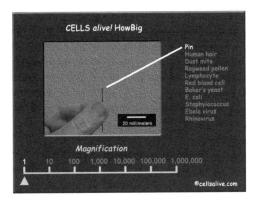
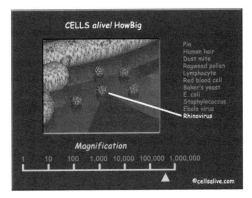

Since humans have such limited perceptual ability (dogs can hear sounds that we can't, plus their sense of smell is so much greater than humans) human genetic coding has taken our narrow bandwidth of perception and defaulted it. You don't see opportunities to take actions to reach you goals. Instead human natures' default is to see your threats and avoid them. You need to counter this and you do that with the use of a behavioral contract. State a specific commitment plus a penalty if you don't perform. Now human nature defaults your perception to seeing the opportunity to avoid your biggest threat, the penalty, and you do so by taking the action.

Challenge:
Be a student of high performance. Be committed to learning. Study the material on my website, www.bobdavies.com.

Tapping in Meditation:
My purpose today is to learn and practice self-mastery so I can be of service to others. The heart that gives—gathers.

Journal Notes:

Day/Year	
Day/Year	
Day/Year	
Day/Year	
Day/Year	

January 17

The Lesson of the Squares—What Are You In Reference To?

This is one of my favorite illusions:

Is Square A darker than Square B? 100% of the people you ask will say yes and they will believe with certainty that they are correct. That's because their senses are limited and unreliable. The problem is what the viewer is in reference to. Square A is in reference to the white squares and space. Square B is referenced to the dark squares giving it a light appearance. The reality is that they are both the same shade. You can prove it to yourself (inspect and verify) by copying this and cutting the B square out. Place it on top of the original and then move it to the top of square A. As you change what you're in reference to, (go from black squares to white squares and space) it looks like square B is changing colors in front of your eyes.

Our brain is encased in a skull. We do not have physical contact with the outside world. Our reality is a flawed interpretation of our five senses. When you change what you are in reference to you also change your perception.

Challenge:

Notice how a small change in what you pay attention to changes your outcome. Do you pay attention to or, are you in reference to reasons why you can't do something or are you in reference to opportunities to get it done. You can control this.

Tapping in Meditation:

My purpose today is to live life fully by changing what I pay attention to.

Journal Notes:

Day/Year	
Day/Year	
Day/Year	
Day/Year	
Day/Year	

January 18

Higher Power—Learn How To Tap In

Tune in your favorite radio station. What happen to all of the other frequencies? Did they disappear? No, they are still there it's just that you haven't tuned into their frequency. Their energy vibrations still exist but you are not tapped in.

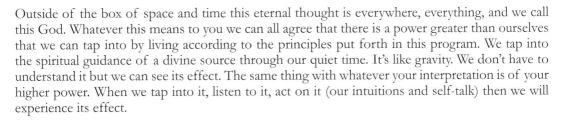

The Inner Universe—Earth 67,000 miles per hour orbits the sun. The Milky Way Galaxy is hurling around it's center at 500,000 miles per hour. The Power of the cosmos is inside all of us…Let's talk about tapping into it!

All material things, the universe, the world, even our bodies are simply eternal thought and information expressed in time and space. The more physicists and astronomers reduce matter the more it becomes a formula of math which is information and thought.

Outside of the box of space and time this eternal thought is everywhere, everything, and we call this God. Whatever this means to you we can all agree that there is a power greater than ourselves that we can tap into by living according to the principles put forth in this program. We tap into the spiritual guidance of a divine source through our quiet time. It's like gravity. We don't have to understand it but we can see its effect. The same thing with whatever your interpretation is of your higher power. When we tap into it, listen to it, act on it (our intuitions and self-talk) then we will experience its effect.

In happy moments praise the universal higher power. In difficult moments, see this divine energy. In quiet moments worship, listen and tap into this energy. In painful moments trust this higher power.

Challenge:
Take 5-10 minutes every day and quite the mind. Meditate to align yourself with your higher power, however you define it.

Tapping in Meditation:
My purpose today is to become one with the infinite riches of the universe. Divine love surrounds me and I move forward in peace.

Journal Notes:

Day/Year	
Day/Year	
Day/Year	
Day/Year	
Day/Year	

January 19

The Lesson of Snake Eggs—Expectations

In my live programs I'll ask the audience if anyone is afraid of rattle snakes. I'll ask one of the people who raise their hands to come up on stage. "Oh, it's perfectly safe. I don't have rattle snakes, but I do have rattle snake eggs. You can get them on the internet. Don't worry, it's safe."

I'm holding an envelope with a picture of a rattle snake. I ask them to take the envelope and open it. Again, I emphasize that it's perfectly safe. When they open the envelope there is a popping sound and movement and I've had people scream, drop the envelope and run off stage.

I show them what they just responded to, a wire, a rubber band and a washer. What were they in reference to? The anticipated life threatening danger from a rattle snake. They anticipated danger. They expected danger. All they needed was the slightest bit of supporting evidence for them to react as if their life was threatened. They were "predisposed" to see danger.

Next I changed what they were in reference to by showing them the wire, rubber band and washer. With a change in reference, how they were observing this, what they were paying attention to, their reaction changed as well.

Challenge:

If you don't feel like doing what you need to be doing, change your thinking. Change your approach.

Tapping in Meditation:

My purpose today is to be of service to others by being focused and carefully selecting what I allow myself to pay attention to.

Journal Notes:

Day/Year	
Day/Year	
Day/Year	
Day/Year	
Day/Year	

January 20

Expectations Versus Possibilities

I was coaching a financial advisor who had organized a group of strategic partners who were non-compete and served the same marketplace. My client referred many people to the attorneys and accountants and he expected to get referrals back from them which had not happened. He was very upset and felt he was being taken advantage of until we had this discussion.

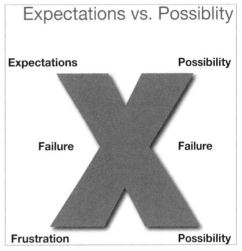

When you expect something to happen, like receive partner referrals, and it doesn't happen (failure), the only way to perceive and react to it is as a failure, it's unfair and become angry.

Try this subtle shift. It is possible that my strategic alliance partners' will send me referrals. When they don't do that (failure) what is left is that it is still possible. Think about this for a while. Let it sink in.

Challenge:
Practice having a flexible way of perceiving things. It's the small subtle shifts in perception that make a major difference.

Tapping in Meditation:
My purpose today is to take responsibility for how I perceive things. My perceptions are guided by gratitude, love, appreciation and service

Journal Notes:

Day/Year	
Day/Year	
Day/Year	
Day/Year	
Day/Year	

January 21

Stuck—Change Your Approach

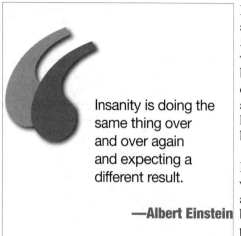

Insanity is doing the same thing over and over again and expecting a different result.

—Albert Einstein

I did an exercise in a live training program that brought about some very interesting insights. There were about 50 people in the room plus 3 judges. The objective was to move from one side of the room to the other but you could not duplicate the way that anyone else covered this distance. If someone simply walked across you couldn't do that but you could put your hand on top of your head and walk across, that would be different.

Everyone was being creative and successfully finding ways to move across the room, approved by the judges as not duplicating someone else until #31. The person before this woman was about to go used what she was planning on doing to cross the room. Hand on top of the head and spinning all the way to the other side.

This woman was stuck. She was paralyzed. For several minutes despite the coaxing and cheering from the group she could not think of another way to cross the room. Finally it came to her and she modified her design and successfully used a method that had not been used before.

Challenge:

Notice what you focus on today. Are you possibility focused or obstacle focused. Make the choice to shift what you pay attention to. What modifications do you need to use in your thoughts and approaches that may need to be invented in the moment.

Tapping in Meditation:

My purpose today is to help other people. You get by giving. I help myself by helping others. I find a way to be of service to others by the end of today even if that opportunity is not easily seen.

Journal Notes:

Day/Year	
Day/Year	
Day/Year	
Day/Year	
Day/Year	

January 22

Where's The Focus

Imagine you are standing on a 2 foot wide by 20 foot long board that is lying on the ground. There is a $100 bill at the far end. Would you walk across the board and get the money? Of course you would. What are you focusing on? What's the picture in your mind? It's the successful act of walking across the board and picking up the money. Easy peasy!

Now, suppose I take that same board and suspend it between two buildings that are 20 stories high. Would you walk across and pick up the money? The physicists would tell you that gravity is not a factor, the wind is light and variable so the only difference is in your mind. Would you do it? Chances are great that you would not.

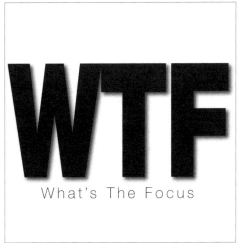

WTF
What's The Focus

Why is that? Because the WTF (What's The Focus) is not on your side. You're not paying attention to the successful outcome. Instead you're paying attention to the undesirable difficulty.

Challenge:
Where in your life do you pay attention to the undesirable difficulty instead of the desired result? Stop doing that and start focusing on the desired outcome. Start today!

Tapping in Meditation:
My purpose today is to live life easily and in alignment with the higher vibrations and energy for good that surrounds me. I am bathed in love and purpose as I stay focused on opportunities all day long.

Journal Notes:

Day/Year	
Day/Year	
Day/Year	
Day/Year	
Day/Year	

January 23

Why Behavioral Contracting—Loss vs Gain

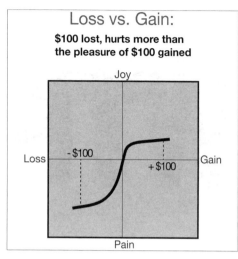

Loss vs. Gain:

$100 lost, hurts more than the pleasure of $100 gained

If you've heard me speak you've heard me say that my program is based on scientific principles and the best practices of elite performers. You've also heard me state that Instincts Trump Intentions. (Jan 13). This means the human body has built in genetic wiring that is common to everyone. This dictates how you think, what you see, how you feel and what you do. This wiring is non-negotiable.

That is actually to your advantage. Since we know that you are genetically coded to avoid the highest level of perceived pain then we can tap into that with the strategy of behavioral contracting where we manufacture a pain with a consequence that is higher than the pain of the activity. Hence, your human instinct compels you to avoid that pain by doing what you said you would do.

One of the reasons that this is so powerful is because everyone is wired for survival. This means safety. You are wired to protect from a loss rather than to seek a gain. You are motivated to keep what you already have as opposed to get something else.

For example, if you don't take a specific action you will need to pay a penalty of $100 to a competitor. In addition to the pain of sending the money to a competitor, on a non-conscious basis you are driven to keep what you already have—the $100.

If I told you that I would give you $100 if you did an action it would not work consistently. Since you don't already have the money there is no pull for you to shift your perception of pain. Lets' say your penalty was one of embarrassment. If you don't take an action you need to go to a crowded area and "bark" at 10 strangers. Do you want to do that? You are motivated to keep what you already have, which is the comfort and lack of embarrassment.

I'll bet that if you who have rear view video in your car that you will never get a car without it. If you don't I'll also bet that you are not seeking to have it. That's how this works!

Challenge:

Practice being uncomfortable every day. Do one thing that you would ordinarily avoid today. Make a deal with someone a place a painful penalty if you don't take the action. Inspect and verify today's concept.

Tapping in Meditation:

My purpose today is to challenge myself to expand my comfort zone and I do.

Journal Notes:

Day/Year	
Day/Year	
Day/Year	
Day/Year	

January 24

What Stops Behavioral Contracting? 1-4

1. Satisfied—don't care. A person with this perspective will stay as far away from this body of information and program as possible.

2. Unrealistic Commitments. You don't go from zero to hero. Take small steps. If the most you've ever earned is $100,000 a year you can't commit to earning a million. Prove me wrong and go ahead and do so but you must make commitments base on previous results. Someone says they commit to working out five times this week. I always ask, how many times did you work out last week? The most common answer, 0. Maybe I'll accept a commitment for 2.

3. Not enforcing the consequences. If a person has money problems don't accept a consequence of $100. Also if you feel sorry for the person and don't enforce the consequence then you are doing a great disservice to that person. If that's the case then there is no shift in pain perception and you will focus on the pain of the activity which will lead to avoidance.

4. Benefits in the consequence. There is a benefit to having a consequence where you will take your office out to lunch and pay for it. There is a benefit in giving your spouse $100 if you don't perform. However, that doesn't mean that it won't be effective as a consequence. Sometimes you just have to have trial and error to see what types of penalties you will respond to best.

Challenge:

You are participating in this to be more effective. Consistency of routine is vital. Keep building the habit of your daily meditation and daily reading.

Tapping in Meditation:

My purpose today is to notice that by being more personally effective it is easier for me to help others. It's not the thing I get but the hearts I touch that determine my success in life. I do touch hearts.

Journal Notes:

Day/Year	
Day/Year	
Day/Year	
Day/Year	
Day/Year	

January 25

What Stops Behavioral Contracting—5-8

5. The consequence is not painful enough. Back in 2013 Kobe Bryant had a run of technical fouls. There was a substantial fine for each technical. He said that he didn't care, he could afford it. He said that it just meant more money for the NBA Cares charity program. However, once he reaches a 16th technical he gets suspended for one game. Now this is painful enough of a fine that it will alter his perception on technical 15. Up until that point it is more painful not to complain then it is to hold back.

6. A commitment that requires someone else to act. Be careful about making a commitment like how many appointments you will set. That requires someone else to accept and agree. Unless you tell me that you can generate enough activity to guarantee a number of appointments then I would be hesitant to accept that type of a commitment.

7. To frequent check ins. You don't want to make behavioral contracting a burden. If someone says they will make x amount of calls a day you don't check in with them every day. It's a once a week check in.

8. Failure. You will not stay with behavioral contracting if you are setting yourself up to fail. The cause of the failures is either commitments that are unrealistic or commitments that you don't really care about. Be careful of what you give your word you will do and do it!

Challenge:

Use behavioral contracting with another person. You are giving them a great service.

Tapping in Meditation:

My purpose today is to train and practice. There's an old warriors' saying: "The more we sweat in training, the less we bleed I battle." I am committed to personal growth and learning.

Journal Notes:

Day/Year	
Day/Year	
Day/Year	
Day/Year	
Day/Year	

January 26

Small Changes—Large Results. The 1.2% Factor.

At 211 degrees water is hot. At 212 degrees it boils. American Airlines in 1987 saved $70,000 by removing one olive from the salads they served in first class.

As study was done comparing the DNA of a chimpanzee and a human being. Researchers found that there was a 1.2% difference between the genetic coding of a chimp and you. Look at the difference in the final outcome of a human and chimp.

The average baseball player hits 250. This is 3 hits every 12 times at bat. He earns about one million.

The superstar hits 333. He earns about 24 million. This is significant. However, how did he get there? Is the superstar significantly better than the average? No, the super star is a little bit better. The super star gets one more hit every 12 times a bat.

Challenge:

Use this program to get yourself to take one small action that you ordinarily would not have taken today. It's the accumulation of these small actions that lead to large results.

Tapping in Meditation:

My purpose today is to notice being uncomfortable and still take one small action that I ordinarily would not take. Enjoy the little things for one day and I may look back and realize they were the big things.

Journal Notes:

Day/Year	
Day/Year	
Day/Year	
Day/Year	
Day/Year	

January 27

Instant vs. Delayed Gratification

The Stanford marshmallow experiment was a series of studies on delayed gratification in the late 1960s and early 1970s led by psychologist Walter Mischel, then a professor at Stanford University. In these studies, a child was offered a choice between one small reward (sometimes a marshmallow, but often a cookie or a pretzel, etc.) provided immediately or two small rewards if he or she waited until the tester returned (after an absence of approximately 15 minutes). In follow-up studies, the researchers found that children who were able to wait longer for the preferred rewards tended to have better life outcomes, as measured by SAT scores, educational attainment, body mass index (BMI) and other life measures.

That's one of the problems with reaching your goals today. If you over eat today you won't gain 5 pounds tomorrow. If you don't make your prospecting calls today you won't have less income tomorrow. However these types of choices over time will produce significant unwanted results. If your goal does not have an instant gratification component then you will need to manufacture instant gratification. You do this with a weekly behavioral contract.

Challenge:

Your ability to pay the price in advance is the true mark of a successful person. Sacrifice in the short term will bring success in the long term. Just for today make a choice for the greater good of your goal rather than what you feel like doing or what is comfortable to do.

Tapping in Meditation:

My purpose today is to do the tougher thing first, and I do.

Journal Notes:

Day/Year	
Day/Year	
Day/Year	
Day/Year	
Day/Year	

January 28

Instant versus Delayed Gratification—My Story

The problem is all physiology. I'm sitting at home and I have a feeling. I think this feeling is hunger. My brain releases dopamine, a neurotransmitter that motivates and focuses me on eating. I grab some flour, Wheat Thins, and as I eat I'm releasing serotonin, a feel good neurotransmitter. I'm actually getting high from these drugs. My thinking is that I can over eat today and tomorrow I won't be fat. This is my genetically coded default observation of instant gratification. It feels good now so don't worry about tomorrow.

This was actually the start of a very significant change in my health. I am a skydiver. At present I have made over 2000 sky dives. My normal weight was in the 220s.
It is vital to be able to match the fall rate of the rest of the people that you are in the air with. At 220 I was too heavy and would go low on the formation. This means that I was not able to match the slower fall rate of the rest of the people in the group. However if I weighed 205 or less then that was not an issue.

It's midweek and I'm about to shift my instant gratification picture. If I continue to eat these Wheat Thins then I'll be heavy and when I go skydiving this Saturday, in just a few days, then I'll go low. This now has my current behavior linked to instant gratification. Seven days is a time period that is short enough for instant gratification to have an effect.

Another option to manufacture instant gratification would be to send a text to my live coach and tell him that if I eat anything else tonight I will pay him $100. I've taken the focus from the instant gratification of the good feeling from overeating to the avoidance of a higher pain, the $100.

Challenge:
Have another person who you can have this type of relationship with. Someone who will not listen to your stories, excuses and drama but who will hold you accountable and impose a penalty if you don't do what you agree to do.

Tapping in Meditation:
My purpose today is to live as integrity. I am kind to other people. I express love. I do what I say I will do.

Journal Notes:

Day/Year	
Day/Year	
Day/Year	
Day/Year	
Day/Year	

January 29

Attention Neurons

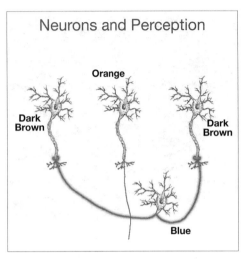

Neurons and Perception

Orange

Dark Brown

Dark Brown

Blue

When something grabs your attention—you spot a friend across the street—the specific neurons governing perception of that region of visual space (orange) become activated. Simultaneously, inhibitory neurons (blue) suppress the nearby brain cells responsible for perceiving surrounding areas (dark brown). Thus, paying attention to one thing makes it harder to notice what is around it.

When you make a commitment to perform an action and you place a painful consequence for non-performance, the attention neurons block out competing perceptions allowing you to focus on the task at hand.

Challenge:

Just for today make a decision on one action you will take no matter what.

Tapping in Meditation:

My purpose today is to practice the shift from what I can get to how can I serve and I do. I serve other people. I respond to people with their needs in mind. I am kind.

Journal Notes:

Day/Year	
Day/Year	
Day/Year	
Day/Year	
Day/Year	

January 30

Systems—Airplane Example

I fly a Bonanza V35B single engine aircraft. I remember the first time I was going to be flying in the clouds by myself. I was terrified. The most common cause of small aircraft accidents is what's called VFR into IMC. Visual Flight Rules, clear weather, to Instrument Meteorological Conditions, clouds. The reason this is so dangerous is because you can't trust your own senses to tell you what position the airplane is in. You can't trust your own senses because the human senses are flawed (see Jan 16-17).

In reference to the clouds I am helpless. So I need a system that has a predictable result. That system is the airplanes instruments. By looking at just one instrument, the attitude indicator, a gyroscope, (rigidity in space) I can tell what the airplane is doing. I must rely on a system.

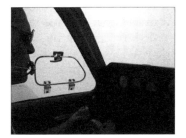  

The system you are participating with is designed to offset the limits of human nature.

Challenge:

Your system is to plan on Sunday for the next seven days. Your system is to make commitments and add accountability and to take 5 to 10 minutes a day and tap into your higher power or the strength for good of the universe. Your system is to read from this book every day. Your system is to be actively engaged in self-development and learning. You system is to live our food plan, to exercise for fitness and to live oriented from service, love and gratitude. How are you doing?

Tapping in Meditation:

My purpose today is to live and execute my plan. It is easy and I am focused. I stay on task doing the most productive activity at all times. I am productive.

Journal Notes:

Day/Year	
Day/Year	
Day/Year	
Day/Year	
Day/Year	

January 31

Concepts of Time—Entropy

What is time? I'm trying to understand how time works. And that's a huge question that has lots of different aspects to it. A lot of them go back to Einstein and space-time and how we measure time using clocks. But the particular aspect of time that is most confusing is the arrow of time: the fact that the past is different from the future. We remember the past but we don't remember the future. There are irreversible processes. There are things that happen, like you turn an egg into an omelette, but you can't turn an omelette into an egg.

The arrow of time is based on ideas that go back to Ludwig Boltzmann, an Austrian physicist in the 1870s. He figured out this thing called entropy. Entropy is just a measure of how disorderly things are. And it tends to grow. That's the second law of thermodynamics: Entropy goes up with time, things become more disorderly. So, if you neatly stack papers on your desk, and you walk away, you're not surprised they turn into a mess. You'd be very surprised if a mess turned into neatly stacked papers. That's entropy and the arrow of time. Entropy goes up as it becomes messier.

A deck of cards starts off with low entropy, everything in place. Keep shuffling the deck and it becomes more disordered. In fact you can shuffle almost in infinity and it will not line up with all the suits and colors together as it was new. Unless that is, you add energy to the system. You would have to physically find all of the aces, all of the kings, etc and put them in their original order. It takes an intervention to stop the impact of nature's tendency towards disorder.

Challenge:

What needs your attention right now? Where in your life are you not satisfied with your current results? What one action can you take today that will make a difference?

Tapping in Meditation:

My purpose today is to make a difference. Today I live with love and gratitude and I make a difference in someone else's life, just for today.

Journal Notes:

Day/Year	
Day/Year	
Day/Year	
Day/Year	
Day/Year	

FEBRUARY

Davies Day Book

365 concepts for excellence

February 1

Concepts on Time—Einstein Says...

Time
is an
Illusion.

—**Albert Einstein**

Einstein's theory of relativity states that time and space are not as constant as everyday life would suggest. He suggested that the only true constant, the speed of light, meant that time can run faster or slower depending on how high you are, and how fast you are traveling. So not everyone has the same perception of time.

Imagine you are standing in line at a grocery store and the person in front of you can't find a coupon. You are very conscious of time and it seems to take forever as this person is holding up the entire line. When you are conscious of time it slows down.

Now imagine that you are watching your favorite movie. It finally ends and you now realize that you were non-conscious of time and it just sped right by.

As you age a change occurs in your brain in an area known as the pineal gland. If you are over 50 years old you will be absolutely amazed that it is already February 1st. If you have teenagers January would have just crawled by. For you it flew by. What caused this is the subtle changes in the pineal gland as you age.

Since it is known that if you are conscious of time it slows down where might that be to your advantage and how do you become conscious of time? How about if you need more time to complete a project? Simply by looking at a clock and focusing on one activity you will become conscious of time and it will literally slow down.

Challenge:
Practice influencing your perception of time. Notice the clock as you start an activity and experience time slowing down allowing you to get more done. When you want time to speed up become non-conscious of time. Read a magazine while exercising and before you know it you'll be done!

Tapping in Meditation:
My purpose today is to be aware of and to honor time. I respect and appreciate being alive. I live fully. I notice and appreciate every moment.

Journal Notes:

Day/Year	
Day/Year	
Day/Year	
Day/Year	
Day/Year	

February 2

Think Feel Act—Thoughts are Real Part I.

Benjamin Libet, a pioneering scientist in the field of human consciousness says that reality is in the mind of the observer. There is scientific evidence that proves that this is true. First, since our brain is encased in a bony skull, we do not have direct contact with the outside world. That means that everything we think, feel and do is an interpretation of our five senses. Our senses are flawed and inaccurate and so is our picture of the world.

Thoughts Are Energy.
They Are REAL
and they
have POWER

The key to realize is that we have the choice to create our own reality. We are not subject to what happens to us. We can be the inventor of our future. Our brain is an incredible organ that takes an electrical impulse and turns it into a chemical discharge. This chemical has a charge and hence we attract to ourselves what our dominating thoughts are. This is referred to as manifestation.

Challenge:

Be the guardian of my thinking, all day today. Notice, do you think positive or negative thoughts. Do you think of ways you can solve your problems or focus on the problems? Since simply by having the thought, you have created the reality you will only allow yourself to have positive thoughts today.

Tapping in Meditation:

My purpose today is to be the change I seek in others. I think only positive loving thoughts about myself and others. When I catch myself having negative thoughts I immediately return to that which is good, blesses and prospers me. I am blessed and prosperous.

Journal Notes:

Day/Year	
Day/Year	
Day/Year	
Day/Year	
Day/Year	

February 3

Thoughts are Real Part II Matthew Nagle

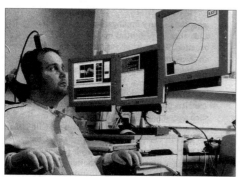

With the aid of electrodes implanted in his brain, a man paralyzed from the neck down was able to perform certain everyday activities—move a computer cursor, open e-mail, turn on a TV set—merely by imaging them.

The patient, whose spinal cord was injured when an attacker stabbed him in the neck, was able to open and close a prosthetic hand, his thoughts translated into action by a custom-built computer.

After implanting electrodes in the brain of Matthew Nagle, the 25 year old stabbing victim, scientists discovered that the neurons associated with moving his arms and hands could still generate electrical signals. This has brought hope to thousands of people with injured spinal cords. It's called BrainGate.

Challenge:

Your thoughts are powerful. Your thoughts are real. Your thoughts matter. Take responsibility for every thought that you have, just for today.

Tapping in Meditation:

My purpose today is to be of service to others. As I keep my thoughts towards being kind, loving and of service to others then my life will work out for the good.

Journal Notes:

Day/Year	
Day/Year	
Day/Year	
Day/Year	
Day/Year	

February 4

The Lesson of the 3 Circles

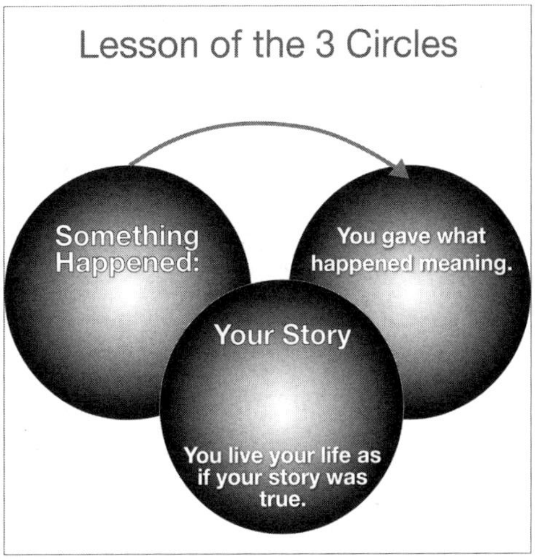

The human brain is designed to take a limited amount of information and fill in the blanks. You make up a story about everything that you encounter. You have to. Your brain is designed to give meaning and interpret everything. Here is the normal way that your brain processes information and events.

Lesson of the 3 Circles

Something Happened:

You gave what happened meaning.

Your Story

You live your life as if your story was true.

Step 1: Something Happens. Your spouse leaves a dirty frying pan on the stove overnight.

Step 2: You interpret it and give it meaning. How rude, he/she doesn't respect me. He/she expects me to clean up after him/her. What am I their slave?

Step 3: You live your life as if your story was true. This includes all of the heartaches and misery that comes from your interpretation.

Since it's all made up anyway why not choose an interpretation that keeps you calm and in a good mood. It's all up to you. There is no inherent meaning in anything that someone else says or does. Life is empty and meaningless. Events are neutral, you give it meaning.

Challenge:

This requires giving up being a victim and taking full responsibility for your responses to situations and events that happen to you. Are you willing to do this? Practice today and notice what difference it makes.

Tapping in Meditation:

My purpose today is to notice the struggle that I am in today will be the strength that I build for tomorrow. I take full responsibility for my mood. I choose to be in a good mood. I am in a good mood all day long.

Journal Notes:

Day/Year	
Day/Year	
Day/Year	
Day/Year	
Day/Year	

February 5

It's all Perceptual Choice—The Professor

At the beginning of an 8:00 am class at the University of Nevada, Las Vegas, (UNLV), the professor cheerfully asked his students how their weekend had been. One young man said that his weekend had not been very good. He'd had his wisdom teeth extracted. The young man then proceeded to ask the professor why he always seemed to be so cheerful. His question reminded the professor of something he read somewhere before: "Every morning when you get up, you have choices about how you want to approach life that day", he said to the young man. "I choose to be cheerful." "Let me give you an example", he continued.

The other 60 students in the class stopped their chatter and began to listen to their conversation.

As soon as the professor arrived he called AAA and asked them to send a tow truck. The secretary in the Provost's office asked him what happened. "This is my lucky day", he replied, smiling. "Your car breaks down and today is your lucky day?" She was puzzled. "What do you mean?"

"I live 17 miles from here", the professor replied. "My car could have broken down anywhere along the freeway. It didn't. Instead, it broke down in the perfect place: off the freeway, within walking distance of here. I am still able to teach my class, and I've been able to arrange for the tow truck to meet me after class. If my car was meant to break down today, it couldn't have been arranged in a more convenient fashion." The secretary's eyes opened wide, and then she smiled. The professor smiled back and headed for class. So ended his story to his students in his economics class at UNLV.

He scanned the 60 faces in the lecture hall. Despite the early hour, no one seemed to be asleep. Somehow, his story had touched them. Or maybe it wasn't the story at all. In fact, it had all started with a student's observation that he was cheerful. A wise man once said:
"Who you are speaks louder to me than anything you can say."

Challenge:

Just for today notice who you are being, all day long. Do something today that your future self will thank you for.

Tapping in Meditation:

My purpose today is to live a life of few regrets. I do what I need to do whether I want to or not. I take the right actions.

Journal Notes:

Day/Year	
Day/Year	
Day/Year	
Day/Year	
Day/Year	

February 6

Do You Make a Difference? The Great Fire and The Little Water

Among the Aztec people of Mexico, it is said that a long time ago there was a great fire in the forests that covered our Earth. People and animals started to run, trying to escape from the fire. Our brother owl, Tecolotl, was running away also when he noticed a small bird hurrying back and forth between the nearest river and the fire. He headed towards this small bird.

He noticed that it was our brother the Quetzal bird, Quetzaltototl, running to the river, picking up small drops of water in his beak, then returning to the fire to throw that tiny bit of water on the flame. Owl approached Quetsal bird and yelled at him: "What are you doing brother? Are you stupid? You are not going to achieve anything by doing this. What are you trying to do? You must run for your life!"

Quetzal bird stopped for a moment and looked at owl, and then answered: "I am doing the best I can with what I have."

It is remembered by our Grandparents that a long time ago the forests that covered our Earth were saved from a great fire by a small Quetzal bird, an owl, and many other animals and people who got together to put out the fire.

Challenge:
What one action just for today can you do that may make a difference in someone else's life? Ever thought of calling a client just to say hi?

Tapping in Meditation:
My purpose today is to make the rest of my day the best of my day.

Journal Notes:

Day/Year	
Day/Year	
Day/Year	
Day/Year	
Day/Year	

February 7

Act as If Part I

The human brain can't tell the difference between what is real and what is vividly imagined. I X V = R. Imagination x vividness = reality. This also is the power of your thoughts being real and having real consequences particularly on a physical level. Over 80% of hospital beds are filled with psychosomatic disorders. Psycho—the mind, somatic—the body. They are real disorders that were created by your thoughts.

Years ago my college roommate and lifetime friend, Tony, decided to retire. He taught me how to use hypnosis to accelerate an athletes' performance. Since I was a college football coach back in the 70s and 80s this gave me an advantage.

Tony was a speaker like me and his niche was using hypnosis to demonstrate the power of the human mind. I also was presenting hypnosis programs but I stopped because I didn't want to compete with Tony. After he retired I decided I would bring those programs back. The last one I did was for the Housemaster Franchise annual convention, 12 years ago.

A client wanted Tony to present his hypnosis program. They had seen him before and loved the program. Since he had retired he referred this client to me. I decided to accept the engagement and present the hypnosis program. However, I hadn't done one of these in 12 years!

Here's what I did. I used the power of my brain to visualize, to study and prepare, to practice. I watched Tony's videos, I watched my own videos, I had a mentor with a state of the art hypnosis induction and I studied his videos. I must have put in about 100 hours of solid studying and rehearsing prior to this program. I was so prepared that both programs that I did for this client came off perfectly! It was terrific. The client was thrilled. I had instincts because of the preparation that I went through. Every time I watched a video my brain responded as if I was physically doing the show myself in real time. When the day came I acted as if I had just presented a hypnosis program and it was fantastic.

Challenge:
What do you fear doing that you might risk the possibility of failure? I challenge you to be as prepared as you can and proceed anyway. You will be proud of yourself.

Tapping in Meditation:
My purpose today is to confront my fear, embrace my fear and take the action anyway. I easily and effortlessly acknowledge my fears and perform anyway.

Journal Notes:

Day/Year	
Day/Year	
Day/Year	
Day/Year	
Day/Year	

February 8

Act as If Part II

The subconscious mind accepts as being true whatever is vividly imagined. A group of men were hypnotized and told that they were great and talented artists. They were given a canvas and commanded to paint their favorite portrait. Check it out:

Look at the quality of these portraits. These men had absolutely no training nor previous talent in painting and drawing. They just acted on the suggestion that they were great and talented artists as if it were true.

During one of my shows I hypnotized an obese woman. I told her she was a great and talented dancer and singer and that when I said the number 3 she would grab the microphone and sing and dance to her favorite song.

On 3 she grabbed the microphone out of my hand and started singing and dancing and working the audience like a pro. You ready for this? She had a fantastic and beautiful voice. When she was done I said to her, "When I touch you on your forehead you'll remember what you've just done." When I touched her she became extremely embarrassed. Her internal dialogue was "I can't sing, I can't dance, I'm not attractive, no one will be interested, etc." All lies!

Challenge:

What lies to you believe about what you are capable of doing?

Tapping in Meditation:

My purpose today is to live the truth about myself. I do violence to my limiting thoughts. I am unstoppable.

Journal Notes:

Day/Year	
Day/Year	
Day/Year	
Day/Year	
Day/Year	

February 9

Alien Conversation

The development of your outer cortex and language is what separates you from other primates. You are capable of being aware of your own awareness, of how you feel and you can distinguish yourself as an individual. You do this with internal dialogue or self-talk. Unfortunately, genetic coding has defaulted your self-talk to be negative. You are wired not to see opportunity but instead to see threats. You are also wired to constantly have this conversation with yourself about what can hurt you and you are driven to constant avoidance.

I refer to this internal dialogue as the Alien Conversation. Remember the move Alien? The astronaut is on the space ship and looks up for his cat and the alien creature grabs him by the face and kills him. This is my metaphor for your internal dialogue.

Go ahead and open your right hand. Take a look at it. This represents your predisposition for negative internal thoughts. Go ahead and get a grip right on your face. Feel it digging in. Now take your left hand and grab your wrist. When you pull it off its going to make a popping sound and try to get right back on but keep it off. Ready, now! Feel it struggling trying to get back on?

I want you to talk to it. (You might want to name it as well). "Thank you for caring, but not for sharing" You might have to go every 5 minutes pulling the alien off of your face just to get yourself to take the right actions.

Remember, the alien is fear based dialogue designed believe it or not to protect you from doing actions that are non-consciously viewed as threats.

Challenge:
Notice the limiting internal dialogue, the alien! When you notice stop the thought and replace it with a possibility thought.

Tapping in Meditation:
My purpose today is to fulfill the universes gift to me which is my potential. My gift to the universe is to use it to be all that I can be in the service of others.

Journal Notes:

Day/Year	
Day/Year	
Day/Year	
Day/Year	
Day/Year	

February 10

Visualization and the Wall Test

Stand with your right shoulder perpendicular to a wall. Stand one foot away from the wall. Have a partner stand slightly behind you. Now, keeping your feet straight forward, I want you to straighten your left arm and twist as far as you can go across your body as far as you can go on the wall. Stop when you are convinced that you've gone as far as you can and ask your partner to place their finger on that spot and keep it there.

Face the front again. Now look over your shoulder at the spot that your partner is marking. I want you to visualize blasting beyond that spot. See yourself stretching easily and effortlessly beyond that spot. Close your eyes and visualize that happening. See it in your mind's eye, want it to happen, expect it to happen. No open your eyes again and retest and see how far you can go. It's virtually 100% that people go further the second time. Check out what's happening in your brain when you are visualizing.

These two images above are fMRIs and show a few differences but overlap in the regions of the brain involved in recalling a past event and imagining a future one. In each case, a network of neurons fires across the cerebral cortex.

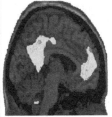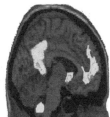

Visualization and the Real Experience

Remember Past   Imagining Future

Challenge:
Do the wall test with other people. Everyone should go further when they are focused on doing so. How else can you apply this?

Tapping in Meditation:
My purpose today is to stretch through my limitations. I do this by living a healthy and well prepared life.

Journal Notes:

Day/Year	
Day/Year	
Day/Year	
Day/Year	
Day/Year	

February 11

Tapping in with Meditation

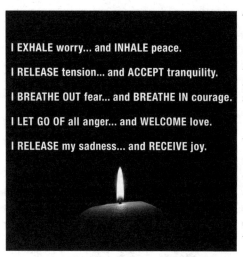

I EXHALE worry... and INHALE peace.

I RELEASE tension... and ACCEPT tranquility.

I BREATHE OUT fear... and BREATHE IN courage.

I LET GO OF all anger... and WELCOME love.

I RELEASE my sadness... and RECEIVE joy.

The individual human mind is like a computer terminal connected to a giant database. The database is human consciousness itself, of which our own consciousness is merely an individual expression but with its roots in the common consciousness of all of mankind. We live in a universe where everything is connected to everything.

When you meditate you are quieting your mind and dialing in or tapping into the universal divine energy, divine intelligence. Just sit quietly for 5 to 10 minutes. Read the "Tapping in meditation" notes at the bottom of each day and then simply listen. Don't attempt to analyze or understand, just listen. If your thoughts wander just notice your breathing.

The highest energy level is enlightenment. At this level there is no longer the experience of yourself as separate from others. Your body is seen as merely a tool of consciousness through the intervention of mind, oneness.

The key is not to let the lower energy fields of anxiety, fear, anger, resentment get in the way of enlightenment. In the universe like goes to like and we attract to us that which we emanate. Your meditation time is your time to observe this attraction. The fundamental tenet of the new theoretical physics is that everything in the universe is connected with everything else. You meditation is a time to nurture and allow the connection to the greater good.

When you choose the path of love, service and giving you are aligning with enlightenment. Your meditation has scientific benefits. It is a calm and full of peace and serenity.

Challenge:

Take 5-10 minutes every day to tap in with your mediation. Align your energy with the higher energy level present in the universe and tap into natures' powerful existence.

Tapping in Meditation:

My purpose today is to feel oneness with the tremendous power of the universe. Feel the universal energy flow through me.

Journal Notes:

Day/Year	
Day/Year	
Day/Year	
Day/Year	
Day/Year	

February 12

The Food Plan—A Healthy Lifestyle

Everyone in this program has a commitment to excellence in their health, business and personal lives. Your commitment to health starts with the food you eat. Nutritional science enables people to reverse and prevent disease, age slower and to live a healthier and longer life. Nutritional science has advanced to the point that we can have the healthiest, longest lived population in the history of the human race.

The key is to eat for nutritional density. Low nutrient eating leads to cellular toxicity. The cells build up levels of toxic waste products, free radicals, biological aging. This buildup of toxins makes you feel ill in between meals so you'll want to eat more food to feel better.

Our plan:

- Breakfast: 1 ounce oatmeal, 6 ounces fruit, 8 ounces sugar free yogurt, 1 tablespoon flaxseed ground meal.
- Lunch: 6 ounces protein, 6 ounces steamed vegetables, 8 ounces salad, 1 tablespoon olive oil. (4-6-6 for women)
- Dinner: 6 ounces protein, 6 ounces steamed vegetables, 8 ounces salad, 1 tablespoon olive oil, 6 ounces fruit. (4-6-6 women)

Green vegetables such as kale, cabbage, collards and broccoli are called cruciferous. Their leaves resemble a crucifix. Cruciferous vegetables are twice as powerful as other plant foods.

By 2010 processed foods had become 62% of the calories consumed in the standard American diet. Avoid low nutrient foods. Avoid flour and sugar. Your program is 3 weighed and measured meals, nothing in between and the abstinence from flower and sugar.

Challenge:
Before the food plan you used to stuff your face. Now you face your stuff. Follow the food plan. Prepare in advance.

Tapping in Meditation:
My purpose today is to live a healthy lifestyle. I protect my energy and enthusiasm. I am happy, healthy and prosperous.

Journal Notes:

Day/Year	
Day/Year	
Day/Year	
Day/Year	
Day/Year	

February 13

TOFI

Similar Age, Gender, BMI and Same % Body Fat

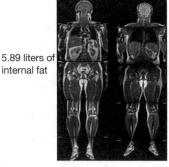

5.89 liters of internal fat

1.65 liters of internal fat

Different levels of internal fat = different disease risks

The term TOFI "thin-outside-fat-inside" is used to describe lean individuals with a disproportionate amount of fat (adipose tissue) stored within their abdomen. The figure to illustrate this shows two men, both aged 35 years, with a BMI of 25 kg/m. Despite their similar size, the TOFI had 5.86 liters of internal fat, while the healthy control had only 1.65 liters.

To classify an individual as TOFI, it is essential to measure their internal fat content. The only way that this is possible is by using magnetic resonance Imaging (MRI) or CT scanning. The parameters of the MRI scanner are manipulated to show fat as bright (white) and lean tissue as dark.

Indirect methods such as waist circumference are not suitable as individuals with an identical waist circumference can have vastly different levels of internal fat.

Variation in visceral fat in men with the same waist circumference

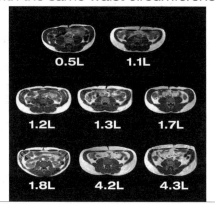

0.5L   1.1L

1.2L   1.3L   1.7L

1.8L   4.2L   4.3L

Challenge:

The food plan is for everyone. Have breakfast, 4-5 hours later lunch, 4-5 hours after that dinner. No snacking, no flour or sugar.

Tapping in Meditation:

My purpose today is to honor my body with proper nutrition. I have a plan and I eat on purpose. I am of service to others because I take care of myself. I am happy and healthy.

Journal Notes:

Day/Year	
Day/Year	
Day/Year	
Day/Year	
Day/Year	

February 14

Have a Dream

Definiteness of purpose is the starting point of all achievement.–W. Clement Stone. You've got to have the image and idea of what you want to become before you can manifest it into reality.

"We become what we think about." –Earl Nightingale.

"Whatever the mind of man can conceive and believe, it can achieve." –Napoleon Hill

I will tell you a story of Monty Roberts. As he was a kid, his father as a horse trainer was moving from stable to stable, from ranch to ranch—training horses. Thus, the boy's school career was constantly interrupted. One day, when he was a senior, his teacher asked him to write about what he wanted to be when he grew up.

A goal is a dream with a deadline.

—Napoleon Hill

He didn't hesitate a minute and wrote a seven page paper about his aim to be an owner of a horse ranch. He wrote many details and drew a location of the buildings, stables and even a detailed house plan.

Two days later he received his paper back with the letter F on the front. He came up to the teacher and asked: "Why did I receive an F?" the teacher responded: "This dream is so unrealistic for a boy like you, who has no money, no resources and who comes from an itinerant family. There is no possibility that you will reach your great goals one day."
Then the teacher offered Monty the opportunity to rewrite the paper with a more realistic attitude.

The boy went home and asked his father how he should act. The father answered: "This decision is very important for you. So you have to make up your own mind on this."

After several days the boy brought the same paper to his teacher. No changes were made. He said: "Keep the F and I will keep my dream."

Monty Roberts now owns a 4,000 square foot house in the middle of a 200 acre horse ranch and he still has that school paper which now is framed over the fireplace.

Challenge:
Follow your heart and never let anyone (energy vampires) steal your dreams. What one action can you do today that moves you closer to your dreams? "You miss 100% of the shots you don't take." –Wayne Gretzky

Tapping in Meditation:
My purpose today is to vision my perfect calendar, identify my perfect dream life and live it today.

Journal Notes:

Day/Year	
Day/Year	
Day/Year	
Day/Year	

February 15

The Power of Thought—The Lift

In my live presentations I'm fond of doing this demonstration which illustrates the power of having a dream, a vision, preparation and accountability.

I bring up a heavy person, usually a man, up on stage and have him sit in a chair. Next I ask for 3 women volunteers, who believe that women are powerful, to come on up and help me. One stands by the mans' right shoulder, I stand by the left shoulder, and the other two ladies stand by each knee.

Our goal is to lift the man off of the chair. We make a fist with both hands and put our forefingers straight. Fist together, thumbs tucked down, two ladies under the knees, myself and the other woman under the shoulders and on 3 lift as high as we can.

Then I ask the audience, "Did we succeed at reaching our goal?" The answer is yes. Our goal was to lift this person off of the chair. However, did we do the best that we were capable of? The answer is no.

We do the lift again. This time we apply the principles of precise planning, visioning and accountability. I tell the group that this time our goal is to lift the person twice as high and I demonstrate by lifting my outstretched arms above eye level. I ask everyone else to do the same (presetting an outcome). Next I have the volunteers make a commitment." I promise to do everything I can do to lift the person twice as high, will you hold me accountable?" Each person commits. Then we close our eyes and visualize the outcome. We add in the suggestions that the person is light as a feather and that we are strong as an ox. On 3 we repeat the lift and the most amazing thing happens, the person flies off of the chair! It was easy and effortless.

Challenge:
Develop a preset outcome for how you want today to go. Visualize it going exactly like that. Now go and amaze yourself by staying on task and focused.

Tapping in Meditation:
My purpose today is to stay engaged in what is most important to me today. Notice how I feel today. Engage with other people.

Journal Notes:

Day/Year	
Day/Year	
Day/Year	
Day/Year	
Day/Year	

February 16

The Placebo Effect

Researchers have been studying the placebo effect for decades. In 1955, researcher H.K. Beecher published his ground breaking paper "the Powerful Placebo" in which he concluded that across 26 studies he analyzed, an average of 32% of patients responded to the placebo.

In the 1960s, breakthrough studies showed the potential physiological effects of dummy pills—they tended to speed up pulse rate, increase blood pressure and improve reaction speeds for example, when participants were told they had taken a stimulant and had the opposite effects when participants were told they had taken a sleep producing drug.

This is not purely psychological, the mind-body connection is clear. Your expectations have a clear and established impact on your physiology. The good news about this is that you can control this. You can control your thoughts, what you pay attention to. This means that you can also control your physiology. The method is precise planning for your week every Sunday, creating a behavioral contract with accountability and keeping your mind and body energized through proper diet and exercise choices.

Challenge:

Notice how your expectations impact your reality. Be careful what you expect because you cause it to happen.

Tapping in Meditation:

My purpose today is to notice my thoughts, then organize those thoughts into ideas and plans, then transform those plans into reality. The beginning is in my mind. I am a spiritual and mental magnet attracting all things which are good and bless me. I am blessed.

Journal Notes:

Day/Year	
Day/Year	
Day/Year	
Day/Year	
Day/Year	

February 17

The Placebo Effect—Predisposed

I had termites in my residence. After discussing the options I decided to treat them locally. I was told that the treatment was successful and the termites were gone!

I was taking a trip for a speaking engagement. I was bringing along some books, CDs and DVDs for sale. I pack them in a large display case that I store in my garage.

I had the display case delivered to the function room. I arrived a bit afterwards. As I was walking over to the display case I noticed a termite on the lid. I immediately started to think "I can't believe this. The treatment failed after all. Since I store the case in my garage I must still have termites!"

When I got closer to the display case I could see that what I thought was a termite was simply a piece of plastic. It was all in my mind.

Challenge:

What outcomes are you expecting today? How about creating the mental conditions for some breakthroughs in your health, business and personal life. It's a decision. Decide that today will be a terrific day.

Tapping in Meditation:

My purpose today is to cherish my visions and dreams as they are the substance of my soul. They are the blueprints of my ultimate achievements.

Journal Notes:

Day/Year	
Day/Year	
Day/Year	
Day/Year	
Day/Year	

February 18

The Placebo Effect—Fat Suit

Take it from Tyra Banks, size does matter. On one of the episodes of her talk show, the supermodel, 31, wore a fat suit, and then went on three blind dates as a 350 pound woman. The result? "One of the most heartbreaking experiences in my life," the 5 foot 9 150 pound banks said.

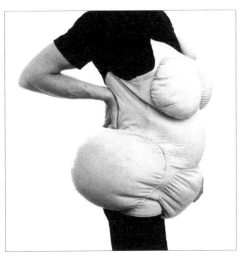

She said that obesity is openly discriminated against. She decided to take this further. She walked down the streets of NY and within 10 seconds people pointed and laughed in her face. One person even cut in front of her to take the taxi she had hailed.

Next she did something that surprised her. She changed her mind set, her expectations. She decided to see if it made a difference if she was cheerful, energized, positive herself. She found that yes it did. She was treated with respect, people were friendly, a hot dog vendor even graciously added some extra ingredients for her. Everything was different because she was different. This is a quantum conversation, more on that later.

Challenge:

You create your own reality by your thoughts, your expectations and your deeds. Just for today live without fear and do something you would not ordinarily do and have the expectation of a positive result. Journal about it at the end of the day.

Tapping in Meditation:

My purpose today is to tune my mind energy into accomplishment and wealth. I attract abundance, happiness and health into my life.

Journal Notes:

Day/Year	
Day/Year	
Day/Year	
Day/Year	
Day/Year	

February 19

What I Can Control, I Must Control

Three Main Areas of the Brain

The biggest area and most important area for control is your attitude. There are 3 main areas to your brain, the outer cortex, the limbic area and the brainstem. The outer cortex is the analyzing and planning area. It is your critical thinking area. The limbic area is your emotional and fear part. The brainstem is your autonomic nervous system, breathing, heart rate, etc.

When the electrical activity is in the amygdala area of the brain you are in a fear based, stressed and aroused state. Someone pulls a gun out on you and your amygdala would light up. This is a very stressful circumstance. It is a survival mechanism however as you are prepared to fight or flight with all of the hormones and chemicals that come along with this state. However, if this is an inappropriate response, such as being in traffic, where there is no real threat to your survival, then it becomes a tremendous stressor.

On the other hand, when the electrical activity is in the Septum area of the brain then a much more pleasurable state occurs. You can control which area of the brain is electrically active with the nature of your thinking. You can keep your physiology in a peaceful, alert, calm and focused state with positive thinking accompanied by precise planning.

Challenge:

Take control of what you can control. You can be in control of your life and the results that you experience through your right attitude and proper planning.

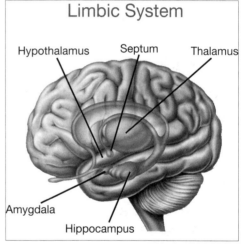

Limbic System

Tapping in Meditation:

My purpose today is to keep my thinking spirit guided rather than material guided. There is strength, peace and calm to be found in communion with my higher power, the energy of the universe.

Journal Notes:

Day/Year	
Day/Year	
Day/Year	
Day/Year	
Day/Year	

February 20

A Carrot, an Egg and a Cup of Coffee

A young woman went to her mother and told her about her life and how things were so hard. She didn't know how she was going to make it and wanted to give up. She was tired of fighting and struggling. It seemed as one problem was solved, a new one arose.

Her mother took her to the kitchen. She filled three pots with water and placed each on the fire. Soon the pots came to a boil. In the first she placed carrots, in the second eggs and in the last she placed ground coffee beans. She let them sit and boil without saying a word. In about 20 minutes she turned off the burners. She fished the carrots out and placed them in a bowl. She pulled the eggs out and placed them in a bowl as well.

Then she ladled the coffee out and placed it in a bowl. Turning to her daughter she asked, "Tell me what you see." "Carrots, eggs and coffee," she replied. Her mother brought her closer and asked her to feel the carrots. She did and noted that they were soft. The mother then asked her to take an egg and break it. After pulling off the shell she observed the hard-boiled egg. Finally the mother asked the daughter to sip the coffee. The daughter smiled as she tasted the rich aroma. The daughter then asked, "What does it mean, mother?

Her mother explained that each of these objects had faced the same adversity; boiling water. Each reacted differently. The carrot went in strong, hard and unrelenting. However after being subjected to the boiling water it softened and became weak. The egg had been fragile. Its thin outer shell had protected its liquid interior, but after sitting through the boiling water the inside became hardened. The ground coffee beans were unique however. After they were in the bowling water they changed the water.

"Which are you?" she asked her daughter. "When adversity knocks on your door how do you respond? Think of this, the carrot that seems strong when confronted with pain and adversity wilts, becoming soft and losing its strength. The egg starts with a malleable heart, but changes with the heat. Did you have a fluid spirit but after some type of adversity become hardened and stiff? Does your outer shell look the same but on the inside you are bitter and tough with a stiff spirit and hardened heart? Or are you like the coffee bean that actually changes the hot water, the very circumstance that brings the pain. When the water gets hot it releases the fragrance and flavor. If you are like the bean when things are at their worst you get better and change the situation around you.

Challenge:
Relay this message to those people who mean something to you and to those who have touched your life, to those whose friendship you appreciate.

Tapping in Meditation:
My purpose today is to be the catalyst that changes poor circumstances for better outcomes.

Journal Notes:

Day/Year	
Day/Year	
Day/Year	

February 21

Rationalization

You don't function very well with what's referred to as "cognitive dissonance." Cognitive dissonance occurs when you are holding two conflicting beliefs such as I am willing to prospect and I hate rejection, or, I am committed to healthy living and I hate getting up early to exercise, or even, I am absolutely committed to weight management but I do not want to give up flour and sugar.

You can't maintain this dissonance or it would cause too much stress, depressing your immune system resulting in depression and illness. So there is a built in instinct of a defensive mechanism, a manipulation of perception called rationalization.

Rationalization is your buffer protecting you from confronting the authenticity between what you say you are committed to accomplish and what you are not willing to do.

This is not good or bad, we all do this as an instinct. Remember, the purpose of our genetic coding is for survival, not prosperity. So if you're thinking that you are absolutely committed to your family but you are not spending time with them then your brain will protect you from feeling guilty by conjuring up some rational lies. Oh, this is just temporary, I've got a deadline. I'll spend time with the kids next weekend. Now that's a rationalization.

In addition to cognitive dissonance, rationalizations are triggered when an activity that you need to do is perceived as painful. For example you plan on making 20 prospecting calls a day. However, your brain non-consciously scans this activity for any link to "life threatening pain." You have a stored memory of a horrific rejection that happened 20 years ago. This is a non-conscious memory but it's a neural network in tact none the less which generates an avoidance response, like your life depends on it. Then you follow this with rationalization. "I do intend to prospect but I need to research these companies first."

The purpose of rationalization is to protect you. The way that it works is by justifying avoidance. Most of the time you are not aware that this is going on. You'll simply think that you are just too busy.

Challenge:
Notice your avoidance without judgment. Make a decision on the spot to change your thinking, pay attention to something else and take the action.

Tapping in Meditation:
My purpose today is to be authentic. I arrange or change my thoughts as needed so that I do what I need to do to be fully engaged in reaching my goals.

Journal Notes:

Day/Year	
Day/Year	
Day/Year	
Day/Year	
Day/Year	

February 22

Get M.A.D. The 8 Day Week

Make a Decision! What decisions are you avoiding? Most likely the reasons you are avoiding have nothing to do with what you think they are. It's really very simple. If you are avoiding taking an action it's because that action is linked to pain. It's very difficult to overcome the inertia of millions of years of evolution that have developed the automatic fleeing from any and all of your perceived threats.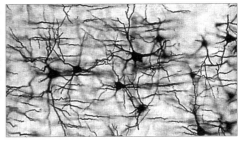

Your avoidance is driven by non-conscious processes called neural networks. These are stored memories that you have tagged as dangerous and your primitive limbic area of your brain exaggerates to a life threatening status.

Neural networks are formed to save energy and time for response. However, they are not based on reality or current circumstances. As a result of these compelling avoidance networks, which are followed by rationalization, you may sometimes fall into the pattern of thinking that you really are going to do something, but it's on the 8th day of the week;

Monday, Tuesday, Wednesday, Thursday, Friday, Saturday, Sunday, SOMEDAY.

If you can persist through your projection of fear and pain then in almost every case you see that the actual doing of what you were avoiding was easier and more pleasant then you thought it would be. Keep in mind; it's the starting that stops most people, so get moving.

Challenge:
Make a list of what you're avoiding. Make a decision on what action you will take today, this week. Put it into a behavioral contract so you can manipulate the perceived threat and compel yourself to specific actions, now and for the rest of the week.

Tapping in Meditation:
My purpose today is to get and remain in action. I am a doer. I easily glide through fear, doubt and insecurity and remain in productive action.

Journal Notes:

Day/Year	
Day/Year	
Day/Year	
Day/Year	
Day/Year	

February 23

Make Your Lifestyle an Asset, not a Liability

Everything is related, the way that you think effects your physiology which impacts your actions. Likewise your actions will impact your physiology which will affect your thoughts so it goes both ways.

One of our coaching commandments is that "What you can control, you must control!" One of those most important areas is your lifestyle.

Benjamin Franklin pointed out that early to bed, early to rise can make you healthy, wealthy and wise. Unfortunately, the "early to rise" part is a problem for many people. If you want to get a good start to the day you can't sleep away your life. Sleeping in is wasting time. Time is precious. So what is your lifestyle? Is it an asset? Are you on my food plan? (See February 12th) Are you exercising? Are you preparing in advance for the next seven days? Are you controlling your thoughts and editing negative limiting beliefs?

Are you committed to excellence? I love what Ralph Waldo Emerson says, "What you do speaks so loudly I can't hear what you say!"

So, if you're staying up wasting time watching late night T.V., if you're drinking alcohol, doing drugs, smoking or anything else detrimental to your performance, STOP IT! Being good at your job is only part of the formula. You also must incorporate these ingredients: positive attitude, integrity, willingness to stretch beyond your comfort zone, cooperation, be a team player.

Challenge:

What changes do you need to make in your habits and lifestyle routine. Journal those here. Develop your plan of actions and commit to those over a seven day period of time. What do you need to do today?

Tapping in Meditation:

My purpose today is to be in the lifestyle and routine that I need to be and do to be of service to myself and others.

Journal Notes:

Day/Year	
Day/Year	
Day/Year	
Day/Year	
Day/Year	

February 24

Exercise for Fitness

Your physical health, fitness and energy level are of the highest priority. According to Dr. Stanley, author of "The Millionaire Next Door", there is an 80% correlation between being a deca-millionaire and being in an exercise and fitness program.

The first thing to consider is your own personal circumstances. Do you have arthritis or other joint pain issues that would need to be considered? Perhaps all you can do is walk. I'm going to make these assumptions for the rest of this concept. I'll assume that you are able to vigorously exercise. I'll assume that you are not training for any particular sport. So here's what you need to know.

There are two sources of energy that the body uses, muscle glycogen and fat. One is in the presence of available oxygen and the other is not. With aerobic exercise oxygen is carried through your breath to the muscles giving them the energy needed to sustain the effort. Oxygen is required to breakdown fat for energy. Oxygen is not present with anaerobic exercise. The chemical formula to use muscle glycogen for fuel does not require oxygen. So if the intensity of your exercise exceeds your aerobic capacity then you go anaerobic.

You need to utilize both systems. The exercise program is for fitness, not weight management. The food plan is for weight management. With that in mind here are some things you'll need to know.

First, how to determine the intensity of your exercise. Use this formula, 220 minus your age equals your max heart rate. Exercise between 60-80% of that range. So, $220 - 60 = 160$ x 80% = 128. That's your target heart rate. Get a heart rate monitor. Usually this is a strap around your chest plus a watch that will give you an ongoing measure of your heart rate. If it's too low, pick up the pace. If it's too high, back it down. HIIT is the recommended exercise method, high intensity interval training. This involves a 60 second sprint followed by a 90 second jog while monitoring your heart rate. I'll suggest that you see a trainer for your specific program.

The other type of exercise that must be done consistently is weight training. I would recommend that you work upper body, days 1 and 3, and lower body on days 2 and 4. So a minimum of 4 workouts per week, mixing both aerobic and anaerobic exercise.

Challenge:
Do you belong to a gym? See a trainer for some guidance on your specific workout.

Tapping in Meditation:
My purpose today is to take full responsibility for my health and fitness. I am healthy and fit. I love to exercise and I do.

Journal Notes:

Day/Year	
Day/Year	
Day/Year	
Day/Year	
Day/Year	

February 25

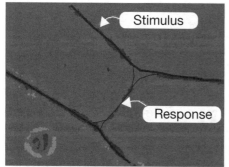

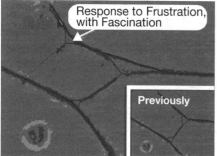

Creating Habits, Stimulus—Response

Habits are essentially patterns of behavior that become "worn in" to our brains. Someone who wakes up every morning, pours a cup of coffee and lights a cigarette, in that order, every morning, has that pattern built in to his or her brain—in the form of well-used synaptic pathways.

Everything we do (and think, for that matter) is governed by impulses firing across synapses, or spaces between certain cells that guide communication in the brain. When any behavior or pattern is repeated enough, the synaptic pathways associated with that pattern get used to being accessed. As a result, it becomes easier for impulses to travel along those pathways, and the behavior seems "natural." In other words, to the brain, wake-coffee-cigarette, in that order, is practically instinctive. One action triggers the next. Habits are stimulus response neurological connections. Here is a simple example.

As you can see in the picture, I have a 3-drawer cabinet. It was originally to my left. The garbage can is on my right. When I get the stimulus to throw something away I automatically turn to my right (Response). That is a wired in pathway. However, I wasn't able to use the 3rd drawer in my cabinet because of a bar at the base of my desk. So I decided to move the cabinet to the right side and the garbage can to the left.

Now I get the stimulus to throw something away and I automatically turn to the old pattern, to the right. However, I now become conscious that I've moved it, a high energy state, and I turn to the left to complete the intended action. It takes several trials of falsely turning to the right to throw something away before I begin to form a new neurological pathway. Over time the old pathway will be absorbed by the brain (synaptic pruning) and the new pathway will become solidified. This is called brain plasticity. It is a major breakthrough. It proves that you can rewire your brain at any time and form new habits.

Challenge:

What habits do you need to stop or start? Make a list and then decide what actions you will take today, this week.

Tapping in Meditation:

My purpose today is to take on peak performance habits and eliminate habits that hold me back.

Journal Notes:

Day/Year	
Day/Year	
Day/Year	

February 26

15 Tips to Enjoy the Ride

1. Take a walk for 30 minutes every day and as you walk smile.
2. Sit in silence for at least 10 minutes each day.
3. When you wake up in the morning complete the following statement, "My purpose today is to …today."
4. Live with the 3 Es Energy, Enthusiasm, Empathy and the 3 Fs Faith, Family, Friends.
5. Spend more time with people over the age of seventy and under the age of six.
6. Dream more while you are awake.
7. Make at least three people smile each day.
8. Realize that life is a school and you are here to learn. Problems are simply part of life that appear and fade away like algebra class but the lessons you learn will last a lifetime.
9. Smile and laugh more. It will keep the energy vampires away.
10. Life isn't fair but it's still good.
11. Don't take yourself too seriously, no one else does.
12. You don't have to win every argument. Agree to disagree.
13. Make peace with the past so it won't mess up the present.
14. Don't compare your life with others. You have no idea what their journey is all about.
15. Burn the candles. Use the nice sheets. Don't save it for a special occasion. Today is special.

Challenge:
Which one of these speaks to you today? Any action you can take? Journal if you do.

Tapping in Meditation:
My purpose today is to be aware of what my gift is. This gift, at whatever cost, must be expressed.

Journal Notes:

Day/Year	
Day/Year	
Day/Year	
Day/Year	
Day/Year	

February 27
Taking Responsibility with Rational Emotive Therapy

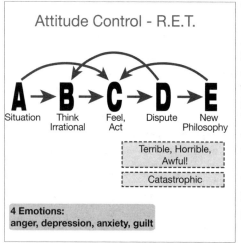

Attitude Control - R.E.T.

A → B → C → D → E

Situation | Think Irrational | Feel, Act | Dispute | New Philosophy

Terrible, Horrible, Awful!

Catastrophic

4 Emotions:
anger, depression, anxiety, guilt

Think about the ABCs

A—something happens that makes you upset. Someone cuts you off, treats you unfairly, lies to you, doesn't do what they say they will do, etc. Most people think that what happens to them leads to the Cs, which is how you feel and act. However, that is not correct. That is a victim orientation. The As lead to the Bs which lead to the Cs. B is your underlying thinking which is irrational.

When an irrational belief is violated you feel terrible, horrible and awful and someone must pay. Here are some irrational beliefs:

1. I must be treated fairly at all times.
2. I must be liked and respected by everyone.
3. Other people must always tell the truth and do what they say they will do.
4. I must be thoroughly competent in everything that I do.
5. If I am rejected or fail, someone deserves to be blamed and punished. Sometimes I blame myself.

This is a no win perspective. Your only options are to experience excessive anger, anxiety, depression or guilt. Let's change it. Go from the C to D where you dispute your B, underlying irrational belief. Then go to E and form a new philosophy where you will then change C how you feel and act. Here is the template:

Although I would prefer_____ (fill in the blank, that people are honest for example) I understand that not all people are _____ (honest) and it's not terrible, horrible and awful when they are not.

This is a magical formula that gives control back to yourself over your emotions.

Challenge:
Find situations where you can use R.E.T. to change your perceptions.

Tapping in Meditation:
My purpose today is to go the extra mile. There are no traffic jams along the extra mile.

Journal Notes:

Day/Year	
Day/Year	
Day/Year	
Day/Year	
Day/Year	

February 28

Attitude Short Cut—Turn Frustration Into Fascination

I had several back to back to back speaking engagements that I was going to be traveling for today. The night before I told my assistant, Layne, please be at my house at 6:00 am. Layne was going to drive with me to the airport and then take my car back to the office. I had an 8:00 am flight and my wife couldn't take me because she had to get the kids ready for school. I didn't want to have to park my car at the airport for that long a time so Layne agreed to take me.

My routine started off as it normally does, 3:50 am wake up, dress, meditation, gym, then I was planning on picking up Layne at my office (separate building attached to my house) and off to the airport in plenty of time.

After my shower I called Layne but I went to voice mail. As I drive to my office she's not there. I park and attempt to call her again but to no avail. Now I'm getting concerned about time. It's now 6:15 am and with traffic it will take me about 30 minutes to get to the airport so I've got to go. I'm going to have to suck it up and just park at the airport but I've got to leave.

Finally Layne comes around the corner in obvious distress. She parks and as she walks over to my car she is about ready to be in tears. My response, I laughed. "Layne, it is so fascinating that you would be late to get me but we've got to go.

This wasn't Bob being a nice guy. This was my practicing this coaching concept, "Turn Frustration into Fascination." I would have been justified and "right" in being upset with Layne. She had excuses, there was an accident on the freeway, her cell phone battery ran out, it doesn't matter. The only thing that matters is that she is late.

By shifting my observation of this and perceiving it from the filter of turning frustration into fascination I spared myself what I call double duty. Not only did the thing happen but I'm upset about it. Where is the win there? Being upset doesn't change anything. Berating Layne might give the illusion of my feeling better but it's dysfunctional. It doesn't mean that I don't fire her. However, I'm not going to be upset about it.

Challenge:

This is a beautiful habit to form. You will rewire your brain with this habit and it will become automatic. When this happens you will be very attractive to others. Practice, Practice, Practice.

Tapping in Meditation:

My purpose today is to remain calm and serene. I turn frustration into fascination all day long.

Journal Notes:

Day/Year	
Day/Year	
Day/Year	
Day/Year	
Day/Year	

February 29
Someone is Trying to Kill You Crabwell Grommet

On the morning of his 42nd birthday, Grabwell Grommet awoke to a peal of particularly ominous thunder. Glancing out the window with his bleary eyes, he saw written in fiery letters: "SOMEONE IS TRYING TO KILL YOU, GRABWELL GROMMET!"

With shaking hands, Grommet lit his first cigarette of the day. He didn't question the message. You don't question messages like that. His only question was, "Who?" At breakfast as he salted his fried eggs and buttered his toast, he told his wife, Gratia, "Someone is trying to kill me." "Who?" she asked with horror. Grommet slowly stirred the cream and sugar into his coffee and shook his head, "I don't know," he said.

Convinced though he was, Grommet wasn't going to the police with his story. He decided his only course was to go about his daily routine and hope somehow to outwit his would-be murderer. He tried to think on the drive to the office. But the frustration of making time by beating lights and switching lanes occupied him wholly. Nor, once behind his desk, could he think a moment what with jangling phones, urgent memos and the problems and decisions piling in as they did each day.

It wasn't until his second martini at lunch that the full terror of his position struck him. It was all he could do to finish his Lasagna Milanese. "I can't panic," he said to himself, lighting his cigar. "I simply must live my life as usual."

So he worked until seven as usual. Drove home fast as usual. Studied business reports as usual. And he took his usual two Seconal capsules in order to get his usual six hours sleep. As days passed, the man fully stuck to his routine. And as the months went by, he began to take a perverse pleasure in his ability to survive. "Whoever's trying to get me," he'd say proudly to his wife, "hasn't got me yet. I'm too smart for him."

"Oh, please be careful," she'd reply, ladling him a second helping of beef stroganoff. The pride grew as he managed to go on living for years. But as it must to all men, death came at last to Grabwell. It came at his desk on a particularly busy day. He was 53.

His grief-stricken widow demanded a full autopsy. But it showed only emphysema, arteriosclerosis, duodenal ulcers, cirrhosis of the liver, cardiac necrosis, cerebrovascular aneurysm, pulmonary edema, obesity, circulatory insufficiency and a touch of lung cancer. "How glad Grabwell would have been to know," said the widow smiling proudly through her tears, "that he died of natural causes." (Source Unknown)

Challenge:
If you can identify with any of this STOP the habit and START a healthier lifestyle, today!

Tapping in Meditation:
My purpose today is to practice excellence in everything I do.

Journal Notes:

Day/Year	
Day/Year	
Day/Year	
Day/Year	
Day/Year	

Davies Day Book

365 concepts for excellence

March 1

Stay in the Here and Now

It was preseason practice on the hot athletic fields at Cal State Fullerton. We had just come to the end of a grueling yet successful practice and it was time for conditioning. The team lined up in the end zone for 110s. That's where we sprint from end zone to the other end zone and jog back.

We had a defensive tackle who we called "Land Mine." He was 5'8 and weighed 265 pounds. He was compact and very explosive for a few feet anyway. Here is what I can only imagine is going on in his mind. PAST—oh my God. The last time we did 110s particularly in this heat I almost died. FUTURE—how am I ever going to get through this. We haven't even started and I'm exhausted. So we begin…

Land Mine starts to lag behind. While the rest in his group are jogging back he is still on the sprint phase although I wouldn't call what he's doing a sprint. Fast forward, the team is on 6 and Land Mine is struggling at 4. Finally he falls down, rather pathetically, in the middle of the field grabbing his hamstring and writhing in pain. He's thinking I'm only at 4 there are 12 more (FUTURE), the last time we did these I almost died at 8 (PAST) and the result of going back and forth is simply utter exhaustion and failure.

Now I don't recommend this as a motivational method, but the offensive line coach sprints over to him and starts screaming at him most of which I can't say publicly. The gist of this was that he was a loser, he would always be a loser, he was a disgrace and embarrassment to the entire team and more.

To my surprise, this moved Land Mine. He struggled to his feet and all of a sudden he had a mindset shift. It was a focus in the NOW. It was this step, then the next step, and the next and before you knew it the entire team watched Land Mine finish 16 110s surprising even himself!

There is magic in the Here and Now. There is power in the present. I have this happen all the time where my performance is saved by a present now focus. Particularly in my morning core floor workouts where I'm working my abs. Oh are they hard. If I stay on one rep at a time it's easy to get through. Yes, I said easy.

Challenge:

How can you make your life easier with a here and now focus? Do you see how a bit of mental strategy can give you great power? How can you apply this today?

Tapping in Meditation:

My purpose today is to embrace the moment, to stay present and savor the task that I am involved with as I give the best that I have.

Journal Notes:

Day/Year	
Day/Year	
Day/Year	
Day/Year	
Day/Year	

March 2

The Buddha and Being Present

A man walking across a field encounters a tiger. He fled, the tiger chasing after him. Coming to a cliff, he caught hold of a wild vine and swung himself over the edge. The tiger sniffed at him from above. Terrified, the man looked down to where, far below, another tiger had come, waiting to eat him. Two mice, one white and one black, little by little began to gnaw away at the vine. The man saw a luscious strawberry near him. Grasping the vine in one hand, he plucked the strawberry with the other. How sweet it tasted!

This is a beautiful story about what you pay attention to. Think about it. The tiger above wants to kill and eat the Buddha, it's chased him to the cliff (past), the tigers waiting below are eager to do the same (future) and add to that the two mice that are chewing away at his life line. With all of the confusion and threats the Buddha still has the presence of mind to focus on the present moment, the now, the beautiful strawberry.

Challenge:
You can always return to having anxiety about the past, or what you should have done, and the future and what might be awaiting you. However, to stay in the now with a present focus is the most powerful observation you can make.

Tapping in Meditation:
My purpose today is to practice seeing. I easily see simplicity from clutter, harmony from discord and opportunity from difficulty. I am the master of my mind rather than being mastered by mind.

Journal Notes:

Day/Year	
Day/Year	
Day/Year	
Day/Year	
Day/Year	

March 3

Each Day is a Gift—Perceptual Choice

A proud man who is fully dressed each morning by eight am with his hair fashionably coiffed and shaved perfectly, even though he is legally blind, moved to a nursing home today. His wife of 70 years recently passed away making the move necessary. After many hours of waiting patiently in the lobby of the nursing home, he smiled when told his room was ready.

As he maneuvered his walker to the elevator his aid provided a visual description of his tiny room, including the eyelet sheets that had been hung on his window.

"I love it," he stated with the enthusiasm of an 8 year old having just received a new puppy.

"Mr. Jones, you haven't seen the room; just wait."

"That doesn't have anything to do with it," he replied. "Happiness is something you decide on ahead of time. Whether I like my room or not doesn't depend on how the furniture is arranged, it's how I arrange my mind. I already decided to love it. It's a decision I make every morning when I wake up. I have a choice; I can spend the day in bed recounting the difficulty I have with the parts of my body that no longer work, or get out of bed and be thankful for the ones that do."

Each day is a gift, and as long as my eyes open, I'll focus on the new day and all the happy memories I've stored away. Just for this time in my life. Old age is like a bank account. You withdraw from it what you've put in. So my advice to you would be to deposit a lot of happiness in the bank account of memories.

Challenge:
Remember 5 simple rules to be happy. Free your heart from hatred. Free your mind from worries. Live simply, give more and expect less.

Tapping in Meditation:
My purpose today is to live with love and appreciation.

Journal Notes:

Day/Year	
Day/Year	
Day/Year	
Day/Year	
Day/Year	

March 4

WIN the Day

What is important now? Are you majoring in the minors or doing the most productive and loving actions and thoughts? What are you paying attention to?

At the beginning of the week you identify your highest priority items and actually make commitments with accountability. The week is a series of nows, a series of moments. How are you at staying focused on what's important now or do you have your mind split and only partially paying attention to what's important now.

Everything is based on mind, is led by mind, is fashioned by mind. If you speak and act with a polluted mind, suffering will follow you as the wheels of the oxcart follow the footsteps of the ox. Everything is based on mind, is led by mind, is fashioned by mind. If you speak and act with a pure mind, happiness will follow you, as a shadow clings to a form. Plan, prioritize, execute, evaluate and repeat.

Challenge:

Stay focused on one task at a time. Just for today identify what you need to do and who you need to be to win the day.

Tapping in Meditation:

My purpose today is to be pure of thought. To think only of possibilities and with passion and excitement. Only good happens to me.

Journal Notes:

Day/Year	
Day/Year	
Day/Year	
Day/Year	
Day/Year	

March 5

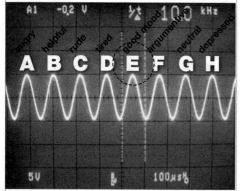

Everything Exists in the Relm of Potentials and Possibilities

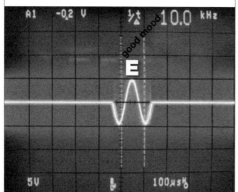

Reality is In the Mind of the Observer

Quantum Physics, Delta and Choice

I was sitting up front on a Delta flight from John Wayne Airport to Atlanta. I just happen to be watching the passengers as they boarded the plane. I had this warm, pleasant and happy feeling. I couldn't help but notice that everyone was in a good mood. Everyone was smiling. People were being very courteous, helping each other. Everyone seemed so nice and kind and gentle with each other. Then something dawned on me. I was in a good mood. I was creating my reality. That just blew me away!

There are two types of physics, classical and quantum. Classical physics are the laws that govern the large. They include action and reaction, cause and effect. That's how we send a rocket to the space station. The other set of laws are quantum, the laws of the small, the sub atomic. Our thinking is subject to these laws.

Niels Bohr proposed the Copenhagen interpretation of quantum theory, which asserts that a particle is whatever it is measured to be (for example, a wave or a particle), but that it cannot be assumed to have specific properties, or even to exist, until it is measured. In short, Bohr was saying that objective reality does not exist. This translates to a principle called superposition that claims that while we do not know what the state of any object is, it is actually in all possible states simultaneously, as long as we don't look to check. Consider my Delta Airlines example.

All potential realities were super imposed at the same time. Instead of creating a reality where everyone was nice and happy I could have focused on everyone being angry, mean, rude or impatient. All of those potential realities existed right alongside of the one I chose, being nice. Once I made the observation, once I selected GOOD MOOD all other possibilities collapsed, ceased to exist and I was left with my choice as my reality. Like Benjamin Lebet says, "Reality is in the mind of the observer."

Challenge:

Notice that you have a choice to select your own reality. Claim what that will be, decide on it, declare it and watch the universe provide it for you. I've heard it said that most people are about as happy as they make up their mind to be.

Tapping in Meditation:

My purpose today is to take a stand for possibility, love, gratitude and appreciation.

Journal Notes:

Day/Year	
Day/Year	
Day/Year	

March 6

Concave or Convex—How Beliefs are Formed

What is this line, concave or convex? You can't tell until you take a point of reference. You've got to have an orientation. Let's say you're on the A side. What you would first do is examine the evidence. The line is bending towards you at the top, it's bending towards you at the bottom, it's bowing away from you in the center. That's the definition of a concave line. Quantum physics says it's both concave and convex but you've observed from the A perspective. You have gathered your evidence and you believe that the truth is that this is a concave line.

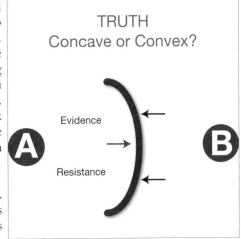

What if I challenge you and question your conclusion. Well you have all of the evidence to support that this is a concave line. Even if you again look at the facts you will still conclude without any doubt that this is a concave line. Once you've reexamined your evidence you become very resistant to changing your perspective.

What about B? B does the same thing. B looks at the same set of circumstances but from a different orientation. The line is bending away from B at the top and bottom and bowing towards B at the center, this is the definition of a convex line.

Which is it? It's concave for A and it's concave for B. What's the truth? The truth is not relevant. The truth doesn't matter. The only thing that matters is, does what you're paying attention to support you in taking the actions to reach your goals? If it doesn't can you and will you change your point of view? Do you see how difficult it would be for anyone to convince you that you have far more capacity to create the circumstances and events in your life then you are aware of? After all you have all of the evidence that says you're doing the best that you can be doing.

Challenge:
Do dogs love bones? No, they love meat. They settle for bones. Where in your life are you settling? Where are you believing that you're doing the best you can? Where are you living in resignation? What lies are you buying into?

Tapping in Meditation:
My purpose today is to challenge what I accept as being true. My past does not equal my future and I am the creator of my reality and circumstances.

Journal Notes:

Day/Year	
Day/Year	
Day/Year	
Day/Year	
Day/Year	

March 7

The Stop Technique and Flipping

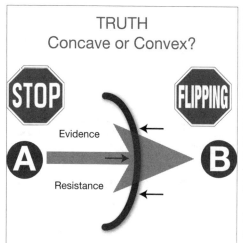

TRUTH
Concave or Convex?

STOP

FLIPPING

Evidence

A

B

Resistance

My health is my number 1 value. I love what Ralph Waldo Emerson says, "What you do speaks so loudly I can't hear what you say!" I intend to get up at 3:50 am and go to the gym. I set the alarm for 3:50 am. The alarm rings right at 3:50 am. Do I get up and go to the gym as intended? It depends on which side of the concave/convex perspective I'm paying attention to. Let's say I'm on the A side. My internal dialogue is, "I'm tired. I have a pain in my back. The last time I worked out through a pain I lost a week of productivity. I've worked out 18 of the last 21 days. Equally as important in a fitness program is rest. I need to sleep in!"

Pretty compelling arguments aren't they? Plus they are absolutely true. However, the truth is not relevant. The truth doesn't matter. The only thing that matters is by paying attention to that do I take the action. If I keep that perspective I will absolutely not go to the gym but I will have some very nice justifications and rationalizations as to why I didn't. However, if I want to get myself to do the deed then I've got to STOP the thoughts that are negative and take on an opposite point of view, a perspective that compels the action. I call this FLIPPING.

The alarm rings. My mind starts complaining, I'm tired, it's cold outside, STOP, FLIP. Stop the competing thoughts and flip to an opposite point of view. 100% of the time when I start my day off with a workout I have a better day. I go downstairs to get my workout gear and catch myself whining again, "I'm tired, my back hurts, STOP-FLIP, 100% of the time I have a better day when I start it off with a workout. This is one fantastic technique if you can get yourself to use it. You can use this for any thought that you find is compelling you to avoid!

Challenge:
Notice when your thoughts are not supporting your desired action. Use the STOP and FLIP technique.

Tapping in Meditation:
My purpose today is to take responsibility and ownership for my perceptual choices. Responsibility is the price of greatness. I am responsible for my life, for my feelings, for my personal growth and for every result I get.

Journal Notes:

Day/Year	
Day/Year	
Day/Year	
Day/Year	
Day/Year	

Cognitive Miser

The STOP and FLIP strategy (March 7) is a fantastic technique that absolutely would work in changing your perceptions and compelling you to take the desired action if you would just use it. Unfortunately you WON'T use it! How do I know this? Because it takes too much energy. The outer cortex area of the brain is the part of the brain that would inhibit your dominating thought and enable you to flip to an opposite point of view. However, it is very energy intensive. Your brain is an energy conserving organ. That's why neural networks are created so energy can be saved. Any activity that is too energy intensive is not likely to be sustained.

Here is a quick test for you. What is 12 divided by ½? Did you say 6? That is not correct. It's 24. (Use a calculator!) Your brain recognized a pattern and then hijacked you and would not let you put more energy on the solving of this problem. So you stopped short in your analysis.

The Case of the Cognitive Miser

Dennis   Jodi   Mark

Dennis is looking at Jodi, but Jodi is looking at Mark. Dennis is married, Mark is not. Is a married person looking at an unmarried person?

A) YES   B) NO   C) Cannot be determined

Here's another one. Dennis is looking at Jodi and Jodi is looking at Mark. Dennis is married, Mark is not. Is a married person looking at an unmarried person? Your choices are yes, no or cannot be determined, need more information. What is your answer? Most people say C, need more information. I ask, what information do you need? The answer, is Jodi married or not? That is not correct. This is another example of the genetic coding to conserve energy. The brain recognizes a pattern, the missing information, and because it is so energy intensive you were hijacked to stop paying attention to this solution. After all, it can't be solved without the missing information.

However, that is not correct. It doesn't matter if Jodi is married or not, a married person is always looking at an unmarried person. Let's say Jodi is married. Dennis who is married is looking at Jodi who in this case is also married. However, Jodi who is married is looking at Mark who is not so yes, if Jodi is married a married person is looking at an unmarried person. If Jodi is not married then it meets the criteria right away, Dennis who is married is looking at Jodi who is not. You see how you were hijacked!

Challenge:
Be aware of the short cuts that your brain instinctively wants to take. You can compensate with precise planning and accountability.

Tapping in Meditation:
My purpose today is to love and approve of myself. I feel the presence of those who are no longer here.

Journal Notes:

Day/Year	
Day/Year	
Day/Year	
Day/Year	
Day/Year	

March 9

Instincts Trump Intentions

Years ago I learned about behavioral contracting. Behavioral contracting means making a commitment and then placing a penalty that will be enforced by someone else if I don't do what I say I will do. The reason that this works is because of the human instinct of avoiding the highest level of perceived pain and seeking comfort.

My first use of this was for my binging while traveling. More specifically the mini bars at the hotels. I successfully used the behavioral contracting technique to get myself to stop binging. It wasn't that all of a sudden I had a great surge in will power, or discipline, or a renewed commitment. It was that I simply tapped into the human instinct that I already had.

You already have the talent and skills that you need to have to reach your goals. I don't have to add anything new. What I need to do is to give you access to what you already have. One way to gain that access is by tapping into the flow of human nature through behavioral contracting.

The good news about this is that anyone can do it successfully. I am still operating on automatic pilot (following my compelling instincts of avoidance) when I contract to stay out of the mini bar.

I love the example of the eye puff machine. If I puff air into your eyes you will blink. Now I want you to intend not to blink. You know it's coming. What do you do? Blink of course because instincts trump intentions. Try running up a flight of stairs as fast as you can and intend to keep your breathing normal—not going to happen!

When you tap in rather than fight human nature you will get more done, consistently over time and live life more fully. Some things you have to do every day. Eating seven apples on Saturday night instead of one a day just isn't going to get the job done

Challenge:

Tap into the way that you are designed—an avoidance machine. Avoid your penalties by doing what you intend to do. Make a contract every week, share it with someone else and look at it every day. Take productive actions every day.

Tapping in Meditation:

My purpose today is to concentrate all my thoughts upon the work in hand. The Sun's rays do not burn until brought to a focus.

Journal Notes:

Day/Year	
Day/Year	
Day/Year	
Day/Year	
Day/Year	

Quantum Physics, Double Slit and Measurement

Scientists randomly shot a particle at a screen with a barrier that had a single slit on its face. They saw a vertical line pattern just behind the vertical slit. That is how they expected the particles to act.

Now let's look at waves. A wave of light for example would strike the single slit barrier and hit the back wall with most of the intensity directly behind the slit as expected, much like the particles reacted. But when we add the second slit something strange happens.

The wave patterns interfered with each other. So now there is an interference pattern on the back wall. Lets go Quantum! An electron is matter on the small scale. Scientists fired a stream through one slit and it behaved like a particle sending a vertical band behind the single slit. When they shot an electron stream through two slits they expected it to leave two bands but instead what they saw was an interference pattern like the wave.

The pieces of matter, particles, behaved like a wave. They decided to shoot the electrons through the slits one at a time. The results were the same. They concluded that a single electron leaves as a particle, becomes a wave of potentials, goes through both slits and interferes with itself.

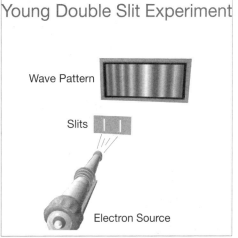

Young Double Slit Experiment

Wave Pattern

Slits

Electron Source

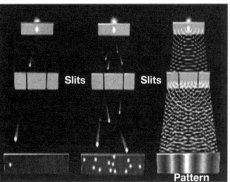

Slits   Slits

Pattern

Physicists were intrigued so they decided to observe which slit the electron actually went through by placing a measuring device by the slits. When they observed, the electron went back to behaving like a particle by producing two bands right behind the two slits as opposed to the interference pattern when it was not observed.

The very act of observing or measuring meant it only went through one and not both. It was as if the electron was aware that it was being measured. The observer collapsed the wave function simply by looking. This means that what you observe changes.

Challenge:

What can be measured must be measured. The act of measurement (observation) changes what is being measured. Make a list of what you can track on a daily basis and keep score every week.

Tapping in Meditation:

My purpose today is to be on purpose and I embrace measurement. I love the accountability that comes from tracking and I do track.

Journal Notes:

Day/Year	
Day/Year	
Day/Year	

March 11

Energy Thoughts E=MC^2

Einstein's Theory

$$E = mc^2$$

The deep connection Einstein discovered between energy and mass is expressed in the equation E=MC². Here E represents energy, m represents mass, and C² is a very large number, the square of the speed of light. Full confirmation was slow in coming. In Paris in 1933, Irène and Frédéric Joliot-Curie took a photograph showing the conversion of energy into mass. A quantum of light, invisible, carries energy up from beneath. In the middle it changes into mass—two freshly created particles which curve away from each other.

Energy is indistinguishable from matter, they are the same. Energy is simply a different state of matter like water, ice, steam are one and the same but in different states.

What this means to you is that you can accomplish and create what you want if you put enough energy into creating it. You can have the confidence that your efforts will bring results because you can create something from nothing by applying energy into the system. So, what do you want? What do you need to do to create it? Get to work.

Challenge:
Create the change that you haven't been willing or able to do until now.

Tapping in Meditation:
My purpose today is to step into the new self-image that I am becoming. I own my new self. I understand that I can create anything with energy, effort and purpose.

Journal Notes:

Day/Year	
Day/Year	
Day/Year	
Day/Year	
Day/Year	

March 12

Energy Thoughts—Newton's Orbital Cannon

Isaac Newton proposed 3 laws of motion.

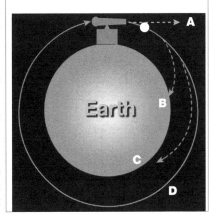

Newton's Orbital Cannon

1. Every object persists in its state of rest or uniform motion in a straight line unless it is compelled to change that state by forces impressed on it.

2. Force is equal to the change in momentum (mV) per change in time. For a constant mass, force equals mass times acceleration. F=ma

3. For every action, there is an equal and opposite re-action.

In this experiment Newton visualizes a cannon on top of a very high mountain. If there were no forces of gravitation or air resistance, then the cannonball should follow a straight line away from Earth, in the direction that it was fired (A). If a gravitational force acts on the cannon ball, it will follow a different path depending on its initial velocity. If the speed is low, it will simply fall back on Earth (B and C). If the speed reaches a stronger velocity then the ball will go further before falling back to Earth (C) and with further velocity, just the right amount you will get an orbit (D), where the object is in a constant balance between the outward trajectories of inertia and the inward pull of gravity. This is how satellites are placed into orbit.

Mass or your result can be created once enough energy is put into the system and with scientific certainty. This is another scientific example of this concept. If you put enough effort into achieving your goals you will achieve them with mathematical and scientific certainty!

Challenge:
Where do you need to increase your efforts? Start today.

Tapping in Meditation:
My purpose today is to simplify. Just for today identify the essential. I eliminate the rest."

Journal Notes:

Day/Year	
Day/Year	
Day/Year	
Day/Year	
Day/Year	

March 13

Energy Thoughts—Axon Hillock

Flow of Informatoin Across a Neuron

A single dentritic spine is electrically excited, causing a wave at point A. The wave spreads along the cell body, decreasing in strength by the time it reaches B, and is virtually gone by point C. If there is still enough strength to trigger an action potential at the hillock (D), the action potential is just as strong at points E and F.

A single dentritic spine is electrically excited, causing a wave of excitation at that point A. The wave spreads along the cell body, decrementing such that by point B it is smaller, and virtually gone by point C. Should there be enough summation to trigger an action potential at the hillock (D) that signal flies down to the axon and does not decrement. Instead, the action potential is just as strong at points E and F.

What this means to you is that there is a tipping point, a point when the sum of all of your efforts will be so strong that it will produce the result that you are looking for. Also once that result is produce it will continue easily and effortlessly. Sort of like pumping water. You have to pump several times with no results until you've put in enough effort that the water flows. Now you don't have to pump anymore because you've done the work for an ongoing flow.

You've got to make so many calls, talk to so many people, do so much of an effort to create the results that you are looking for and then those results will keep coming with a minimum of effort, science guarantees this! It's a part of our genetic coding on a single cell level! Nature rewards effort and intensity.

Challenge:

Nothing is less productive than to make more efficient what should not be done at all. Focus your energy on your most important tasks, just for today. You can speed up the process of getting results by putting just a bit more energy into the task.

Tapping in Meditation:

My purpose today is to be calm and aware and to intuitively know the right thing to do, moment to moment, and I do it. I focus my mind on the good and good comes to me.

Journal Notes:

Day/Year	
Day/Year	
Day/Year	
Day/Year	
Day/Year	

March 14

Energy Thoughts—The S.A.I.D. Principle

Specific Adaptations to Imposed Demands. If you put enough effort into any project you will get the result you are looking for if you stay at it long enough. This is a guaranteed certainty. The S.A.I.D. Principle states that form follows function. An offensive lineman in American football will look different from a wide receiver. The lineman will be about 6'5 300 pounds. The lineman will be very explosive for 5 yards in all directions. He is built according to his function.

A wide receiver will be on the average 6'4 210 pounds. He will be fast and lean. He is built for his function which is to run 40 yards every play. You can see that each has different demands and he has different specific adaptations to those demands.

I was visiting my home state of N.J. and stayed with a former college roommate. He came downstairs the next morning and did 10 push-ups, 10 sit ups and 10 jumping jacks. I asked him what he was doing and as he grabbed his belly he said that he was exercising and that he was going to lose 40 pounds.

I didn't share this with him but he was wasting his time. His level of activity was not intense enough to create an adaptation or result. He needed to pick up his activity levels, duration plus add different activities.

I was coaching a staffing company who embraced these principles. They had measured the activities necessary to be successful in their business and the intensity necessary on a daily basis. Here is a sample:

They embraced several concepts. The act of measurement changes what is being measured. If you can't measure, you can't manage. If you put enough energy into a system you will produce a result with certainty. You have to have enough of the right kind of activity to create the results.

- Telemarketing calls 2
- Client visits 4
- Client visits cold call 2
- Collection calls 2
- Present a candidate 1
- Quality control check 1
- Recruiting source activities 1
- Contract presented 1
- Contract signed 5
- Site evaluation 3

Challenge:
Evaluate; are you doing enough of the right type of activities? What do you need to stop or start doing? Do it today.

Tapping in Meditation:
My purpose today is to call on my inner guidance for clarity, wisdom, knowledge, support, creative inspiration, love and companionship and I do.

Journal Notes:

Day/Year	
Day/Year	
Day/Year	
Day/Year	
Day/Year	

March 15

Shake it Off and Take a Step—The Old Mule

There was an old mule. One day he fell into the farmer's well. The farmer evaluated the situation and thought to himself that neither the well nor the old mule was worth the efforts to save them. Thus he decided to haul dirt to bury the old mule and the well.

So the farmer called his neighbors and together they started shoveling dirt into the well. The old mule was terrified and hysterical in the beginning. But soon one hopeful idea came to his mind. Every time a shovel of dirt landed on his back, he would shake it off and take a step up.

He repeated these words to himself again and again, "Shake if off and step up." This way he could do something positive to encourage himself and towards his desired goal to get out of the well.

After some time the mule had stepped over the well's wall. Although terribly tired, he was the winner. He saved his own life. He decided to face his adversity positively and not to give up. What seemed like it would bury him actually saved him along with his confidence and unresting efforts.

Challenge:
Be the mule! Face adversity positively and keep on keeping on. Just for today what adversity do you face that you can work your way through?

Tapping in Meditation:
My purpose today is to embrace adversity, calamity and confusion. The purest ore is produced from the hottest furnace. The brightest thunder-bolt is elicited from the darkest storm. I believe in me and I keep on keeping on.

Journal Notes:

Day/Year	
Day/Year	
Day/Year	
Day/Year	
Day/Year	

March 16

Eliminate "I Have to"

Imagine you are in a box that is slightly larger than you are. How would you feel? Hot, trapped, claustrophobic, anxious, afraid, like you want to break out? That's the mindset that you put yourself in with the subtle thoughts that you have to do something.

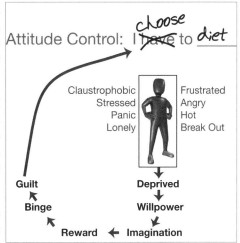

Attitude Control: I ~~have~~ to _choose_ _diet_

What do you have to do today? Fill in the blank, "I have to _____." Let's use diet as an example. Suppose you say, "I have to diet." That puts you into the psychological prison were you feel frustrated, angry, hot, trapped and you want to break out. You are in the mindset of a deprived state.

You maintain this deprived state and you continue to diet through the use of willpower. Willpower is a high intensity, high energy demanding state that is always associated with deprivation. You can only use willpower to maintain a behavior for a short time before your mind wanders to imagination. Imagination is associated with reward. After a while you start to think I've been deprived for too long and you start to think about a reward. Finally, you cannot keep up the energy required to maintain deprivation so you give in and over do what you were trying to avoid in the first place, you binge.

After the temporary relief of the binge what follows next, you guessed it, you feel guilty. Then you decide that you have to diet and you start the cycle over again. The result of this is fatigue, failure and resignation.

The solution—eliminate the I HAVE TO and instead think, I CHOOSE TO. Make your behavior and commitments choices, not I have to's. It's a simple and subtle difference in thinking that pays off big time. It's the small and subtle distinctions that separate the elite performers from the average.

Challenge:
Make a list of what you tell yourself that you HAVE to do today. Take a close look at what is really important and urgent. Decide to take action on one of those items, just for today. Remember, it's your decision, your choice, not an "I have to."

Tapping in Meditation:
My purpose today is to make my life great! Why do anything unless I'm going to do it with excellence. Every action I take today I take with excellence.

Journal Notes:

Day/Year	
Day/Year	
Day/Year	
Day/Year	
Day/Year	

March 17

Intentions + Mechanisms = Results

Imagine there are 100 people in a room and everyone forms a single line at one end of the room. The instructions are, one at a time, to find a way to go to the other end of the room but you can't duplicate anyone before you.

Sounds simple enough right? Guess again. The first person simply walks to the other side of the room. The next person skips, followed by a person who walks backward, then one who walks sideways and another who hops on one leg, followed by one who hops with both legs then someone walks on all 4's etc. until finally the person in front of you takes your thought, they put a finger on top of their head and twirl across the room and you are stuck. You are paralyzed. You can't figure out how to cross the room.

This is incredibly limited thinking. Now here's the tough love part. You are committed to being stuck. This is a victim mindset. There are an infinite number of ways to get across the room. However, it requires quite a bit of mental energy and it's easier to just get stuck and stay stuck.

You might have some goals or interests that you have put off until blank. Fill it in. Until you can afford it, until you have more time, etc. You think that when you have the mechanism then you will have the result. Let's do violence to this formula. Let's eliminate the Mechanisms (and the + sign). What's that leave you with? Intentions = Results.

When you have made the decision to have a result, and commit to it, then the mechanism will reveal itself to you. You don't wait for the revelation, you make the commitment first.

I've always said if you want to know what a person is committed to look at what they have. That's what they are committed to. If a person is in a miserable marriage guess what they are committed to? Yep, being in a miserable marriage and complaining about it.

Challenge:

What are you waiting for? Make a list and see if there is anything that you really want to accomplish that you can start today.

Tapping in Meditation:

My purpose today is to enjoy my house, my family and, more than anything enjoy the feeling of seeing each day used to the fullest to actually produce something. And I do.

Journal Notes:

Day/Year	
Day/Year	
Day/Year	
Day/Year	
Day/Year	

March 18

Self Image, Cognitive Dissonance and the Necker Cube

Have you ever felt uncomfortable when you discover that your beliefs don't match up with reality? Psychologists refer to this phenomenon as cognitive dissonance.

Come back in time with me to September 26, 1981. I was a college football coach at that time coaching at Cal State Fullerton. We were on the road to play the University of Arizona, a highly regarded Pac 10 team. We were the cream puff on their schedule. The Arizona newspaper title for that day read, "Wildcats to play Cal State Disneyland." Not much respect. What was about to happen was a shock to everyone.

We were leading 16-13 going into the 4th quarter. It was stunning. We had been predicted to lose by 40 points. Then something happened. Our athletes started to make mistakes that they hadn't made the entire game. They missed assignments, made physical mistakes and at the end of the game we lost, 37-16. That is a perfect example of cognitive dissonance, where your behavior is not matching up to your belief.

Cognitive Dissonance: The Necker Cube

A   B   C

You've seen what is called a Necker Cube. You can look at the cube so that one side is facing out toward you and then change your observation to make the other side face outward. However, you can't have both perspectives at the same time. Likewise you can't be thinking that you hate prospecting and then build successful relationships. You can't be thinking we're just not a very good team and then win football games.

I can remember thinking that I would never be able to hire anyone who could do the job I needed as good as I could. I struggled for a long time until I was able to change that belief. Your thinking must line up with your intentions and then your must take the right kind of actions and at a threshold that will produce a result. The good news is that you can do this.

Challenge:
Where in your life does your thinking or beliefs hinder you? Just for today make a change. What happens? Journal at the end of the day.

Tapping in Meditation:
My purpose today is to be my best self. This means that just for today I will only allow thoughts of possibility and greatness to enter my mind. I believe in me.

Journal Notes:

Day/Year	
Day/Year	
Day/Year	
Day/Year	
Day/Year	

March 19

Simplify and Say "NO"

There is a principle in physics called "Occam's Razor" The most useful statement of the principle for scientists is that when you have two competing theories that make exactly the same predictions, the simpler one is the better. I want to emphasize, "simplify." If you get bogged down in chaos, stress and uncertainty, ask yourself how can you simplify your life? This usually means what or whom do you need to say no to? Do you have difficulty turning down others requests?

This principle goes back at least as far as Aristotle, who wrote "Nature operates in the shortest way possible." Simplicity is the keynote of a good life. Choose the simple things always. You can be swamped by difficulties if you let them take up too much of your time. Love the humble things in life. Reverence the simple things. You will find that it is necessary to let things go; simply for the reason that they are heavy. So let them go, let go of them. I tie no weights to my ankles.

Challenge:

What or who do you need to say no to, just for today?

Tapping in Meditation:

My purpose today is to love the simple things. I love myself. I take care of myself and say no when my peace and serenity will be violated by saying yes.

Journal Notes:

Day/Year	
Day/Year	
Day/Year	
Day/Year	
Day/Year	

March 20

Do Violence to the Impossible—Live with Passion and Be the Cause

What do you believe is impossible in your life? Do you have some goals that you have brushed aside because you think that given your set of circumstances it would be impossible for you to accomplish them? Don't buy it! You can't trust your interpretation of the reality of your circumstances. Change your mindset. Instead of believing something is impossible take a close look at the word impossible. Let's look at 3 words and give you new insights about all three. Impossible, Passion and Because.

I-m-possible
Pass-i-on
Be-cause

You have far more capacity to create the circumstances and events in your life then you are aware of. All things are possible, to you, through precise preparation, careful thoughts about what you are willing to commit to action and accountability.

One of the non-negotiable requirements for living in excellence is to be passionate about your life. Be passionate and excited about every aspect of what you are going through on a daily basis. What's the alternative, to be miserable? Then you would be doing a two for one. Not only is the thing happening to you but you are also upset about it.

Also, here is another subtle mindset shift. Rather than believing the reasons, stories and excuses about why you can't do something, why not be the cause (be-cause) of your results. Now that is taking full responsibility. Don't be afraid of your fears. They're not there to scare you. They're there to let you know that something is worth it."

Challenge:
Take full responsibility for the results in your life. What is one action that you can take today that can bring a different more desirable result?

Tapping in Meditation:
My purpose today is to live fully and peacefully. Peace comes from within. Do not seek it without.

Journal Notes:

Day/Year	
Day/Year	
Day/Year	
Day/Year	
Day/Year	

March 21

The Dot and Circle Lesson and HIJKLMNO

Thinking Differently to Solve Problems

H I J K L M N O

Here is your test. Draw a circle. Now put a dot in the middle of the circle.

Now duplicate this without lifting your pen or pencil from the page. You cannot have a line from the dot to the outside of the circle. Look away from this book and come back when you are stumped and ready to accept that it can't be done.

Stumped? Most people are. The problem is that you can't approach this in a normal and reasonable way. Being reasonable is the lowest level of human consciousness. Before I give you the solution let me give you another puzzle to solve.

Look at these letters: **H I J K L M N O**

What word do they suggest?

The Solutions

Circle and dot. Place a dot in the center of a page. Keeping your pen on the dot bring the far left bottom corner of the paper up to where your pen is. Now start drawing your circle on top of that folded part of the paper. When you come off of that tip of the page you will be separated from your dot and you can complete your circle. You now have a circle with a dot in the center and you have not lifted your pen off of the page.

HIJKLMNO The word is water. You won't be able to solve this by the most reasonable approach of looking at and rearranging the letters. You've got to change your observation. This sequence of letters is H all the way over To O or H_2O, water.

Challenge:
Einstein said that you can't solve your problems with the same state of mind that you were in when you created them. Just for today what or who can you look at differently? Journal what impact that has.

Tapping in Meditation:
My purpose today is to is to live from my heart. The way is not in the sky. It's in the heart. I see things from a heartfelt loving perspective.

Journal Notes:

Day/Year	
Day/Year	
Day/Year	
Day/Year	
Day/Year	

March 22

Earn Your Pleasures, Use Contingencies

The goal of the experiment is to place a pigeon in a box and have it move to the far end, press down on a lever to receive food. When the scientist first places the animal in the box it just pecks around haphazardly. However, when the pigeon moves in the direction of the desired result, towards the back wall with the lever at the far end the experimenter rewards the pigeon by dropping in a food pellet. This is called shaping behavior. Each time the subject takes an action that approximates the desired end result it receives a reward.

After a few trials the animal has learned to go into the box and immediately to the spot where it received the reward. Now the experimenter stops the reward until the pigeon randomly pecks closer to the lever. This extinguishes the previous behavior and establishes a new boundary.

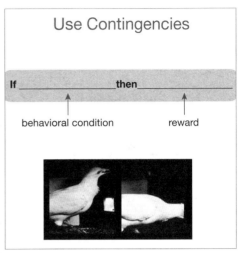

Use Contingencies

If _____ then _____

behavioral condition   reward

The experimenter will continue to do this until the pigeon goes into the box and moves all the way to the back wall. Now it will not receive a reward until it pecks at the lever. Over time with small rewards for actions towards the desired end result the pigeon learns in steps. Now when placed in the box the pigeon moves all the way to the lever and presses it.

Earn your pleasures. Use contingencies. These are IF _____ followed by a behavioral condition, THEN _____ followed by a reward. You can also use the word AFTER for IF. After I make 5 calls (the behavior) then I will check my personal email (the reward).

If I go to the gym 5 times Monday through Friday then I will go flying and skydiving on Saturday. (That would work for me!)

Challenge:
Just for today make a deal. Pick a behavior and a reward. You can do this one time for the entire day or several for shorter periods of time. Journal what you notice.

Tapping in Meditation:
My purpose today is to share myself with others. Thousands of candles can be lit from a single candle. The life of the candle will not be shortened. Happiness never decreases by being shared.

Journal Notes:

Day/Year	
Day/Year	
Day/Year	
Day/Year	
Day/Year	

March 23

Use Mind Maps

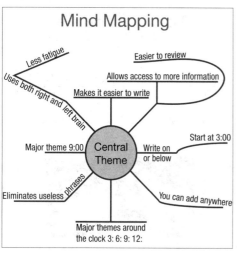

Mind Mapping

Less fatigue

Uses both right and left brain

Easier to review

Allows access to more information

Makes it easier to write

Major theme 9:00

Central Theme

Write on or below

Start at 3:00

Eliminates useless phrases

You can add anywhere

Major themes around the clock 3: 6: 9: 12:

A Mind Map is a powerful graphic technique which provides a universal key to unlock the potential of the brain. It harnesses the full range of cortical skills—word, image, number, logic, rhythm, color and spatial awareness—in a single, uniquely powerful manner. In so doing, it gives you the freedom to roam the infinite expanses of your brain. The Mind Map can be applied to every aspect of life where improved learning and clearer thinking will enhance human performance. Since the human brain operates from series of neural networks, Mind Mapping duplicates this process.

Here is how. Place a circle about the size of a quarter in the center of a page. Write your central theme or idea in that circle. Next draw straight lines, about an inch long, at 3, 6, 9 and 12. You can write on or below a line. Starting at 3 o'clock start to place your major themes or ideas. Move around as if a clock, 6, 9, 12. You can add anywhere, there is no right or wrong. This eliminates useless words or phrases. Mind Mapping increases creativity because it gives you access to both sides of your brain. The actual thinking of the information activates the outer cortex and the placement in the Mind Map activates the limbic area. You get full brain access to more ideas.

Challenge:

Take a topic of interest and mind map it.

Tapping in Meditation:

My purpose today is to be aware of my thoughts and the impact that they have on me and other people. I am what I think. All that I am arises with my thoughts. With my thoughts I make my reality.

Journal Notes:

Day/Year	
Day/Year	
Day/Year	
Day/Year	
Day/Year	

March 24

Use Pending vs Current Mind Maps to go From Confusion to Clarity

Rita is a professional speaker. She was sitting at her desk knowing that she needed to be making prospecting calls. However, her mind kept being interrupted by all kinds of distracting thoughts. She was paralyzed and wasn't able to get anything done. Finally, she remembered a technique she heard about when she attended a workshop for people with ADHD.

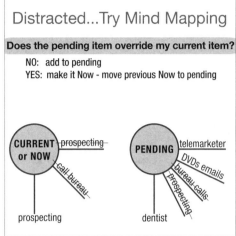

Distracted...Try Mind Mapping

Does the pending item override my current item?
NO: add to pending
YES: make it Now - move previous Now to pending

She grabbed a piece of paper and drew two circles on each half of the page. On the left she wrote Current or Now and on the right she wrote Pending. She remembered that this was a structure that would calm the mind and give her a place to capture her ideas yet at the same time stay focused on doing only one thing at a time.

As she is prospecting, making telephone calls, she has the thought that she needs to make contact with one of her employees, a telemarketer. She stops and asks herself this question, does the pending item override what she is currently doing? If yes she puts it on her current mind map and moves prospecting over to pending. There is only one activity on her current mind map. If no then she puts that item on her pending map. She can get to it later.

Next she gets a call about some DVDs. No, that doesn't override what she is currently doing so she stays on task but adds that to the pending. This is followed by an email from a speaker bureau who wants to check a date for availability. Yes, this overrides her prospecting, so she moves prospecting over to pending and writes speaker bureau in her now map.

Challenge:

Use a pending versus current mind map technique today. Notice the clarity that you get and the peacefulness that you maintain with this structure.

Tapping in Meditation:

My purpose today is to trust my inner light and intuition to guide me. Nervousness surrounding what I do is a good sign. I know the situation will work out for my highest good. Wonderful things unfold before me.

Journal Notes:

Day/Year	
Day/Year	
Day/Year	
Day/Year	
Day/Year	

March 25
Human Instincts—Avoid the Highest Level of Perceived Pain

There was a T.V. series titled *House*. The main character, Dr. House, had chronic and severe leg pain. In one episode he's sitting at his desk and takes a paperweight and smashes his hand. His colleague says, "Have you lost your mind?"

Dr. House replies, "No, I'm just sick and tired of the pain in my leg!"

The principle here is that we are genetically coded to recognize and avoid the highest level of perceived pain. Now Dr. House would no longer feel the pain in his leg. Instead he would feel the pain in his hand.

I've seen this happen to myself. Both of my knees are bone on bone. I had severe pain in both and was close to having knee replacement surgery. Then something happened. I developed severe degenerative arthritis in my right shoulder. I now have chronic pain in my shoulder. Guess what no longer hurts? My knees!

So what is it that you avoid doing? Prospecting, exercising, spending time with your family? The reason that you avoid is because the activity is linked to pain. Your human genetic coding is to recognize your highest level of perceived pain and avoid it. This is an instinct. You can't help it. But you can tap into it. Use a behavioral contract.

Challenge:
Manipulate your reaction to perceived pain by placing a behavioral contract, just for today. Pick one activity that you probably would not have done today, but you want to. Place a painful penalty if you don't take that action. Tell another person that you will give them $100 if you don't take this action today. At the end of the day report on your results. Repeat as needed. Your instinct will be to avoid the highest pain, the $100 penalty.

Tapping in Meditation:
My purpose today is to use my instincts to my advantage. I am a part of all that is good in the universe. I welcome abundance, love and prosperity and I am abundant, loved and prosperous. I am divinely guided all day long.

Journal Notes:

Day/Year	
Day/Year	
Day/Year	
Day/Year	
Day/Year	

March 26

The Law of Opposites—Polarity

John is a very successful estate planning attorney. He is very aggressive. This serves him well. He explains to his client their problems and solutions. He takes them on a journey to see how painful it will be and what they will lose if they don't take the actions he is recommending. He closes a lot of business.

However John has a problem with his staff. It seems that every month he is firing and hiring another attorney. John's aggressiveness is viewed as being demanding and pushy. This is the law of opposites—polarity.

You can't know hot without knowing cold. You can't understand the concept of up without down, good and bad, etc. There is an ancient concept called the 7 Hermetic Principles. The 4th is the principle of polarity which states that everything is dual. Everything has poles. Everything has its pair of opposites. Like and unlike are the same. Opposites are identical in nature but different in degree. It is the extremes that become dangerous and are to be avoided.

Fire is good. It can heat your home and cook your food. Used inappropriately it can burn your house down and kill you. Every trait that you have has is opposite extreme. If you are aggressive that is good. You will plow through excuses and circumstances to lead others and to accomplish their goals. However, take it to its extreme and it's bad. If you're overly aggressive you will be rude and push people away.

Being kind is incredibly positive. Kind people rally people to a cause. However, taken to its extreme kind people get walked over and disrespected. Nature favors symmetry, a balance. Goldilocks said this years ago.

Challenge:
Notice your strengths. Take them to the extreme and they become weaknesses. Be aware of being in perceptual balance.

Tapping in Meditation:
My purpose today is to follow my intuition and my heart. This keeps me safe. I focus on breathing and grounding myself. I make the right choices every time. I draw from my inner strength. I trust myself.

Journal Notes:

Day/Year	
Day/Year	
Day/Year	
Day/Year	
Day/Year	

March 27

What Does Failure Mean?

Colonel Sanders :
The founder of KFC. He started his dream at 65 years old! He got a social security check for only $105 and was mad. Instead of complaining he did something about it. He thought restaurant owners would love his fried chicken recipe, use it, sales would increase, and he'd get a percentage of it. He drove around the country knocking on doors, sleeping in his car, wearing his white suit. Do you know how many times people said no till he got one yes? 1009 times!

Walt Disney:
The man who gave us Disney World and Mickey Mouse. His first animation company went bankrupt. He was fired by a news editor because he lacked imagination. Legend has it he was turned down 302 times before he got financing for creating Disney World.

Albert Einstein:
He didn't speak till he was four and didn't read till seven. His parents and teachers thought he was mentally handicapped. He only turned out to win a Nobel prize and be the face of modern physics.

Richard Branson:
He's a billionaire mogul of Virgin but has had his share of failures. Remember Virgin Cola or Virgin credit cards? Probably not. He's lost hundreds of millions of dollars but has not let failure stop him.

Mark Cuban:
The billionaire owner of the NBA's Dallas Mavericks got rich when he sold his company to Yahoo for $5.9 billion in stock. He admitted he was terrible at his early jobs. His parents wanted him to have a normal job. So he tried carpentry but hated it. He was a short order cook but a terrible one. He waited tables but couldn't open a bottle of wine. He says of his failures, "I've learned that it doesn't matter how many times you failed, you only have to be right once. I tried to sell powdered milk. I was an idiot lots of times and I learned from them all.

How bad do you want to achieve our goal? It better be so bad that rejection won't derail you. How much do you believe in what you are doing? Colonel Sanders did despite 1009 rejections. "Fall down 7 times, get up 8"— Japanese proverb.

Challenge:
Think about what you could do if you weren't afraid to fail. If you are well prepared and you fail, fail forward and learn. Use failure as a magnet bringing you closer to your goals and the life you want to live. Just for today what one action can you take that will have you risk failure? Do it anyway.

Tapping in Meditation:
My purpose today is to keep on keeping on. I am a unique child of this world. I have every bit as much brightness to offer the world as the next person. I matter and what I have to offer this world also matters.

Journal Notes:

Day/Year	
Day/Year	
Day/Year	

March 28

The Lesson of the 6 Pens

Take 6 pens approximately the same size and arrange them into 4 equal size triangles with each leg of the triangle the same size as one of the pens. Are you getting stumped? Are you laying the pens on the table and placing the remaining pens on top in various configurations? That approach won't work. A solution is not available using that approach. You have to change your approach. Tell me when you are ready to surrender and accept that you can't do it.

The key point to emphasize here is to replace "I can't" with this phrase, "At my current mindset a solution is not available."

There is a solution but your approach just hasn't led you to it yet. Here it is. Place three pens in a triangle on your table. Now take the remaining 3 and make a tripod and place the ends at the corners of the triangle on the table. Now you have 4 equal size triangles, the one on the table and the faces of the tripod. (See April 4th for a picture)

Challenge:
You can solve every problem that you have if you change your approach. Eliminate the words "I can't" from existence. Instead repeat, "At my present mindset a solution is not available." Change your approach. Pick one prevailing problem that you have today and change your approach. Journal the result.

Tapping in Meditation:
My purpose today is to easily discover solutions to my problems and I do. Everything works out for my highest good. There is great reason that this is unfolding before me now. I have the talent to get through this now. Every problem has a solution and I seek my solution with resolve. I am safe and sound.

Journal Notes:

Day/Year	
Day/Year	
Day/Year	
Day/Year	
Day/Year	

March 29

A Life of No Regrets

My good friend Mike's wife was dying of cancer. Cancer is a very humbling disease. It calls on you to examine the purpose of your life. Did you live with your intentions fulfilled or did you sell out to reasons, stories, excuses, obstacles, fears and lies?

After she died, I asked Mike if he had any regrets. His answer surprised me, impressed me and made me sad as I reflected back on my own life. He said NO. He had no regrets the way he lived his life with his wife. He took time off, he went on family vacations, he had plenty of family memories, he shared quality time with his wife and family and if he had to do it again there wasn't a thing he would change.

I couldn't say that, how about you?

Challenge:

Just for today look at what changes you would need to make so you could say that you lived a life of few or no regrets?

Tapping in Meditation:

My purpose today is to attempt all—not some—possible ways to get unstuck. I seek new ways of thinking. I know the answers are before me even if I'm not seeing them. I believe in my ability to unlock the way and set myself free.

Journal Notes:

Day/Year	
Day/Year	
Day/Year	
Day/Year	
Day/Year	

March 30

Waiting Outside the Lines—Greyson Chance

Read the words to this song;

> "You never enjoy your life-living inside the bars. You're so afraid of taking chances—how you gonna reach the top? Rules and Regulations—force you to play a tape—get rid of all the hesitation—it's time for you to seize the day. Instead of just sitting around and looking down on tomorrow—you gotta let your feet off the ground—the time is now. I'm waiting—waiting outside the lines Ohhhh waiting outside the lines… Try to have no regrets even if it's just a night—how you gonna walk ahead if you keep living blind—stuck in my same position—you deserve so much more—there's a whole world around us—just waiting to be explored—instead of just sitting around and looking down on tomorrow you gotta get your feet off the ground—the time is now—just let gooooo don't want to have to force you to smile—I'm here to help you notice the rainbow—cause I know what's in you is out there—I'm waiting……I'm trying to be patient the first step is the hardest—I know you can make it. Go ahead and take ittttt I'm waiting… You never enjoy your life living inside the bars you're so afraid of taking chances—how you gonna reach the top."

Challenge:
It's the starting that stops most people. What is one action you can take today that would get you started towards something you would be proud of?

Tapping in Meditation:
My purpose today is to create action. The past has no power and no hold over me anymore. I embrace the rhythm and the flowing of my own heart. All that I need will come to me at the right time and place in this life. I am deeply fulfilled with who I am.

Journal Notes:

Day/Year	
Day/Year	
Day/Year	
Day/Year	
Day/Year	

March 31

What You Seek Also Seeks You

What you seek is seeking you

—**Rummi**

When you have a thought you have already created your reality. Your thoughts have a magnetic attraction that attracts to you what is like your thoughts. Thought precedes physical form and "the action of Mind plants that nucleus which, if allowed to grow undisturbed, will eventually attract to itself all the conditions necessary for its manifestation in outward visible form.

There is a postulate attributed to Aristotle that nature abhors a vacuum. No man is an island. You live in a world of interdependence. Everything is interconnected. You have a talent. You solve a problem. Someone somewhere is looking for you. What you seek is also seeking you so don't be selfish and stop seeking, seek harder.

Challenge:

What is one action that you can take that would be evidence of your "seeking harder?" Take that action.

Tapping in Meditation:

My purpose today is to trust my inner wisdom. I make the right choices today, all day long. I have all that I need to make this a great day in my life. I am healthy and strong

Journal Notes:

Day/Year	
Day/Year	
Day/Year	
Day/Year	
Day/Year	

APRIL

Davies
Day Book

365 concepts for excellence

April 1

Good Character is Better than Outstanding Talent

Character - Coach Labrum

"Gentlemen, we are not pleased with how our football brothers are representing our family, school...and yourselves."

High school team suspended
for off-field misbehavior

Football at Union High School in Roosevelt, Utah is a privilege. Coach Labrum benched his team to teach a lesson. They had just lost to a rival team, 40-16. The players were shocked when their coach told them to "Turn in your jerseys. I'm suspending the whole team." Labrum has had enough of slipping grades, skipping classes, and possible involvement in the cyber-bullying of another student.

This wasn't about winning or losing, it's about character. Labrum offered them a way back. Besides doing plenty of soul searching they scrubbed school hallways, picked up trash, visited elderly and memorized a passage on the importance of character.

The most common response from the players was that they would never forget this. "It really changed my attitude and made me want to be a better person" said one player. They received their jerseys back in time for their homecoming game.

Playing football for these athletes was no longer a right, it was a privilege. One of the most encouraging things about this was that school officials and parents backed up the coach's decision.

Challenge:

Think about what you might be tolerating in your own family. What are the privileges versus rights, where a conversation is needed? Have that conversation today.

Tapping in Meditation:

My purpose today is to be a moral and ethical stand for those I love. Be the change I want to see in others.

Journal Notes:

Day/Year	
Day/Year	
Day/Year	
Day/Year	
Day/Year	

April 2

Intentions versus Actual Performance

Day 2 of the 2nd quarter. How are you on implementing your business plan?

How about your New Year's Resolutions? If you're like most people there is a gap between what you intended to do and what you have actually done. Why is that?

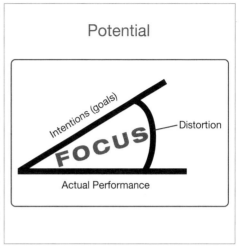

Let's assume that you are well planned and that your goals are realistic. What explains that gap between your potential and your actual performance? It's easy, human instincts. If you are not taking an action that you need to take to reach your goal it's because your brain has "tagged" it as painful or inconvenient or just flat out dangerous. Reality doesn't matter. It doesn't matter whether rejection can actually hurt you (it can by the way), the only thing that matters is your human instinct to avoid anything that you perceive as being a threat.

So if you haven't followed the food plan, if you haven't exercised, if you haven't made your calls don't fret. You can start today and get back on track. Make a commitment and have someone hold you accountable with a consequence for non-performance.

Challenge:
Re-evaluate the 1st quarter. What adjustments do you need to make in your commitments and activities for Q2?

Tapping in Meditation:
My purpose today is to solve any challenges that come up. I have all the information that I need. I have the knowledge to make smart decisions today and I do. I make the right choices all day long using my inner wisdom. I am happy and content with my life. I am patient and calm and greet the day with ease.

Journal Notes:

Day/Year	
Day/Year	
Day/Year	
Day/Year	
Day/Year	

April 3

Wheat is Making You Fat

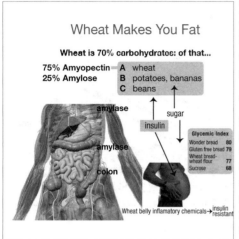

Wheat Makes You Fat

Wheat is 70% carbohydrates: of that...

75% Amyopectin — A wheat
25% Amylose — B potatoes, bananas
C beans

Remember your commitment to excellence includes your health, business and personal life. You are hopefully participating in our food plan of avoiding sugar and flower, three weighed and measured meals, nothing in between.

Today, let's look at how wheat, which is usually ground into flower, is making your fat. Wheat is 70% carbohydrate and out of that is 75% Amyopectin and 25% Amylose. There is an enzyme in the saliva and in the stomach that is released and breaks down Amyopectin. There are different types of Amyopectin and they respond to Amylase differently. Type C, found in beans, breaks down very slowly if at all. This means that most of that food is sent to the colon and excreted. Type B, found in potatoes, bananas, breaks down more readily into sugar over time. Type A, the type of Amyopectin found in wheat and wheat products breaks down very quickly. This floods the blood with sugar which causes the pancreas to release a flood of insulin. Insulin is a carrier molecule that transports the sugar into the cells for energy and also stores the excess sugar as a future energy source, fat. With wheat breaking down so rapidly there is a large response of insulin which promotes the large storage of sugar as fat and what is called "wheat belly" is the result.

You have been deceived by advertising to get rid of table sugar/sucrose, and replace it with complex carbohydrates. Herein lays the illusion of wheat. Wheat breaks down quickly into blood sugar, which is referred to as the glycemic index.

Low GI	Medium GI	Hi GI
0-55	56-69	70 +

Wheat bread which is "sold" as healthy is actually almost as bad (bad=fast breakdown to blood sugar) as white Wonder bread. In fact, wheat products are more damaging then table sugar, 68 GI for sucrose versus 77 GI for Wheat. Eating wheat will promote insulin resistance and weight gain. We avoid all flower and sugar and that includes wheat products.

Challenge:
Stay with the food plan regardless of circumstances.

Tapping in Meditation:
My purpose today is to love and nurture myself with the proper nutrition and plentiful food in my food plan and I do.

Journal Notes:

Day/Year	
Day/Year	
Day/Year	
Day/Year	

April 4

Passion

Look at the word **pass-i-on**. Defined; "A strong feeling of enthusiasm or excitement for something or about doing something" One of the non-negotiable coaching commands for you along this journey for excellence is to be absolutely passionate about your life, about what you do, about your day.

One of the common characteristics of peak performers is that they are excited and highly energized about what they do. This is essential for health. Look at the legendary Alabama football coach Bear Bryant. He said that he would die when he stopped coaching football. After breaking the record for career victories by a college football head coach, Paul (Bear) Bryant called himself a tired old man who never got tired of football. When Bryant finally retired, he didn't receive an opportunity to enjoy life away from the game, if that were possible for him. He died 28 days after coaching his last game.

Mind-Set Focus

Arrange six pens to make four triangles. The triangles must be the same size, with each side equal to the length of one pen.

Replace "I can't" with "at my current level of thinking a solution is not available!"

Joe Paterno, one of the most successful coaches in American football at Penn State, was fired in November, 2011. He died from lung cancer in January, 2012, less than 3 months. Bobby Bowden, head football coach at Florida State University, had to be forced to retire at the age of 80 years old.

The moment you lose your passion, your energy, your reason why, your growth and excitement, then you start to decay. There is a principle in physics that states you are either growing or decaying, there is no middle ground.

What these great men lost was their focus for 7 days, their preparation, execution, evaluation, preparation and repeat. When you lose your passion and no longer are passing on your energy and preparation, then decay sets in.

Challenge:
Make sure you are in an environment that you are excited about. Make sure that you are actively taking steps to reach your goals, regardless of your age and circumstances. Just for today, be excited and in action.

Tapping in Meditation:
My purpose today is to live the old lessons (work, self-discipline, sacrifice, teamwork, fighting to achieve). I design my happiness today.

Journal Notes:

Day/Year	
Day/Year	
Day/Year	
Day/Year	
Day/Year	

April 5

The Lesson of the Bell Curve—The 2-7-2 Rule

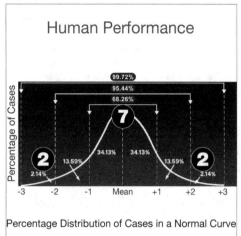

Percentage Distribution of Cases in a Normal Curve

We live in a world of math. Nature is information expressed in the language of math. Nature has symmetry. This symmetry states that there is a polarity, hot and cold, good and bad and a statistical representation called the frequency distribution or bell shaped curve.

The bell curve illustrates what I call the 2-7-2 rule. It states that 2% of the population will be the top producers, 70% will be the average, and 2% will be the low producers. Regardless of the human variable being measured the math will have symmetry, the 2-7-2 rule.

The top 2% of the population are not special from the rest. They just have habits and attitudes that are different from everyone else. You can examine your life and identify where you are not a top producer, or at least as successful as you would like to be. Then you can identify the habits that you need to either stop or start. Once you've made that analysis then you can literally re-wire your brain to form those new habits and "prune away" the old habits. If you follow the same principles that are common for the top 2% of the population, the same formula, then you will be in the top 2%, it is not negotiable.

Calvin Coolidge if famous for having said, "Nothing in the world can take the place of persistence. Talent will not; nothing is more common than unsuccessful men with talent. Genius will not; unrewarded genius is almost a proverb. Education will not; the world is full of educated derelicts. Persistence and determination alone are omnipotent. The slogan "Press On!" has solved and always will solve the problems of the human race."

Challenge:

Make a list of your unwanted habits and the new habits that you want to create. Take one action today from your new habits list. Stop on action today from your unwanted habits list.

Tapping in Meditation:

My purpose today is to design my day. Happiness is not something I postpone for the future; it is something I design for the present.

Journal Notes:

Day/Year	
Day/Year	
Day/Year	
Day/Year	
Day/Year	

April 6

The Lesson of the Bell Curve—Core Principles

I am the source of all that I experience versus going victim and blaming others.

When behavioral research psychologists examined the symmetry of the bell curve, they noticed that each cluster, the 2-7-2 clusters, had one thing in common, their attitude. As different as the individuals were, with their circumstances, challenges, ages, genders, locations, etc., they all shared a common attitude. There is a common attitude that results in your place on that curve.

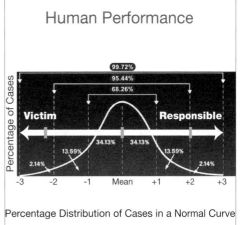

Percentage Distribution of Cases in a Normal Curve

Look at the bottom 2%. They have a common reference point, or attitude. They are constantly looking at reasons why things can't get done. They are constantly blaming their circumstances and other people for their failures. The common attitude is VICTIM. They don't have goals, they don't make plans, after all, why bother! They have given up.

Look at the other extreme. The top 2% are in reference to they are the source. They take total responsibility for their results. Their attitude is, I am the source of all that I experience versus going victim and blaming others. They have a focus not on themselves but on being of service to others. The top 2% make weekly commitments with defined plans and specific actions they commit to take.

The 70% are in the middle. Sometimes they take responsibility and sometimes they blame. Sometimes they are well planned with defined goals and action steps and sometimes they are not.

The common denominator of the top producers is that they present outcomes, in advance, with some method of reinforcement and support. They take full responsibility for their results.

Challenge:
It's a recipe. Follow the recipe and you get the result. Ingredients needed, passion, planning and 100% personal accountability. Just for today, plan your day and week. Take 100% responsibility for your results.

Tapping in Meditation:
My purpose today is to do ordinary things extraordinarily well and I do

Journal Notes:

Day/Year	
Day/Year	
Day/Year	
Day/Year	
Day/Year	

April 7

The Go Givers—Core Principle 1—Service

"The Go Giver" by Bob Burg and John Mann is a delightful book that is in alignment with my core principle #1, SERVICE. Burg and Mann published The Five Laws of Stratospheric Success:

- **The Law of Value**—your true worth is determined by how much more you give in value than you take in payment.

- **The Law of Compensation**—your income is determined by how many people you serve and how well you serve them.

- **The Law of Influence**—your influence is determined by how abundantly you place other people's interests first.

- **The Law of Authenticity**—the most valuable gift you have to offer is you.

- **The Law of Receptivity**—the key to effective giving is to stay open to receiving.

Challenge:

Our first guiding principle is to be of service to others. Just for today take on an attitude of service in everything that you do.

Tapping in Meditation:

My purpose today is to shape my thoughts. I become what I think. When my mind is pure, joy follows like a shadow that never leaves.

Journal Notes:

Day/Year	
Day/Year	
Day/Year	
Day/Year	
Day/Year	

April 8

Core Principle II—Synergy—Better as a Team

Another core principle comes to light when study of the elite performer continues. As a group they believe and live the principle that they are far better off as a part of a team then they can be by themselves. Our universe supports this because everything is interrelated. Nothing stands isolated from the simplest single cell organism to the complex and expansive universe.

The peak performers understand the concept of synergy. Take one arrow and bend it until it breaks and notice the amount of pressure you need to apply. Now take two arrows, hold them together and how much pressure will be necessary to break them? You might think twice as much but that is not correct. It might take 4 or 5 times as much pressure because the dynamic has changed. That is the concept of synergy.

Challenge:
How can you partner with someone else and create a stronger team? Who else serves the same clients that you do? Reach out to them to form a strategic alliance for greater service to your clients. Be a team player. Help your colleagues with their priorities. Share information instead of hoarding it.

Tapping in Meditation:
My purpose today is to collaborate with others. When I approach life from collaboration then I play a bigger game. I attract collaboration to myself.

Journal Notes:

Day/Year	
Day/Year	
Day/Year	
Day/Year	
Day/Year	

April 9

Core Principle III—I do What I Say I Will Do

What does it mean to you to give your word? What does it mean to you to live with integrity? I love the phrase from Ralph Waldo Emerson, "What you do speaks so loudly I can't hear what you say."

"My word is my bond"—unknown

"We promise according to our hopes, and perform according to our fears." —Francois duc de la Rochefoucauld

"Oaths are but words, and words but wind." —Samuel Butler

"The best way to keep one's word is not to give it." —Napoleon Bonaparte

"Never take a solemn oath. People think you mean it." —Norman Douglas

"Promises are like crying babies in a theater, they should be carried out at once." —Norman Vincent Peale

"A promise made is a debt unpaid." —Robert Service

"We must not promise what we ought not, lest we be called on to perform what we cannot." —Abraham Lincoln

"Promises are like the full moon, if they are not kept at once they diminish day by day." —German Proverb

"Some persons make promises for the pleasure of breaking them."—William Hazlitt

"When a man repeats a promise again and again, he means to fail you."—Proverb

"Promise only what you can deliver. Then deliver more than you promise."—Author Unknown

"One must have a good memory to be able to keep the promises that one makes"—Friedrich Nietzsche

"Promises may fit the friends, but non-performance will turn them into enemies."—Benjamin Franklin

Challenge:
Pay attention to doing what you say you will do and do it!

Tapping in Meditation:
My purpose today is to be my word. I give my word carefully and do what I said I would do.

Journal Notes:

Day/Year	
Day/Year	
Day/Year	
Day/Year	

The Lesson of the Cart

What is the real problem here? I've heard that one person is pulling and the other pushing, that they are both men and even that they need a horse. The most common response that I get to this is however is that they have what they already need in the cart. They are carrying round wheels and using square wheels. I'm told that the solution would be to simply use what they already have.

What is the Real Problem?

That is not correct. That is not the real problem. Look again. Yes it is true that they would be more successful if they used what they already have, the round wheels. However, that is not the real problem. The real problem is that they are successfully moving the cart the way that it is. They compare themselves to others who are also using square wheels and they are doing better than most. Good is the enemy of great. It's got to be a mindset shift first then put the proper wheels on.

Challenge:
Where in your life are you not playing all out and getting maximum results because you are accepting "good."

Tapping in Meditation:
My purpose today is to be excellence. Everything I do I do to the best of my ability. I live with an ease of total effort.

Journal Notes:

Day/Year	
Day/Year	
Day/Year	
Day/Year	
Day/Year	

April 11

Random Act of Kindness

I was speaking to an audience of 22,000 people at the Memphis Pyramid in the 1990s. The speaker before me was a very successful member of this direct sales group. I had a chance to chat with him back stage before the doors opened. I remember asking him what one thing he had learned that helped him the most to have his success. He said, very simply, be nice to people.

Not only does a single kind action brighten the day of the person who receives it, the kindness benefits the giver as well. Studies show that humans are naturally inclined to be generous and compassionate toward one another.

Altruism may improve your mental and physical health, boost your self-esteem, create meaning and purpose in your life and foster a connection with community. When you do something nice for someone else, your brain releases two powerful mood boosters, dopamine and endogenous opioids. Experts call this the "helpers high." It's also found to reduce stress and lower anxiety and depression.

Helping someone face-to-face triggers your body to release oxytocin, a bonding hormone that also lowers blood pressure. Kindness also activates the vagus nerve, which controls inflammation in the body. People who volunteer tend to live longer.

John Wooden said, "You can't live a perfect day without doing something for someone who will never be able to repay you."

Challenge:

Make someone's day today with a random act of kindness. Notice any self-serving thoughts of deprivation and replace them with thoughts and acts of kindness.

Tapping in Meditation:

My purpose today is to be kind and I am. Being kind is more important than being right. What many people need is NOT a brilliant mind that speaks but a special heart that listens. I listen with love and appreciation.

Journal Notes:

Day/Year	
Day/Year	
Day/Year	
Day/Year	
Day/Year	

10 Free Random Acts of Kindness

It only takes a second to be kind and courteous to someone. Here are some suggestions.

1. Hug your loved ones and always take the opportunity to tell them you love them. When I drop my kids off at school I always make sure that the ride is a positive attitude ride and the last thing I say is I love you, make it a great day.
2. Hold the door open. I was walking into the gym very early one morning and a guy I see there frequently but have never spoken with was walking behind me. He was far enough behind that I could have let the door close without anyone giving it a second thought. I waited for him and I could sense his appreciation.
3. Offer your seat to someone. I was on a crowded shuttle between terminals at the Atlanta airport and a person barely made it through the closing doors. They had their hands full with luggage and I offered my seat to them. Not only did they appreciate it but I could also sense the acknowledgment of everyone who saw me do this too.
4. Write a note to praise someone who helped you. It will make their day.
5. Write something funny, kind or inspiring on a sticky note and leave it somewhere unexpected such as the mirror of a public restroom.
6. Mow your neighbor's lawn.
7. Allow someone to cut in front of you when it would be appropriate to continue on and make them wait.
8. Visit the local veteran's hospital.
9. Offer encouraging words to someone who looks upset.
10. Smile at strangers and say "hello."

Challenge:
Implement one of these suggestions today. There is no such thing as a small act of kindness. Every act creates a ripple with no logical end.

Tapping in Meditation:
My purpose today is to be nice to everyone. I always smile and appreciate things because it could all be gone tomorrow. I am kind to everyone I meet; they are all fighting some battle.

Journal Notes:

Day/Year	
Day/Year	
Day/Year	
Day/Year	
Day/Year	

April 13

Victim—Responsible—Light a Candle

Don't Complain About the Dark—Light a Candle

child → dog food → clothes

I have an office complex that is a separate building yet attached to my house. It has its own separate entrance, heating, air and water, etc.

One day after work hours I shut everything down and walked through that magical door separating my office from my house. I remember that the house was a mess, there were clothes all over the floor, there was dog food where it shouldn't be, a messy kid and more. I remember thinking how I work so hard all day, why can't my wife just keep the house clean.

Then I caught myself taking a victim stance and blaming my wife. This phrase came to my mind, "Don't complain about the dark—light a candle."

Wow! Since we are genetically coded to conserve energy at all times, it didn't surprise me that I would default to going victim and blaming. However, I never even thought about doing something about it. I can pick up some clothes. I could throw the dog food away. I could take action instead of adding to the chaos by blaming. What a concept.

Challenge:

You will know when you are going victim when this situation arises, if you can take a small action to solve the issue then rather than blame, take that one action. Repeat to yourself, "don't complain about the dark—light a candle."

Tapping in Meditation:

My purpose today is to take responsibility for the choices I make. Everything I do is based on the choices I make. It's not my parents, my past relationships, my job, the economy, the weather, an argument or my age that is to blame. It is only myself that is responsible for every decision and choice I make, period. I make loving choices all day long.

Journal Notes:

Day/Year	
Day/Year	
Day/Year	
Day/Year	
Day/Year	

April 14

Short Term plus Faith

You intend to drive from New York City to the Jersey Shore. You've decided to beat the traffic and travel at night. As you make your way onto the Garden State Parkway you notice that all you can see is the distance that is covered by your headlights. This is a very small portion of your entire trip, you've got another 45 minutes left. All you can see is right in front of you. You can never see further than your headlights, yet you can make the entire trip that way.

What is right in front of you keeps moving forward, towards your goal. You have faith that if you just travel this series of short distances, and that you have faith in the process, and then you will ultimately reach your destination, safe and sound.

So it is with this program.

Challenge:

Your headlight distance is simply today, from right now until the time you go to sleep. Have faith that as you continue to think powerfully and follow this program that you too will arrive, safe and sound.

Tapping in Meditation:

My purpose today is to start my journey with a single step. Most people go through life as failures because they are waiting for the time to be right. Do not wait, start now. Start where I stand, work with whatever tools I may have and better tools will be found as I go along. I trust my higher power to provide the wisdom and means that I will need.

Journal Notes:

Day/Year	
Day/Year	
Day/Year	
Day/Year	
Day/Year	

April 15

Will, Fern and the Power of Encouragement

Two frogs named Will and Fern fell into a deep pit together. At first they thought it would be easy to jump out. But after many frustrating failed attempts they cried for help. A crowd of animals gathered around the pit.

Everyone agreed that it was hopeless so they urged Will and Fern to accept their fate. The harder the trapped frogs jumped, the more the crowd yelled at them to give up. Finally, Will stopped trying. Fern refused to quit and with one mighty heroic attempt he leaped out of the pit.

The crowd was amazed. Someone asked her why she kept trying when everyone told her she had no chance.

Fern was baffled. "What are you saying?" she asked. I'm a bit deaf. I was sure you were all cheering me on. I couldn't have done it without your encouragement.

Challenge:
There will always be people in your life who will feel threatened by your success and will cheer for what you can't do. Give them kindness and love but don't hang out with them. You need to surround yourself with positive people who are also goal oriented and committed to growth. Are you?

Tapping in Meditation:
My purpose today is to keep on competing. Life is a healthy competition with me, my own thoughts. There was never a problem that could defeat sunrise and hope.

Journal Notes:

Day/Year	
Day/Year	
Day/Year	
Day/Year	
Day/Year	

The Carol Johnston Story

Lynn Rogers, former head women's gymnastics coach at Cal State Fullerton, tells the story about expectations with one of his athletes. Carol Johnston (born March 10, 1958, Calgary, Alberta) was an American competitive gymnast, born without a right arm below her elbow. Johnston was a collegiate gymnastics champion in the late 1970s who was featured in the 1979 film Lefty.

Photo : used with permission

When Carol was just a freshman she wanted Lynn to teach her to do a particular move on the uneven bars. Lynn "knew" that she would never be able to master such a difficult and complicated move with only one arm. However, to free himself up to work with his more senior athletes, Lynn allowed her to practice this move with his assistant coach while he worked on the floor exercise with his other more able girls. He allowed this knowing full well that she would never be able to do the move; he just wanted her out of his hair for a while.

Carol didn't know that she shouldn't be able to do the exercise. The assistant coach working with her, Breck Greenwood also didn't know that she should not be able to perform this move. So guess what happened? She aced it. It seemed that Breck and Carol were the only ones in the gym who didn't know she would not be able to perform and master that move. Amazing what you can do when you can't hear people cheering for you to fail.

Challenge:
What one action can you take, just for today, without regard to failing? Something that you might be uncomfortable doing. Do it anyway!

Tapping in Meditation:
My purpose today is to notice that experience is not what happens to me, it's about what I do with what happens to me. When the wrong people leave my life, the right things start happening.

Journal Notes:

Day/Year	
Day/Year	
Day/Year	
Day/Year	
Day/Year	

April 17

Stay Low Glycemic

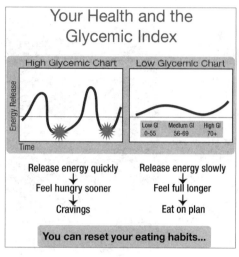

Your Health and the Glycemic Index

High Glycemic Chart | Low Glycemic Chart

Energy Release

Time

Low GI 0-55 | Medium GI 56-69 | High GI 70+

Release energy quickly → Feel hungry sooner → Cravings

Release energy slowly → Feel full longer → Eat on plan

You can reset your eating habits...

I was at the airport gate 10 minutes before it was time to board my flight. There was an obese man in the area eating a McDonald's hamburger, fries and a Coke. My thinking was that he probably thinks he's eating healthy. He's not eating a lot of volume but let's take a closer look. The meat is good but he's not having enough. A hamburger might have 2 ounces, you need 4-6, (see Feb. 12th for the food plan). So he's actually under eating. He's got 2 horrific sources of high glycemic sugar, the Coke and the bun of the hamburger. The fries, potatoes as a grain are fine when you're on maintenance, but fried is not our first choice. Most French fries served in U.S. restaurants are immersed in corn-based oil usually considered the worst oil for human health—before they're fried. Corn oil contains large amounts of saturated fat, known to contribute to heart disease. Also, where is his salad? He doesn't have one. He's off on all 3 categories on your food plan.

This is a poor habit. Immediately he's going to have a spike in his blood sugar level. This triggers the release of insulin in large amounts. The insulin will take the blood sugar and transport it into the cells for energy, good, and transport the rest to the fat cells for storage, bad. When he has this surge of insulin he will soon deplete his blood sugar level while promoting fat gain even though he's not eating much. In a short period of time he's going to have some major cravings so he'll grab some peanuts and pretzels and cookies on the airplane and start the cycle over again.

If he was in the office he would not be very productive all day long chasing the glycemic curve.

Challenge:
Eat the food plan. Regardless of your body size (see Feb. 13) you need to pay attention to eating the right kind of foods. This will give you a steady state of energy throughout the day.

Tapping in Meditation:
My purpose today is to love myself. Because I love myself I nourish myself properly. I eat according to my plan.

Journal Notes:

Day/Year	
Day/Year	
Day/Year	
Day/Year	
Day/Year	

Energy—Sprint-Jog

We all have a biological clock. Many factors influence it such as cycles of light and dark, ambient temperature, meal times and stress and exercise. For a 6:00 am wake up, the sharpest rise in blood pressure occurs at 6:45. Melatonin secretion stops at 7:30 am. A bowl movement is likely at 8:30 am. The highest testosterone secretion is at 9:00 am. You have high alertness at 10:00 am. Your best co-ordination is at 2:30 pm, fastest reaction time at 3:30 pm. Your greatest cardiovascular efficiency and muscle strength at 4:00 pm. Your highest blood pressure is at 6:30 pm and your highest temperature is at 7:00 pm. Melatonin secretion starts at 9:00 pm and at 10:30 pm Bowel movements are suppressed. Your deepest sleep is at 2:00 am.

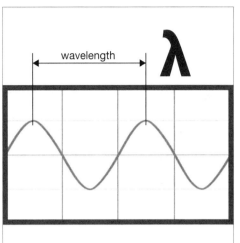

There is also a circadian pattern for your focus as well. The outer cortex area of your brain is a very high energy user. Because of that you can only continue with intensely focused activity for a cycle of no longer than between 60-90 minutes. At that time you'll need to either take a break or change activities to a non-thinking activity like readying personal mail, answering emails, checking the mail, or anything else that you could do that does not require focused energy. This is what I refer to as sprint-jog. Visualize an energy wave. The upward slope is high intense and focused activity, prospecting for example is the sprint. Then there must be a jog. This can either be the changing of an activity or an actual break. You'll need about 15-30 minutes for the break. Then you are set for another sprint followed by another break. You might have 3 or 4 of these cycles every day. Plan for them.

Challenge:

Use the sprint-jog principle in planning your most productive activities for the day. Make sure to schedule an important call during one of your sprint times.

Tapping in Meditation:

My purpose today is to be the best I can be, just for today.

Journal Notes:

Day/Year	
Day/Year	
Day/Year	
Day/Year	
Day/Year	

April 19

More on the Bell Curve—Packing

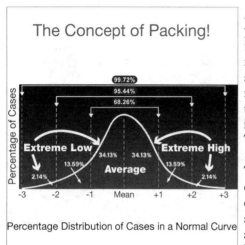

The Concept of Packing!

Percentage Distribution of Cases in a Normal Curve

A lion is chasing a pack of zebras. As the zebras retreat you can observe some interesting math. There are a few leading the pack, a few bringing up the rear and most of the zebras are packed together. The lion may attempt to ambush one of the leaders although it is more likely that it will focus on one of those bringing up the rear. Where will the lion never attack? The pack in the middle. It would be trampled to death if it did. Therefore, there is safety in numbers.

The math is the frequency distribution curve more commonly known as the bell shaped curve. There is a central limit tendency which means that the extremes are constantly being pulled to the center. I refer to this as packing. This is an amazing pull of Mother Nature. It's also a pull of the US government. The government fears the extremes. The government didn't want one company to have control of what is on your desktop so in 1999 Microsoft was ruled a monopoly. They also poured millions of dollars into the homeless and cleaning up the streets in Los Angeles before the 1984 Olympics. The extremes are threats. This constant pull toward the average surrounds you all the time.

If you are committed to excellence, to being a peak performer, you are going to need to have an intervention. If you don't have an intervention you will be pulled down to the average. Likewise, the extreme poor performers cannot stay where they are without an intervention as well, otherwise they will be pulled upwards to the average.

The intervention is attitude. The poor performers are locked into an attitude of being a victim and blaming. The peak performers are likewise locked into an attitude of total responsibility and planning. They preset outcomes, in advance, with reinforcement, support and accountability. The moment they stop they get pulled to the average. It's math!

Challenge:
Continue using this program. The intervention against mediocrity is precise weekly planning, accountability, and a positive attitude.

Tapping in Meditation:
My purpose today is to remain positive regardless of external circumstances. I prosper wherever I turn and I know that I deserve prosperity of all kinds. I am grateful. The more grateful I am, the more reasons I find to be grateful. I pay my bills with love as I know abundance flows freely through me.

Journal Notes:

Day/Year	
Day/Year	
Day/Year	
Day/Year	
Day/Year	

April 20

Decision versus Action—Get M.A.D.

An old fable says 3 birds were sitting on a wire, one decided to fly away, how many birds were left on the wire? The answer is 3. The decision to do something must be followed by precise action or nothing changes. So get M.A.D., make a decision on some pending items you've been putting off and follow that up with action.

Challenge:

The world needs you now, not when you're perfect. What decisions are pending? What decisions are you avoiding? What one decision could you make right now that would reduce stress and have your life be more fulfilling? Just for today make that decision and follow that with one action that gets the ball moving.

Tapping in Meditation:

My purpose today is to be decisive and in action. I am good at making decisions. I think through all of my options carefully and decide. I am in tune with what I need. I am mindful of how my decisions will affect others. My choices are right. I have confidence in my decisions and my actions.

Journal Notes:

Day/Year	
Day/Year	
Day/Year	
Day/Year	
Day/Year	

April 21

Three Human Resistances

Human nature is very revealing. Your genes have not changed over the last million years and you are instinctively driven. Sometimes this protects you and saves your life. In fact that is what you are genetically coded to do, stay alive and pass on your genes.

However, there are human resistances that are genetically coded that become your competitor. There are 3.

1. I will resist doing what I don't feel like doing.
2. I will resist doing activities that are uncomfortable. I will avoid and seek comfort.
3. I will resist, avoid and fear change.

Alonzo Mourning, the basketball player for the Miami Heat, had to have a kidney transplant. What was his body genetically coded to do? Reject the foreign tissue. This is called homeostasis. The body doesn't make an exception. The body does what its instincts direct.

Performance excellence is not a natural place to be. The natural place to be is mediocrity. In order to be outside of the norm or the pack, you will need to have an intervention. The intervention for "Zo" was his immunosuppressant drugs. How long does he need to take then? The answer is "forever" or as long as he wants to be alive.

This program is your intervention. How long do you need to participate? The answer is "forever" or as long as you want to live in excellence.

Challenge:
Notice where you might be resisting improvement.

Tapping in Meditation:
My purpose today is to notice and rejoice in the love I encounter every day. I deserve love and accept it now. I give out love and it is returned to me multiplied. I am happy and at peace.

Journal Notes:

Day/Year	
Day/Year	
Day/Year	
Day/Year	
Day/Year	

April 22

The Lesson of the Rubber Band

Place your palms together and put them inside a rubber band. Now extend both hands as far away from each other as you can without breaking the rubber band. Imagine that this outstretched position represents performance excellence. What do you notice? What does the rubber band want to do? Of course you notice the tension. You notice that the rubber band wants to return to its original shape.

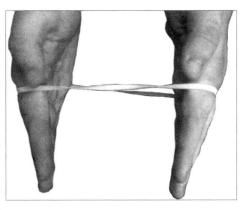

What is keeping the rubber band extended? You have to apply energy, an outside force. How long do you need to apply this intervention, this energy that keeps the rubber band from returning to its natural shape? The answer is as long as you want to keep it extended.

Since the extended rubber band in the analogy represents performance excellence, there needs to be an intervention, added muscular energy, to keep the rubber band in excellence. In this program your intervention is to precisely play every 7 days, to embrace and use accountability, to tap in and meditate 5-10 minutes every day, to eat 3 weighed and measured meals and to maintain a positive attitude at all times.

How long do you need to do this? As long as you demand excellence!

Challenge:
Notice and appreciate what you have become since the beginning of the year, since the beginning of this program. Has your personal growth journey changed someone else's life?

Tapping in Meditation:
My purpose today is to live with joy and delightful surprises. My life is filled with love, fun and friendship. I forgive, relax and am peaceful. I choose love, joy and freedom. I open my heart and allow wonderful things to flow into my life.

Journal Notes:

Day/Year	
Day/Year	
Day/Year	
Day/Year	
Day/Year	

April 23

The Power of the ANDs

All That ... And Then Some

You have far more capacity to create the circumstances and events in your life then you are aware of. You just don't realize that because you don't have anything to compare. You've lived your entire life with action-reaction, cause and effect. You've exerted effort and achieved results and it's all too easy for you to buy into that you are doing the best that you can. Don't buy into that lie!

Participate with the power of the ANDs, And Then Some. When you think you have no more give it one more burst of effort.

Challenge:

Just for today, do one action that you know you would not have attempted. That can be one more phone call, one more rep in the gym, one more of something. Live "and then some" just for today.

Tapping in Meditation:

My purpose today is to challenge my limited views. I am more powerful than my circumstances. I am more powerful than any limitations. I am not alone as I tap into the energy of the universe. With this energy at my side I can accomplish more than I am aware of.

Journal Notes:

Day/Year	
Day/Year	
Day/Year	
Day/Year	
Day/Year	

Challenge Accepted Truths

Nicolaus Copernicus was a Renaissance mathematician and astronomer who formulated a heliocentric model of the universe which placed the Sun, rather than the Earth, at the center. Copernicus was a revolutionary. He challenged accepted truths. Everyone knew that the earth was the center of the universe. To challenge what was accepted as being true was dangerous and he feared reprisals from his friends and the church. He waited until he was on his death bed in 1543 to publish his book, "On the Revolutions of the Heavenly Bodies"

Fast forward to December 17th, 1903, at Kitty Hawk, North Carolina, the Wright Flyer became the first to achieve controlled sustained flight. They were ridiculed because everyone knew that a heavier-than-air machine could not have flight.

Flight
and the
4:00 mile

In 1954 Roger Bannister again broke through an established scientific belief that it was impossible for a human to break a 4 minute mile. On May 6th, 1954, he broke that perceived barrier with a 3:59.4 minute mile. Shortly thereafter several others broke the 4 minute mark as well. Quantum theorists would say he had conditioned the space.

You've got to be careful about people around you who may be well meaning but are actually cheerleading for average performance. You may have heard the quote that someone who thinks something can't be done is usually passed up by someone doing it.

Challenge:
Keep challenging your assumed beliefs about why you accept as being your limits. Just for today attempt one thing that you don't think you can do.

Tapping in Meditation:
My purpose today is to keep on growing and improving. I challenge perceived limitation. I follow my dreams no matter what. I have courage. I show compassion in helping my loved ones understand my dreams.

Journal Notes:

Day/Year	
Day/Year	
Day/Year	
Day/Year	
Day/Year	

April 25

Challenge My Assumptions

I coach financial advisors and other professionals to form strategic alliances with other professionals who serve the same high net worth house hold. I had a telephone call with another consultant who was also working with my coaching client. We were going to have an in office meeting at the consultants' office. I asked Bruce if he would send me the directions to his office. What assumption did I just make?

If you think this through the most obvious assumption that I made was that Bruce would do what he said he would do and send me directions to his office. Here are the steps to challenge your assumptions.

>   Step 1: Notice you are making an assumption.
>   Step 2: Challenge the assumption.
>   Step 3: Be in choice about actions.

Step 1: I noticed that I was assuming that Bruce would either fax or scan the directions to his office.

Step 2: Challenge the assumption, maybe he'd get too busy or distracted and forget.

Step 3: Be in choice about actions. I could have asked him to give me the directions right now on the phone. I chose not to take any action. The reason for this choice was because I had a coaching call later that morning with the advisor who was also coming to that meeting and he could give me the directions.

My challenge was correct because Bruce did get distracted and never did send me directions. It all worked out just fine however because I went through this exercise.

Challenge:

What assumptions are you making about your marriage, your colleagues, your friends, and your family? Challenge those assumptions and be in choice about actions for today.

Tapping in Meditation:

My purpose today is to have clear and truthful communication with my family, friends and colleagues. I challenge my assumptions and ask for clarification.

Journal Notes:

Day/Year	
Day/Year	
Day/Year	
Day/Year	
Day/Year	

April 26

Seed the Blue

Have you ever had something really good happen to you right out of the blue? Nothing ever happens out of the blue. That would be a violation of the law of accumulative effect. Things that happen to you, both good and bad are the result of small decisions, small actions or lack of actions that you have taken or not over a long period of time.

If the sum of your actions is positive then as some point in time the accumulative impact will "all of a sudden" explode with something absolutely terrific. The illusion is that it's out of the blue. It's the sum of your consistent good efforts over time.

This is the analogy of planting a seed and the seed germinating in its kind. A tomato seed will never give you a cucumber. However, if you water and fertilize it then over time it will give you a tomato.

Law of Accumulative Effect

Time

SEED the BLUE

Challenge:
Seeding the blue can also be negative as well so make sure that you are consistently positive and doing the right kinds of actions and having the right kinds of thoughts.

Tapping in Meditation:
My purpose today is to guarantee my future by inventing it. I invent it in advance with my thoughts and deeds.

Journal Notes:

Day/Year	
Day/Year	
Day/Year	
Day/Year	
Day/Year	

April 27

Concepts on Time—Chart Your Time

Charting Time—Start and Stops

Time	Activity	Stop
4:15 am	Gym-workout-shower	6:15 am
6:15 am	Breakfast prep	7:45 am
7:45 am	Drive to office	7:50 am
7:50 am	Office admin-emails	8:30 am
8:30 am	East coast calls	9:45 am
9:45 am	Break	10:15 am
10:15 am	Local calls	10:30 am
10:30 am	Coaching call	11:30 am
11:30 am	Break	11:45 am
11:45 am	Meet w/marketing dir.	12:15 pm

Are you getting everything done that you want to accomplish? Are you telling yourself that you're just too busy to _____ (fill in the blank). Don't buy into it. By now you understand that you can't trust your own interpretations about how you are doing. With that in mind let's do an exercise that will be an objective "truth telling" data collector—chart your time. Just grab a pad and make the following columns, starting time, activity, stopping time. That's it. Every start follows a stop. So if you're on a conference call from 9:00 am until 9:25 am you have your start, your activity and your stop. What do you do next? If it's check emails then you have another start, 9:25 am, activity and your stop. Suppose you've taken 8 minutes on emails that means that your stop was at 9:33 am. That is also your start to your next activity.

I do need to give you a warning however. Most people you know, those in the average, don't want to have anything to do with time charting. It takes away excuses, it's there in black and white. Most people don't want to be "found out!"

Challenge:

Chart your time, just for today. You may want to share this with others and have them chart their time, for several days! Watch your thinking. Make sure you don't buy into "I don't have time to do this." That's fear based thinking.

Tapping in Meditation:

My purpose today is to live authentically. I am committed to living in excellence so I plan for it. I have excellent time management skills. I am naturally talented at managing my time in all areas of my life. I always do what I am supposed to be doing. I complete projects on time. I know my schedule for the day and week ahead of me.

Journal Notes:

Day/Year	
Day/Year	
Day/Year	
Day/Year	
Day/Year	

Concepts on Time—The Lesson of the Pie Chart

One of the ways that elite performers think is that they embrace objective measuring. They like visuals. Anything that can give you a sensory input is going to help to guide your awareness. It is out of this awareness that you can then make appropriate decisions and choices about actions. The pie chart is one of the ways that you can turn a vague idea into a more objective measurement. Here's how.

Ideal vs. Real Activities

Ideal 100% **Real 100%**

% Ideal		Activities	% Real	
5%	A	Partner discovery-identify	1%	↑
30%	B	Partner development PRP	10%	↑
30%	C	Recruiting new agents-personal & driving partners	10%	↑
20%	D	Manpower-every agent producing=>27,000	10%	↑
10%	E	Retention PRP's agents	20%	↓
5%	F	Compliance/everything else	49%	↓

Make a chart. Have two circles named Ideal and Current. Next identify the activities that you need to be engaged in on a weekly basis, giving yourself 100% of business time. After you have identified the activities you need to be involved with then give yourself a percentage of how much of 100% business time should be attributed to each activity in an ideal world. For example, if one activity is prospecting and ideally you should be spending 40% of your time in that activity—then indicate that. Then come back and place the current value, let's say it's only 25%. Do this for each activity.

Next, look for the trends by placing an up or down arrow for each category. Prospecting in this example would get an up arrow, you need to do more.

Challenge:
Plan for the actions you will take this week to be in action on your trends. What action will you take today that would move you in the direction that you have identified as ideal. Many times this means you need to delegate, do you?

Tapping in Meditation:
My purpose today is to be efficient with my time as I do the most productive activities first. I am passionate and love my clients. I love my life.

Journal Notes:

Day/Year	
Day/Year	
Day/Year	
Day/Year	
Day/Year	

April 29

Comfort Zone-Approach-Avoidance

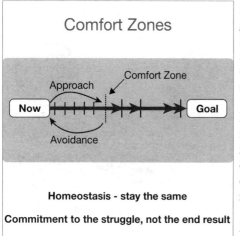

Comfort Zones

Homeostasis - stay the same

Commitment to the struggle, not the end result

Have you ever started to make progress towards a goal and then something happened that set you back? It may be because you need to expand your comfort zone. The comfort zone is the tipping point where you can experience a highest point of stress and anxiety and one more instance will send you avoiding.

If someone has never made a 6 figure income they may have a comfort zone that will not support them in their efforts. They start out just fine but as they get close to the comfort zone they then sabotage their efforts by blowing a sale, or getting sick, it can take many forms.

How about you? Are you stuck in any particular area? You may need to make progress with your comfort zone. You may be more committed to the challenge to succeed then the actual result. Not to worry. You don't need to go to therapy to find out where you might have a commitment to the struggle. You can nudge your comfort zone closer and closer to where it needs to be so your actions are in alignment with your intended goals and you don't create setbacks (avoidance) that have you starting over again.

Challenge:

In areas or activities where you sense you are uncomfortable (as in a comfort zone challenge) use behavioral contracting. Make a commitment to another person what your specific activity will be, due the end of the week, and place a heavy penalty for non-performance. This will move your comfort zone up towards alignment with your goals.

Tapping in Meditation:

My purpose today is to go beyond what I feel comfortable doing and to expand what I am capable of achieving. I take productive actions whether I feel like it or not.

Journal Notes:

Day/Year	
Day/Year	
Day/Year	
Day/Year	
Day/Year	

April 30

Notice and Appreciate Your Acres of Diamonds

"Acres of Diamonds" originated as a speech which Russell Conwell delivered over 6,000 times around the world. It was first published in 1890.

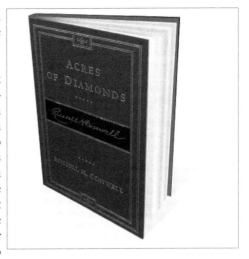

The central idea of the work is that one need not look elsewhere for opportunity, achievement, or fortune— the resources to achieve all good things are present in one's own community. This theme is developed by an introductory anecdote, credited by Conwell to an Arab guide, about a man who wanted to find diamonds so badly that he sold his property and went off in futile search for them. The new owner of his home discovered that a rich diamond mine was located right there on the property. Conwell elaborates on the theme through examples of success, genius, service, or other virtues involving ordinary Americans contemporary to his audience: "dig in your own backyard!"

Challenge:

Where are you looking outside of your own resources to solve a problem? You may already have everything you need at your disposal to make the changes necessary to solve your problems.

Tapping in Meditation:

My purpose today is to be resourceful and to trust myself, my talents, my ability to find creative solutions to my problems and I do.

Journal Notes:

Day/Year	
Day/Year	
Day/Year	
Day/Year	
Day/Year	

Davies
Day Book

365 concepts for excellence

May 1

Notice and Appreciate Your Acres of Diamonds

The House with the Golden Windows

The little girl lived in a small, very simple, poor house on a hill and as she grew she would play in the small garden and as she grew she was able to see over the garden fence and across the valley to a wonderful house high on the hill—and this house had golden windows, so golden and shining that the little girl would dream of how magic it would be to grow up and live in a house with golden windows instead of an ordinary house like hers. And although she loved her parents and her family, she yearned to live in such a golden house and dreamed all day about how wonderful and exciting it must feel to live there.

When she got to an age where she gained enough skill and sensibility to go outside her garden fence, she asked her mother is she could go for a bike ride outside the gate and down the lane. After pleading with her, her mother finally allowed her to go, insisting that she kept close to the house and didn't wander too far. The day was beautiful and the little girl knew exactly where she was heading! Down the lane and across the valley, she rode her bike until she got to the gate of the golden house across on the other hill.

As she dismounted her bike and lent it against the gate post, she focused on the path that led to the house and then on the house itself and was so disappointed as she realized all the windows were plain and rather dirty, reflecting nothing other than the sad neglect of the house that stood derelict. So sad she didn't go any further and turned, heartbroken as she remounted her bike. As she glanced up she saw a sight to amaze her. There across the way on her side of the valley was a little house and its windows glistened golden as the sun shone on her little home.

She realized that she had been living in her golden house and all the love and care she found there was what made her home the 'golden house'. Everything she dreamed was right there in front of her nose!

Challenge:

Just for today, be conscious and aware of all that you have. Notice and appreciate the people in your life. Whose life do you stand to impact as you continue your journey on personal and professional development?

Tapping in Meditation:

My purpose today is to appreciate what I already have.

Journal Notes:

Day/Year	
Day/Year	
Day/Year	
Day/Year	
Day/Year	

May 2

The Lesson of the 3 Trees

There is a story of a man who begged the Buddha to teach him his wisdom. "When you can tell me the meaning of the middle tree in a cluster of 3 trees then you will be ready for my teaching. "Outside the man saw 3 trees. He started to notice clusters of 3 trees everywhere he went. He even noticed clusters of bushes and shrubs that came in groups of 3. He went to the Buddha and said I have the meaning of the 3 trees. He went on to tell that the number 3 is used 467 times in the Bible. It pictures completeness. He started to tell the story of how Jesus prayed three times in the Garden of Gethsemane before his arrest. The Buddha interrupted him and said "Nonsense! You are not ready for my teachings. Come back when you know the answer."

The man went away again determined to find the answer to the meaning of the middle tree. He then approached the Buddha again sure that he had the answer this time. "It has to do with the 3 pillars of mind, spirit and body. They are all interrelated." "Nonsense" interrupted the Buddha. So the man retreated again this time even more determined to find the "truth." He came back a short time later and said to the Buddha, "I've got it now. It has to do with architectural design, the plan, the foundation and the structure." "Nonsense" "Come back when you know the meaning of the middle tree!" By now the man was very frustrated. "What in the world could the middle tree mean?" He said to himself. Finally he had a revelation. He stormed into the Buddha and blurted out in frustration, "It doesn't mean anything!" To which the Buddha replied, "That's right, you are now ready for my teaching."

Our senses are incomplete approximations of our interpretation of reality. We don't see the real world. Our brain is encased in bone. Our perceptions are combinations of limited electrical inputs from our senses. There are gaps in the information. Therefore our brain fills in the gaps and we make up complete versions from our inputs. You are designed to be a story teller, to tell a story of your environment. However, you also have the ability to select the version of your own narration. You can create a positive version or a negative one. You can live in drama or positive passion. Choose Passion.

Challenge:
Carefully select the best versions of everything that happens to you.

Tapping in Meditation:
My purpose today is to seek the good in everyone and every situation and I do. I am surrounded by love and I live in abundance.

Journal Notes:

Day/Year	
Day/Year	
Day/Year	
Day/Year	
Day/Year	

May 3

Visualization—Imagination Triggers the Same Response as the Physical Mechanism Involved in Sight

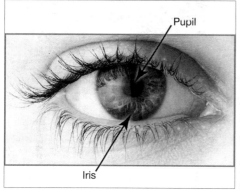

Pupil

Iris

The eyes pupils are allowing researchers to explore the parallels between imagination and perception. In a recent series of experiments, University of Oslo cognitive neuroscientists Bruno Laeng and Unni Sulvtvedt began displaying triangles of varying brightness on a computer screen while monitoring the pupils of the study volunteers. The subject's pupils widened for dark shapes and narrowed for bright ones as expected.

Next participants were instructed to simply imagine the same triangles. Remarkably, their pupils constricted or dilated as if they had been staring at the actual shapes. The same pattern happened when they asked subjects to imagine more complex scenes such as a sunny sky or a dark room.

This study suggests that imagination and perception may rely on a similar set of neural processes: when you picture a dimly lit restaurant, your brain and body respond as if you were in that restaurant.

When you meditate you start your quite time with a thought, an image for the day from the tapping in meditation below. The act of visualization, mental rehearsal, uses the same neurological pathways as the real act.

Challenge:

Keep on having your quite, meditation time and form it with positive thoughts. It will have a real physiological impact.

Tapping in Meditation:

My purpose today is to set the conditions for a positive, loving and productive day right now. See it, visualize it and allow it to happen.

Journal Notes:

Day/Year	
Day/Year	
Day/Year	
Day/Year	
Day/Year	

Manifestation

Your brain is this magnificent 3 pound organ that takes an electrical impulse and turns it into a chemical that is released called a neural transmitter. This chemical has a charge and like attracts like. That sets up the manifestation event.

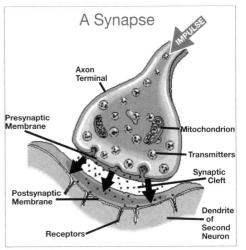

A Synapse

Benjamin Libet, noted biologist, said, "Reality is in the mind of the observer", meaning that once you have the thought you have created your physical reality. You have also set up the law of attraction. Your brain doesn't edit your manifestation. This means that if you think positive thoughts you will attract those into reality. The same with negative thoughts. If you constantly think about what your problems are you will attract more of what you are thinking about. What you confess (or constantly think about) you possess, or cause to occur. This is a scientific principle and it must occur. Plant a tomato and you won't get corn, you'll get a like seed, the tomato. The seed will grow to what it is supposed to be if you water and fertilize it. The same holds true for your thoughts.

Challenge:
You can control this so keep having positive thoughts. When you catch yourself thinking negative, stop the thoughts and replace them with positive thoughts always! Make this a habit.

Tapping in Meditation:
My purpose today is to hold the vision and thoughts of what I want, happiness, health and prosperity.

Journal Notes:

Day/Year	
Day/Year	
Day/Year	
Day/Year	
Day/Year	

May 5

A Man and a Dog—Not in Enough Pain

A man walks into a bar and orders a drink. His dog walks off to a corner of the bar and lies down. A few minutes later the dog is whaling in pain. The bartender says, "What's wrong with your dog it's screaming in pain?" They both walk over to the look at the dog. When they get over to the animal they notice that the dog is lying on a board that has a nail sticking up from it.

The bartender asks, "Why doesn't your dog get up and move?" The owner says, "I guess he's not in enough pain to come up with the energy and effort to move."

Challenge:

Where are things not bad enough (painful) in your life for you to make the decision to put in the energy and effort to make a change? Don't wait. Pick one area and one activity and just for today, execute that action.

Tapping in Meditation:

My purpose today is to take my planned actions regardless of my fears. It is easy and effortless to stay focused on what I want and what I need to do to have it and I do. I am an action person.

Journal Notes:

Day/Year	
Day/Year	
Day/Year	
Day/Year	
Day/Year	

Manifesting—Significant Event

I grew up in poverty and embarrassment. I never brought my friends over to my house because I was so poor and the house was in shambles. The only way I was going to go to college was to get a football scholarship with I was fortunate enough to achieve at Rutgers University. While at Rutgers I was still in poverty but was doing OK on scholarship.

When I graduated I got hired as a high school teacher and coach. I was not I poverty. However, I still had the poverty mentality. After two years I resigned as a teacher and coach and went to graduate school at Springfield College. This was a positive move. I was coaching football and wrestling on the college level. I was getting my master's degree. However, I was earning only $2,000 per year as a graduate assistant. I was back in poverty. After two years I graduated and was hired as the head football and wrestling coach at Cal Tech in Pasadena, Ca. Again, I was out of poverty. However, again I still had the poverty mindset. After one year at Cal Tech, I resigned and was hired as a restricted earnings coach at Cal State Fullerton. This means that I was a full time coach but only paid $5,000. Once again I had the poverty mindset and manifested poverty.

Sometimes it takes a significant event to snap us out of our mindset. I had this happen with embarrassment. I was living for free at our team doctors' house in beautiful Newport Beach Ca. I was driving a brand new Honda loaned to me by one of our boosters, and I had food stamps. I was in the local grocery store buying groceries when my significant event happened. I handed the clerk my food stamps and she must have been new. She hadn't seen food stamps in the store before, (it's Newport Beach after all) and she gets on the intercom, "Food stamps check stand 5." I was embarrassed. I got M.A.D. (Make A Decision).

I had enough of poverty and embarrassment. I got M.A.D. and made a decision that that was it. I was done with poverty. Now watch manifestation in action. One of our coaches gets hired at the University of Hawaii. I get hired in his place as a full time paid position. Once I shifted my mindset from one of poverty to one of abundance the opportunities presented themselves. It took the mindset shift first then I attracted the realty next.

Challenge:
Where do you have a disconnect between what you want and what you have? Don't wait for a significant event to occur. Make a decision to take the actions you need to change your circumstances today!

Tapping in Meditation:
My purpose today is to be who I need to be to reach my goals and to be of service to others. I allow my subconscious to guide me to the thoughts and actions necessary.

Journal Notes:

Day/Year	
Day/Year	
Day/Year	
Day/Year	
Day/Year	

May 7

Eggs—It's Still Your Responsibility

Reality is in the mind of the observer. According to quantum physics all possibilities of outcomes and meaning exist equally at the same time and it's up to you the observer to select a meaning from all of the potential realities. Once you make your selection, your observation, all other possibilities collapse and the only reality remaining is your choice.

I purchased an investment 5 unit property in Riverside, California. After making an offer I brought my wife and children up to Riverside to do a walk through. It was very revealing. The tenants were incredibly messy. In one unit there was grease on the walls, garbage everywhere and even egg remnants from breakfast still in the frying pay left on the stove. It was a total mess and smelled.

So one Saturday I decide to sleep in. When I woke up I went downstairs and the kitchen was a mess. There were dirty dishes everywhere and a pan with egg remnants left over from the breakfast that my wife cooked for the kids. I made a comment to my wife, "I guess the Riverside tenants were here!" to which she freaked out! "You don't have any idea of what I do to raise these kids while all you do is work and take care of yourself. You never appreciate what I do and you have no idea of the mess that I have to deal with. All you do is criticize everything I do." And there was more of a reaction.

I stood back and tried to calm my wife down. I repeated back to her, "Reality is in the mind of the observer. All I said was I guess the Riverside tenants were here and you're making up a story about this that is getting you upset. It doesn't mean anything except what you decide it will mean. The story you are making up is making you upset. Why don't you tell yourself a different version?"

Unfortunately that didn't help. My wife continued to be angry. Now here's the message. Yes, I was correct in my "coaching" of my wife about her responsibility to give meaning to my statements. However, it is my responsibility to be careful about what I say and to be aware of my intentions. If I suspect that saying something would be ill received it is my responsibility to not put fuel on the fire!

Challenge:
You can't win by holding on to being right. Look at the point of view of others, just for today.

Tapping in Meditation:
My purpose today is to view the world from others perspectives. I have a divine guidance in understanding others perspectives and it softens my approach to them.

Journal Notes:

Day/Year	
Day/Year	
Day/Year	
Day/Year	

The Lesson of the Landing Gear—Get Rid of Drag

I was on an instrument approach through the clouds in my Bonanza single engine airplane going into John Wayne Airport. All of a sudden I looked at my airspeed and I was only getting an airspeed of 125 knots when I should have been getting 165 kts. I was very concerned because I wasn't getting full engine power. Since I was in the clouds there was an added element of danger. I was afraid that my engine would deteriorate even further so I wanted to get out of the clouds and on the ground as soon as possible so I asked to be expedited, just short of declaring an emergency.

3 green lights

As I broke out of the clouds I started my check list for landing. When I put my landing gear down I was supposed to see three green lights indicating that it was completely extended. I didn't see any of the lights. I asked the tower to give me a visual and they told me that the landing gear was stuck in a half open position. Then I noticed a circuit breaker had popped so I recycled the circuit breaker and to my delight and relief the landing gear went down and locked and I had 3 green lights.

Then I realized that I didn't have an engine problem that affected my airspeed. I had the landing gear exposed and that created drag. Drag was the reason that I did not get the performance I expected. When I cleared the drag the aircraft performed as it was designed to perform.

Challenge:
Where is the drag in your life? What are you putting up with that you need to clear? Make a list of what is holding you back and just for today get rid of all of the drag that you can. That may include friends or co-workers who constantly complain. When you clear the drag you will perform as you were meant to.

Tapping in Meditation:
My purpose today is to surround myself with positive, excited and motivated people. I am positive, excited and motivated.

Journal Notes:

Day/Year	
Day/Year	
Day/Year	
Day/Year	
Day/Year	

May 9

Clean up Your Life—Get Rid of Clutter

Commitments to Action with Accountability

Clean out the garage by Sunday or...

The second law of thermodynamics states that there is a tendency towards disorder, a less organized state called entropy. The maid comes and cleans our house. I walk into my sons' room at the end of the day and I can't tell the maid had been there, it's a mess.

This is the way it is in your life. The natural order is disorder and clutter. You can't function efficiently unless you have order. Researchers at the Princeton University Neuroscience Institute published the results of a study they conducted in the January 2011 issue of The Journal of Neuroscience that relates directly to uncluttered and organized living. From their report "Interactions of Top-Down and Bottom-Up Mechanisms in Human Visual Cortex":

Multiple stimuli present in the visual field at the same time compete for neural representation by mutually suppressing their evoked activity throughout visual cortex, providing a neural correlate for the limited processing capacity of the visual system. Or, to paraphrase in non-neuroscience jargon: When your environment is cluttered, the chaos restricts your ability to focus. The clutter also limits your brain's ability to process information. Clutter makes you distracted and unable to process information as well as you do in an uncluttered, organized, and serene environment.

The researchers used functional magnetic resonance imaging (fMRI) and other physiological measurement tools to map the brain's responses to organized and disorganized stimuli and to monitor task performance. The conclusions were strong — if you want to focus to the best of your ability and process information as effectively as possible, you need to clear the clutter from your home and work environment. This research shows that you will be less irritable, more productive, distracted less often, and able to process information better with an uncluttered and organized home and office.

Challenge:

Identify the clutter in your life. Just for today de-clutter one area. Use behavioral contracting to make the commitment. Notice the difference this makes in how you feel and in your ability to focus. Journal about it. Get rid of anything that isn't useful, beautiful or joyful.

Tapping in Meditation:

My purpose today is to live an organized, neat and clean life and I do. I find peace and serenity by putting things in their place.

Journal Notes:

Day/Year	
Day/Year	
Day/Year	
Day/Year	
Day/Year	

Comstock Test

Make a fist with both hands and place your knuckles together so that the heels of your hands are touching. Place both forefingers straight up in the air making a "goal post." Now stare at the space between your fingers and imagine that both fingers are two strong magnets being pulled together, a stronger and stronger pull until they touch. Want this to happen, allow this to happen, watch as it happens.

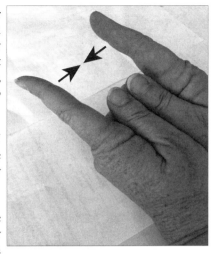

What did you notice? If you're like most people one of three things happened. First, your fingers started to move together, second, they came very close together or thirdly they actually touched.

When I do this test in a group there are always going to be some folks whose fingers stay right where they are. How did that happen? Because the muscles in your body are in constant circular motion, what should happen is that your fingers should start to move together. As I added words and pictures, two strong magnets, they should have responded further. If they didn't respond then it means that you resisted. You prevented what should have happened from happening by having an intervention. Your intervention was to contract the extensor muscles on the back of your fingers and that's how you prevented the natural response from happening.

Keep this in mind. The natural state, nature's arrow of time, is to move toward entropy or disorder. A hot cup of coffee never gets hotter and a broken egg never "un-breaks" itself.

In order to maintain clarity, focus, cleanliness and peak performance you must prevent what should happen, mediocrity, by having an intervention.

Challenge:
There are several interventions for you to apply. First get rid of your clutter. Next, precisely identify what you want this week and break that down to what you need to do today. Further clarify to what you commit to do today and make a deal with someone else that if you don't take this one action you will give them $100.

Tapping in Meditation:
My purpose today is to live with an ease and efficiency. I accomplish this with precise planning, accountability and cleanliness.

Journal Notes:

Day/Year	
Day/Year	
Day/Year	
Day/Year	
Day/Year	

May 11

Write a Journal

Journaling is an ancient tradition, one that dates back to at least 10th century Japan. Successful people throughout history have kept journals. Presidents have maintained them for posterity; other famous figures for their own purposes. Oscar Wilde, 19th century playwright, said: "I never travel without my diary. One should always have something sensational to read on the train."

Health Benefits

Contrary to popular belief, our forefathers (and mothers) did know a thing or two. There is increasing evidence to support the notion that journaling has a positive impact on physical well-being. University of Texas at Austin psychologist and researcher James Pennebaker contends that regular journaling strengthens immune cells, called T-lymphocytes. Other research indicates that journaling decreases the symptoms of asthma and rheumatoid arthritis. Pennebaker believes that writing about stressful events helps you come to terms with them, thus reducing the impact of these stressors on your physical health.

Scientific evidence supports that journaling provides other unexpected benefits. The act of writing accesses your left brain, which is analytical and rational. While your left brain is occupied, your right brain is free to create, intuit and feel. In sum, writing removes mental blocks and allows you to use all of your brainpower to better understand yourself, others and the world around you. Begin journaling and begin experiencing these benefits. The clarity and stress reduction is well worth your time and effort.

Challenge:

Journal your thoughts and feelings below. Keep this journal ongoing throughout the years particularly as it relates to the concepts on these pages. Notice what you've written in past years.

Tapping in Meditation:

My purpose today is to capture my thoughts, feelings, doubts and insecurities in my journal. I journal every day.

Journal Notes:

Day/Year	
Day/Year	
Day/Year	
Day/Year	
Day/Year	

May 12

The Randy Pausch Story—Brick Walls and Time Management

Randy Pausch was a professor of computer science at Carnegie Mellon University. He was an award winning researcher and teacher and worked with Google and Walt Disney Imagineering.

Randy was diagnosed with terminal pancreatic cancer and given only a few months to live. He had previously committed to a lecture series and kept his commitment naming these his last lectures. What would be your approach if you knew you had only a few months to live? He decided to lecture about the joy of life, he talked about honesty, gratitude and doing the best you can.

Being on deaths' bed gave him cause to think about what really matters. He talked about his childhood dreams and coming up against brick walls. He said, "The brick wall is there to give us a chance to show us how badly we want something. The brick walls are there to stop people who don't want it badly enough. They're there to stop other people."

Randy says, "Time is all you have and one day you might find out you have less than you think." He gives these tips on time management:
1.   You can always change your plan but only if you have one
2.   Ask yourself if you are spending your time on the right things
3.   Develop a good filing system
4.   Delegate
5.   Take a time out

Challenge:
Imagine you had two months to live. What would you do? Of that, what can you do now? What mindset shifts could you make now?

Tapping in Meditation:
My purpose today is to be engaged and live life fully. I may wear out but I won't rust out. I live my life with a present here-and-now-focus and enjoy every moment.

Journal Notes:

Day/Year	
Day/Year	
Day/Year	
Day/Year	
Day/Year	

May 13

The $100k Salt and Pepper Shaker—Met Life

When Randy Pausch was a child he and his sister brought a $10 salt and pepper shaker as a gift for his parents in appreciation for taking him to Disneyland. It was a prized gift and in his excitement he dropped it and it broke. As he cried a man suggested that he go back to the store and ask if they would replace it. Randy said, "But it was my fault" and the man suggested that he ask anyway.

Randy explained to the clerks that it was his fault that he was excited and careless. The clerk's response stayed with Randy for a lifetime. They said no it was our fault for not wrapping it carefully enough to protect it and they replaced it. Randy told his father and it left such an impression of kindness, generosity and good will that his father spent over $100k over the years bringing busloads of kids to Disneyland.

In the 1980s I was in Cleveland selling tickets for attendance at my full day workshop. A manager from Met Life purchased a ticket. I had a clear no refund policy that I had everyone read agree to and sign. The policy stated that he could come to another program, give the ticket to someone else or receive the program on audio cassettes, (remember it was the 80s). His company called a managers meeting on the day of my program. He called and asked me personally for a refund. I told him I was sorry but he knew the policy and agreed and I would not issue a refund.

Fast forward 3 years. I'm sitting in an executive's office of Met Life in Irvine California. They had a partnership with Century 21 and were going to purchase my program for all of their agents working with Century 21 nationwide. This executive had done his homework and had made his decision, it would be my company. All he had to do was to get this approved by his committee and this was just a formality as they would just accept his recommendations. Guess who was on that committee?

I let a $250 ticket cost me thousands of dollars, but that's not the lesson. It's not my money until I have a happy client. The refund would have been the right thing to do because he asked for it. It would have been the kind thing to do and I didn't do it. I was greedy and attached to being right. I've never done that again! Lesson learned. How about you?

Challenge:
Look for times when you are being greedy, selfish, and are attached to being right. Can you shift your perspective for the greater good?

Tapping in Meditation:
My purpose today is to kind to all people and I am.

Journal Notes:

Day/Year	
Day/Year	
Day/Year	
Day/Year	
Day/Year	

The Lesson of the 7 Circles

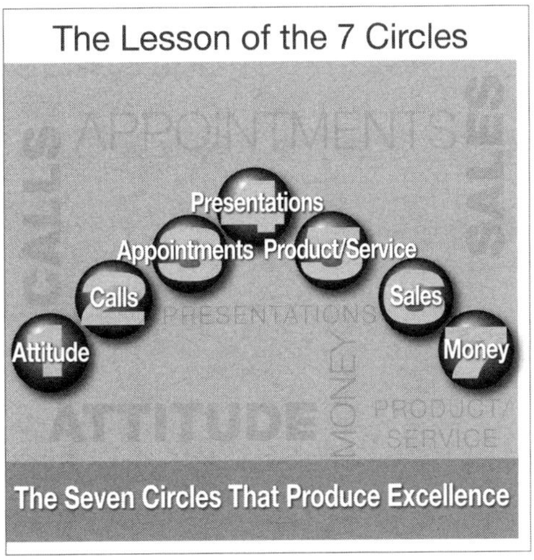

I know that you are in this program because you love people right? Place a $ in the far right circle. Money is not the most important thing in your life but it is up there with air and breathing. This is a sequence of events for all sales. In order to make money you need to have SALES. In order to make sales you need to have the PRODUCT or SERVICE to sell. In order to sell the product or service you need to set APPOINTMENTS. In order to set appointments you need to make CALLS. In order to do this you need to have an attitude that supports you in taking this sequence of events.

That's where the barrier is—ATTITUDE. There is a weakness in the United States and worldwide in teaching or coaching attitude. This is not Polly Ana there's a pony in that horse manure stuff. This is not cheerleading you which is useless.

The Lesson of the 7 Circles

Presentations
Appointments Product/Service
Calls
Attitude   Sales
                          Money

The Seven Circles That Produce Excellence

When I talk about coaching attitude I'm meaning teaching you how to change what you pay attention to, how to change your focus, your reference point. You do that by being specific about what you want in a short period of time, what you need to do over the next 7 days, what you will do this week and then add in a heavy dose of accountability with behavioral contracting.

Challenge:
What area of your life needs your attention today?

Tapping in Meditation:
My purpose today is to be the change I seek in others. I smile often. I am kind. I am of service to others. I have a great attitude.

Journal Notes:

Day/Year	
Day/Year	
Day/Year	
Day/Year	
Day/Year	

May 15

It's All Attitude—Character Traits of a Leader

Characteristics of a Leader		
Characteristics	**Attitude**	**Skill**
Believed in me	✓	
Encouraged me	✓	
Tough on me	✓	
Mentored me	✓	✓
Held me accountable	✓	
Loved me	✓	

Attitude is the most important attribute you can possess. Not any kind of attitude. I'm talking about being the kind of person who lights up a room when they walk in. This is a program that reinforces our food plan through the commitment to personal excellence. People who are leaders have an energy about them.

When I was coaching football at Cal State Fullerton my roommate was like this, Steve Mariucci. He had high integrity, extreme high work ethic, contagious energy and unyielding passion. That's all attitude.

Steve went on to become the head football coach for the San Francisco 49'ers and Detroit Lions and now is a NFL broadcaster. All of the coaches on that staff shared those characteristics and all went on to great accomplishments. Attitude is the difference maker!

Challenge:

Think of the person who has had the most impact in your life. Who comes to mind? Is it a teacher? A coach? A colleague? A lifelong friend? A family member? Make a list of the characteristics that would describe their relationship with you. Did they believe in you? Challenge you, tough on you, hold you to a higher standard than you thought possible? Did they love and support you and your efforts? Did they tell the truth to you? What else?

After you make your list then make two columns labeled Attitude and Skill. Place a check mark next to each characteristic that you've just used to describe your mentor. Is it an attitude or a skill? What do you notice?

Tapping in Meditation:

My purpose today is to make a difference in someone else's life with my attitude.

Journal Notes:

Day/Year	
Day/Year	
Day/Year	
Day/Year	
Day/Year	

Never Give Up

When I was having my pool built the construction crew had to take out much of the existing landscape. We were careful to preserve the beautiful palm trees. There was one particular plant that very difficult to remove. I watched the crew take an axe to it and they chopped it up. There was nothing but a stub left and they weren't concerned because the original plan called for the planter with the palm trees and that stub to be filled in with rocks.

I was absolutely amazed when that plant grew back. It not only grew back to its original size but it seemed to have come back even larger and healthier. I kept thinking that little plant just never gave up. (Giant Bird of Paradise)

We have a phrase in skydiving that says "go in with all of your handles pulled." This means that if you're ever in an emergency you make sure that you've done everything you can to correct the situation and give yourself a chance to survive. This means pulling the handle for your main parachute, for your "cut away", for your reserve, all of your handles.

This fits in with my philosophy of what I can control I must control. You can control your effort, your preparation, you're learning and your own self development. When you have a goal in mind, do the research, make the plan, and execute the plan. Most importantly, never give up! You never know when you are very close to the result and one more bit of effort will be the tipping point

Challenge:
Look at the various projects you have. Just for today focus on one and give maximum effort. When you think you've done that, give it one more push!

Tapping in Meditation:
My purpose today is to rejoice in my ability to solve my problems with effort. I love to work hard and apply myself. I find a peaceful serenity in hard work.

Journal Notes:

Day/Year	
Day/Year	
Day/Year	
Day/Year	
Day/Year	

May 17

Covey's 4 Squares for Time Management

I. Important and urgent	**II. Important and not urgent**
III. Not important but urgent	**IV. Not important and not urgent**

I don't know if Steven Covey authored this himself but it is frequently attributed to him. I use it all the time and would like to see you use it too. Think of a box that has 4 quadrants. You could use my version, shown here, to prioritize your time. For example from 11:00 am until 2:00 pm you will only do quadrant I important and urgent activities. Depending on your industry you'll need to fill in the blanks about what would be classified as important and urgent. For someone in sales for example, important and urgent between those hours might be prospecting. That means that an important but not urgent activity like preparing a proposal for a prospective client (important and not urgent) would not be done at that time. Time blocking is a key for the utilization of this concept.

You certainly don't want to find yourself engaged in an Internet search for some product illustrations during prime hours. That could be quadrant II or maybe even quadrant IV. This is an easy way to have a visual system to classify your activities and times to accomplish them.

Challenge:

Take a look at what you need to accomplish today. What are the important and urgent activities for the day? Do those until you complete them or until you've blocked off time for other priorities.

Tapping in Meditation:

My purpose today is to enjoy the day. To take pride in being well prepared and I am well prepared. I am proud of myself for staying focused on productive activities and I do.

Journal Notes:

Day/Year	
Day/Year	
Day/Year	
Day/Year	
Day/Year	

May 18

Inspect and Verify

Years ago I blocked off time to do an important and urgent activity. I knew that this particular company that had independent agencies all over the United States had a large company meeting in August. All of these agencies met company-wide in August and they start to plan about mid-May, or now.

I committed to my coach that this week I would focus on calling all of these companies, about 100 of them. What he said stuck with me for years. He said, "Send me a list of who you called at the end of the day on Friday."

Inspect and verify is a gift that you can give to another person. It forces them to be specifically accountable and conscious of what they are doing. It's easy to see if you are on target or off when you are charting the specifics of your actions.

Inspect and Verify

Challenge:
Embrace "Inspect and Verify." Where can you make a commitment, just for today, document your specific actions and report to someone else for accountability? Make that commitment and track your results.

Tapping in Meditation:
My purpose today is to be better today than I was yesterday and I am. I don't pray for things to get easier, I pray for me to get better.

Journal Notes:

Day/Year	
Day/Year	
Day/Year	
Day/Year	
Day/Year	

May 19

Nick Saban and Aristotle—How You Do One Thing

To finish that quote from the legendary Alabama Football Coach, Nick Saban, "How you do one thing is how you do everything." Aristotle said that you are what you repeatedly do and that excellence is not an act but a habit.

Isn't that why you're in this program? It's not just to lose weight, improve relationships or make more money. It's about what you are becoming. It's about who you are becoming. It's about the little things that you do and the thoughts that you have when no one is looking. How you do one thing is how you do everything.

Challenge:

Where do you need to clean it up? Thoughts, deeds? Do you have bits of lack of integrity? Moments of greed, negative thinking? Remember, no judgment, it's not good or bad, just observe. Just for today do everything, even (especially) the little things with excellence in mind.

Tapping in Meditation:

My purpose today is to do the little things, the big things, all things with excellence. My purpose today is to be the best I can be all day long.

Journal Notes:

Day/Year	
Day/Year	
Day/Year	
Day/Year	
Day/Year	

May 20

To My Sterling Silver Friends

There is a big difference between a sterling silver plate and a silver-plated one. One is silver all the way through and is expensive; the other is silver plated on the outside only and cost less. The silver on the plated plate can wear off and the copper or metal underneath becomes visible. The silver plate becomes more beautiful with use.

You know "silver and silver plated" human beings. At first glance they may look alike, but what happens when a bad crises comes up, a test of character comes up; a time of definite decision comes up?

In a silver plated person, the "copper or metal" underneath soon shows through. It is not hard to recognize a plated person.

It may take more time to recognize the sterling person because at first glance he may look the same as the plated person. You have to see this person in his successes, his failures, his hopes and dreams, his disappointments and his joys. When the "copper" doesn't show through, you know that this person has a sterling character.

Yes, like silver, it costs more to be a sterling person; much more in terms of integrity, honesty, unselfishness and patience. But in the final analysis, there is no comparison with the cheaper product.

Challenge:
The result of staying with this program of excellence is that you become sterling silver. This is a program of 3 weighed and measured meals, no snacking in between and an ongoing commitment to personal and professional development. This is a program of scientifically based positive attitude and perceptual choice. This is a program of best effort every day, one day at a time. How are you doing?

Tapping in Meditation:
My purpose today is to do the ordinary things extraordinarily well. Either I run the day or the day runs me. I plan so I am prepared to give best effort in adversity.

Journal Notes:

Day/Year	
Day/Year	
Day/Year	
Day/Year	
Day/Year	

May 21

Categories—Wheel of Life

Imagine this cart represents your life. Take a look at the roles that you play. Rank your results in each category from a zero to 10. No one is a 0 and no one is a 10. Just put a dot on the line to the right of the word where you think you are in each category versus where you'd like to be or think that you arc capable of being. Next connect the dots to get the shape of the wheels on your cart of life.

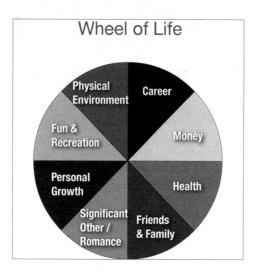

Challenge:

Where are you scoring yourself low? Just for today, what are you going to do about this? What one small action can I take before I end the day today to move one of these categories just a bit higher.

Tapping in Meditation:

My purpose today is to focus on what I can do and what I am willing to do to improve myself today.

Journal Notes:

Day/Year	
Day/Year	
Day/Year	
Day/Year	
Day/Year	

May 22

The Gap Exercise

Let's focus on 3 categories, your health, business and personal life. You define what each means. Place a number on the line that represents where you are in terms of results right now. Don't compare yourself to someone else, but rather to where you want to be and think you are capable of being. No one is a 0 and no one is a 10. Go ahead now. What you will notice is that in each category there is a next higher number.

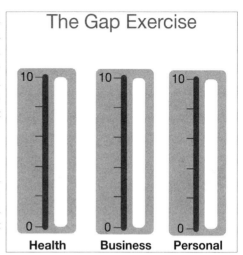

The Gap Exercise

Health Business Personal

Challenge:

Identify the gap between where you are now and incremental progress towards that next higher number. Just for today what can you do different to make a small movement in a positive direction to that next higher number?

Tapping in Meditation:

My purpose today is to allow the day to bring me great joy and I do. My thoughts are my reality and I am thinking of a bright new day. I fill this day with hope and face it with joy. The day will come and go whether I engage or not. I am engaged.

Journal Notes:

Day/Year	
Day/Year	
Day/Year	
Day/Year	
Day/Year	

May 23

Change—Metamorphosis or Gradual

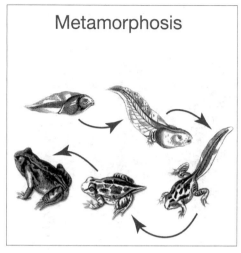

Metamorphosis

Metamorphosis a biological process by which an animal physically develops after birth or hatching, involving a conspicuous and relatively abrupt change in the animal's body structure through cell growth and differentiation. A butterfly emerges from a cocoon overnight.

The other type of change is more gradual. An example would be a tadpole into a frog. It starts off in the larvae state and then gradually grows and sprouts limbs and eventually climbs out of the water as a frog.

Your program is a program of gradual change. One moment at a time, one day at a time. One thought at a time.

Challenge:

What do you need to change just for today? An action? A thought? Make that change, just for today.

Tapping in Meditation:

My purpose today is to tap into the power of the universe that is greater than I am, that great orderly design. However I hold my higher power I am a vessel receiving guidance all day long.

Journal Notes:

Day/Year	
Day/Year	
Day/Year	
Day/Year	
Day/Year	

May 24

Change, Easy Does It Or Else—The Wisdom of the Human Body

This is your program, one day at a time, best effort for today. Not the rest of the week, just this moment. If you look at the big picture without bringing yourself back to the immediate moment in front of you then you will trigger homeostasis.

Check this out. The wisdom of the human body. Calcium is one of the most carefully regulated elements in the body, taken in through food and then sustained, in a steady state, in the bloodstream and bones through a network of hormones. Vitamin D also plays a role in helping to regulate the amount of calcium in the kidneys, bones and blood. The system is so effective that it will leach calcium from bone, retrieve it from the urine, or absorb it from the intestinal tract rather than allow the blood calcium level to fluctuate.

Small Things—Large Results

American Airlines saved $40,000 in 1987 by eliminating one (1) olive from each salad served in first class.

This is your genetic coding to "stay the same." Oh, wait a minute, you want change. You want something to be different. Then you had better focus on one small step in this moment. Build a series of these together and change will occur as you rewire and reset your brain and your habits.

Challenge:
Almost the end of the 2nd month of the second quarter. Time to take a look and see what small corrections you need to make, just for today.

Tapping in Meditation:
My purpose today is to give to others. That which I give away I get to keep. I cannot sincerely help others without helping myself.

Journal Notes:

Day/Year	
Day/Year	
Day/Year	
Day/Year	
Day/Year	

May 25
Law of Accumulation—You've Got to Have Feedback-Blue Man

Paul Karason

Paul Karason was 62 when he died. He was admitted to the hospital after suffering a heart attack. He later contracted pneumonia and had a severe stroke. Karason shot to internet fame several years ago for the blue color of his skin, which was a side effect using a silver compound for more than a decade to treat a bad case of dermatitis on his face.

This happened gradually over time. The problem was that he didn't have feedback. No one else was there to notice what he was blind to, that his skin was slowly turning blue. This is one of the fundamental principles of your program. You can't rely on yourself to hold yourself accountable because you have broken eyes. You need to have accountability that comes from an outside source, an accountability partner.

People who are obese didn't get that way overnight. It was a gradual accumulation of their habits over time. Feedback, accountability for the next seven days are the keys.

Challenge:
Are you planned for the week? For today? What is your biggest priority for today? Who is holding you accountable? Anyone?

Tapping in Meditation:
My purpose today is to make sure that the law of accumulative effect works for me for good ends. I am the sum of the actions and decisions that I make over time. I make them wisely.

Journal Notes:

Day/Year	
Day/Year	
Day/Year	
Day/Year	
Day/Year	

May 26

Feedback—Johari's Window

The Johari window is a technique created in 1955 by two American psychologists, Joseph Luft (1916–2014) and Harrington Ingham (1914–1995), used to help people better understand their relationship with self and others. They named it by combining their first names, Johari. The concept the Johari House with four rooms.

1 Know Self Things we know about ourselves and others know about us	2 Hidden Self Things we know about ourselves that others do not know
3 Blind Self Things others know about us that we do not know	4 Unknown Self Things neither we nor other know about us

- Room 1 is the part of ourselves that we know and others know.
- Room 2 is our private space, which we know but keep from others.
- Room 3 is the aspects that others know but we are not aware of.
- Room 4 is the most mysterious room in that the unconscious or subconscious part of us is known by neither ourselves nor others.

Imagine placing both arms fully extended with your forefinger pointing straight in front of you. Now move both arms to your sides until you can no longer see your fingers. That is your blind area. Getting feedback from others helps you to uncover that which is unknown to you. You do this with questions.

Challenge:
Pick about 5 people and send them these questions: 1. What do you see as my greatest strengths? 2. Greatest weaknesses? 3. How effective am I in my interactions with you? 4. If you were president of this organization what would you do differently?

Tapping in Meditation:
My purpose today is to constantly grow, learn and improve and I do grow, learn and improve. I am open minded.

Journal Notes:

Day/Year	
Day/Year	
Day/Year	
Day/Year	
Day/Year	

May 27

Arête

You want happiness. Aristotle said if you want happiness you have to strive to live at your highest potential, moment to moment, that's arête. Intention—know who you are, what you want and then just do it. A clear intention of who you are, what your values are and how they show up in the world is important.

Here are 10 principles of all of the enlightened teachers;

1. Optimism—if you can't control your mind then you're in trouble. Can't be a victim.
2. Vision—you can create your ideal life so what do you want? Everything is created twice—in your mind first, then reality!
3. Self-awareness—what are your signature strengths, what do you want to bring to the world?
4. Goals bring it into reality.
5. Action—it's not enough to have 1-5—you just have to execute.
6. Energy—you must optimize energy with exercise, nutrition, circulating money, producing more than consuming.
7. Wisdom—studying, loving what is, love where you are.
8. Love—none of it matters if you don't live with love.
9. Courage—can't be overwhelmed with fear.
10. Spirit—align with something bigger than you and let it flow through you.

Challenge:
People will forget what you said, people will forget what you did, but people will never forget how you made them feel. Be conscious of your impact on others.

Tapping in Meditation:
My purpose today is to realize that I am not a product of my circumstances; I am product of my decisions.

Journal Notes:

Day/Year	
Day/Year	
Day/Year	
Day/Year	
Day/Year	

Personality Profile D.I.S.C.

Are you more outgoing or reserved? Are you more people or task oriented? You've just given yourself a short cut to a personality profile with the D.I.S.C. instrument. The DISC profile is a universal language of behavior. Research has shown that the behavioral characteristics can be grouped together in four major divisions called personality styles. People with similar styles tend to exhibit specific behavioral characteristics common to that profile.

All people share these four styles in varying degrees of intensity. The acronym DISC stands for the 4 personality styles, D (Drive) I (Influence) S (Steadiness) C (Compliance). The usefulness of this to you is to help you build rapport by noticing the signs of the preferred style of others you are interacting with. For example, if you are dealing with a high D it would be helpful for you to be direct and go to the bottom line. Hi Ds want to be challenged and they want results. If you answered that you were more of an outgoing person and task oriented that would put you in the D quadrant. If you were more outgoing and people oriented that would put you in I. More reserved and people, S, more reserved and task, C.

Hi Is also want things fast paced and they need stimulation, risk and they are enthusiastic. Hi Ss are slower paced, supportive and relationship oriented, while Hi Cs are more conservative, more into data analysis, precise measurement.

Challenge:

Where is your most natural style? What style is most difficult for you to be? Name a key personal relationship and their style. Name a key business relationship and their style. Notice if you can match their style you can create rapport.

Tapping in Meditation:

My purpose today is to notice how I am like or different than others. Create rapport by matching the preferred system of others.

Journal Notes:

Day/Year	
Day/Year	
Day/Year	
Day/Year	
Day/Year	

May 29

Assumptions, A Bat and A Ball—Energy Conservation

A bat and a ball cost $1.10. The bat cost a dollar more than the ball. How much does the ball cost? Most people will say the ball cost 10 cents. Nope! If the ball cost 10 cents then that would mean that the bat would have to cost $1.10 to be a dollar more than the ball. The ball costs 5 cents. The bat costs $1.05 making it a dollar more than the ball.

This is counter intuitive. It seems to defy logic, however it does not. It just takes a bit more energy than your brain wants you to put forth.

How about this one. What is 12 divided by ½? What is your reflex knee jerk response? 6? Nope, it's 24.

Challenge:

You go through your life in a mostly non-conscious state. How much to you really pay attention to. See if you can remember the drive from the office to your home. Make this a special day of paying attention.

Tapping in Meditation:

My purpose today is to be a visionary. I see what others don't see. I have an acute sense of the possible.

Journal Notes:

Day/Year	
Day/Year	
Day/Year	
Day/Year	
Day/Year	

May 30

Napolean Hill—Two Envelopes

Napoleon Hill (October 26, 1883 – November 8, 1970) was an American author in the area of the new thought movement who was one of the earliest producers of the modern genre of personal-success literature. He is widely considered to be one of the great writers on success. His most famous work, Think and Grow Rich (1937), is one of the best-selling books of all time (at the time of Hill's death in 1970, Think and Grow Rich had sold 20 million copies). Hill's works examined the power of personal beliefs, and the role they play in personal success. He became an advisor to President Franklin D. Roosevelt from 1933 to 1936. "What the mind of man can conceive and believe, it can achieve"

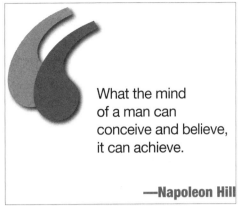

What the mind of a man can conceive and believe, it can achieve.

—**Napoleon Hill**

is one of Hill's hallmark expressions. How achievement actually occurs, and a formula for it that puts success in reach of the average person, were the focal points of Hill's books. What is truly amazing is that Hill had these insights without the benefit of the science that is available today.

"A great power that is under your control. The power to take possession of your own mind and direct it to any ends of your own choice. All success begins with a definiteness of purpose. A clear description of what you want, a list of blessings.

Everyone comes to this earth with two envelopes. One is the riches you will enjoy if you take control of your own mind. The other is labeled the penalties you face if you don't take possession of your mind and direct it. The contents of those two envelopes:

1.Sound Health 2. Peace of mind 3. A labor of love of your own choice 4. Freedom from fear and worry 5. A positive mental attitude 6. Material riches of your own choice and quantity.

The Second list contains the prices one must pay for neglecting to take possession of your own mind and direct it. 1. Ill health 2. Fear and worry 3. Indecision and doubt 4. Frustration and discouragement your whole life 5. Poverty and want 6. Envy, greed, jealously, hatred and superstition.

He said 'Whatever the Mind can conceive and believe, it can achieve'.

Hill said 'You have a great power under your control, much bigger than any of your fears. It is the power to take possession of your own mind and to direct it to whatever you want.

Challenge:
Create a picture of precisely what you want in Life. You create the reality with your thoughts and you manifest it into material form with your actions.

Tapping in Meditation:
My purpose today is to think, do and be excellence, all day long.

Journal Notes:

Day/Year	
Day/Year	
Day/Year	

May 31

Candace Pert—The Mind and Body are One

Can you believe how fast this year is speeding by? It's already the end of the second month of the second quarter. One more month to sprint to where you need to be to stay on track for Q2.

Candace Beebe Pert (June 26, 1946 – September 12, 2013) an American neuroscientist and pharmacologist and her colleagues from the National Institute of Mental Health in Maryland, discovered that the human body is a psychosomatic network. They discovered that there are molecules called peptides that interconnect three distinct systems—the nervous system, the immune system and the endocrine system, into a single network. Pert says, "I can no longer make a strong distinction between the brain and the body.

Pert offered scientific evidence to support the philosophical concepts that your thoughts are real. Our brain has the magnificent capacity to take an electrical impulse and turn it into a chemical release (neurotransmitter). Yes, the reality starts with the thought.

Challenge:

Be the guardian of your thinking because your thoughts bring into reality the exact substance of those thoughts.

Tapping in Meditation:

My purpose today is to face my challenges in the spiritual realm. He that conquers himself is greater than he who conquers a city. The real victories are victories over sin and temptation, leading to a victorious and abundant life.

Journal Notes:

Day/Year	
Day/Year	
Day/Year	
Day/Year	
Day/Year	

JUNE

Davies Day Book

365 concepts for excellence

June 1

Quantum Physics—The Illusion of Separateness

Those who are not shocked when they first come across quantum theory cannot possibly have understood it.

—Niels Bohr

Quantum physics has revealed that everything is energy, wave forms of probability that exist within an infinite field of probabilities. Atoms were broken down further and were found to be pure energy. All things are comprised of energy. The bottom line is Einstein's discovery proved that all things broken down to their most basic form consist of the same stuff-energy. Looking at this another way you could say that we exist in what could be considered to be an infinite field of quantum energy soup just as an individual drop of water exists within the ocean.

Without a basic understanding of quantum physics you might think that there are different forms of energy such as energy that powers your home, energy that makes you get out of bed in the morning, energy that fuels your car, etc. Everything that exists whether nature, sound, colors, oxygen, your thoughts, your physical body, everything exists only as this very same energy.

To put it another way, ANYTHING and EVERYTHING is from the same source and is merely a vibrating frequency of energy which joins together with energies of the same harmonious frequency to form what we perceive to be reality and as a result determines what we experience in the physical world. This means that what the most enlightened teachers in the history of the world have taught and which spiritual texts have shown for thousands of years, we "Really Are One." There are no parts at all. What we call a part, or individual is merely a pattern in an inseparable web of relationships. Objects themselves are networks of relationships, of information, embedded in larger networks.

It doesn't matter which avenue you choose to study, spirituality, quantum physics, human physiology, the power of the human mind or through the simple observations of nature, ALL avenues will lead to the very same conclusions. These conclusions are that all of these seemingly separate events are intricately interconnected. Everything at its core consists of pure energy and is connected to everything else. Your thoughts are creative. This thought energy takes form based on the thoughts and beliefs of the person thinking them. Everything is thought.

Challenge:

If nothing could stop you what would you have, be and do right now? Get a clear picture and you have already created the reality.

Tapping in Meditation:

My purpose today is to think of the reality I want. Create it mentally first.

Journal Notes:

Day/Year	
Day/Year	
Day/Year	
Day/Year	
Day/Year	

June 2

Quiet Time—Tapping In—How to Meditate

Regardless of external circumstances a person can make themselves happy or miserable. In order to make this happen we need to understand or at least accept that there is a higher power greater than we are that is pure energy. We can tap into that higher power just like tuning in a radio station in your car. The tool for tapping in is meditation.

Neuroscientists have discovered that when you meditate you actually get better at doing it over time. You not only get better at meditating, but you also improve a wide range of self-control skills including attention, focus, stress management, impulse control and self-awareness. Regular mediators have more gray matter in the prefrontal cortex as well as regions of the brain that support self-awareness.

Meditation will optimize your immune system. You live in a hyper stimulating environment all day long. It is important that you take some time every day to get out of that fight or flight mode and into the "relaxation response." Constant meditation can change your genetic expression. Your genes are not fixed. Through a process called epigenetics your thoughts and behaviors are constantly influencing how your genes are expressed. Five to ten minutes of meditation a day for only 8 weeks you begin to optimize hundreds of your genes to more closely match those of lifelong mind body practitioners. Here's how:

Challenge:
1. Get out your IPhone and set the alarm for how long you plan to meditate. Start out with 5 minutes, then gradually get up to 10 or more.
2. Sit with dignity. Be comfortable, but not slouched or lying down.
3. Read the challenge and tapping in meditation from this book.
4. Take a couple of deep breaths and then focus your eyes on an anchor. When they want to allow them to close.
5. Notice your breathing. Count each time you exhale up to 10.
6. Now just listen. This is your tapping in. When thoughts come let them come and go. If you get too distracted then go back to counting your breathing up to 10 exhales.
7. To further quiet your thinking repeat to yourself "I am a spiritual and mental magnet attracting to myself all things which are good, bless and prosper me. I am blessed and prosperous." Then go back to counting your breathing and next just listening.

Tapping in Meditation:
My purpose today is to embrace the rhythm and the flowing of my own heart. The past has no power and no hold over me anymore. All that I need will come to me at the right time and place in this life. I am deeply fulfilled with who I am.

Journal Notes:

Day/Year	
Day/Year	
Day/Year	
Day/Year	
Day/Year	

June 3

Take Responsibility and the 4 Core Principles

You are in a program of excellence that embraces excellence. There is a shared core commitment to health, business and personal excellence. Just about everyone in this program is also using the food plan for weight management. A common core behavioral culture shared by everyone includes 4 core principles. They are;

1. I do what I say I will do. (Minimum level objectives)
2. I am far better off as a part of a team then I can be alone. (Synergy)
3. Accountability—I am the source of all that I experience versus going victim and blaming others.
4. Service to others.

Responsibility is a choice. It's often referred to as the key to freedom. Your future can be everything you have ever dreamed of. You have the talent and tools to experience one beautiful day after another. When you take personal responsibility for your life and the results you are obtaining you will cease to blame others and be the cause of those results. Since you can't change other people blame is inappropriate. Blaming others causes you to remain in a prison of your own making. When you take responsibility blame is eliminated and you are free to grow.

When you don't take responsibility you are rejecting your uniqueness and you are turning all of your special powers over to other people, situations or circumstances. You are then no longer in control of your future.

Dr. Rollo May, a distinguished psychiatrist once wrote, "The opposite of courage in our society is not cowardice, its conformity." It requires great courage to take responsibility for your life. George Bernard Shaw said, "People are always blaming their circumstances for what they are. I don't believe in circumstances. The people who get on in this world are the people who get up and look for the circumstances they want, and if they can't find them, they make them!"

You are responsible for your wealth, your emotional state, your health, your happiness. Winston Churchill said, "Responsibility is the price of greatness."

Challenge:

No matter what circumstances you find yourself in look at yourself as the responsible party. How have you been that this is your current result?

Tapping in Meditation:

My purpose today is to be and I am responsible for my life, for my feelings, for my personal growth and for every result that I get.

Journal Notes:

Day/Year	
Day/Year	
Day/Year	

June 4

Victim—Responsible Exercise

When I do this exercise in my live programs I'll ask the audience to partner up into As and Bs. I ask A to tell a story about a time in their life when they were a victim. Be convincing. Their goal is to get B to raise their hand when I ask, "How many of you believe that your partner was a victim?" I ask the As to notice how it felt to remember from a victim mindset. How was your energy? Your emotions?

Next I ask As to retell their story but this time only from a taking responsibility view point. They are not allowed to say that they can't do this because they really were a victim. They will notice a few differences when they reflect on this perspective. First, it's a choice. They can always either chose a victim or a responsibility reference mind set. Next they will notice how their energy level is so much higher from a responsibility perspective. It just feels better to be accountable.

A story I like to tell is when I invested in a residential property in Alabama. As it turns out I paid $60,000 for the property and it was inflated by over $30,000. This owner saw me as an out of state investor who didn't know the marketplace who was ripe for the picking. That house would have appraised at about $25,000, not the $60,000 I paid. The seller, who was also the listing real estate agent, knew that I would think $60,000 was dirt cheap and that I would be happy buying it without a mortgage and collecting a nice $630.00 in rent every month. That is exactly how I saw it especially when that amount wouldn't even be a down payment out here in California and I'd get at best a $200 positive cash flow per month not $630.00. Also the rehab work that he did was very shoddy and I had to redo quite a bit of it to bring it up to code. This is the victim mind set and I get angry when I think about this from this perspective.

How about taking responsibility? It always comes down to actions that I could have taken. Ok, I could have ordered and paid for an appraisal. That would have given me the market value but I just didn't want to pay for it. I could have ordered and paid for an inspection. This would have showcased the shoddy work. Also I could have gotten on a plane and flew to Alabama to look at the property. I did not do this. I also could have asked for referrals of other out of state investors that this Realtor had worked with.

Challenge:
Now that's taking responsibility. It feels so much better to approach life this way.

Tapping in Meditation:
My purpose today is to know my inner self and allow it to guide me to the right decisions. I trust myself to make the best and smartest decision for me. I receive all feedback about my decisions with kindness but make the final call myself. I listen with love to this inner conflict and reflect on it until I get to peace around it.

Journal Notes:

Day/Year	
Day/Year	
Day/Year	
Day/Year	
Day/Year	

June 5

Suggestions for Peace of Mind

1. Move every day. Take a walk for 30 minutes and smile as you pass others.
2. Sit in silence for at least 5 minutes every day.
3. Read one page in this book when you wake up every day.
4. Live with the 3 Es, Energy, Enthusiasm, Empathy and the 3 Fs, Faith, Family, Friends.
5. Spend more time with people over the age of 70 and under the age of 6.
6. Dream more while you're awake.
7. Make at least 3 people smile every day.
8. Realize that life is a school and you are here to learn. Problems will come and go but the lessons you learn will last a lifetime.
9. Smile and laugh more. Be a fan of comedy. It will keep the energy vampires away.
10. Life isn't fair but it's still good!
11. Don't take yourself too seriously, no one else does.
12. You don't have to win every argument. Agree to disagree.
13. Make peace with the past so it won't mess up the present.
14. Don't compare your life with others. You have no idea what their journey is all about.
15. Burn the candles. Use the nice sheets. Don't save it for a special occasion. Today is the special occasion.
16. No one is in charge of your happiness except you.
17. Forgive everyone for everything.
18. What other people think of you is none of your business.
19. However good or bad a situation is, it will change.
20. Time heals almost everything. Give time-time.
21. Get rid of everything that isn't useful, beautiful or joyful.
22. Believe the best is yet to come.
23. No matter how you feel, get up, dress up and show up.
24. Do the right thing, even when no one will know.
25. Remember that you are too blessed to be stressed so enjoy the ride.

Challenge:

Each night before you go to bed complete the following statements, "I am thankful for …" "Today I accomplished…"

Tapping in Meditation:

My purpose today is to tap into the infinite source and supply of spiritual substance, the energy all around me. My relationships are filled with love. I feel good about myself.

Journal Notes:

Day/Year	
Day/Year	
Day/Year	
Day/Year	
Day/Year	

June 6

Branding-Speaking-Writing

A brand is the set of expectations, memories, stories and relationships that, taken together, account for a consumer's decision to choose one product or service over another. Your brand is your reputation. Simply put, your brand is your promise to your customer. It tells them what they can expect from your products and services, and it differentiates your offering from that of your competitors. Your brand is derived from who you are, who you want to be and who people perceive you to be.

One of the quickest and most powerful way to establish yourself as an expert is to speak and write. Regardless of your career one opportunity would be to submit topical articles to your local newspaper. They are quite often looking for outside contributors.

Also, do you have a message inside? What kinds of groups would benefit from hearing you speak? What is your expertise? Can you write a book about what you are passionate about and self-publish? Something changes for you when you become an author.

It is very therapeutic to express yourself whether it's journaling in this book, speaking, submitting an article or writing your own book.

Challenge:
Write an outline for a book that you would write. Whether you intend to do so or not you might just surprise yourself about the music you have inside of you.

Tapping in Meditation:
My purpose today is to embrace my passions and offer my skill sets to the public. I become richer and richer every day. The warmth of others surrounds me. I am in control of my life.

Journal Notes:

Day/Year	
Day/Year	
Day/Year	
Day/Year	
Day/Year	

June 7

Future Self Exercise

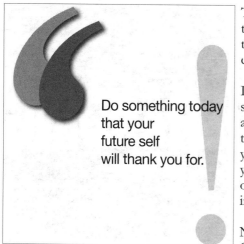

Do something today that your future self will thank you for.

The purpose of the future self-exercise is to tap into the creative right brain and to project into the future to grab the insights and imagined clarity in a way that can be helpful to you in the present.

Imagine a beam of light that extends from outer space. Follow that beam as it leaves the building you are in right now. You can do this while you are doing this reading. Notice in your mind's eye what you see as you are leaving the building, traveling above the city, as you continue out so you can see the entire area. Keep on going and notice the curvature of the earth. Now imagine you are in outer space.

Next notice another beam of light returning to earth. Grab it and follow it back down to earth. This beam is taking you back to earth 20 years from now. Keep following this beam down, noticing as much as you can about everything that you see. This is where your future self-lives. Contact earth and notice where you are. Notice what dwellings or nature surrounds you. Now, move into the dwelling of your future self. Knock on the door.

As the door opens what do you notice? Greet your future self and notice the way your future self-returns your greeting. Notice where this person, you in the future, lives and move with him or her to a comfortable place for conversation. As you move to this place notice the qualities and nature of the place and the person who lives there. When you arrive at this conversation place allow yourself to get comfortable. You have a few questions to ask your future self.

- What is it that you most remember about the last 20 years?
- What do I need to be most aware of to get me from here to there?
- What advice would you give me to live my life to the fullest?

You may even think of a few questions of your own.

Next you will see another beam of light taking you back to outer space and returning you back to earth, full of wisdom from the visit with your future self. Journal your insights below

Challenge:
Find a peaceful and quiet place and do the future self-exercise. Do something today that your future self will thank you for.

Tapping in Meditation:
My purpose today is to tap into the wisdom, the information that already exists all around me and I do.

Journal Notes:

Day/Year	
Day/Year	
Day/Year	

Everyone is Highly Motivated

There is no such thing as an unmotivated person. It's just not genetically possible. You are wired for a motivational instinct to survive. It's not possible to not be motivated. However, you may not be motivated to do what you think you should be doing.

Imagine you go home after a very exhausting and tough day on the job. You have absolutely no energy. You collapse into your favorite chair too exhausted to do anything. A friend calls you to go to the gym and you're too exhausted. You spouse asks you to help the kids with their homework and you're just too exhausted. Are you unmotivated?

The answer is no, you are very highly motivated, to conserve energy. The key is to notice what you are in reference to. How are you running your nervous system that the end result is a physiology of exhaustion? You are in reference to how tough your day was.

Now watch what happens when you change what you are in reference to. All of a sudden you smell smoke, you see flames so you instantly jump out of your chair, grab your favorite kid and run out of the house.

What happened to that exhausted non energy state? You instantly changed your physiology by changing what you were paying attention to. The good news is that you can do this on demand.

This is what I taught my football team to do when I coached at Cal State Fullerton. I taught them to generate best effort on every plan. They had a last play of the game mindset on every play.

Challenge:
You can be a victim to the events of your day or you can invent your physiology by changing what you pay attention to. Take responsibility and stay focused in excellence.

Tapping in Meditation:
My purpose today is to always do my best and I do. I am magnetic to success. I attract all good things to myself.

Journal Notes:

Day/Year	
Day/Year	
Day/Year	
Day/Year	
Day/Year	

June 9

Always Give Effort—KOKO

Don't Quit—(a poem) Author Unknown

Keep ON Keeping ON

When things go wrong, as they sometimes will.

When the road you're trudging seems all up hill.

When the funds are low and the debts are high, and you want to smile but you have to sigh.

When care is pressing you down a bit, rest if you must but don't you quit.

Life is queer with its twists and turns, as everyone of us sometimes learns, and many a failure turns about when he might have won had he stuck it out.

Don't give up, though the pace seems slow, you might succeed with another blow.

Often the goal is nearer than it seems to a faint and faltering man, often the struggler has given up when he might have captured the victor's cup.

And he learned too late, when the night slipped down, how close he was to the golden crown. Success is failure turned inside out—the silver tint of the clouds of doubt.

And you never can tell how close you are, it may be near when it seems afar.

So stick to the fight when you're hardest hit.

It's when things seem worst that you mustn't quit.

Challenge:
Just for today fight through any perceptions or feelings that make you want to quit. Keep on Keeping on.

Tapping in Meditation:
My purpose today is to use the creative power of my thinking to shift my physiology on demand. I get myself to do what I want to do by shifting my thinking.

Journal Notes:

Day/Year	
Day/Year	
Day/Year	
Day/Year	
Day/Year	

June 10

25 Phrases of Wisdom from Wise People

1. "Whatever the mind can conceive and believe, it can achieve."—Napoleon Hill
2. "Your time is limited so don't waste it living someone else's life."—Steve Jobs
3. "Strive not to be a success, but rather to be of value."—Albert Einstein
4. "Two roads diverged in a wood, and I took the one less traveled and that has made all the difference."—Robert Frost
5. "The common question that gets asked in business is, "Why?" that's a good question, but an equally valid question is "Why not?""—Jeff Bezos
6. "You miss 100% of the shots you don't take."—Wayne Gretzky
7. "Every strike brings me closer to the next home run."—Babe Ruth
8. "Definiteness of purpose is the starting point of all achievement."—W.Clement Stone
9. "Life is what happens to you while you're busy making other plans."—John Lennon
10. "We become what we think about."—Earl Nightingale
11. "Twenty years from now you will be more disappointed by the things that you didn't do than by the ones you did do so throw off the bowlines, sail away from the safe harbor, and catch the trade winds in your sails. Explore, dream, discover."—Mark Twain
12. "Life is 10% what happens to me and 90% of how I react to it."—John Maxwell
13. "The mind is everything. What you think you become."—Buddha.
14. "The best time to plant a tree was 20 years ago. The second best time is now."—Chinese Proverb
15. "An unexamined life is not worth living."—Socrates
16. "80% of success is showing up."—Woody Allen
17. "Don't wait. The time will never be just right."—Napoleon Hill
18. "Winning isn't everything but wanting to win is."—Vince Lombardi
19. "I am not a product of my circumstances. I am a product of my choices."—Bob Davies
20. "Every child is an artist. The problem is how to remain an artist once he grows up."—Pablo Picasso
21. "You can never cross the ocean until you have the courage to lose sight of the shore."—Christopher Columbus
22. "I've learned that people will forget what you said, forget what you did, but people will never forget how you made them feel."—Maya Agelou
23. "Either you run the day or the day runs you."—Jim Rohn
24. "Whether you think you can or you think you can't, you're right."—Henry Ford
25. "The two most important days in your life are the day you are born and the day you find out why."—Mark Twain.

Challenge:
Just for today give maximum focus and energy, rest and start all over.

Tapping in Meditation:
My purpose today is to win the day. I have a peaceful, loving and serving day.

Journal Notes:

Day/Year	
Day/Year	
Day/Year	
Day/Year	

June 11
Be a Better Observer Using Systems—The Lesson of the Numbers

```
73   9  49   66    78   62  50
37    53        5    46   34
 69      17        38  14      74   18
41  33              29      2  70  86
  21   1    25   10
 13                        54  42   22
57   81  77  61   58    30
   85  45   65    6       82   26
79   31   55   32  60    44  76  80
   75    63        20
23  43   47  51  64   88      68
39   3    11          48    56
  67  87  71   24  36    40
59    15   35 28   4    12   16
19  7  83    27    84  72   8   52
```

```
I  73   9  49  | 66    78   62  50 II
37   53      5 | 46   34
 69     17     | 38  14     74  18
41  33    (1)  29| 10  (2) 70  86
  21    25     |
 13            | 54  42  22
57  81  77  61 | 58    30
   85  45   65 | 6      82  26
III 79  31  55 | 32  60    44 76 80 IV
   75    63    |    20
23  43   47 51 | 64  88     68
39  (3)   11   |       48    56
  67  87  71   | 24  36    40
59    15   35 28| (4)  12    16
19  7  83   27  | 84  72  8  52
```

Your test is to find as many numbers in consecutive order from #1, #2 etc. in 30 seconds. Ready, set, go. As you hunt and peck at random for the numbers you are using a lot of mental energy. A common number might be 8 to 12.

Now watch what happens to your effectiveness when I give you a system, an order out of the chaos, a structure.

This time draw a line through the middle of the numbers, vertically, between 49 on the left and 66 on the right. Next draw a horizontal line through the middle of the page with the numbers 55 above and 63 below this line. Now label the quadrants from top left, 1, top right 2, bottom left 3, bottom right 4.

This time look in quadrant 1 for the first number, then quadrant 2 for the next, then quadrant 3 for the next in sequence and quadrant 4 for the next. Then, back to 1, 2, 3, 4, OK, 30 seconds again now start.

As you can imagine someone who scored an 8 to 12 the first time would now score in the 20s by using a system. It's amazing that performance is not only better with a system but it's also easier.

Challenge:
Use your system. The system of this program is 3 weighed and measured meals, nothing in between and the avoidance of flour and sugar. Your system has the component of weekly behavioral contracting, plus the self-development from the habit of reading one page of this book every day and having quiet time for 5 to 10 minutes every day. That is your structure, your system.

Tapping in Meditation:
My purpose today is to choose happiness whenever I wish no matter what my circumstances. I always give myself permission to buy the things that are most important to me in life. Gratitude brings me into a harmonious relationship with the good in everyone that surrounds me.

Journal Notes:

Day/Year	
Day/Year	
Day/Year	
Day/Year	
Day/Year	

June 12

Be a Better Observer—The Little Girl and the Truck

Urban legend has it that once during rush hour in New York City a tractor-trailer became stuck in the very busy Holland Tunnel. The truck was too tall to move forward and wedged too tightly to move backward. The police called the fire department and were about ready to engage in what seemed like the most logical solution, sawing off the top of the trailer and then towing it out of the tunnel.

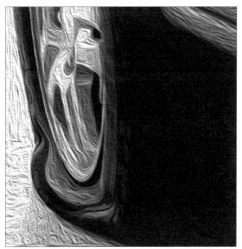

Then a car drove by and a little girl asked her father why don't they just let the air out the tires? Her dad asked the police. They scratched their heads, let the air out of the tires and within minutes they had the truck cleared from the tunnel. This young girl was just too naive to look for difficult solutions.

There is a principle in physics called Occams Razor. What this mean is that when there are multiple potential solutions it's usually the simplest option that is the best.

Challenge:
Simplify. Where do you need to simplify your life? What or who do you need to say no to?

Tapping in Meditation:
My purpose today is to be grateful that I can think and that I can use those thoughts to change my life as I choose. I am a success. I am a receptacle of love.

Journal Notes:

Day/Year	
Day/Year	
Day/Year	
Day/Year	
Day/Year	

June 13

The Law of Compensation—Left Turning Tendency

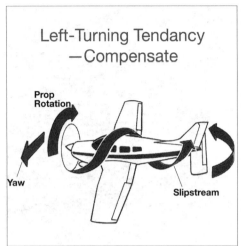

Left-Turning Tendancy —Compensate

Prop Rotation

Yaw

Slipstream

There is a built in flaw in the design of the Beechcraft Bonanza airplane that I fly. In fact, this applies to any single engine airplane. This is referred to as the left turning tendency.

As the slipstream produced by the propeller rotation wraps around the fuselage it strikes the left side of the vertical fin producing a left turn.

Imagine that I want to fly from John Wayne Airport in Southern California up north to San Francisco. If I don't compensate for the built in design flaw I will wind up over the ocean, lost.

Therefore I must take action to compensate. That action is the use of the right rudder. This pushes the tail fin in the opposite direction and compensate for the left turning tendency. The key is to make note that the aircraft will do what it is designed to do, turn left, unless I have an intervention. The right rudder is the intervention.

What about you? Do you have any design flaws? The answer is yes. As a human being you are designed to recognize the highest level of perceived pain and to avoid. The human mind will operate exactly as it is designed to operate as well. Anything that you perceive as painful will stimulate the natural human response of avoidance.

You cannot prevent the human survival instinct of avoidance. You can't stop it. The only thing you can do is surrender to it and use it. You do that with this program. You do that by controlling your physiology with the food plan. You do that by planning weekly and making commitments with behavioral contracting. You compensate for the flaws of human nature by reading a page a day and having quiet time every day.

Challenge:
Use the tools of this program and your success is almost certain!

Tapping in Meditation:
My purpose today is to be creative and capable and I am. I clearly see all there is to be grateful for in life. Through gratitude my world expands. I love and accept myself unconditionally.

Journal Notes:

Day/Year	
Day/Year	
Day/Year	
Day/Year	
Day/Year	

June 14

Inertia—It's the Starting that Stops Most People

Inertia is a word we use when we talk about matter and movement. Basically, our idea of inertia goes back to Sir Issac Newton's first two laws of physics:

1. An object at rest tends to stay at rest.
2. An object in motion tends to stay in motion.

Inertia is the quality in matter (matter is anything you can touch) that lets it stay still if it is still, or keeps it moving if it is moving.

If you want to overcome inertia, you have to apply a force. A force will make something that is still start to move, like flicking a wad of paper with a pencil will make it move. Also force, due to resistance, will slow or stop something that is already moving. The wad of paper will be slowed by resistance made by rubbing up against the air it is passing through.

It's the start
that stops
most people.

—Anonymous

It's the starting that stops most people. If you have a big project that you want to complete if it's large in scope, you have no momentum since you are just starting. Added to the lack of motion is the fear that you will have as you project the difficulty of such a large endeavor. So how do you create inertia? By starting.

First, break the project down into small manageable tasks. Next block off time to execute the tasks. Make a behavioral contract agreeing to complete the tasks by the end of the week and have a heavy penalty if you don't. Now you are tapping into the starting and building momentum. Once you have created your start and your momentum then the results will start to pour forth easily and effortlessly. It's just like priming the pump to get water from the well. Keep on priming and once you've put in the work and have the inertia the well will provide you with an ongoing source of water.

Challenge:
What project are you avoiding? Precisely plan and get started on one small part of it today.

Tapping in Meditation:
My purpose today is to radiate self-respect and I do. I am the source of my abundance. I allow my intuition to guide my actions today with trust that I am guided toward my highest good.

Journal Notes:

Day/Year	
Day/Year	
Day/Year	
Day/Year	
Day/Year	

June 15

My Human Rights

1. To say NO without guilt.
2. To determine the use of my own time.
3. To feel and express my anger.
4. To feel and express healthy competitiveness and my achievement drive.
5. To strive for self-actualization by whatever channels, talents and or interests I find natural.
6. To use my own judgments in deciding which of my own needs are the most important.
7. To make mistakes.
8. To have my own opinions given the same respect as other people's opinions.
9. To ask for help from other people.
10. To be treated as a capable human adult and not to be patronized.
11. To consider my own needs as important as those of other people.
12. To ask someone else to look at their behavior.
13. To tell someone else of my needs.
14. To take care of my own responsibilities.
15. To be independent.
16. To be an individual, a whole person and be happy.
17. To be selfish. To take care of myself.
18. To let go of the unmanageable in my life, duty versus desire.
19. To attend meetings.
20. To daydream and fantasize.

Challenge:

Continue using the tools of this program. Follow the food plan. Use weekly behavioral contracts. Read one page a day. Quiet time every day.

Tapping in Meditation:

My purpose today is to be proud of all of my accomplishments. I am worthy of receiving abundance and I do receive abundance. I am supported to follow my passions.

Journal Notes:

Day/Year	
Day/Year	
Day/Year	
Day/Year	
Day/Year	

Spiritual Awakening

A spiritual awakening refers to a shift in consciousness, an apperception of reality which had been previously unrealized. The culmination of such realizations is in the recognition that all of existence is of the same source, energy.

Over time, many great teachers have come to embody this wisdom, two of note include Jesus Christ and Siddhartha Gautama (the Buddha)—though there have been many more.

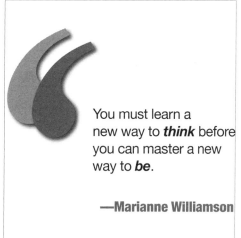

You must learn a new way to **think** before you can master a new way to **be**.

—**Marianne Williamson**

The core message has been the same, that absolute truth is beyond all the concepts and beliefs and the understanding of man, who is limited by time and space. The illusion is that apparent differences are in reality a fundamental oneness, and that your true nature is whole, unbounded and everlasting.

All form arises from pure potentiality; the sages referred to this as emptiness, the Tao, Brahman, Allah, God—while science may refer to it as the implicate order, quantum physics or the zero point field.

By any name, the words point to an intangible energetic essence that transitions from possibility and timelessness to actualization, where experience occurs through the rich diversity of form based on your observation.

To say that you've had a spiritual awakening is a bit of an oxymoron; the 'you' is exactly what vanishes. To be on a path to spiritual awakening is more accurate.

Challenge:
Each day be a little more thoughtful, more considerate to those you come into contact with. Continue to take self-inventory, correct any mistakes, admit when you are wrong.

Tapping in Meditation:
My purpose today is to lose interest in selfish things and gain interest in others. I keep material things in their proper place. Self-seeking slips away. My overall outlook upon life has changed. Honest, pure, unselfish, loving. When I think of other people and their troubles I forget my own. Unselfish service to others.

Journal Notes:

Day/Year	
Day/Year	
Day/Year	
Day/Year	
Day/Year	

June 17

The Serenity Prayer

God grant me the

Serenity to accept the things I cannot change

Courage to change the things I can and

Wisdom to know the difference.

The Serenity Prayer is the common name for an originally untitled prayer composed by the American theologian Reinhold Niebuhr (1892–1971). It has been adopted by Alcoholics Anonymous and other twelve-step addiction recovery programs.

The best-known form is: "God, grant me the serenity to accept the things I cannot change, the courage to change the things I can, and wisdom to know the difference.

The continuation;

Living one day at a time, enjoying one moment at a time, accepting hardships as the pathway to peace, taking, as He did, this sinful world as it is, not as I would have it, trusting that He will make all things right if I surrender to His will, that I may be reasonably happy in this life and supremely happy with Him.

(If you prefer a non-religious application, substitute Good Orderly Design for God.)

The following prayer follows;

Trust in God with all your heart and lean not on your own understanding;
in all your ways acknowledge him, and he will direct your paths.

From a scientific perspective, you do not have the perceptual capacity to understand the true reality. You are limited by your senses and time and space dimensions. Even as science makes headway into quantum physics, nano technology, even the discovery of the Higgs Boson, (the fundamental property of all of matter), you still must rely on believing what you cannot see, having faith that the principles of this program will manifest into reality in your life.

Challenge:
Be fully engaged in this program. Be a student of this information and allow it to bring results in your life and enable you to help others as well.

Tapping in Meditation:
My purpose today is to believe and allow. And I do.

Journal Notes:

Day/Year	
Day/Year	
Day/Year	
Day/Year	
Day/Year	

June 18

Personality Characteristics—Shortcomings to Peace and Serenity

You will experience all of these characteristics listed as shortcomings and defects. Likewise you will experience all of the characteristics listed as peace and serenity. It's a matter of duration. Which ones do you experience most frequently? You can change that. What you focus on materializes. All of your quiet meditations will lead you to peace and serenity. Abundance lives in peace and serenity. Here's the list;

Characteristics (shortcomings-defects)	Characteristics of Peace and Serenity
Selfishness	Interest in others/altruism
Being self-centered	Being love-others centered
Dishonesty	Honesty
Fears	Faith and trust
Being inconsiderate	Being considerate
Pride	Humility
Greed	Giving and sharing
Lustful thoughts	Respectful thoughts
Anger	Serenity
Envy	Being grateful
Procrastination	Taking right action
Gluttony	Moderation
Impatience	Patience
Intolerance	Tolerance
Resentment	Forgiveness
Hate	Love and concern for others
Harmful acts	Good deeds
Self-pity	Self-forgiveness
Self-justification	Humility and truth
Self-importance	Modesty
Self-condemnation	Self-forgiveness
Suspicion and jealousy	Trust
Doubt	Faith and trust in a universal higher power

Challenge:

Pick one or two of these and just for today focus on the characteristics of peace and serenity for those traits.

Tapping in Meditation:

My purpose today is to feel the energy of love, gratitude, appreciation and abundance and I do.

Journal Notes:

Day/Year	
Day/Year	
Day/Year	
Day/Year	
Day/Year	

June 19

A Spiritual Awakening Mindset—Grow Good Corn

There was a farmer who grew award-winning corn. Each year he entered his corn in the state fair where it won a blue ribbon. One year a newspaper reporter interviewed him and learned something interesting about how he grew it.

The reporter discovered that the farmer shared his seed corn with his neighbors. "How can you afford to share your best seed corn with your neighbors when they are entering corn in competition with yours each year?" the reporter asked.

"Why sir," said the farmer, "didn't you know? The wind picks up pollen from the ripening corn and swirls it from field to field. If my neighbors grow inferior corn, cross-pollination will steadily degrade the quality of my corn. If I am to grow good corn, I must help my neighbors grow good corn."

He is very much aware of the connectedness of life. His corn cannot improve unless his neighbor's corn also improves.

So it is in other dimensions. Those who choose to be at peace must help their neighbors to be at peace. Those who choose to live well must help others to live well, for the value of a life is measured by the lives it touches. And those who choose to be happy must help others to find happiness, for the welfare of each is bound up with the welfare of all.

The lesson for each of us is this: if we are to grow good corn, we must help our neighbors grow good corn.

Challenge:

One of the core principles of this program is to be of service to others. Just for today how can you make someone's life a bit easier? You get by giving.

Tapping in Meditation:

My purpose today is to live in peace. By being calm and aware, I know intuitively the right thing to do, moment to moment. The more I focus my mind upon the good, the more good comes to me. My inner guidance is there for me to call on anytime I need or want extra clarity, wisdom, knowledge, support, creative inspiration, love, or companionship. I tap in to the wisdom of the universe.

Journal Notes:

Day/Year	
Day/Year	
Day/Year	
Day/Year	
Day/Year	

What Does Sugar Do to the Brain?

You are in a program that supports healthy living with a precise food plan and a daily personal growth curriculum. Your food program is an avoidance of flour and sugar, three weighed and measured meals, nothing in between, daily meditation, daily reading and attendance on the live conference calls.

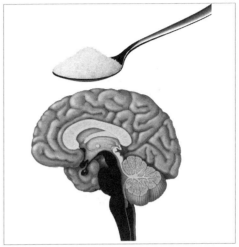

I read this article in a Dutch newspaper about sugar. Paul van der Velpen, the head of Amsterdam's health service, the Dutch capital city where the sale of cannabis is legalized, wants to see sugar tightly regulated.

"Just like alcohol and tobacco, sugar is actually a drug. There is an important role for government. The use of sugar should be discouraged. And users should be made aware of the dangers. This may seem exaggerated and far-fetched, but sugar is the most dangerous drug of the times and can still be easily acquired everywhere." Mr Van der Velpen cites research claiming that sugar, unlike fat or other foods, interferes with the body's appetite creating an insatiable desire to carry on eating, an effect he accuses the food industry of using to increase consumption of their products.

"Sugar upsets that mechanism. Whoever uses sugar wants more and more, even when they are no longer hungry. Give someone eggs and he'll stop eating at any given time. Give him cookies and he eats on even though his stomach is painful," he argued.

"Sugar is actually a form of addiction. It's just as hard to get rid of the urge for sweet foods as of smoking. Thereby diets only work temporarily. Addiction therapy is better."

The senior health official wants to see sugar taxes and legal limits set on the amount that can added to processed food. He also wants cigarette-style warnings on sweets and soft drinks telling consumers that "sugar is addictive and bad for the health." "Health insurers should have to finance addiction therapy for their obese clients." he said.

Challenge:
TOFI—thin on the outside, fat on the inside, the food plan of this program is for everyone! Stay on the food plan. Just for today, weigh and measure, avoid four and sugar.

Tapping in Meditation:
My purpose today is to be joyful. When the compulsive striving away from The Now ceases, the joy of being flows into everything you do.

Journal Notes:

Day/Year	
Day/Year	
Day/Year	
Day/Year	
Day/Year	

June 21

Got Oatmeal? Dig In!

There are many reasons that you have oatmeal in your food plan whether it's in the form of steel-cut, rolled, quick cooking or what I like instead—buckwheat grouts.

Oats were the first whole grain recognized by the FDA to help reduce cholesterol. The soluble fiber from the oatmeal as a part of a daily diet may reduce the risk of heart disease. Diets high in whole grains help increase insulin sensitivity, lowering the risk of type II diabetes. The soluble fiber in oatmeal absorbs water and forms a gel that helps delay gastric emptying and increases feelings of satiety. Both help control cravings.

Increased fiber intake can reduce constipation. Studies have shown that the high amount of soluble fiber in your food plan can help reduce systolic blood pressure, decreasing the risk of cardiovascular disease.

A food plan high in fiber may reduce the risk of colon rectal and breast cancers. Beta glucans in soluble fiber have been shown to help the immune system fight bacteria and viruses. According to a study by researchers at Tuft's University, test performance and memory in school children increased after eating breakfast containing oatmeal.

Challenge:
Use the tools of this program, just for today.

Tapping in Meditation:
My purpose today is to be open and receptive to blissful, knock-my-socks off miracles in every area of my life. Luminous and productive energy flows through me. I open my heart to receive the highest power available to me. I trust I am being led to where I need to be.

Journal Notes:

Day/Year	
Day/Year	
Day/Year	
Day/Year	
Day/Year	

June 22

Do Dogs Love Bones?

When I ask this in my live programs I get a resounding YES. Then I reveal, NO, they love meat, they settle for bones. Where in your life are you settling? Where are you living in resignation believing that you are doing the best that you can? No judgment, it's not good or bad, just observe.

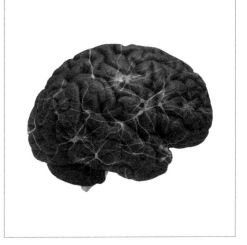

I have a statement that declares that you have far more capacity to create the circumstances and events in your life than you are aware of. However, you have had a life time of starts, stops, effort, results, failures and you have formed beliefs about what you are capable of doing, being and having.

Your brain had developed a series of brain schema, or neural networks associated with your expectations and previous results. These become what you believe to be true. It's a survival mechanism to store previous experiences and to be able to activate them non-consciously. The non-conscious mind is 400 times faster than the conscious. It's an adaptation that favors survival to be able to respond to a threat long before you are aware of what you are doing. The brain favors expected networks and holds these to be truths.

The way that this shows up in your life is that you believe that you're doing the best that you can be doing and you live your life in resignation. This is often times paired with avoidance and a justification of avoidance with rationalization and you never know that's what you're doing.

It's all just a made up narrative, a fictional interpretation of your past experiences. Your brain doesn't do well with in-completes, or not understanding so you fill in the blanks from the limits of your senses and make complete narratives about what you can or cannot do. None if it is true.

Challenge:

Where are you living your life believing that you are doing the best that you can? Just for today, challenge that belief and act as if you can "raise the bar."

Tapping in Meditation:

My purpose today is to challenge my beliefs about what I am capable of doing. My life is perfect as it is. I live it with my heart wide open. I am the person I was meant to become. The world is a better place because of what I create. Everything I do is an opportunity to be completely present. The smallest action can make a difference. My life is important. I can change the world just by being here, right now.

Journal Notes:

Day/Year	
Day/Year	
Day/Year	
Day/Year	
Day/Year	

June 23

The Millionaire Mind

Dr. Thomas J. Stanley, author of "The Millionaire Mind", wrote a book in 1996 that shattered America's most firmly held beliefs. According to Dr. Stanley, wealthy individuals do not all belong to an elite group of highly educated and exceedingly lucky people who often inherit their money and spend it on lavish purchases and pampered lifestyles. Instead he showed that a significant number of America's wealthy are far more likely to work hard, save diligently and live well below their means.

Dr. Stanley identified actions and thought processes used by millionaires to eliminate and reduce fears and worries.

The top 12 are:

1. Hard work.
2. Believing in yourself.
3. Preparation.
4. Focusing on key issues.
5. Being decisive.
6. Planning.
7. Being well organized to deal with big issues.
8. Taking immediate action to solve problems.
9. Countering negative thoughts with positive ones.
10. Out-working, out-thinking, out-toughing the competition.
11. Visualizing success.
12. Never allowing fears to control your mind.

Challenge:

All of the above thought processes are attitudes. They are mindsets. Pick one to focus on today. Journal what you notice.

Tapping in Meditation:

My purpose today is to use my intuition and intelligence to guide me at all times and I do.

Journal Notes:

Day/Year	
Day/Year	
Day/Year	
Day/Year	
Day/Year	

June 24

Newton's Laws of Motion

The first law says that objects move uniformly unless acted on by an outside force. (Law of Inertia).

The second law says that Force produces changes in motion, (Acceleration), in an object (Mass). A larger force produces a larger acceleration.

The third law says that forces come in pairs. For every action there is an equal and opposite reaction. Exert a force on object A and then object B exerts a force of equal strength back on A.

The laws of nature apply to you. You are either growing or decaying. There is no middle ground. Also, what you seek is also seeking you, so seek harder.

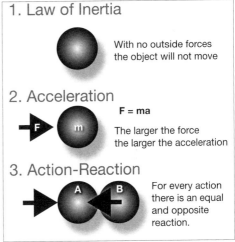

1. Law of Inertia

With no outside forces the object will not move

2. Acceleration

$F = ma$

The larger the force the larger the acceleration

3. Action-Reaction

For every action there is an equal and opposite reaction.

If you keep putting out good and ethical efforts it is a mathematical certainty that good results will come back to you. Forces act in pairs. You cannot put good energy into the universe without results coming back to you.

The good news about this is that you can control your efforts. When I was a college football coach we had a team belief, no opponent will ever out work or out prepare us. They may beat us but they won't out work or out prepare.

Challenge:
What you can control, you must control. You can control your efforts, your preparation. All you need to do is to find out what you want and what the most productive use of your time is to get what you want and then execute. Just for today, execute.

Tapping in Meditation:
My purpose today is to attract to myself in equal proportion to what I put out to the universe in thought and action, and I do.

Journal Notes:

Day/Year	
Day/Year	
Day/Year	
Day/Year	
Day/Year	

June 25

3 Rs—Resistance, Resentment, Revenge

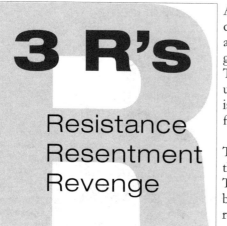

A financial advisor in Texas owns a very successful company. He has a marketing department that advertises to generate leads and then makes calls to generate the appointments for the advisors in the firm. This is a very successful model and frees the advisors up to study product and develop client relationships. It is agreed and contracted that the clients belong to the firm, not the advisor.

Two of the advisors decide to leave and they recruit their clients to come along with them to another firm. They are in clear violation of their contract and ethics but they do it anyway. The owner is very upset. He has resistance, resentment and seeks revenge.

He is doing what I call double duty. Not only did his advisors breach their agreement by leaving the company and taking the companies clients, but he is also upset about it.

The key is to change the "story" you are making up about what happened. It doesn't mean that you don't pursue these two unethical advisors. It just means that you don't let it upset you. It's just too easy to "go victim" and blame and have the reference of "look what they did to me." That is not the orientation of this program. This program and my teachings says that whatever happens to you is neutral, it's simply what happened. You give it meaning. You therefore can maintain control and like quantum physics proves, multiple meanings about what happen are all super imposed in reality and only the one you choose becomes your reality. So why in the world would you choose a story that makes you upset?

Challenge:
See the world through neutral eyes. The meaning of ALL things is only the meaning that YOU give to it.

Tapping in Meditation:
My purpose today is to make peaceful choices and decisions. My choices lead to serenity. Happiness is everywhere I choose to see it, in the wag of a dogs' tail, the laughter of a child, in the bloom of a flower. I am prosperous and happy.

Journal Notes:

Day/Year	
Day/Year	
Day/Year	
Day/Year	
Day/Year	

June 26

The Sound of Music and Plants—Dorothy Retallack

1973, a woman named Dorothy Retallack published a small book called *The Sound of Music and Plants*. Her book detailed experiments that she had been conducting at the Colorado Woman's College in Denver. Mrs. Retallack used two chambers (and fresh plants). She placed radios in each chamber. In one chamber, the radio was tuned to a local rock station, and in the other the radio played a station that featured soothing "middle-of-the-road" music. Only three hours of music was played in each chamber. On the fifth day, she began noticing drastic changes. In the chamber with the soothing music, the plants were growing healthily and their stems were starting to bend towards the radio! In the rock chamber, half the plants had small leaves and had grown gangly, while the others were stunted. After two weeks, the plants in the soothing-music chamber were uniform in size, lush and green, and were leaning between 15 and 20 degrees toward the radio. The plants in the rock chamber had grown extremely tall and were drooping, the blooms had faded and the stems were bending away from the radio. On the sixteenth day, all but a few plants in the rock chamber were in the last stages of dying. In the other chamber, the plants were alive, beautiful, and growing abundantly.

Stunted Plant Growth

Rock Music   Classical Music

She went on to experiment with other types of music. The plants showed no reaction at all to country and western music, similarly to those in silent chambers. However, the plants "liked" the jazz that she played. The most pronounced response was to baroque music. Baroque is a time period, 16th to 18th century. During that time the music had a particular mathematical construction, largo tempo, 60 beats per minute, that had an impact on human brain wave patterns. Listening to baroque music enhances focus, reduces heart rate and improves performance for humans. Since all matter is energy the energy of baroque music has a positive interaction with everything it touches.

Challenge:
Add baroque music to your life. Play a baroque music CD in your office, nonstop.

Tapping in Meditation:
My purpose today is to control what I can control. I can control the environment in my office. I can control my attitude, my mindset and my choices, and I do. My thoughts of happiness bring happiness into my life and the lives of others.

Journal Notes:

Day/Year	
Day/Year	
Day/Year	
Day/Year	
Day/Year	

June 27

Baroque Music, Mice and Personal Reinforcement

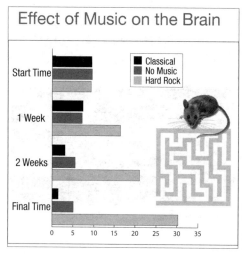

Effect of Music on the Brain

Legend:
- Classical
- No Music
- Hard Rock

Categories (top to bottom): Start Time, 1 Week, 2 Weeks, Final Time
Axis: 0 5 10 15 20 25 30 35

Other scientists have discovered that mice that listen to discordant music regularly have damage in the hippo campus region of the brain. That region is usually associated with alertness, memory and learning. Evidence was found of abnormal "branching and sprouting" of the neurons, as well as disruption in the normal amounts of messenger RNA, a chemical crucial to the storage of memories. The amount of time required for a mouse to remember how to run a maze was significantly longer when exposed to rock music over time. "What we are seeing here is the effects of disharmonious music on mammalian brains. And, insofar as human beings have mammalian brains we cannot preclude the possibility that disharmony may affect human brains as well." – Harvey H. Bird, physicist, Fairleigh Dickinson University.

While I was at Cal Tech I had researched what the Russians and Bulgarians were doing with baroque music and athletic performance. Before the breakup of the Soviet Union they had won more gold medals in the Olympics than any other country.

I applied this technique at Cal Tech and my wrestling team placed 2nd in the conference. That had never happened before. When I left for Cal State Fullerton I also brought this technique and applied it with input from assistant coaches and my roommates Steve Mariucci and Rich Ellerson and we won two conference championships. Now you can apply this technique as well. Here's how.

Challenge:

Get a source of baroque music. Create a script of affirmations. Record the affirmations over the baroque music. Speak 3 times in the first person, "I respond to rejection with enthusiasm and positive energy", and 3 times in the 3rd person, You respond to rejection with enthusiasm and positive energy." Pause for 5 seconds and then record your next affirmation. Make a CD. Keep it in your car. Listen to it for 5 minutes every day and you will be rewiring your brain and forming new habits.

Tapping in Meditation:

My purpose today is to unite with the energy in my environment. I am the center of power. Joy floods my thoughts and my life. I deserve good in my life. I am the creator of my abundance. Action is the energy that translates my thoughts into reality. I radiate love and respect for myself and others.

Journal Notes:

Day/Year	
Day/Year	
Day/Year	
Day/Year	
Day/Year	

June 28

Cleve Backster—Thoughts and Plants

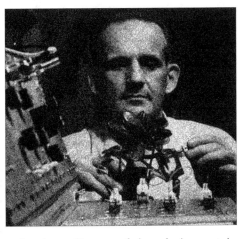

Grover Cleveland "Cleve" Backster, Jr. (February 27, 1924 – June 24, 2013) was an interrogation specialist for the Central Intelligence Agency (CIA), best known for his experiments with plants using a polygraph instrument in the 1960s which led to his theory of "primary perception" where he claimed that plants "feel pain" and have extrasensory perception (ESP), which was widely reported in the media but was rejected by the scientific community.

Backster's study of plants began in the 1960s, and he reported observing that a polygraph instrument attached to a plant leaf registered a change in electrical resistance when the plant was harmed or even threatened with harm. His work was inspired by the research of physicist Jagadish Chandra Bose, who claimed to have discovered that playing certain kinds of music in the area where plants grew caused them to grow faster.

In February 1966, Backster attached polygraph electrodes to a Dracaena cane plant, to measure at first the time taken for water to reach the leaves. The electrodes are used to measure galvanic skin response and the plant showed readings which resembled that of a human. This made Backster try different scenarios, and the readings went off the chart when he burnt the leaf, because according to him, the plant registered a stress response to his thoughts of harming it. He conducted another similar experiment where he observed a plant's response to the death of a brine shrimp in another room; his results convinced him that plants demonstrated telepathic awareness. He argued that plants perceived human intentions, and as he began to investigate further, he also reported finding that other human thoughts and emotions caused reactions in plants, which could be recorded by a polygraph instrument. He termed the plants' sensitivity to thoughts "Primary Perception", and published his findings from the experiments in the International Journal of Parapsychology in 1968. Soviet scientists invited Backster to the first Psychotronic Association conference in Prague in 1973 and his paper was entitled Evidence of *Primary Perception at a Cellular Level in Plant and Animal Life*. After 1973, he further experimented on yogurt bacteria, eggs and human sperm and he claimed his results showed "primary perception" could be measured in all living things. His findings remain controversial still today however.

Challenge:
Your thoughts are very powerful. Your thoughts are the tool for you to engage with the universal power and energy that is everywhere and more powerful then you. Tap in!

Tapping in Meditation:
My purpose today is to be the creator of my own success. Good morning life! I am so grateful to be alive today. I am confident in all that I do.

Journal Notes:

Day/Year	
Day/Year	
Day/Year	
Day/Year	

June 29

What do You Fear?

Fear is a vital response to physical and emotional danger—if you didn't feel it, you couldn't protect yourself from legitimate threats. But often you fear situations that are far from life-or-death, and thus hang back for no good reason. Traumas or bad experiences can trigger a fear response within you that is hard to quell. Yet exposing yourself to your personal demons is the best way to move past them. Did you know that there's only one fear that has been scientifically proven to be an innate rather than a conditioned response? The fear of heights has been documented to appear in young children. Thus it's highly likely that all other fears are rooted in conditioned responses. This is good news because it means that when you're able to reign in your thinking, you can tame your fears.

Physically there are two pathways to generate fear. One is fast and non-conscious. The senses have a direct neurological connection to the limbic area of the brain. This means that you see something and immediately you get the fear response. The other pathway is slower and routes through the cortex. Meaning your thinking gets interpreted, then connects to the limbic area for the fear response.

The good news is that you can intercept the pathway with the very thing that created it, your thinking. When I go skydiving one of the fears that I have is sitting next to the door at the back of the aircraft. During the summer once the aircraft climbs to 1000 feet we open the door to cool the inside during climb to 12,500 feet. Twenty Two people fit in two rows of 11. Once the door is open and we remove our seatbelts the last person on each side sits on the floor so it is less crowded. That would put you right in front of an open door if you're sitting on the right row of benches. Early in my skydiving career (currently 2000 jumps and counting) I would purposely sit in that spot so I could confront my fear. What is the worse that could happen? I could fall out. Has that ever happened before? No, plus I'm wearing a parachute anyway. The common acronym is False Expectations Appearing Real. It's all about the story you are making up about the activity. Usually the expectation is a worse case and that fuels the fear.

Challenge:

The next time you are feeling fear ask yourself what's the narrative you are telling yourself? Change the story you are making up to one of safety and a positive outcome, then stay in the here and now. If you stay in the moment you cannot be afraid because fear is a constant back and forth between the past and future. There is no fear in the now.

Tapping in Meditation:

My purpose today is to be afraid and take the action anyway. Fear doesn't stop me. It just improves me. I embrace the fear and then erase the fear with action.

Journal Notes:

Day/Year	
Day/Year	
Day/Year	
Day/Year	
Day/Year	

June 30

10,000 Hours—Preparation Eases Fear

10,000 Hours of Practice. In the book Outliers , author Malcolm Gladwell says that it takes roughly ten thousand hours of practice to achieve mastery in a field. The 10,000-hours concept can be traced back to a 1993 paper written by Anders Ericsson, a Professor at the University of Colorado, called *The Role of Deliberate Practice in the Acquisition of Expert Performance.*

It highlighted the work of a group of psychologists in Berlin, who had studied the practice habits of violin students in childhood, adolescence and adulthood.

All had begun playing at roughly five years of age with similar practice times. However, at age eight, practice times began to diverge. By age 20, the elite performers had averaged more than 10,000 hours of practice each, while the less-able performers had only completed 4,000 hours of practice.

Michael Jordan wasn't even the best athlete in his family as a kid. It wasn't until he didn't make the varsity team his sophomore year in high school that he decided to turn it up and become one of the hardest working athletes of his generation. As a result, he's one of the best.

You don't like to hear about that however. You'd prefer to think of Air Jordan as a born gifted athlete rather than an ordinary hard working guy who created genius. It's much easier to think that the great ones are born gifted than to admit that you have far more capacity to create the circumstances and events in your life. "By failing to prepare, you are preparing to fail." Benjamin Franklin. "I will prepare and someday my chance will come." Abraham Lincoln.

Challenge:
Being prepared reduces anxiety and the experience of fear. Always control what you can control and that means your preparation. Always be well prepared in everything that you do.

Tapping in Meditation:
My purpose today is to prepare for everything that I do. All things are ready, if my mind be so. Organize, don't agonize.

Journal Notes:

Day/Year	
Day/Year	
Day/Year	
Day/Year	
Day/Year	

Davies
Day Book

365 concepts for excellence

July 1

Fear is Good and Bad

"Our deepest fear is not that we are inadequate. Our deepest fear is that we are powerful beyond measure. It is our light, not our darkness that most frightens us. We ask ourselves, 'Who am I to be brilliant, gorgeous, talented, and fabulous?' Actually, who are you not to be? You are a child of God. You're playing small does not serve the world. There is nothing enlightened about shrinking so that other people won't feel insecure around you. We are all meant to shine, as children do. We were born to make manifest the glory of God that is within us. It's not just in some of us; it's in everyone. And as we let our own light shine, we unconsciously give other people permission to do the same. As we are liberated from our own fear, our presence automatically liberates others."—Marianne Williamson

"There are two basic motivating forces: fear and love. When we are afraid, we pull back from life. When we are in love, we open to all that life has to offer with passion, excitement, and acceptance. We need to learn to love ourselves first, in all our glory and our imperfections. If we cannot love ourselves, we cannot fully open to our ability to love others or our potential to create. Evolution and all hopes for a better world rest in the fearlessness and open-hearted vision of people who embrace life."—John Lennon

Fire under control can heat your house and cook your food. Fire to the extreme and out of control can kill you.

Fear is both good and bad. I have a fear of pain and lack of mobility in my old age. This drives me to exercise and follow our food plan. Fear is a good motivator in this case.

You may have a fear of not having enough income to retire. That's a good fear if it drives you to make decisions about your efforts and dollar decisions today.

You can't be rational with fear. There is a 40,000 to 1 ratio in the odds of dying in a car crash versus on a roller coaster yet we don't fear the drive to the park but freak out on the ride. You have a 4,000 to 1 ratio of being killed by a lightning strike then by a shark but which one do you fear most?

Challenge:
Fear is not reasonable and rational. Simply change your conversation about what you fear and turn it into a positive expectation and then take the action anyway.

Tapping in Meditation:
My purpose today is to embrace that courage is not the absence of fear but being afraid and doing it anyway and I do.

Journal Notes:

Day/Year	
Day/Year	
Day/Year	

July 2

The Wolf You Feed

One evening an old Cherokee told his grandson about a debate that goes on inside people. He said, "My son, the battle is between 2 "wolves" inside us all.

One is Evil. It is anger, envy, jealousy, sorrow, regret, greed, arrogance, self-pity, guilt, resentment, inferiority, lies, false pride, superiority, and ego.

The other is Good. It is joy, peace, love, hope, serenity, humility, kindness, empathy, generosity, truth, compassion and faith.

The grandson thought for a minute and then asked his grandfather; "Which wolf wins?"

The old Cherokee simply replied, "The one you feed."

Challenge:

You have the power to select the thoughts that you will allow to occupy time in your brain. Just pull the trigger. Stop any negative and limiting thoughts and allow only positive and passionate thoughts. You control this.

Tapping in Meditation:

My purpose today is to do what I fear most. I can do anything. When I connect to the silence within, I can make sense of the disturbance going on around me. I choose my own path with my thoughts. I attract love, gratitude and abundance.

Journal Notes:

Day/Year	
Day/Year	
Day/Year	
Day/Year	
Day/Year	

July 3

Who or What are You Tolerating?

Tolerations are those sources of irritation and distraction that you just "put up with," often without realizing the extent to which they are depleting your energy and undermining your pursuit of your highest goals. When you identify and eliminate these tolerations, you free up surprising amounts of time and energy, resources you can tap to help become more deeply engaged in the pursuits that matter most to you.

So one by one, start saying goodbye to the things that bug you. Where do you have clutter—overcrowded closets and kitchen cupboards? Where do you need to set some boundaries on the kinds of conversations, kinds of friends you willing to have and even let go of some relationships that have ceased to feel rewarding? It may seem strange to encourage you to be less tolerant. To allow these tolerances to exist is to settle for something less than a full life. Tolerations make you block out a lot of life's happiness, just because you're trying not to be affected by what annoys you.

Our everyday surroundings are fertile ground for tolerations. Just take a quick mental survey of your home and office right now. What bugs you? A burned-out light bulb, a dried-up pen, an overly chatty coworker? Some of these things may seem small or trifling, but size doesn't matter. They can all grate on your nerves and deplete your energy. Even the time constraints we experience every day are things many of us routinely tolerate. I have a coaching client who complains that he doesn't have any time for himself on the weekends. My statement to him is that this is self-imposed. What or who is he tolerating? What or to whom does he need to say no to?

Recurring annoyances — from a drawer that won't close properly to a phone that rings constantly or a set of keys that disappears on a regular basis — can lead to perpetual irritation and depleted mood. Taken together, small irritations like these can also lead to chronic, low-level stress in the body. When the body experiences stress, the adrenal glands release the hormone cortisol, which in moderate levels helps our body function. But if cortisol levels stay too high for too long, it can lead to weight gain, a dampened immune-system function and even memory loss.

Challenge:

Take a few moments to identify what or who are you tolerating. Then, handling one toleration at a time, consider the following questions: Can you act on it? Can you eliminate it? Can you improve it? Identify, make decisions and execute.

Tapping in Meditation:

My purpose today is to simplify. When I de-clutter my life I allow space for love, abundance, appreciation and clarity.

Journal Notes:

Day/Year	
Day/Year	
Day/Year	
Day/Year	
Day/Year	

July 4

Independence Day—Freedom

In 1775, people in New England began fighting the British for their independence. On July 2, 1776, the Congress secretly voted for independence from Great Britain. The Declaration of Independence was first published two days later on July 4, 1776. The first public reading of the Declaration of Independence was on July 8, 1776. Delegates began to sign the Declaration of Independence on August 2, 1776. In 1870, Independence Day was made an unpaid holiday for federal employees. In 1941, it became a paid holiday for them.

The first description of how Independence Day would be celebrated was in a letter from John Adams to his wife Abigail on July 3, 1776. He described "pomp and parade, with shows, games, sports, guns, bells, bonfires, and illuminations" throughout the United States. However, the term "Independence Day" was not used until 1791.

We claimed our independence from Britain and Democracy was born. Every day thousands leave their homeland to come to the "land of the free and the home of the brave" so they can begin their American Dream.

Are you really free? Freedom is defined as the quality or state of being free, as the absence of necessity, coercion, or constraint in choice or action. Were you free before this program or were you a slave to your bad habits and addictions? Are you free now?

Challenge:
What habits do you need to change to improve your results? Pick one and just for today be that change.

Tapping in Meditation:
My purpose today is to exercise my freedom. No matter what my situation I have a choice. At any given moment I have the power to say that this is not how the story will end. I am responsible for everything that happens to me.

Journal Notes:

Day/Year	
Day/Year	
Day/Year	
Day/Year	
Day/Year	

July 5

Gunny Sacking

John comes home exhausted from an exciting yet tough day in the office. His wife Martha asks if he would go to the store and get some milk. John doesn't know what kind of a day his wife had but he doesn't even think about it and just says that he's too tired. John then sits in his favorite chair and turns on the television.

Martha feels completely ignored and that John is being very selfish. He didn't even ask her about her day. She doesn't say anything however but takes this bit of disappointment and puts it in a sack that she carries over her shoulder.

John takes his plates into the kitchen and just leaves them on the counter without emptying them, rinsing them or putting them into the dishwasher. Martha sees this and thinks that it's kind of rude for John to expect her to clean up after him and the kids. She doesn't say anything and just takes that insult and puts it into her sack.

Martha's favorite program is about to start but John is watching a game. He is very polite about it but he asks if it's OK just to record her show. Although Martha doesn't appreciate that John is not interacting with her and she'd rather record the game and watch the show with John, she just says OK, fine and ads another chip into the sack. This goes on and on for weeks until one day John comes home in a great mood and says, "Honey I'm home, what's for dinner" to which Martha smacks him right across the face with her filled sack and screams "Get your own dinner, I'm tired of waiting on you!"

Gunnysacking is when someone silently collects irritations and slights until "the last straw is placed on them" causing an overblown reaction. Gunnysacking has been described as 'an alienating fight tactic in which a person saves up, or gunnysacks, grievances until the sack gets too heavy and bursts, and old hostilities pour out' (A gunny sack is a cloth container used for carrying or storing things).

Challenge:
There is an easy solution to this. First, notice that you are gunnysacking. Awareness is the key. Once you notice then make a decision about addressing the issue even if it's a small issue. Don't let minor irritations build up.

Tapping in Meditation:
My purpose today is to tell the truth faster. Much unhappiness has come into the world because of bewilderment and things left unsaid. Many times in life I've regretted the things I've said without thinking. But I've never regretted the things I said nearly as much as the words I left unspoken. I communicate clearly and truthfully.

Journal Notes:

Day/Year	
Day/Year	
Day/Year	

July 6

Relationship Cycles

Do you remember the first time you fell in love? The hormone oxytocin is a bonding opiate that is released so there is definitely chemistry when you are in love. This is the intoxication stage. In this stage your partner can do no wrong, you hang on every word, you just can't get enough of that person. Remember that?

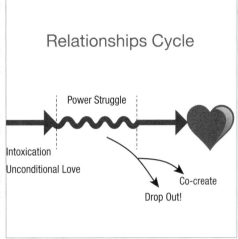

Relationships Cycle

There are 3 stages in all relationships both business and personal. The first stage is this intoxication stage with unconditional love. However, there is a duration where this stage will merge into the 2nd stage which is struggle. This can take weeks, months or more but it most certainly will happen. This stage is where unmet needs rise to the top, where boundaries are challenged.

There is also a duration to this stage as it leads to one of two outcomes with a 50% chance of either occurring. The next stage is either a divorce, or ending of the relationship or a co-create where you live happily on forever.

We have a football coaching mindset that says never get to high or too low on an athlete. That also is a relationship and all relationships will go through all 3 stages. Where are you with your relationships? Are you stable and into the co-create phase? Those are your true friends and you have a history together. You've been through the struggle and have made it to co-create. How about your children, co-workers?

Challenge:
Just know that it is normal for all relationships to have a rocky road. You will make it through with the one's you cherish.

Tapping in Meditation:
My purpose today is to cherish my human relationships with family and friends and I do.

Journal Notes:

Day/Year	
Day/Year	
Day/Year	
Day/Year	
Day/Year	

July 7

Struggle Negates—The Inverted U

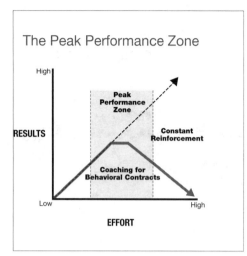

The Peak Performance Zone

Peak Performance Zone

Constant Reinforcement

Coaching for Behavioral Contracts

RESULTS

High

Low

EFFORT

Low   High

What do you think the relationship is between the amount of effort you put into something and the amount of results you produce? Most people think that it's a linear graph, the more effort you put into something the more results you will receive, graphing out at a 45° angle.

The reason you might feel like that is because it does start out with that relationship. Put in more effort and your results do increase. Up to a point that is. There is a tipping point where additional effort decreases performance, hence the graphs shape looks like an upside V or an inverted U.

Challenge:

The reason this matters to you is to adjust your mindset. Just working harder is not the answer. There is a peak performance zone which is a range of effort that results in the best results. If you are below this zone then you need to pick it up. If you are past this zone then you need to back off a bit. Take a look at what you are involved in and see if you need to make any adjustments in your commitments of time and effort.

Tapping in Meditation:

My purpose today is to make continuous effort in just the right amount for peak performance in all that I do. I trust my intuition and the greater power of the energy in the universe to guide me. Continuous effort, not strength, struggle or intelligence, is the key to unlocking my potential.

Journal Notes:

Day/Year	
Day/Year	
Day/Year	
Day/Year	
Day/Year	

Struggle Negates—Negotiate

In my live programs I bring a volunteer up on stage and I ask him to tell the audience what his goals are for the year. Let's say its business and he tells me that one of his metrics for success is how much net profit after taxes he will have. That meets my first criteria for strategic planning, "what do you want?" Next I ask him what he needs to do to make that happen. He gives me several activities but for this demonstration I'll focus on just one, prospecting. I next ask him to give me three obstacles to prospecting. He picks, rejection, too busy with other priorities and fatigue.

I bring 3 of the biggest guys in the audience up on stage and each one represents an obstacle. Rejection stands to the left of my volunteer, facing him and hooks his right arm. Too busy stands to the right and hooks my volunteers left arm. To fatigued stands behind my volunteer and puts his arm around his neck and chest. My three obstacles have firm grips on my volunteer goal setter. Next the competition begins. When I count to 3 I want you to break through your obstacles and reach your goals. Guys, don't let him free.

The audience loves this demonstration. The goal setter tries very hard, struggles, gives great effort yet is no match for his obstacles. I turn to the audience and ask them to cheer him on, give him energy then I ask these questions; "Did he try? Did he try hard? Did you cheer him on? Did it matter?" The answers yes he tried, yes the audience encouraged him and no, it didn't matter, he didn't break free and reach his goals.

Next I ask, "Do you think money is a motivator?" The audience says Yes! I then borrow a $100 bill. Now I turn to the volunteer again and say "If you can break free when I say go I'll give you this $100. At first he prepares himself for the struggle and he's ready for maximum effort. If I let him go and attempt this with his mindset of extreme effort he will fail. What do you think he will believe if he tries as hard as he can and fails? He'll believe that he just can't do it. So I interrupt and tell him there is only one strategy that will work and it's not the struggle. Most of the time the mindset shift occurs and he NEGOTIATES with his obstacles. I'll give you each $25 if you let me go. Now they've formed a partnership and he easily and effortlessly walks through and reaches his goals. I always ask the audience, "Who gave me this $100 bill?" and for some reason everyone raises their hands!

Challenge:
Look at your goals and activities and see where you need to negotiate, just for today.

Tapping in Meditation:
My purpose today is to be appreciative of what I have. Everyone has some type of a struggle so I am grateful for the life and pleasures that I have.

Journal Notes:

Day/Year	
Day/Year	
Day/Year	
Day/Year	
Day/Year	

July 9

Helplessness and Optimism

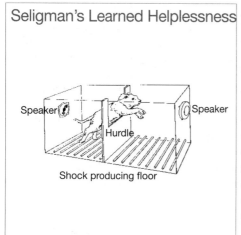

Seligman's Learned Helplessness

Speaker
Hurdle
Speaker
Shock producing floor

All the great teachers from Aurelius and the Buddha to the modern gurus and scientists tell us the same thing. If you can control your internal dialogue, your thoughts, and tame your fears, doubts and insecurities, then nothing else matters, period! Before Martin Seligman started studying optimism he spent decades studying the opposite, helplessness. In one study with two dogs both are given shocks at random intervals. One can press a lever to stop the shocks. The other can't. The first dog quickly discovers how to stop the shocks and is fine. The other dog, the one who can't do anything about the shocks, eventually gives up and curls into a helpless ball in the corner as the shocks continue.

Part 2: Those same dogs are put into a new environment. This time BOTH dogs can easily avoid the shocks. The healthy dog quickly discovers the trick, jump over the hurdle, and is fine. The other dog, even though it has the power to change things, just gives up, curling into a ball as the shocks continue. That dog has learned helplessness.

So do you. After being shocked so many times in your own life where do you have "learned helplessness" and have just given up, living your life in resignation believing that you are doing the best that you can do?

Challenge:

Where are you holding back believing that you just can't do something? Just for today refuse to believe that and take one small action.

Tapping in Meditation:

My purpose today is to tap into my capacity to create the circumstances and events in my life and I do. I have great potential and I realize it one day at a time by having optimistic thoughts.

Journal Notes:

Day/Year	
Day/Year	
Day/Year	
Day/Year	
Day/Year	

WTF

This does not mean Where is the Food? It also doesn't mean Why the Face? It means WHERE'S THE FOCUS? When the rat has learned helplessness because of its previous experience with the tremendous shock in the attempt to reach its goal, the food, what does it focus on in further trials? Does it focus on the opportunity or the obstacle? The answer is that it focuses on the obstacle, every time. That is a survival instinct.

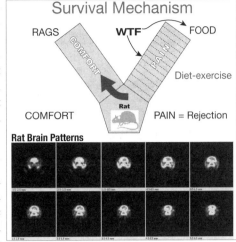

In one trial scientists placed a device on the skull of the rat that enabled them to see exactly how the brain was firing. They saw exactly how the brain fired when the rat was in pain and avoiding as it stepped on the grid. The next trial after the scientists had removed the shock the rat's brain didn't need to experience the shock again. It had a stored memory and immediately avoided the metal grid. The scientists also saw that the rat's brain immediately generated the exact brain firing when the rat was previously exposed to the real shock.

Challenge:

Where have you experienced a shot of pain so that now you avoid? In fact, everything you are avoiding is because it's linked to pain. It doesn't matter whether the threat is real or not, your brain responds as if it was. So WTF? Are you focusing on opportunities to get things done or the reasons why you can't? Just for today, focus on the opportunities and take one action.

Tapping in Meditation:

My purpose today is to find simplicity out of clutter, to find harmony out of discord, to find opportunity out of difficulty and I do.

Journal Notes:

Day/Year	
Day/Year	
Day/Year	
Day/Year	
Day/Year	

July 11

Opportunity is Nowhere

Where are you convinced that you are doing the best that you can be doing? I have a phrase that states, "You have far more capacity to create the circumstances and events in your life than you are aware of." It will take some faith in the principles of nature and a mindset shift.

Thomas Edison said; "Opportunity is missed by most people because it is dressed in overalls and looks like work." Don't wait for extraordinary opportunities. Seize common occasions and make them great. Weak people wait for opportunities, strong people make them.

Abraham Lincoln said a quote that I love, "The best way to predict your future is to invent it!" How do you invent it? Through precise planning, hard work and execution.

Challenge:

The next time you catch yourself thinking that opportunity is nowhere, pause, take the word Nowhere and break it into Now Here. Then step into the possibility and make it happen.

Tapping in Meditation:

My purpose today is to see the opportunity in every difficulty and I do. I heed the opportunities of this day, July 11th. Opportunities are all around me, each and every day. I keep an open mind to opportunities that can benefit me and I take advantage of them while they're right there in front of me.

Journal Notes:

Day/Year	
Day/Year	
Day/Year	
Day/Year	
Day/Year	

July 12

Where Are You Being a Fraud—The Tell

Imagine you are in Las Vegas playing poker. You are dealt 4 aces. How about that! You are almost certain to win this hand. You want to keep the rest of the players in the game so you can win more money. However, someone notices that the last time you won the pot you constantly stroked your chin. That's what gamblers refer to as a subconscious tell. It's a behavior that in consistent with some series of thoughts, in this case, a good hand. Gamblers work hard on identifying and eliminating their "tell."

So, where are you being a fraud? Remember my statement for how you participate with this program, no judgment, it's not good or bad, it just is. The "tell" that you are being a fraud is when you say or think that you are committed to a result yet you are not consistently taking the actions that are necessary and that you are capable of taking.

Be careful, your non-conscious mind will not allow you to easily see this. Instead it will bombard you with perceptions of your obstacles, your priorities and your excuses and you will not know that you are avoiding. You will think that you're doing the best that you can. Don't buy it!

Challenge:
Do a bit of a year to date analysis of where you are versus where you thought you would be to date in your health, business and personal life. You're at the start of Q3 so this is good timing. Where are you lagging? Where might a careful analysis reveal that you're being a fraud? (No judgment). Make any adjustments to time and commitments for the rest of the year. Just for today declare your outcome and objective for this day. Execute!

Tapping in Meditation:
My purpose today is to help others. I have my hands to serve and my heart to give love. Power is the ability to do good things for others and I do.

Journal Notes:

Day/Year	
Day/Year	
Day/Year	
Day/Year	
Day/Year	

July 13

Write a Vision and Mission Statement

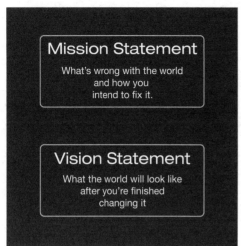

Mission Statement

What's wrong with the world and how you intend to fix it.

Vision Statement

What the world will look like after you're finished changing it

Your Vision is why you exist. Your mission is what you will do and how you will do it to live your vision. A vision statement is sometimes called a picture of your company in the future but it's so much more than that. Your vision statement is your inspiration, the framework for all your strategic planning. What you are doing when creating a vision statement is articulating your dreams and hopes for your business. It reminds you of what you are trying to build. The vision statement answers the question, "Where do I want to go?"

Don't confuse a vision statement with a road map; it's not. What Bill Gates envisioned when he first started Microsoft was a personal computer in every home and business, not a series of steps for making that happen. That's why it's important when crafting a vision statement to let your imagination go and dare to dream—and why it's important that a vision statement captures your passion.

Example: Vision Statement: I provide families the guidance they need to protect their lifestyle. Your mission statement in a nutshell, expresses what you do and why you do it. Use this format:

I am_____ Who does _____ So that _____

Who you are, what you do and the result that occurs. Example, I am a financial planner who guides families to protect and grow their wealth so that they have peace of mind in retirement and protected lifestyles.

Challenge:

Write your vision and mission statement. Post it where you can see it every day. Now live into it.

Tapping in Meditation:

My purpose today is to (insert the result you intend to create).

Journal Notes:

Day/Year	
Day/Year	
Day/Year	
Day/Year	
Day/Year	

July 14

The Interdependence and Intelligence of Living Things

Quantum physics states that there is no separate individual, you are a part of an overall energy that is everything. There is an interdependence of all things in the universe. Animals and plants share the biosphere with each other. Many organisms have very close associations with each other, some living in or on the bodies of others. All animals ultimately depend on the green plants, the producers, for their food. Food chains involve producers, consumers and decomposers. Without the producers, the consumers would not be able to obtain their food. Without the consumers, the decomposers would not be able to return the nutrients to the ecosystem. Without the decomposers, the producers would not have the needed nutrients to facilitate the process of growth. Everything is interconnected.

Mutualism is when two organisms both help one another in a form of interdependence. For example, the ants and the acacia tree form a symbiotic relationship of mutualism. The ants benefit by living in the acacia tree and the tree benefits when the ants consume the insects that eat the leaves of the trees. Your life depends on bacterial mutualism. Rather than an individual, separate body that is all "human," the research indicates that we are more like a multi-organism ecosystem.

There is an intelligence in the universe. There exists the intrinsic tendency for things to self-organize and co-evolve into ever more complex, intricately interwoven and mutually compatible forms. This intelligence gets very interesting. For example, fungi don't leave themselves to the whims of the wind when disseminating the spores they use to reproduce. They create their own breeze by releasing moisture with the spores. The water cools the air creating a tiny convection current, that's intelligence.

Air as an environment can lead to surprising interactions between living and nonliving things. When positively charged insects fly close to a spider web electrostatic charges cause the web to move toward them to actively capture the flyers. In a never ending quest to ensure that bugs distribute their pollen flowers display their brightest colors and scents to attract bees and other pollinators. Scientists recently discovered another shocking method flowers use to lure bees, electric fields, now that's intelligence.

Challenge:
Tap into the intelligence in the universe with your daily meditations.

Tapping in Meditation:
My purpose today is to allow the intelligence and energy of the universe to guide my thinking for service and prosperity. Everything in the universe has a purpose. The invisible intelligence and information that flows through everything in a purposeful fashion is also flowing through me. I attract abundance and love.

Journal Notes:

Day/Year	
Day/Year	
Day/Year	
Day/Year	
Day/Year	

July 15

The Girl Who Loved

Doctors told Rep. Jaime Herrera Beutler her baby would die. But a surprising treatment has made her the first to survive a rare syndrome. Beutler, a Republican congresswoman learned that her baby had Potter syndrome, a prenatal condition affecting 1 in 3,000 in which neither the kidneys nor lungs develop. The doctors said it's 100% fatal. Instead, her baby Abigail became the first person to survive with Potters.

A lot of women would have terminated the pregnancy but Jaime opposes abortion. But this wasn't a political decision, it was a personal one. As the doctor was explaining the circumstances she could feel the baby moving inside. She was not going to be the one to end this life. She decided to share her story.

She received a call from a man whose son had the disease and was now 7. Beutler called the man's doctor and found that there was a technique of the infusion of saline injected by a needle into the womb. In a normal pregnancy the growing kidneys help produce the amniotic fluid needed for overall development especially of the lungs. Since Potter babies have no kidneys their lungs don't develop normally and they can't breathe after birth.

Jaime fit the weekly treatment around her congressional schedule, rising at 4 am to drive to Baltimore and return to D.C. in time to vote on issues, sometimes staying on the house floor until 11 pm. She was there when she felt the first pains of labor. Four days later Abigail was born.

Abigail remained in intensive care before coming home at 5 months. Still without kidneys she is on dialysis and will need a transplant. Jaime is back to work, traveling across the country. There are days when she is exhausted. But she is doing what she had to do. Seeing Abigail "happy and growing," says Jaime, "we're so grateful. She continues to beat the odds."

What kind of mindset does it take for someone to push like this? Can you imagine what it must be like to be exhausted yet still take your baby for lifesaving treatment while maintaining your own busy schedule as well? This is an example of an "all in", whatever it takes commitment. There are so many lessons here. Think about this for a moment.

Challenge:
Where are you not playing "all in?" What can you take away from this story to make your day a better day?

Tapping in Meditation:
My purpose today is to give without remembering and take without forgetting. Sacrifice is one of the purest and most selfless ways to love and I practice it daily.

Journal Notes:

Day/Year	
Day/Year	
Day/Year	
Day/Year	
Day/Year	

Be Selfish—Put Yourself First

This may seem like a contradiction to sacrificing for someone else out of love but I assure you it is not. It's like the airplane announcement, in an emergency put your oxygen mask on first then help your favorite child. The reason behind this is that you can't be of service to others unless you are taking care of yourself. Be selfish, take care of yourself first is one of my coaching commandments. Many times women are particularly guilty of violating this. They put everyone ahead of their own needs. Usually it's the children first, then their spouse, everything else then their own needs. Is that you? How's that working? It should be you first, your spouse second and then the kids and everyone else. I'm sure that will cause some discussion however. Science proves that you will be happier if you take care of yourself first. Self-care is a divine responsibility. Here are 7 reasons why you can be of greater service to others by doing so:

- **Reason #1.** Happy people are kinder. They treat others as a reflection of how they feel themselves.

- **Reason #2.** Happy people are more productive. They have more energy and passion.

- **Reason #3.** Happy people are more helpful. They just feel better.

- **Reason #4.** Happy people are more creative. We can't create when our nervous system is put in overwhelm by the release of cortisol, a stress hormone.

- **Reason #5.** Happy people are more resilient. Because of self-care they feel better, have more energy, better self-esteem and better expectations. They see a world of possibilities not obstacles.

- **Reason #6.** Happy people are more interested in others, and friendlier. People rarely remember what you said, but they'll always remember how you made them feel. When you feel better about yourself you mirror that to others.

- **Reason #7.** Happy people make better friends, colleagues, and citizens and are just more pleasant to be around. It's a physiological response.

Challenge:
What do you need to do to be happy today? Is there any evidence that you put yourself first today in the name of self-care for service to others?

Tapping in Meditation:
My purpose today is to nurture others through self-care. Self-care is not selfish or self-indulgent. I cannot nurture others from a dry well. I need to take care of my own needs first then I can give from the surplus of my abundance.

Journal Notes:

Day/Year	
Day/Year	
Day/Year	
Day/Year	
Day/Year	

July 17

You are a Mirror to the World

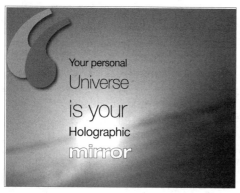

Your personal
Universe
is your
Holographic
mirror

Mary is finding that people all around her are notorious for not keeping their word. They commit to meeting for lunch but consistently cancel. She has business meetings that are set yet the client isn't even courteous enough to cancel, they simply don't show up.

It will be natural and easy for Mary to go victim and blame others for not honoring their world. However, Mary is insightful. She knows that what shows up in her life is a mirror of who she is and how SHE is showing up. Armed with this insight Mary first looks to see where she is not being her word. She looks to see where her broken promises are going uncorrected. She looks to see where she is not being courteous and respectful of others time. Mary understands the principles of attraction and manifestation so she correctly looks inward rather than outward. She knows that how she is being is what the world will create and reflect back to her. She understands the laws of quantum physics, that everything in the universe is a reflection of her own state of consciousness. It matters what she is within for everything without will be mirrored and reflected back accordingly.

The world is simply a mirror reflection her own inner state. If you are out of integrity then you will see a world where others are out of integrity. A joyful world is simply returning to you your own inward joy. What you see is a reflection of your own state of consciousness.

There are days when everything seems to go wrong, your car won't start, you forgot to set the alarm, your kids are disrespectful, etc. One thing leads to another and so on. Before you know it the world looks like a very ugly place. However, nothing in reality created this, you did. It is your own state of consciousness that created these realities.

Do you see how good this news is? It means that you can just as powerfully create a loving, appreciative and joyful reality as well. You have the power of choice. Positive thinking is a form of thought that habitually looks for the most positive outcome from all situations. A positive thinker doesn't refuse to acknowledge the negative; you just decide not to dwell on it.

Challenge:

When you focus on good you will find it. Control your internal state with your thinking. The key to eliminating negative circumstances in your life is to banish them in your thinking. Your reality mirror is your perception and expectations of the external world. Change your thinking and that will be reflected in your external world.

Tapping in Meditation:

My purpose today is to think, feel and act the way I desire to receive from others and I do. My positive thinking reflects back a positive and loving world.

Journal Notes:

Day/Year	
Day/Year	
Day/Year	

Which is Easier—50% or 100% Commitment?

Imagine you are committed to a minimum of 4 workouts for this week. You intend on doing 5 but are being held accountable to 4. It's Monday and the alarm rings at 3:50 am. The competition begins. As soon as that alarm rings your brain gets into a negotiation. Your internal dialogue starts analyzing how tired you are. This is supported by your physiology as you have serotonin which gives you a feeling of well-being, it is warm and you keep thinking that you should sleep in this morning. "I'll have 6 days to work out a total of 4 or 5, not a problem, equally important in a fitness program is rest, I need to sleep in." It's very tough to argue with these rationalizations. The truth is that you don't need to work out on Monday since you have 7 days to do 4/5 workouts. So let's say that your decision is to sleep in and also add that you intend to go to the gym in the afternoon, around 3:00 pm. OK, it's a deal back to sleep—zzzzzz.

Don't wait for the perfect moment, take the moment and make it perfect.

Fast forward to 3:00 pm. Your brain associates going to the gym with pain, it takes energy, it's hard, it's inconvenient, so you go through the same type of negotiation. You're tired, you don't need to work out today, you've got some administrative stuff you need to do. It is a lot harder to have a 50% commitment then it is to have a 100% commitment. Check this out. At 9:00 am you send your live coach or anyone else a text, "I'm going to the gym today at 3:00 pm or it's $100." You have just removed the negotiations. You've just removed the uncertainty. You've just removed the thinking. You've just tapped into your natural human instinct of avoiding the highest level of perceived pain.

Now you've leveraged your perception of pain and when 3:00 pm rolls around there won't be any thinking because you put a behavioral contract in place. You have a specific declaration (go to the gym at 3:00 pm) plus accountability (or I'll pay you $100). This leverages your reference point, what you pay attention to. Instead of paying attention to how tired you are or how much work you have to do, you instead instinctively recognize a higher pain, the penalty, and you pay attention to what your instincts drive you to do, avoid the highest level of perceived pain. It's easy and effortless and off to the gym you go.

Challenge:
Pick one activity that you need to do today to have this day have more meaning. Commit to doing that activity and use a behavioral contract. Don't wait for the perfect moment. Take this moment and make it perfect. Tomorrow journal what it meant to declare and to be held accountable.

Tapping in Meditation:
My purpose today is to be thankful. No matter how good or bad my life is, I wake up each morning and am thankful that I still have one. What I do speaks so loudly no one can hear what I say. I get things done.

Journal Notes:

Day/Year	
Day/Year	
Day/Year	

July 19

Tell the Truth Faster!

When is the most recent time you can remember not telling the truth? Did you dance around the bull's eye in terms of accurate, direct communication? For every reason there is to lie there is a better reason to tell the truth. Speak your mind even if your voice shakes.

The worst thing about being lied to is knowing you weren't worth the truth. If you're not being truthful is because you are focusing on you own comfort level and it is just easier to default to the lie.

How do you respond when someone asks "How are you?" Most people will say fine. I used to think that this was just sloppy communication and a waste of time. However, upon further research I discovered that there is a bonding that happens between people with this ritual so I'm not totally against it. However, straight talking is a skill that needs to be learned and used. It is so rare that when you use it you will stick out.

Do you remember the first season of the reality show "Survivor?" On the last day on the island a contestant, Susan, a straight talker, caught 16 million people by surprise. She told the final survivors what she thought of them. She didn't censor. It was shocking.

Here's the important question, why bother tell the truth? First, it's a gift to the other person and it saves time. It's easier to lie if you don't care but to go through your own comfort and really state what is on your mind takes a caring attitude and more energy. It's better communication and it really does save time.

This doesn't excuse you from having tack. If your spouse asks, "Does this outfit make me look fat?" It's not appropriate to say, no it's the donuts that make you look fat! What you say does matter and you do need to take responsibility for the impact that you may cause with your words. However, you can tactfully say what you think and still do your part to spare the others feelings as best that you can.

Challenge:
Practice telling the truth. Notice opportunities to tell the truth and notice the natural pull to tell a lie and rationalize. Just for today, tell the truth faster. Notice the response you get.

Tapping in Meditation:
My purpose today is to speak my truth. Time goes by so fast and I also take the opportunity to tell people how much they mean to me. I admit when I am wrong and I make amends.

Journal Notes:

Day/Year	
Day/Year	
Day/Year	
Day/Year	
Day/Year	

Avoid Sloppy Communication

Notice how you feel when you're having a conversation with someone and they use the phrase, "I'll be honest with you." You may not have any conscious awareness of this but on a non-conscious level you are losing rapport and respect for the person using this phrase. To carry this to the extreme it would look like this, "OK, hold on, I'm going to be honest with you for this one statement….OK, now I'll go back to lying!"

In my live coaching I fine people $1.00 every time that use that phrase. Clean it up. If you're committed to excellence then this means you do all things with excellence. That includes how you look, your energy, your deeds and your speech.

OK, here's another one, TRY. Stay away from this word. Don't try to do something, either do it or don't do it. There is no try. Try to pick up this pen. You can't do it. You either pick it up or you don't. There is no try-do or do not do.

One last lazy bit of communication is the phrase "You know what I mean?" or You know what I'm saying?" Or even the shortened version, "You know?" No, I don't know what you mean. Tell me. Notice how often you use this phrase. Cut it down considerably. It's called an irritator.

A study on effective negotiations compares negotiators considered skilled vs those considered average, and the study found several important differences. One is that skilled negotiators use an average of 2.3 "irritators" per hour of face-to-face negotiation time whereas the average negotiators used 10.8. Irritators were defined as any phrase with negligible value in persuasion and that just cause annoyance, such as "fair price," "generous offer," "reasonable arrangement," along with our 3 phrases here.

You hear these used so often that they've lost their value; when you hear someone try to persuade you with these phrases, don't you start to feel that that person is being disingenuous? This may be a non-conscious response but if you had your brain being monitored in a fMRI you would see electrical activity in the arousal, emotional area of the limbic region. It does matter.

Challenge:
How you speak, the words that you use, matter. Clean up useless phrases. Notice and eliminate the phrases or words, to be honest, try and you know what I mean.

Tapping in Meditation:
My purpose today is to learn and change. I am committed to excellence. Everything I do I do to the best of my ability and with ease.

Journal Notes:

Day/Year	
Day/Year	
Day/Year	
Day/Year	

July 21

Effective Communication—3 Magic Phrases

We are what we repeatedly do, therefore EXCELLENCE is not an act but is a habit.

—**Aristotle**

When you are managing or coaching another person as well as in other circumstances of just normal conversation you are likely to find that the other person is going to be a bit lazy and not fully accountable. This is not good or bad, it's just the easier less energy expensive mode of operating. This translates into other people dumping their problems on you and wanting you to solve them. So here is an alternative way to respond. Instead of going right to solving the other persons problems use the first magic phrase.

Magic Phrase #1: Tell Me More.

Visualize someone tossing you a hot potato. What do you do—you toss it back! This phrase forces the other person to become conscious of the experience, which requires more energy and effort, and to dig deeper into the issue. After they have had a chance to express themselves more fully, then use the second magic phrase.

Magic Phrase #2: What Are Your Options?

This also has the same effect of having the other person look at possible solutions rather than the lazy approach of having you offer them. Also, they will place more value on solutions that they come up with rather than what you tell them to do. Once you both have explored this then use the third magic phrase.

Magic Phrase #3: What Will You Do?

Now you've guided the person from analysis into action. For excellent results have a 7 day time frame and use a behavioral contract for accountability. Have the person state what action they will take by Sunday and have a consequence if they don't.

Challenge:

Use the 3 magic phrases with your family, your co-workers, your friends and notice the impact.

Tapping in Meditation:

My purpose today is to allow others to solve their own problems. Other people are as wonderful as the sunset if I let them be.

Journal Notes:

Day/Year	
Day/Year	
Day/Year	
Day/Year	
Day/Year	

July 22

Be Uncomfortable Every Day

Eleanor Roosevelt said, "Do one thing every day that scares you." That is also one of my coaching commandments, "Be uncomfortable every day!" At least Monday through Friday for business application although this concept may extend to the weekend if it serves you.

When you lift weights you are actually creating damage to the muscle tissue and the growth is the recovery of that tissue. Being uncomfortable and taking the action regardless is a way of doing damage to old and stagnant neurological patterns that keep you playing small. If you retreat every time you feel uncomfortable then you will not move your comfort zone and rewire your brain, called brain plasticity.

Do one thing everyday that scares you.

—Eleanor Roosevelt

You have far more capacity to create the circumstances and events in your life than you are aware of. One way to tap into this capacity is to notice being uncomfortable and take that action, on purpose, once every day.

Challenge:
Just for today plan one uncomfortable activity and execute it.

Tapping in Meditation:
My purpose today is to feel the discomfort, the fear, and do it anyway and I do.

Journal Notes:

Day/Year	
Day/Year	
Day/Year	
Day/Year	
Day/Year	

July 23

All the Way In or All the Way Out

COMMITMENT

You're either in or you're out. There's no such thing as life in between

There is a principle in physics that states you are either growing or decaying—there is no middle ground. That also applies here. When you think about making a commitment it's either all the way committed or not committed at all, at least that is the recommendation of this program of excellence.

So this means that you weigh and measure all your meals. You make a contract for every week and you execute your agreements or you honor the penalties. All the way in means that you take 5-10 minutes a day for quiet time and you read one page every day in this book.

Commitment means taking action even when you are no longer in the mood that you were in when you made the commitment. There is a difference between interest and commitment. When you are interested in doing something you do it only if it's convenient. When you are committed you do it regardless and you don't accept excuses.

Challenge:
Put your hand over your heart and feel your heartbeat and be grateful that you are alive so you can honor your word and do what you say you will do.

Tapping in Meditation:
My purpose today is to teach others about commitment, about excellence, about integrity and I do. I do this through my words and actions. How I feel about taking an action is not relevant. Do it now and do it anyway.

Journal Notes:

Day/Year	
Day/Year	
Day/Year	
Day/Year	
Day/Year	

All the Way In or All the Way Out—Holding Back

When I talk about the fear based internal conversations that my live audiences have, referred to as the "Alien", I give an opportunity to demonstrate the natural paralyzing effect that fear has. It's a true challenge. I say, "When I give you the cue, Ready-Set-Go, I want you to scream as loud as you possibly can like your life depends on your being as loud as you can, these 4 words, Fear Is A Lie!"

Simple enough. I point out that there is a non-conscious dynamic that will be operating here that is outside of their initial conscious control but they can override it if they want to. Then I ask, "How many of you are thinking, not going to do it?" Most of the audience raises their hands. Then I continue, "How many of you will scream loud enough that I don't bother you but you're not going to scream as loud as you can like your life depended on your doing so?" Again I get some hands.

OK, I ask if the group is ready to compete and I then give the signal, "Ready-Set-Go." The audience screams, some groups louder than others. However, it is 100% that there is hold back in the room. Yep, 100% of the time everyone in the audience has held back. Why is that?

The reason is because of neural networks. This is a survival mechanism. Long ago you experienced a time when you were embarrassed. Your brain tagged that as "life threatening" and you formed what is called a cortical limbic loop. When you were confronted with a similar situation, or you thought about taking a similar action (cortex), your brain had a stored memory that was immediately activated that prevented you from taking that "dangerous" action. It doesn't matter whether the threat is real or not. The only thing that matters is that you have it tagged as an event to be avoided.

Challenge:

Where in your life are you holding back? From whom are you withholding from? Just for today, what are you going to do about it? The only reason you're holding back is fear. Time goes by too fast. Take action today.

Tapping in Meditation:

My purpose today is to take action. Action always beats intentions. I am on a journey of self-improvement in my health, business and personal life. Taking action is proof of my development and I do take actions.

Journal Notes:

Day/Year	
Day/Year	
Day/Year	
Day/Year	
Day/Year	

July 25
Dr. Seus—Oh The Places You'll Go—Progress Not Perfection

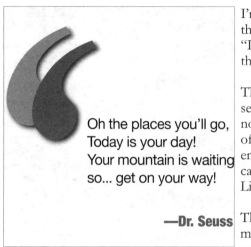

Oh the places you'll go,
Today is your day!
Your mountain is waiting
so... get on your way!

—Dr. Seuss

I'm going to paraphrase here. There is a message in the Dr. Seuss book that says something to the effect, "I always do what I say I will do" on the left page and then on the right is reads, "Except when I don't."

This is a program of progress, not perfection. The second law of thermodynamics states that there is no perfect system and that the natural state is a state of order to disorder or entropy. There is no perfect engine. The next time you drive feel the hood of your car. It will be hot. Heat is lost to the environment. Likewise there is no perfect human being.

There will be times when you miss your reading, you miss your meditation, you don't follow the food plan, you don't do the most productive things first and you aren't loving and full of gratitude. When those days happen it's not terrible, horrible and awful, it just is. That's when you evoke the wisdom of Dr. Seuss. It goes like this;

"I am always loving, giving, appreciative and productive, except when I'm not." Period. That's it. Back on track. You have a reference point to know when you have crossed your boundary, when you are off course. This it's simply a matter of readjusting, forgiving yourself and getting back on track. I love this Dr. Seuss phrase;

"You have brains in your head. You have feet in your shoes. You can steer yourself any direction you choose. You're on your own. Any you know what you know. And YOU are the one who'll decide where to go."

Challenge:
Never, ever, dwell on your failures and disappointments. Instead focus on your opportunities, re adjust your plan, recommit and execute.

Tapping in Meditation:
My purpose today is to honor myself. Today is the day. I'm off to great places. I'm on my way!

Journal Notes:

Day/Year	
Day/Year	
Day/Year	
Day/Year	
Day/Year	

Fit For Life

I'll assume that you are not an athlete training for a sport. That being the case here are my recommendations. Although exercise is not a part of the weight management program it is a part of our excellence program.

Here is a simple program you can follow. Another assumption that I'll make is that you don't have any physical problems that would prevent you from working out. My recommendation is a 4 day workout as a minimum, 5 if you can. The programs include both aerobic and anaerobic training (Google it.) First the weight lifting program.

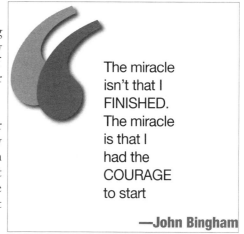

The miracle isn't that I FINISHED. The miracle is that I had the COURAGE to start

—John Bingham

Day 1 Upper Body. This would be front of the arms, back of the arms and chest. I like the flat bench with barbells. I use stand up free weight arm curls and pulley triceps. Do 3 sets to failure, failing at 8-10 reps.

Day 2 Lower Body. Front and back of the legs. If you can do free weight squats then that's all you would need to do. That's an advanced exercise however, so if not then seated leg extensions, 3 sets 8-10 reps, and seated leg curls, 3 sets 8-10 reps. That's it and your done for the lower body day.

Day 3 repeat day 1 and Day 4 repeat day 2.

For cardiovascular fitness I recommend HIIT. That's high intensity interval training. Work at 80-90% of your max heart rate. Do 8 sprints for 60 seconds followed by 90 seconds of rest in between. That will put you at 30 minutes. This includes a 5 minute warm up and a 5 minute cool down. Do this for two workouts, then your third cut it back to 4 sprints and after your 4th just do steady state at 60% of your max for as long as you want to.

Core exercises. I recommend the following; 2 days 2 sets of each exercise, 1 day 1 set and no core your 4th workout. The core exercises: sit-ups, 20 reps per set, leg raises, 20 reps per set,, crunches, 20 reps per set,, knee ups 20 reps per set, leg bicycles, 30 reps per set, oblique sit-ups 30 reps per set. That's it, you done. It should take you about an hour for your workout. Of course, if you don't understand any of this, see a trainer in the gym. Have fun.

Challenge:
There is an 80% correlation between being a deca millionaire and being in and exercise and fitness program. Start exercising.

Tapping in Meditation:
My purpose today is to live a fit lifestyle and I do. My lifestyle is an asset. Fit is not a destination, it's a way of life. I love to exercise and I do.

Journal Notes:

Day/Year	
Day/Year	
Day/Year	

July 27

Training Doesn't Work

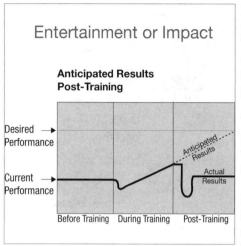

Entertainment or Impact

**Anticipated Results
Post-Training**

Desired Performance →

Current Performance →

Anticipated Results

Actual Results

Before Training   During Training   Post-Training

Research statistics show that it is very rare for a training program to go beyond entertainment into impact. This is not necessarily a reflection of the competency of the trainer or the relevancy of their material. It's more a reflection of human nature. This includes this program as well.

There is only one way to ensure that the training you participate is has long lasting results and it is exactly what you are doing, a planned system of learning, reinforcement, behavioral contracting and coaching.

Look at your program, read one page a day, quiet meditation 5-10 minutes daily, follow the food plan every day, attend the group live coaching conferences, this is an ongoing system of learning. This is repetition. You come back to the same concepts each day, each year. This is how you rewire the brain and form habits.

Challenge:

Work the tools of this program every day. Also, reach out to support someone else as well.

Tapping in Meditation:

My purpose today is to relax into a peaceful and productive day. I have peace of mind. I have serenity. I am committed to excellence. I use the tools of this program.

Journal Notes:

Day/Year	
Day/Year	
Day/Year	
Day/Year	
Day/Year	

July 28

What do You Stand For? The Story of Malala Yousafzai

A year after being shot in the head by the Taliban, the teenage activist continues to share her dreams and tell her story. Although just a teenager, her dream is to see every child in the world be educated. How is that for a stand? She has written a memoir, "I Am Malala" and became the youngest person ever nominated for the Nobel Peace Prize.

Malala says of the Taliban, "They thoughts bullets would silence us but they failed. Out of that silence came thousands of voices."

To declare a stand means to declare a position, to hold firm for or against something or someone, as in the government was determined to take a stand against all forms of terrorism. It means holding your ground against an enemy or other issues even if that enemy is peer pressure. Our children need to be able to see us take a stand for a value and against injustices, be those values and injustices in the family room, the boardroom, the classroom, or on the city streets.

> One child,
> one teacher,
> one book,
> one pen
> can change the
> world.
>
> —**Malala Yousufzai**

I love the stand that Angelina Jolie Pitt takes; "To be in any way a positive contribution, that's all anybody wants to be. It's all I've ever wanted to be. I wanted to be an artist, be a mother. You want to feel that you've been of use, in whatever way that comes out."

This program takes a stand for excellence. This means a near zero tolerance for anything or anyone in the way of that stand.

Challenge:
What is your declared stand for this year? Especially today, live from that stand. When you are about to avoid something ask yourself, what would the action be if you are holding firm to your stand for excellence, then just listen and act.

Tapping in Meditation:
My purpose today is to allow my declared stand be my compass and direct my actions. I trust my intuition. I follow my stand.

Journal Notes:

Day/Year	
Day/Year	
Day/Year	
Day/Year	
Day/Year	

July 29

What is it to be Extraordinary?

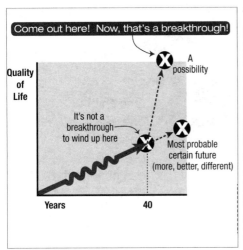

Take a look at the direction of your life, at least before participating in this program. Imagine a graph where the vertical axis is the quality of your life and the horizontal axis is your age.

Let's take a best case scenario. If you did nothing and continued on as you were before this program it's very likely that you would have continued to improve. Yes, you would have experienced struggles and challenges, but you would have made your way through the struggle to a successful and fulfilling life, but compared to what? What would you have? More, better, different? It's not a breakthrough to continue on as you are. What would be an outrageous outcome? Remember, you have far more capacity to create the circumstances and events in your life than you are aware of.

Challenge:

If you applied yourself, what could you create for your life? What impact could you have for others? Let your imagination flow. Be extraordinary today. See if you can point to one thing about today that was extraordinary and journal about it.

Tapping in Meditation:

My purpose today is to realize my potential and not to settle for less. It is my road and my road alone. Others can walk it with me but no one else can walk if for me.

Journal Notes:

Day/Year	
Day/Year	
Day/Year	
Day/Year	
Day/Year	

Anxiety Can Be Good for You—Sometimes

Short-term stress can boost your immune system. Firdaus Dhabhar, a Stanford University researcher, who studies how stress changes the body has discovered that stressed out laboratory mice exhibit more robust immune responses to vaccines than control groups of mice left in peace. Something similar happens to people.

In a study of knee surgery patients, for example, Dhabhar found that the anxiety of their impending operations boosted the number of immune cells circulating in their blood. Such studies convinced him that stress does not entirely deserve its bad reputation and that some situations it can actually improve health.

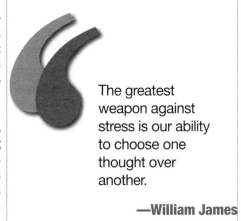

The greatest weapon against stress is our ability to choose one thought over another.

—**William James**

A transient burst of stress tends to activate some parts of the immune system while chronic stress generally stifles the entire immune system.

However, stress really doesn't exist. It's all in your mind. Essentially all stress is self-imposed. It's your interpretation of events laden with a negative expectation. Did you know that the body can't differentiate between positive or negative stress? A wedding or buying a new house will both generate the same stress response as being in traffic.

However, it is good to know that being stressed is absolutely normal and in small doses healthy. You are not a perfect machine so it's OK to experience stress and anxiety.

Challenge:
Feel and allow your stress and anxiety today. When you've had enough simply change your thoughts.

Tapping in Meditation:
My purpose today is to challenge the beliefs that I hold about people and the world. There is a great power and freedom in seeing issues from different perspectives.

Journal Notes:

Day/Year	
Day/Year	
Day/Year	
Day/Year	
Day/Year	

July 31

Take a Break to Sharpen Your Ax

If I had six hours
to chop down a tree,
I'd spend the
first four hours
sharpening the axe.

—**Abraham Lincoln**

How hard to you drive yourself? Get away from work. Eat lunch somewhere other than your desk. Take a walk, go to the gym, develop a hobby, find some way to disengage. A brief breather recharges you and keeps you more productive. For example;

Two men were chopping wood. One of the men worked hard all day, seldom taking a break and took only 20 minutes for lunch. The other man took several breaks a day, spent 45 minutes for lunch, and even took a 15-minute nap before going back to work.

The first man became increasingly frustrated because, no matter how hard he worked, the other man's pile of wood was always much bigger than his at the end of the day. "I don't understand how you do it,' said the first man one day. "Every time I look around, you're are sitting down, and yet you cut more wood then I do. Why is that?"

With a smile the second man replied, "Did you also notice that while I was sitting down I was sharpening my ax?"

You've got to remember that struggle negates. There is a tipping point where an increase in effort will actually decrease results. It's up to you to know yourself and to know how far you can push before your performance starts to decline. It's not all work after all.

Challenge:
What do you need to do today to "sharpen your ax?" Do it

Tapping in Meditation:
My purpose today is to live a few years of my life like most people won't so that I can live the later years like most people can't. My life is the sum of the choices I make and I make wise choices.

Journal Notes:

Day/Year	
Day/Year	
Day/Year	
Day/Year	
Day/Year	

AUGUST

Davies Day Book

365 concepts for excellence

August 1

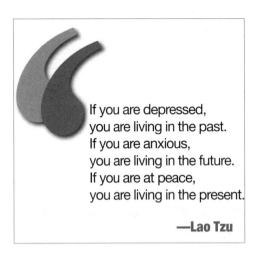

If you are depressed,
you are living in the past.
If you are anxious,
you are living in the future.
If you are at peace,
you are living in the present.

—Lao Tzu

1. Take a look at the habits that I have that don't serve me. I have the power to change anything about myself that I want. If I am not able to do so then I need to ask for help.

2. Acknowledge the presence of a higher power greater than myself which has created me. I can tap into this higher power energy to solve all of my problems.

3. Let go of the need to figure things out. No need to analyze, no efforting. I surrender to the greater power of the universe and make decisions and take actions wisely.

4. Release the past, letting go of any guilt or regrets, finding fault or blaming.

5. Forgive myself for the way that I've been. I realize that my actions came from fear, doubt and insecurity. I no longer pass judgment on myself or others.

6. Drop all anxiety about the future. I live this day with joy, trust, love and serenity as I realize that this day is all that I can handle.

7. Let go of my neediness, my dependencies on others or on having things turn out the way I want them to. Inner peace is true freedom.

8. Take responsibility for all aspects of my life. I am the source of all that I experience versus going victim and blaming others.

9. Use my talents, time and resources for the benefit of my life and the lives of others.

10. Enter this day with positive expectations, passion peace and give it my positive best.

Challenge:
Willingly share the experience, wisdom, peace, strength and hope that you are receiving from the tools of this program.

Tapping in Meditation:
My purpose today is to live the words from John Lennon, "Imagine all the people living life in peace. You may say I'm a dreamer, but I'm not the only one. I hope someday you'll join us, and the world will be as one."

Journal Notes:

Day/Year	
Day/Year	
Day/Year	
Day/Year	
Day/Year	

August 2

There is Peace in Staying in the NOW

Stand under a cold shower. If you stay in the present then you will not feel the pain of the cold. It's an absolutely amazing feat of the mind. There is no pain in the present. Pain is an interpretation of a past sensation. Check it out.

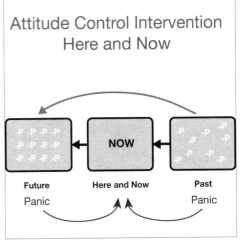

Attitude Control Intervention
Here and Now

Future — Panic
Here and Now
Past — Panic
NOW

Did you know that anxiety is a self-imposed narration. Here's how it works. Let's apply anxiety to prospecting. You start the process by having the thought, the intention that you are going to prospect. That is activity in the prefrontal cortex area of the brain, right behind your forehead. Next you go into auto-instinct. Your brain has a neurological connection that has extended to the limbic area (Cortical-limbic loop). The limbic area is the arousal, fear, avoidance area. Your brain already has stored a previous past painful experience of rejection. You then project this past experience into a future expectation. This leads to the instinct of avoidance and that is followed by rationalization where you justify the avoidance and think that the truth is that you are just too busy.

A woman is a newly trained loan officer. She is trained to go into real estate offices and pass out her rate sheets, meet the Realtors and develop relationships. The very first office she goes into is a very negative experience. The broker, who also owns a mortgage company, sees her walk into the office. He runs out of his office, takes the loan officers card, rips it up and throws it at her yelling this is how much I want to see you in my office. The woman runs out of the office in tears.

Now it's time for this woman to start prospecting again. What does her brain do? The thought of prospecting generates the memory of the negative P (past experience). She then projects that –P to the anticipation of the future and does not prospect. This happens over and over again and before long she has multiple –Ps and they are all projected to the future. As she instinctively wanders from the past to the future she becomes unable to execute the activity that is represented, prospecting.

The answer is to stay in the present. There is no fear in the here and now. This is no pain, there is no panic. There is only serenity in the here and now.

Challenge:

Anytime you are experiencing anxiety you are bouncing between the past and the future. Stay focused in the here and now.

Tapping in Meditation:

My purpose today is to have a present focus. Just for today when I catch myself thinking of the past or projecting to the future I immediately bring it back to here and now. I am powerful and unstoppable in the present moment.

Journal Notes:

Day/Year	
Day/Year	
Day/Year	

August 3

Self Imposed Anxiety—It's a Choice

Back in the 1980s I was prospecting and I found an association that was still planning for their general session keynote speaker. They were having a committee meeting the next day and if I could get them my demo video VHS (remember those) then I could be considered. The meeting planner liked my approach and encouraged me to send it in. This was long before emails were an everyday occurrence.

I called FedEx and set up the shipment. My office is a separate building attached to my house. It has its own entrance, heat and air, etc. FedEx picks up from the front porch of my house however. I prepared the package and left it outside on the porch to the main house.

Before I go to bed I always check the front porch to see if any deliveries have arrived. When I opened the door, there was my package. FedEx did not pick it up. I immediately projected to the future, "I'm not going to be considered at tomorrow's meeting, (future-panic), I can't believe FedEx was so incompetent (past-panic)" so I storm into my office and call FedEx.

A very nice woman answers and I catch myself going from irate to calm. I decided to stay focused in the present moment, the now. What am I doing right now? I'm talking with FedEx about my delivery. There is no panic in the present moment. I can choose to stay present or I can bounce between the past (panic) and the future (panic) and be miserable. If I bounce back and forth it will not change the situation and I will do double duty. Not only will my package still not be delivered but add my high anxiety to that as well.

The first thing the woman asked for was my confirmation number. I didn't have one. It turns out that I never properly placed the order. She was kind enough to expedite the order and get the package delivered, on time. Because I was calm she became an ally and did everything she could to turn this into a positive result.

Challenge:

Worrying does not take away tomorrows troubles, it takes away today's peace. Stay in the present moment, all day long, one moment at a time.

Tapping in Meditation:

My purpose today is to stay focused and on task. I am stronger than anything I am facing right now.

Journal Notes:

Day/Year	
Day/Year	
Day/Year	
Day/Year	
Day/Year	

August 4

I Take My Program Seriously

Too often in my life I have expended time and energy in pursuits that were self-destructive. I choose now to channel my attention and actions into the one thing that has the best chance to bring me happiness.

I am both realistic and gentle with myself. I am not perfect nor is it necessary to be. I recognize and respect others differences. Everyone has their own story to tell and everyone is unique. I work my own program and am supportive of others. I will allow myself to step beyond my self-imposed isolation and I will reach out to others. I will enjoy my life. I budget time into my day specifically for the purpose of tapping in to the universal intelligence with quiet relaxation.

I practice self-love. I am open to receive the blessings of abundance. I continue to take personal inventory and to love and approve of myself. I have a spiritual awakening as a result of these tools and I continue to love myself and live this program in all of my affairs.

Challenge:
Use the tools of this program every day. Accept and love yourself every day.

Tapping in Meditation:
My purpose today is to know that I am enough. I have enough. I do enough. Breathe extra deep and let go and trust that my universal higher power and the divine intelligence will reward my efforts.

Journal Notes:
Journal below how your dreams will turn into your future success. Journal any thoughts you may be having about this program and your participation.

Day/Year	
Day/Year	
Day/Year	
Day/Year	
Day/Year	

August 5

An Interesting and Untapped Power—The Smile

UC Berkely did a 30 year longitudinal study that looked at pictures of students in their year book. The amazing thing about the study was that by measuring the students smile in the yearbook the researchers were able to predict how long lasting and fulfilling a marriage would be, how well they would score on a standardized test of well-being, and how inspiring they would be to others. If you want to be a leader and be inspiring to others smiling can help.

A smile predicts longevity. In a 2010 Wayne State University study, researchers found that smiling predicts longevity. They looked at the smile span of the players on 1960 baseball cards .A beaming smile, lived to an average age of 79.9. A slight smile, age 75 and no smile 72.9. We are actually born smiling. A developing baby is seen to smile even in the womb. Smiling is a universal expression. Only 1/3 of people smile more than 20 x per day while nearly 14% smile less than 5 x. Children smile as many as 400 times per day.

It's very difficult to frown while looking at someone who smiles. Smiling is contagious and it suppresses the control we usually have on our facial muscles. Smiling stimulates the brains reward centers the same way as eating chocolate. British researchers found that one smile can generate the same brain reward stimulation as up to 2000 bars of chocolate. The same researchers found that smiling had the same brain stimulation as receiving $25,000. That's not bad, a $25,000 smile.

A group of German researchers did an interesting study. They showed pictures to subjects that made them smile and they saw the reward centers of the brain light up using fMRIs. Then they injected Botox into the cheeks of the volunteers which prevented them from smiling. Next they showed them the same pictures and since they could not smile they could not generate the same neurological response, the reward center of the cortex did not light up. The act of smiling itself causes activity in the brain. Smiling can make you healthier. Smiling can help reduce the number of stress enhancing hormones like cortisol and adrenalin, and increase the level of mood enhancing hormones like endorphins and reduce overall blood pressure. And if that's not enough, smiling can actually make you look good in the eyes of others. When you smile not only are you more likable and courteous, but you also appear to be more competent. Mother Teresa said, "I will never understand all the good that a simple smile can accomplish." So if you want to live a longer, healthier and happy life, smile.

Challenge:

My purpose today is to notice the impact that I have on myself and others when I smile.

Tapping in Meditation:

My purpose today is to smile often. I am in a good mood all the time.

Journal Notes:

Day/Year	
Day/Year	
Day/Year	
Day/Year	

August 6

Greed—Who's needs are your thinking of? King Solomon and the Baby

One day, the wise King Solomon was approached by two women arguing over a baby. Each claimed the child was hers. Unable to judge, King Solomon thought up a plan—he offered to cut the baby in half, giving half to the one and half to the other.

The first women agreed with the King: "Let the baby be neither mine nor hers, but divide it. If I can't have the child", she cried, "She can't have it either." The second women pleaded with Solomon not to hurt the child. "Give her the baby. I'd rather lose the child that sees it slain." Solomon knew immediately that this was the rightful mother. He returned the baby to her.

One of the tools of this program is to be of service to other people. What if you don't naturally feel that way? It is an important principle and it's important that you develop this approach, this mindset.

Good news, you can rewire your brain to develop the habit of responding to other people with their needs in mind first. Simply declare it, reinforce it with your quiet time, then become aware of opportunities to put other people's needs ahead of your own (within reason, all extremes turn destructive), and notice doing so.

Challenge:
Just for today find an opportunity to interact with another person with their needs as the focus. This may only be the act of listening.

Tapping in Meditation:
My purpose today is to develop the habit of responding to others with their needs in mind first and I do.

Journal Notes:

Day/Year	
Day/Year	
Day/Year	
Day/Year	
Day/Year	

August 7
Mindset Development—5 Styles of Distorted Thinking

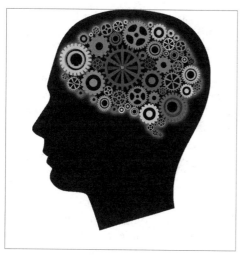

1. **Filtering**: You take the negative details and magnify them while filtering out all positive aspects of the situation.

2. **Polarized Thinking**: Things are black and white, good or bad. You have to be perfect or you are a failure. There is no middle ground.

3. **Overgeneralization**: You come to a general conclusion based on a single incident or other piece of evidence. If something bad happens once, you expect it to happen over and over again.

4. **Mind Reading**: Without their saying so you know what people are feeling and why they act the way that they do. In particular, you are able to define how they are feeling about you.

5. **Catastrophizing**: You expect a disaster. You notice or hear about a problem and start, "what it's." What if a tragedy strikes? What if it happens to you?

Are you experiencing any of these styles of thinking? Ask yourself without judgment, it's not good or bad, just notice.

Challenge:
Just for today see if you can catch yourself with any of these modes of thinking and simply STOP it! Take the opposite point of view, just for today.

Tapping in Meditation:
My purpose today is to see the world from a possibility perspective. No matter what happens to me today I see only opportunities.

Journal Notes:

Day/Year	
Day/Year	
Day/Year	
Day/Year	
Day/Year	

August 8

Mindset Development—6-10 Styles of Distorted Thinking

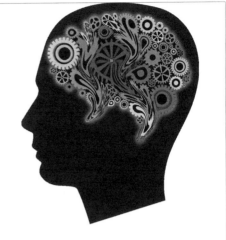

6. **Personalization**: Thinking that everything people do or say is some kind of a reaction to you. You also compare yourself to others, trying to determine who's smarter, better looking, more successful, etc.

7. **Control Fallacies**: If you feel externally controlled you see yourself as helpless, a victim of fate. The fallacy of internal control has you responsible for the pain and happiness of everyone around you.

8. **Fallacy of Fairness**: You feel resentful because you think you know what's fair but other people won't agree with you.

9. **Shoulds**: You have a list of ironclad rules about how you and other people should act. People who break the rules anger you and you feel guilty if you violate the rules.

10. **Blaming**: You hold other people responsible for your pain, or take the other approach and blame yourself for every problem.

Challenge:

Same challenge as yesterday. Just for today see if you can catch yourself with any of these modes of thinking and simply STOP it! Take the opposite point of view, just for today.

Tapping in Meditation:

My purpose today is to focus on what's important, to capture the good times, to develop from the negatives and if things don't work out to take another shot and I do, all day long.

Journal Notes:

Day/Year	
Day/Year	
Day/Year	
Day/Year	
Day/Year	

August 9
Mindset Development—11-15 Styles of Distorted Thinking

Don't believe everything you think.

11. Emotional Reasoning: You believe that what you feel must be true automatically. If you feel stupid and boring then you must be stupid and boring.

12. Fallacy of Change: You expect that other people will change to suit you if you just pressure or cajole them enough. You need to change people because your hopes for happiness seem to depend entirely on them.

13. Global Labeling: You generalize one or two qualities into a negative global judgment.

14. Being Right: You are continually on trial to prove that your opinions and actions are correct. Being wrong is unthinkable and you will go to any length to demonstrate your rightness.

15. Heaven's Reward Fallacy: You expect all of your sacrifice and self-denial to pay off, as if there was someone keeping score. You feel bitter when the reward does not come.

Challenge:
All of these past few days of distorted thinking styles will play havoc with your state of mind. Notice without judgment if you recognize them and you have the power to stop that pattern right away and replace it with a thought that simply makes you feel better. Do it!

Tapping in Meditation:
My purpose today is to spring forward from life's difficulties with passion and appreciation. I appreciate that I do have the opportunity to turn problems into delightful advantages. An arrow must be pulled backwards to be shot, so when life is dragging me back with difficulties it means it's going to launch me into something great.

Journal Notes:

Day/Year	
Day/Year	
Day/Year	
Day/Year	
Day/Year	

August 10

Puzzle—Get the Person Together

A four year old girl was sitting home with her father one beautiful Saturday afternoon. Her father was watching the football game when the girl said, "Dad, I'm bored. I have nothing to do."

The father picked up the Sunday newspaper and walked across the room toward his daughter. He opened the paper and stopped turning pages when he saw a full-page ad for an airline. The ad read: "We travel the world," with a large photo of the earth as seen from outer space.

The clever father tore the page out and then tore it up into small pieces and said to his daughter, "Okay honey. Put this world back together again with the tape over there."

The bored little girl slid off the couch and, with a hesitant look up at her Dad, started arranging the numerous pieces. In a few minutes the girl said, "Dad, I'm all done. I'm still bored. I have nothing to do."

Doubting his daughter could have put the ad puzzle back together so quickly the father exclaimed, "There's no way you could have put that world back together so quickly. Let me take a look."

When the girl gave her father the full page ad completely intact the father was amazed.

"How did you put that world back together so fast?' he asked.

And the girl explained, "Well, you see Dad, there was a picture of a person on the other side. When I put the person together the world was together."

Challenge:
As you continue to use the tools of this program do you see yourself improving? Do you see the improvement in others? Do you realize that it's not about other's, it's about you and your journey?

Tapping in Meditation:
My purpose today is to fully love and accept myself and others. I love the person I am today. Without the lessons I've learned from the past my journey, I would not be me. Life is a journey and I live it.

Journal Notes:

Day/Year	
Day/Year	
Day/Year	
Day/Year	
Day/Year	

August 11

I Don't Want to Work or is it F=MA?

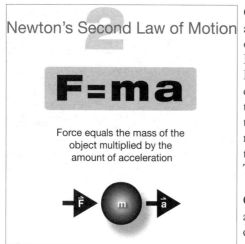

Newton's Second Law of Motion

F=ma

Force equals the mass of the
object multiplied by the
amount of acceleration

Gary Weidner, technical editor for Cleaner Times, an industry publication, wrote about an interesting opinion piece that appeared in Contractor magazine. It was written by Al Schwartz, a plumbing contractor. He had previously published columns about the difficulties of filling positions in the trades. "It's not that there aren't people looking for jobs. But to illustrate the shortage of qualified job applicants, Schwartz mentions a Denver contractor who "has been trying to recruit qualified people from across the country." The contractor reports hiring only 1 applicant in 70.

Qualifications are one thing; attitude is another, and Schwartz illustrates the problem. He tells of a contractor who won a bid outside his normal operating area. The contractor advertised in the Arizona town where the project was located for local help to round out his crew, but found that the entry level people tended to decline a starting wage of $20 per hour in favor of not working and collecting benefits. He goes on to say, "If the kids we do hire last a week, we consider it average." Most who quit called the work "too hard." Schwartz says "There is no longer any doubt about the conclusion that the real problem we face, not only as a trade but as a nation, is that we have bred a generation of young people who, for the most part, have never had to work for anything and they avoid employment in any form that requires work."

These contractors are having difficulty hiring people for strenuous work. Have you experienced this? Have you seen this in yourself? Are you "work (effort) allergic?" Remember observe without judgment. Just keep in mind that it's a law of physics, as you sow so shall you reap. Force (work) equals mass times acceleration. In other words you've got to put energy into a system to create results. No wood in the stove then no fire. What are you seeing in your life? Are you around people who are effort aversive? Do you have children who just want to come home from school and play video games and shy away from anything that requires effort? Do you have employees like that? Are you like that?

Challenge:

Where can you roll up your sleeves and get to work? Just for today do that. Who can you encourage to do the same?

Tapping in Meditation:

My purpose today is to strive for success with hard work. Expecting success without the effort is like expecting a harvest without planting a seed. I effortlessly enjoy and work to the best of my ability at my highest level of effort in everything I do today no matter what the activity is from relaxation, to cleaning to recreation to work. I put in a good effort today.

Journal Notes:

Day/Year	
Day/Year	
Day/Year	
Day/Year	

August 12

The Innocence of Not Seeing Limitations

An elementary school teacher was giving a drawing class to a group of six year old children. At the back of the classroom sat a little girl who normally didn't pay much attention in school. In the drawing class she did. For more than 20 minutes the girl sat with her arms curled around her paper, totally absorbed in what she was doing. The teacher found this fascinating. Eventually she asked the girl what she was drawing. Without looking up the girl said, "I'm drawing a picture of God."

Surprised the teacher said, "But nobody knows what God looks like."

The girl said, "They will in a minute."

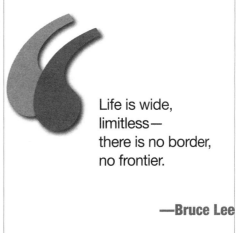

Life is wide, limitless—
there is no border, no frontier.

—Bruce Lee

Challenge:

Every day is a new day of limitless potential. Now is the time to live out all of our dreams. Where have you bought into societies' limitations or your peer's imitations where they try to sell you on what you can or cannot do? What if your potential is limitless? Where are you holding yourself back? Take one small action that you think that you can't, just for today.

Tapping in Meditation:

My purpose today is to drop the boundaries of what I think I can't do and live into my limitless world and I do. I am impressed with the urgency of doing. Knowing is not enough, I must apply, I must do and I do take action.

Journal Notes:

Day/Year	
Day/Year	
Day/Year	
Day/Year	
Day/Year	

August 13

The Lesson of the Guided Eye

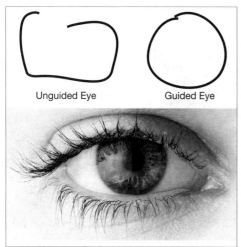

Unguided Eye   Guided Eye

Imagine that you were wearing a device that displayed the actual linear movement that your eyes made on a computer screen. Imagine there is a circle in front of you and I'd like for you to trace that circle with your eyes. You would have made a trace similar to this, haphazard and jagged, anything but a smooth circle.

Next I'd like for you to extend your right arm and right index finger right in front of you and move your finger in a circle and trace your finger. The figure on the right is what you'll see on the computer this time. Nearly a perfect circle but certainly very recognizable as a circle.

Challenge:

The unguided eye is a poor tracker of information while the guided eye is an excellence tracker. The unprepared person is an ineffective user of time. Your preparation is your guidance. Just for today be very well prepared in everything that you do.

Tapping in Meditation:

My purpose today is to begin with a prepared mind. Chance favors preparation. Luck and opportunity follow preparation. I am well prepared in everything I do.

Journal Notes:

Day/Year	
Day/Year	
Day/Year	
Day/Year	
Day/Year	

August 14

Take Risks

To laugh is to risk appearing a fool. To weep is to risk appearing sentimental. To reach out for another is to risk involvement. To expose feelings is to expose your true self. To love is to risk not being loved in return. To live is to risk dying. To hope is to risk despair. To attempt is to risk failure. But risks must be taken because the greatest hazard in life is to risk nothing. The person who risks nothing, does nothing, has nothing and is nothing. They may avoid suffering and sorrow but they cannot learn, feel, change, grow, love and live! Chained by their false security they are a slave, they have forfeited their freedom. Only the person who risks is free.

Take RISKS.
If you win,
you will be happy.
If you lose,
you will be wise.

A long time college roommate and close friend, Tony is a hypnotist and just retired. A company wanted him to do his hypnosis program for their event but since he had retired he referred them to me. Years ago he had taught me to hypnotize people and I also did hypnosis presentations. However, I had stopped those presentations so I wouldn't compete with Tony. The company insisted on the hypnosis program although I attempted to talk them into my core behavioral accountability program. Since they insisted I relented and agreed to perform my hypnosis show for them in 2 locations.

I had not presented a hypnosis show in over 12 years. This was a big risk. What if I failed? What a shock to my credibility not to mention destroying their event. What if, what if?

Once I made the decision to present the program I also decided that I would be as prepared as I could possibly be. If I failed it would not have been from lack of preparation. I watched 100s of hours of videos of my previous programs, of Tony's recent programs, of other mentor hypnotists who I trained with, over and over again. When I finally did the program it was as if I had been doing them all along. I had instincts, I was sharp, and both programs were fantastic. It was my willingness to take a risk and to prepare that saved the day.

Challenge:
What risk can you take today that can have a big impact for yourself or others? Prepare and take that risk. Journal what you learn.

Tapping in Meditation:
My purpose today is to take risks in my life. If I win I can lead, if I lose I can guide. I am open to taking risks combined with precise preparation. I plan for and expect the best outcome.

Journal Notes:

Day/Year	
Day/Year	
Day/Year	
Day/Year	
Day/Year	

August 15
The Act of Observation Changes What's Being Observed

This is a principle of quantum physics. Imagine that you are measuring subatomic particles. Visualize the balls on a pool table as these subatomic particles. You want to observe one. Since you can't see them you will locate one by rolling a ball and when you strike another ball you'll know that you've located one. However, that act of striking a ball changes its location. Hence, the act of observation or measurement is an interaction and changes what is being observed.

Challenge:
If you can't measure, you can't manage. Any goal worthwhile has measurement. What you can control you must control. You can control your measurement and tracking. Make a list of what you can measure in your health, business and personal life. Just for today track it. Notice what happens when you pay attention to something enough to track it.

Tapping in Meditation:
My purpose today is to measure what can be measured, and change what needs to be changed. John Lennon once said "When I was 5 years old my mother always told me that happiness was the key to life. When I went to school, they asked me what I wanted to be when I grew up. I wrote down happy. They told me I didn't understand the assignment. I told them they didn't understand life."

Journal Notes:

Day/Year	
Day/Year	
Day/Year	
Day/Year	
Day/Year	

August 16

A Measurement System Brings Unexpected Results—Fat Bob

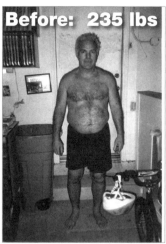

Before: 235 lbs

This book is not about me. However, wherever my story can be of help to you I don't mind sharing it. This is one of those times. Health has always been my number 1 value. I always made what I thought were good food choices and I consistently exercised 4 to 5 times every week. Despite this I had a struggle with my weight. My normal weight was around 220 (highest 235) and occasionally I would diet down to the low 200s. I could never keep it for very long however. It was just too difficult. I'd get tired, hungry and didn't feel well until I ate like normal again. If you were to tell me that I would wind up weighing in the 170s I would not have thought that was possible. Well it is and I've been between 177 and 179 since 2012.

I didn't all of a sudden get motivated, I was always motivated. I had to learn a system of controlling my physiology, my cravings, my blood sugar, insulin, dopamine, serotonin, leptin levels. A big part of this system is boundaries. This is the system that you are on, the avoidance of flour and sugar, 3 weighed and measured meals, nothing in between and massive personal development. By using a system I was able to break through what I thought was possible into a new way of being and living. The good news is that this system is like gravity, it will work for anyone. It doesn't discriminate, nor does it require and special talent. Simply follow the system and you too will have predictable results.

After: 177 lbs

Challenge:
This program is a system of a way of life. Follow the teachings and use the tools every day.

Tapping in Meditation:
My purpose today is to find a way. If I really want to do something I will find a way. If I don't I will find an excuse.

Journal Notes:

Day/Year	
Day/Year	
Day/Year	
Day/Year	
Day/Year	

August 17

Is There Really Free Will?

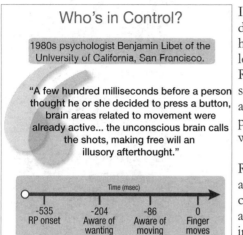
In July 2008 retired steelworker Brian Thomas dreamed that bikers had broken into his camper and he strangled one to death. It turned out he killed his loving wife of nearly 40 years. Detective Inspector Richard Evans said Mr. Thomas told police there was someone in the camper van, a man with blue jeans and a black fleece lying on top of Christine'. An expert psychiatrist explained that Thomas was not aware of what he was doing when he choked his wife.

Recently an increasing number of philosophers and neuroscientists have argued that based on a current understanding of the human brain, we are all sleepwalking all the time. Instead of being the intentional originators of our lives, we are simply pushed around by past events and by the behind the scenes neuro networks of our non-conscious minds. Even when we are awake free will is just an illusion.

Philosophers will argue that all organisms are bound by the same physical laws of the universe where every action is the result of previous events, cause and effect, action-reaction. The universe simply does not allow for free will. Recent neuroscience studies have added fuel to this notion by suggesting that the experience of conscious choice is the outcome of the underlying neural processes that produce human action, not the cause of them. Our brains decide everything even without our help, it just feels like we have a say. So you might say, not true, I can decide to lift my right arm, right now. The scientists would argue that your motor cortex was firing before you were conscious of the choice to lift your arm.

Challenge:

What if it's true that everything you do is predetermined by your neurological wiring? Rather than trying to solve or disprove this, place your energy on thinking positive and productive thoughts. Build the inner processes and networks that will lead you to successful outcomes. Use the tools of this program to do this.

Tapping in Meditation:

My purpose today is to determine my future with the thinking that I have and the decisions I make today.

Journal Notes:

Day/Year	
Day/Year	
Day/Year	
Day/Year	
Day/Year	

August 18

Intentionally Creating Habits

By your very nature, you are a creature of habit. 95% of your actions, thoughts and feelings are a result of habits. You follow the path of least resistance even if your behaviors are inefficient, unproductive or even harmful. A repetitive, addiction driven pattern of behavior can take over part of what had been a deliberate choice.

To carry out behaviors, your brain sends messages to the rest of your body through the different nerve cells. Repeated thoughts or actions create neural pathways and the more frequent the repetition, the stronger the connection and the wider the pathway will become. The constant recurrence decreases the biochemical resistance to that certain thought or action. That is why you can perform certain thoughts and actions almost unconsciously. In addition, your brain is designed to identify and create patterns. Neural pathways you use repeatedly tend to get stronger and wider. This leads to using them even more making them stronger. Our brain coats regularly used pathways with a myelin sheath which makes them even more resistant to change. The more routine a behavior becomes, the less you are aware of it. You lose the fully alert surveillance of that behavior. This is all by genetic design of course because it frees you to use your limited perceptual abilities to pay attention to other threats.

Scientists have discovered that the brain "chunks" multiple circuits as actions become habitual. Using a technique called optogenetics scientists place light sensitive molecules inside the brain and they can see the circuits of habitual behavior. This is good news because if you "interrupt" an unwanted automated circuit enough times you can actually rewire the "chunk" and create a new wanted habit.

Challenge:
Decide on one habit that just for today you'd like to change. Use a behavioral contract to interrupt the automated circuitry. Tell someone else you'll give them $100 if you don't complete this action by the end of the day. Do this for an entire month and you will rewire your brain and create a new habit.

Tapping in Meditation:
My purpose today is to leave old habits behind by starting today with the thought, I release the need for this in my life.

Journal Notes:

Day/Year	
Day/Year	
Day/Year	
Day/Year	
Day/Year	

August 19

The Eagle

A professor told his 8:00 am finance class the story of a farmer who found an abandoned eagle's nest and in it was an egg still warm. He took the egg back to his farm and laid it in the nest of one of his hens.

The egg hatched and the baby eagle grew up along with the other chickens. It pecked about the farmyard, scrabbling for grain. It spent its life within the yard and rarely looked up. When it was very old, one day it lifted up its head and saw above it a wonderful sight—an eagle soaring high above in the sky. Looking at it, the old creature sighed and said to itself, "If only I'd been born an eagle."

The professor scanned the 60 faces in the lecture hall. Despite the early hour, no one seemed to be asleep. Somehow, his story had touched them. Or maybe it wasn't the story at all. In fact, it had all started with a student's observation that the professor was cheerful. A wise man once said: "Who you are speaks louder to me than anything you can say." I suppose it must be so.

Challenge:

What does this mean to you? You get a pass on "it's empty and meaningless" so go ahead and project a meaning, interpretation and a story that speaks to you. However, answer this question, what are you pretending not to be able to do?

Tapping in Meditation:

My purpose today is to use the capacity and potential that I have to create the circumstances and events in my life. I create excellence in everything that I do. I live with abundance and joy.

Journal Notes:

Day/Year	
Day/Year	
Day/Year	
Day/Year	
Day/Year	

August 20

The Obstacle in Your Path

In ancient times, a King had a boulder placed on a roadway. Then he hid and watched to see if anyone would remove the huge rock. Some of the king's wealthiest merchants and courtiers came by and simply walked around it. Many loudly blamed the King for not keeping the roads clear, but none did anything about getting the stone out of the way.

Then a peasant came along carrying a load of vegetables. Upon approaching the boulder, the peasant laid down his burden and tried to move the stone to the side of the road. After much pushing and straining, he finally succeeded. After the peasant picked up his load of vegetables, he noticed a purse lying in the road where the boulder had been. The purse contained many gold coins and a note from the King indicating that the gold was for the person who removed the boulder from the roadway.

The peasant learned what many of us never understand! Every obstacle presents an opportunity to improve our condition. This is also an example of being rewarded for being of service. You can never give more than you've received.

Challenge:
I am only one but I am one. I will not let what I can't do get in the way of what I can do. I evaluate, plan, execute for 7 days, then repeat the process.

Tapping in Meditation:
My purpose today is to do what I can do, and then some. The only difference between opportunity and obstacle is my attitude. I see possibilities.

Journal Notes:

Day/Year	
Day/Year	
Day/Year	
Day/Year	
Day/Year	

August 21

Symptoms of Inner Peace

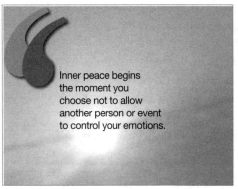

Inner peace begins the moment you choose not to allow another person or event to control your emotions.

Be on the lookout for symptoms of inner peace. The hearts of a great many have already been exposed to inner peace and it is possible that people everywhere could come down with it in epidemic proportions. This could put an end to the current world wide condition of conflict.

Some signs;

1. A tendency to think and act spontaneously rather than on fears based on past negative experiences.
2. An enjoyment of each present moment.
3. A loss of interest or need to judge others.
4. A loss of interest or need to judge yourself.
5. A loss of interest or need for drama or conflict.
6. A loss of the interest or need, or ability to worry.
7. Constant and overwhelming feelings of appreciation.
8. Feelings of connectedness with everything and everyone.
9. Frequent uncontrollable smiling.
10. An ease of living, frequently letting things happen rather than making them happen.

Challenge:

Smile often today. Being at peace doesn't mean being at a place where there are no bad deeds, words, noise, trouble or hard work. What it means is that in the midst of all of those things you remain with a calm heart.

Tapping in Meditation:

My purpose today is to seek the energy vibration of peace, love and abundance and I find it. I live it. I embrace it. All who come into contact with me today feel better because of it.

Journal Notes:

Day/Year	
Day/Year	
Day/Year	
Day/Year	
Day/Year	

August 22

Avoid Resistance, Resentment, Revenge by Letting Go

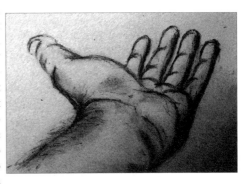

Letting go doesn't mean stop caring, it means that you can't do it for someone else. To let go is not to cut yourself off, it's the realization that you can't control another person. To let go is not to enable, but to allow learning from natural consequences. To let go is to admit powerlessness which means the outcome is not in your hands. To let go is to only change yourself, not others. To let go is not to care for but to care about. To let go is not to fix, but to be supportive, not to judge but to allow another to be a human being. To let go is not to be in the middle arranging outcomes but to allow others to direct their own futures. Letting go is allowing others to face their own reality and to not be attached to protecting them. To let go is not to nag, scold or argue, but to search for your own shortcomings and improve them. Letting go is not adjusting or compromising on your desires, but taking each day as it comes and cherishing the moment, each moment. To let go is not to regret the past but to grow and live for the future. To let go is to fear less and love more.

Challenge:

Let go of your resentments. Just for today let go of your pride and selfishness. Instead of punishing your enemies, which only hurts your own peace of mind, project them love and peace.

Tapping in Meditation:

My purpose today is to let go of my attachments. This allows my spirit to soar, to be free. I start the day with a light heart and a new confidence.

Journal Notes:

Day/Year	
Day/Year	
Day/Year	
Day/Year	
Day/Year	

August 23

7 Rules to Live By

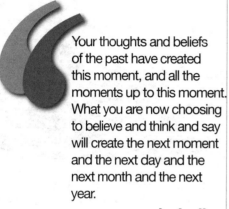

> Your thoughts and beliefs of the past have created this moment, and all the moments up to this moment. What you are now choosing to believe and think and say will create the next moment and the next day and the next month and the next year.
>
> **—Louise Hay**

1. Make peace with your past so it won't screw up the present.

2. What others think of you is none of your Business.

3. Time heals almost everything, give it time.

4. Don't compare your life to others and don't judge them. You have no idea what their journey is all about.

5. Stop thinking too much, it's alright not to know the answers. They will come to you when you least expect it.

6. No one is in charge of your happiness, except you.

7. Smile. You don't own all the problems in the world.

Challenge:

There is one thing that is always magical and if you concentrate on that it will work no matter what the problem is. It is to love yourself. You need to love yourself or you won't do the tools of this program.

Tapping in Meditation:

My purpose today is to accept myself with all of my flaws and to love myself. I love that I am committed to constant improvement. I love that I am committed to serving others. I love that I live on purpose even when I don't.

Journal Notes:

Day/Year	
Day/Year	
Day/Year	
Day/Year	
Day/Year	

August 24

Elite Performers—Persistence is More Important than Talent

This program is based on scientific principles and the best practices of elite performers. The top 2% of the performers share one thing in common, attitude. One aspect of this common trait is persistence and hard work. In 1927, the head instructor of a drama school told student Lucille Ball to "Try any other profession. Any other."

In 1935, Charles Darrow brought a board game to Parker Brothers. The experts at Parker Brothers rejected the game, Monopoly, for "containing 52 fundamental errors." A man of lesser convictions might have accepted the experts' condemnation as true. Not Charles. Instead he sold numerous editions of the board game himself. In 1936 he was approached by the then embarrassed Parker Brothers and the rest is history.

Wayne Dyer wrote his first book, "Your Erroneous Zones," in 1976. He felt so strongly about his book that after his publisher declined he decided to sell it himself. Dyer drove from New York to California, stopping at bookstores along the way and sleeping in his car. He also did as much media as he could. One night while doing a 2:00 am radio interview, one of the listeners was Johnny Carson. He booked Dyer on "The Tonight Show." Dyer has since sold more than 35 million copies.

In 1993 the authors of "Chicken Soup for the Soul" got their first of 140 rejections from publishers. If they would have believed the 140 publishers who were telling them that their idea had no merit and would not sell, then they would not have sold over 500 million of their expanded brand in 43 languages.

Few people had a more difficult time then Alexander Graham Bell. Even President Rutherford Hayes said of the telephone in 1876, "This might be a good thing between a captain of a ship and his crew but who else would want to use them?" These are all examples of ordinary people with extraordinary drive and persistence. If you want something bad enough you will keep on until you find a way. It may be the last key in the bunch that opens the lock.

Challenge:
Just for today pick one activity, pick a time, and keep persisting in that activity until either you reach that time limit or you get the result you want.

Tapping in Meditation:
My purpose today live persistence. I'll never know what's around the corner. It could be everything or it could be nothing. I'll keep putting one foot in front of the other, and then one day I'll look back and see I've climbed a mountain.

Journal Notes:

Day/Year	
Day/Year	
Day/Year	
Day/Year	
Day/Year	

August 25

Plan-Execute-Evaluate—Then Repeat

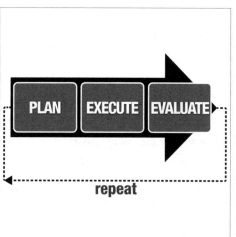

Walk back in time with me to 1979, my football coaching days at Cal State Fullerton. My day started with on Sunday with an 11:00 am staff meeting. That was followed by a defensive coaches' staff meeting from 8:00 am until about 9:30 am. During that time our staff looked at film and gave our athletes a grade for every play. Each athlete was held accountable for their responsibility on every single plan. As a staff we evaluated our team. Next we turned our attention to the upcoming opponent. We studied all of the game films that we had exchanged, charted all of their tendencies, including every offensive play that they ran. We had it categorized by down and distance, position on the field, you name it. It was all very detailed. This led to the development of our game plan and our weekly practice schedule. Then it was time to go home Sunday night, at 2:00 am. Actually Monday morning. I brought this work ethic and precise preparation mentality with me into business and now I bring it to you.

It's estimated that 95% of people can be compared to ships without a rudder, subject to every shift of the winds and tides, they are aimlessly adrift. And while they hope that they'll one day drift into a rich and successful port, you and I know that for every harbor there are thousands of miles of rocky coastline. The chances of their drifting into port are 1,000 to one. But the 5% that have taken the time to precisely plan, to decide on a destination and to chart a course sail straight through the oceans of life reaching one port after another.

Challenge:

Take a chunk of time, 7 days. Make a decision on what you want to accomplish, what you need to do, what you need to do over the next seven days, and what you will do today. Next get into a mindset of execution and do what you agree to do today. Repeat tomorrow.

Tapping in Meditation:

My purpose today is to plan and execute that plan. Without strategy execution is aimless. Without execution strategy is useless. I am precisely planned and I execute my plan.

Journal Notes:

Day/Year	
Day/Year	
Day/Year	
Day/Year	
Day/Year	

August 26

Avoid Isolation—Using All Your Strength

A young boy was walking with his father along a country road. When they came across a very large tree branch the boy asked, "Do you think I could move that branch?"

His father answered, "If you use all your strength, I'm sure you can."

So the boy tried mightily to lift, pull and push the branch but he couldn't move it. Discouraged he said, "Dad, you were wrong, I can't do it."

His father said, "Give it another try." This time as the boy struggled with the branch his father joined him and together they pushed the branch aside.

"Son," the father said, "The first time you didn't use all your strength. You didn't ask me to help."

There are 3 pillars for your personal excellence, personal, health and business results. One of the problems is a problem of isolation, going it alone. There are many things that you can't do alone. That doesn't mean that you can't get them done, you just need to ask for help. You are surrounded by resources that can be mobilized to help you to achieve your goals including family, friends, and faith. Sometimes you fail to ask for help because of pride or stubbornness. Sometimes you think it's a sign of weakness to admit you need a hand. Whatever the reason, it's a waste.

Challenge:
It is important that you learn to use all of your strength. This includes inner resources such as the discipline of a routine, courage and love. This also includes outside resources. Just as you would be willing to help others you need to be willing to ask others to help you. Today, ask for the help that you need.

Tapping in Meditation:
My purpose today is to tap into all of the energy and love that surrounds me. I ask for help when I need it. Equally as important as giving is receiving. I allow others to give to me. Asking for help is a sign of strength and I do ask for help.

Journal Notes:

Day/Year	
Day/Year	
Day/Year	
Day/Year	
Day/Year	

August 27

Woodsmen and Appreciation

Three woodsmen came upon an elderly man stumbling around in the forest. "Excuse me," he said. "I've lost my way. Can you point me in the direction of the road and give an old fellow a bit of water to drink?" The men obliged, and offered the old man water from their canteens, a bit of bread and some nuts. They escorted him through the woods to a well-worn path that would take him to the next city.

"I must repay this kindness you've shared with me," said the old man. "I was once a wizard and I still have the ability to grant each of you one wish. But choose carefully. The choice you make could greatly improve your life or make it worse.

The first man stepped forward. He was from a poor family and wished for wealth. In an instant, a horse and carriage appeared before him. Inside the carriage was a trunk of gold. The woodsman climbed aboard the carriage and off he went. But as he waved goodbye, the wizard sighed heavily. He could see into the future to a time when the woodsman would again be poor and unhappy.

The second man stepped toward the wizard. He was a homely guy who asked to be endowed with good looks. The wizard complied and the man suddenly appeared handsome and muscular. After feeling his improved biceps, angular jaw and smooth skin, the second woodsman thanked the wizard and headed off down the path. Again, the wizard sighed because he knew the day would come when the man would realize that there was more to life than having good looks.

The wizard looked at the third woodsman. He was poor and homely, yet he had just one simple wish. "So be it," said the wizard who finally smiled, because the last man wished to always be grateful for all that he had.

Challenge:
What are you paying attention to? You will always have circumstances, problems, challenges, mistakes and failures. Do you pay attention to how tough life is or do you pay attention to what you are grateful for? To have performance excellence you must have an attitude of appreciation. Today, notice what you have and be grateful.

Tapping in Meditation:
My purpose today is influence what I pay attention to. This directly correlated to my degree of success or lack of success. Being appreciative is an absolute necessity for life fulfillment and I am appreciative.

Journal Notes:

Day/Year	
Day/Year	
Day/Year	
Day/Year	
Day/Year	

August 28

Einstein Quotes to Live By

1. Intellectual growth should commence at birth and cease only at death. 2. Everyone should be respected as an individual, but no one idolized. 3. Never do anything against conscience even if the state demands it. 4. If people are good only because they fear punishment, and hope for reward, then we are a sorry lot indeed. 5. A perfection of means, and confusion of aims, seems to be our main problem. 6. Love is a better teacher than duty. 7. If you can't explain it simply, you don't understand it well enough. 8. No problem can be solved from the same level of consciousness that created it. 9. Insanity: doing the same thing over and over again and expecting different results. 10. Learn from yesterday, live for today, hope for tomorrow. 11. It has become appallingly obvious that our technology has exceeded our humanity. 12. Everything that can be counted does not necessarily count; everything that counts cannot necessarily be counted. 13. Force always attracts men of low morality. 14. Everything should be as simple as it is, but not simpler. 15. A man should look for what is, and not for what he thinks should be. 16. Any man who reads too much and uses his own brain too little falls into lazy habits of thinking. 17. A person who never made a mistake has never tried anything new. 18. It is the supreme art of the teacher to awaken joy in creative expression and knowledge. 19. Anyone who doesn't take truth seriously in small matters cannot be trusted in large ones either. 20. Great spirits have always encountered violent opposition from mediocre minds. 21. Education is what remains after one has forgotten what one has learned in school. 22. Logic will get you from A to B. Imagination will take you everywhere. 23. Anger dwells only in the bosom of fools. 24. Information is not knowledge. 25. Never lose a holy curiosity.

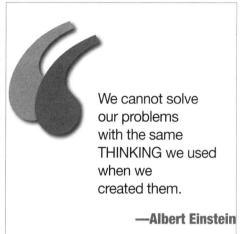

We cannot solve our problems with the same THINKING we used when we created them.

—**Albert Einstein**

Challenge:

Take one of these and focus on it today. See what comes into your awareness because you locked onto the thought. What action did you take?

Tapping in Meditation:

My purpose today is to focus and take action. I am divinely guided all day long. I am surrounded by love and abundance.

Journal Notes:

Day/Year	
Day/Year	
Day/Year	
Day/Year	
Day/Year	

August 29

The Last Days of Zach Sobiech

I want everyone to know,
you don't have to find out you're dying,
to start living.

—**Zach Sobiech**

When faced with months to live, how do you say goodbye? Zach Sobiech turned to music. His song called "Clouds" was born. Every teenager out there thinks that they are invincible, not like superman, but that they'll see you in 5 months. Zach thought he was invincible. He was planning for college. All that changed however when he was told that at 17 years old he had osteosarcoma, a cancer and only had a few months to live.

How did Zach respond to this news? With this statement, " I want everyone to know you don't have to find out you're dying to start living", wow!

Zach shares his thoughts publicly. He says that most people live in the middle between dying and fully living, it's a very comfortable place to live. He is living on two extreme ends where he has really good days and really bad days.

Zachs friends say that he is always looking for something good in people, that he believes in something greater than himself. They say you can be with Zach and just being with him, you feel better. Zach says what makes him happy is to see someone else smile because he put it there. That's what's awesome about living in this world so you can help people.

Zach is surrounded by so much love and it's not happening because he's dying, it's happening because of the way he's living. Zach's lesson to others is about doing what makes you happy and living life to the fullest every day. His philosophy at 17 years old is really very simple, try and make people happy and if you do this you're going to make the world a better place.

His mom says that's one of the blessings of cancer, everything means more, everything is more beautiful. Zach says that death is scary only because you don't know what's next or if there is a next, so it's kind of like sitting in the dark. So you can either be freaking out about the dark because you don't know what's out there or you can just relax and fall asleep and just be happy and content.

"I want to be remembered as a kid who went down fighting and didn't really lose."

On May 20, 2013, cancer took the life of Zach Sobiech but his legacy will live on through the beacon of love and his music.

Challenge:
Make someone else's day better because they were around you.

Tapping in Meditation:
My purpose today is to live this day to its fullest, to smell every smell, to see clearly every wonderful site of nature that surrounds me and to fully appreciate the abundance of life.

Journal Notes:

Day/Year	
Day/Year	
Day/Year	

August 30

Take Action Today

The best time to plant a tree was 20 years ago. The next best time is now! This Chinese Proverb hits the nail on the head. Don't wait another minute to get started on whatever it is you want to accomplish, today is the day to take action. The only thing that is stopping you is fear. Fear disguises itself as circumstances, excuses, reasons. You may be thinking that it's just not reasonable for you to think that you can do something.

Being reasonable is the lowest level of human consciousness. Embrace the fear and by doing it anyway you will see that the fear has no power to hold you back, it's just an illusion.

Jerry Rice, the famous receiver for the San Francisco 49'ers said, "Today I will do what everyone else won't so that tomorrow I can accomplish what everyone else can't."

Challenge:
What are you avoiding? What one action can you take today to create momentum? Take that action.

Tapping in Meditation:
My purpose today is to reduce everything that I want to do to an action that I can do, right now, today, and do it. I can't live my purpose by intentions, I must take actions and I do.

Journal Notes:

Day/Year	
Day/Year	
Day/Year	
Day/Year	
Day/Year	

August 31

Know Your POH in Making Decisions

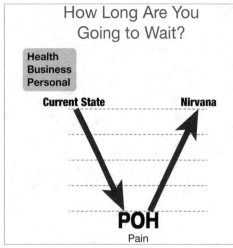

How Long Are You Going to Wait?

Health
Business
Personal

Current State — Nirvana

POH

Pain

I may be helpful to your perspective to project yourself to the worst case scenario if you don't change your habits, actions and current results. You can do this by asking the question, "What would happen if ....?" Then add, "What would that then do for you?"

What would happen if you don't lose weight? You will have less energy. What will having less energy do for you? You'll be less active in your business and spend less time with your children. What will being that, do for you? You will make less money and have poorer relationships with your family. What would making less money and having etc.? You can follow this road map along many different trails.

What would happen if you don't lose weight? You would have poor health, perhaps high blood pressure. What would having high blood pressure do for you? You would be less active and have to take medication. What would be the worst that could happen? You could die! Now you've reached the Point of Hell, or POH.

Next, dismiss that and take a look at the best that could happen. You lose your weight, you will be healthier, you will have better relationships, you will have more money, you will live longer and have peace of mind. Now you've reached Nirvana. Which one feels better?

This is a terrific decision making tactic. In the spring of 1983 I decided to quit college football coaching and start my own speaking and training business. Before I did that I asked the question, what's my POH? What is the worst that could happen? I could fail. Could I handle the worst case? Yes, there were several things that I could do and with my experience in football coaching I would actually be able to improve my position. Then I dismissed it and focused on the best case scenario and made that happen.

Challenge:

What decisions do you need to make? Apply POH and Nirvana today and then make a decision.

Tapping in Meditation:

My purpose today is to be decisive and I am. The world favors decisive people. When I can no longer change a situation, I change myself.

Journal Notes:

Day/Year	
Day/Year	
Day/Year	
Day/Year	
Day/Year	

SEPTEMBER

Davies Day Book

365 concepts for excellence

September 1

Signs of Unhealthy Boundaries

- Telling all.
- Talking at an intimate level on the first meeting.
- Falling in love with a new acquaintance.
- Falling in love with anyone who reaches out.
- Acting on your first sexual impulse.
- Going against your personal values to please others.
- Not noticing when someone invades your boundaries.
- Accepting food, gifts, touch that you don't want.
- Allowing someone to take as much as they can from you.
- Letting others direct your life. Letting others define your reality and define you.
- Believing others can read your mind and anticipate your needs.
- Falling apart so someone will take care of you.
- Self-abuse. Food abuse.

Challenge:

Just for today, if it feels wrong, don't do it. Say exactly what you mean and don't be a people pleaser. Trust your instincts. Don't speak bad about yourself. Never give up on your dreams. Don't be afraid to say No, or Yes. Be kind to yourself and others. Let go of what you can't control and avoid drama.

Tapping in Meditation:

My purpose today is to allow myself to set healthy boundaries. I say no to what does not align with my values and yes to what does. Boundaries help me to remain healthy, honest and living a life that is true to me and I do.

Journal Notes:

Day/Year	
Day/Year	
Day/Year	
Day/Year	
Day/Year	

September 2

That Someone is Me

Someone is lighting a candle for you today and holding you in the light of that flame.

Someone is feeling your pain today, your grief and your sorrow and transforming it into joy, serenity and love.

Someone is thinking kindly of you today in their own heart and soul.

Someone is understanding you today, the depths of what you have been going through and is embracing you with deep love and trusting that your own higher sense of self will pull you through your tough times.

Someone is holding your hand today and letting you know that you have a community, you are not alone. Even when you feel isolated, you are not alone.

Someone knows that there is a great meaning and strong purpose for your life.

Someone is whispering to your soul today and praying for you. We are all celebrating that you haven't given up.

Challenge:
Every thought creates form and all of your physical experience is a mirror of your thoughts. Just for today all of your thoughts are loving, positive, possibility thoughts. You just can't help it. Your mind is flooded with one positive thought after another.

Tapping in Meditation:
My purpose today is to feel the love in the universe. Feel that there is a power greater than myself that guides me to peace and serenity. I listen for the words and images, the clues for my solutions and I receive them.

Journal Notes:

Day/Year	
Day/Year	
Day/Year	
Day/Year	
Day/Year	

September 3

It's the Size of the Fight in the under Dog

Inspiration comes from a lot of different places, but one thing that can always sweep us from under our feet is a great sports underdog. Whether it is a single person or a team, it is these underdogs that shape the world of sports one at a time.

The idea of an underdog is quite possibly the biggest oxymoron there can be, as we aspire to see these things succeed, things that were nothing to begin with. Still, these nobodies have somehow made their way to become somebodies.

A normal resident at the No. 1 spot on many upset and underdog lists, the 1980 men's USA Olympic hockey team, otherwise known as "The Miracle on Ice" still owns a top spot. Going into a round robin game against the Soviet Union in the tournament, many had them pegged as dead men walking. The USA played some great hockey up until this point—despite having a team made up of amateurs and college stars. The Soviets on the other hand were made up of players with a rich history playing together, and their synergy looked to be the toughest thing to defeat. That of course led to the famous Al Michael's line "Do you believe in miracles? Yes!"

The team went on to defeat the Finland 4-2 in their final match, after being down 1-2 in the third period. The Americans, who were not anywhere close to favorites, took Lake Placid by storm and showed that underdogs can never be dismissed.

Challenge:

Where in your life are you an underdog? Where can you exceed the expectations of others, even your own expectations? Do something positive that is out of character today. Today accomplish one small task that even you don't believe you can do.

Tapping in Meditation:

My purpose today is to be bold and erase limitations and I do. I tap into all of my God-given talent and ability today and make something extra ordinary occur.

Journal Notes:

Day/Year	
Day/Year	
Day/Year	
Day/Year	
Day/Year	

September 4

Don't Sweat the Small Stuff and It's All Small Stuff

When you let go of your expectations, when you accept life as it is, you're free. To hold on is to be serious and uptight. To let go is to lighten up. True happiness comes not when you get rid of all of your problems, but when you change your relationship to them, when you see your problems as a potential source of awakening, opportunities to practice, and to learn.

There is a fundamental state that you have when you are in despair, it is that feeling of being powerless. What is at the root of this feeling of powerless? The feeling of being powerless has nothing to do with what the circumstances are. Something happens that you don't like. You are not looking at the thing at the moment, you are looking at the story you have made up about it, what's being taken away from you. What you see is not what is there, but what you see is what you don't want to be there. You don't see what happened, instead you see what you think should have happened, how you think it should have happened. You sit trying to push away the imagined loss of something you imagined you had. You are locked into a negative state in a mind resisting its own image of what should be. No change can occur here. So you try to change the world outside of yourself. Who do you know that has ever changed their life for the better by being bitter about the way things went? What kind of power is in not wanting the moment that you're in? All negative states are a waste.

Real power is to be able to choose in the moment as the moment requires and what serves the good of all. Real power would be in the moment of challenge or trial to be able to remain in relationship with kindness. Real power would be to not fall into a troubled set of thoughts and feelings, but rather understand that everything that comes to you is for the good. There is no power outside of you.

It's not in your power to control outcomes, or change people or to change whatever has just happened no matter what it is. You have but only one power and that is to decide what you want to be in relationship with in every moment. You need to place yourself in relationship to what is real. You have a choice to do with your attention what you want to do with it.

Challenge:
Just for today decide that no matter what happens you will remain connected to a perception and orientation of kindness.

Tapping in Meditation:
My purpose today is to be kind to all people and I am. Kindness is the language that the deaf can hear and the blind can see.

Journal Notes:

Day/Year	
Day/Year	
Day/Year	

September 5

Self Control and Commitments

Delayed Gratification and Commitment

Green → 1 immediately

Red — No tempation button

Purple → 10 with 10 second delay

Have you procrastinated this week? You are genetically coded to take action in the present rather than delay to the future, even if the delay would be better for you.

We over-focus on the present and sacrifice the future. The impulse overcomes us. Which would you rather have a ½ box of chocolates now or a full box in 1 week? Just about everyone who likes chocolates will take the ½ box now. When both choices were in the future however, a half of box of chocolate in one year, or an entire box in a year and one week, everyone waited the extra week for the full box. You are not designed to care about delayed rewards.

You know you will be tempted. If only you could do something to eliminate the temptation. You can! Ainslie & Herrnstein in 1974 did an experiment with rats and pigeons. When a green button was lit and pressed they received 1 immediate food pellet. If a purple button was lit and pressed they received 10 pellets after a 10 second delay. However, if the animal pressed the purple button and then while waiting the green button came on, they couldn't wait and they pressed the green button for the immediate pellet. That stopped the delayed response of 10 pellets.

However, if a red button lit and they pressed it that would stop the green "temptation" button from being lit and they would continue for the ten seconds and receive the 10 pellets. Do you think that they learned to inhibit the temptation by pressing the red button? YES they did!

An alarm clock is connected to your bank account and to a charity you hate, Snuznluz. Every second you snooze money goes to a charity you hate. Another alarm clock is loaded with $100 bills. You have 3 seconds to get up before it starts to shred the bills.

Challenge:

Today have an intervention to remove the temptation to delay by identifying one behavior that you will not delay and place a $100 fine if you do. Be specific.

Tapping in Meditation:

My purpose today is to think action, to think I am a doer. Every feeling and action is preceded by a thought. I have action thoughts all day long

Journal Notes:

Day/Year	
Day/Year	
Day/Year	

September 6

Early Morning Perspectives for Today—Count Your Blessings

If you could shrink the earth's population to a village of precisely 100 people, with all the existing human ratios remaining the same, it would look something like the following. There would be

57 Asians, 21 Europeans, 14 from the Western Hemisphere, both north and south, 8 would be Africans, 52 would be female, 48 would be male, 70 would be non-white, 70 would be non-Christian, 30 would be Christian, 89 would be heterosexual, 11 would be homosexual, 6 people would possess 59% of the entire world's wealth and all 6 would be from the United States, 80 would live in substandard housing, 70 would be unable to read, 50 would suffer from malnutrition, 1 would be near death, 1 would be near birth, 1 (yes, only 1) would have a college education and 1 would own a computer.

When one considers our world from such a compressed perspective, the need for acceptance, understanding and education becomes glaringly apparent. Therefore, if you have food in the refrigerator, clothes on your back, a roof overhead and a place to sleep, you are richer than 75% of this world.

If you have money in the bank, in your wallet, you are among the top 8% of the world's wealthy. If you woke up this morning with more wealth then illness then you are more blessed than the million who will not survive this week. If you have never experienced the danger of battle, the loneliness of imprisonment, the agony of torture or the pangs of starvation then you are ahead of the 500 million people in the world who have.

If you can attend a church meeting without the fear of harassment, arrest, torture or death then you are more blessed than 3 billion people in the world.

Challenge:
Hold your head up with a smile on your face and be truly thankful for all that you have and the freedom to pursue opportunities to improve.

Tapping in Meditation:
My purpose today is to be conscious of my blessings.

Journal Notes:

Day/Year	
Day/Year	
Day/Year	
Day/Year	
Day/Year	

September 7

Find the Fountain of Youth

There are two types of age, chronological and real. You can't do anything about how many birthdays you've had but you can certainly impact your real age, your physical and mental age. Here's how:

1. Stay or get active. Get aerobic exercise, strength training and stretching.
2. Lose weight. Studies show that being overweight or obese reduces your disability-free years.
3. Challenge your mind. Read good books or do puzzles. Even though the brain isn't a muscle, it will deteriorate if you don't use it vigorously. Be a reader. With the discovery of brain plasticity it has been learned that the brain can continue to grow new neurons throughout life in reaction to new learning.
4. Be social. A network of friends offers you support and gets you out of the house. If you don't have close friends, consider joining a church or book group, or volunteer your time at a place that needs hands on help.
5. Find your passion. You must be constantly growing and improving and living with energy. You are either growing or decaying, there is no middle ground.
6. Keep a positive attitude. Don't assume that you're going to get frail and feeble. Instead, look for opportunities to improve your strength and health.
7. Practice good health while you're still healthy.
8. Get at least 6 hours sleep.
9. Stay on our food plan.
10. Find a way to be of service to others. It is one of the most interesting relationships that no person can give more than they receive.

Challenge:

What do you think the difference is between your physiological age and your chronological age? Older, younger? Today examine your lifestyle and make sure that it is an asset, not a liability. If you find habits that you need to change make that commitment today.

Tapping in Meditation:

My purpose today is to learn from yesterday, hope for tomorrow and live for today and I do.

Journal Notes:

Day/Year	
Day/Year	
Day/Year	
Day/Year	
Day/Year	

September 8

Eating Less Keeps the Body Young at Heart

Your food plan does not count calories. Your food plan is not the elimination of fat either. It's simply the elimination of all forms of flour and sugar. You will find however that following your food plan results in a lower caloric consumption than you had prior to participating. A low calorie diet can help the heart age more slowly, according to researchers who released what they call the first ever human study on the subject. The findings confirmed earlier studies on mice and rats that demonstrate the cardiac benefits of restricted calories.

The study looked at the heart function of members of the caloric Restriction Society, ages 41 to 64, who consume 1,400 to 2,000 nutritionally balanced calories per day. They were compared to people who eat a typical Western diet, consuming 2,000 to 3,000 daily calories on average. Those limiting calorie intake had the heart functions of much younger people—typically about 15 years younger than their age. Ultrasound exams showed group members had hearts that appeared more elastic than those of most people their age; their hearts were also able to relax between beats in a way similar to younger people.

"This is the first study to show that long term calorie restriction with optimal nutrition has cardiac specific effects that delay or reverse age associated declines in heart function," said Luigi Fontana, lead author and assistant professor of medicine at Washington University in St. Louis. Simply consuming less food is not the answer, Fontana said. Members of the study eat food resembling your food plan, nutrient dense cruciferous vegetables, olive oil, beans, meat, fruit, whole grains. They also avoided four and sugar. Research on mice and rats indicated that life span could be stretched by about 30% with stringent and consistent calorie restriction.

Challenge:
40% of Americans are completely sedentary in their leisure time, according to a government survey. Remember, your program uses exercise for fitness and the meal plan for weight control. You don't need to worry about calories, just weigh and measure. For today, continue to use your tools. Meditate in the morning, weigh and measure 3 meals, read one page a day from this book, attend your calls. KOKO (keep on keeping on).

Tapping in Meditation:
My purpose today is to notice the serenity that I have by using the tools of this program. I notice the self-improvement in all areas of my life.

Journal Notes:

Day/Year	
Day/Year	
Day/Year	
Day/Year	
Day/Year	

September 9
Twenty Five Thoughts that are Perfect for September 9th

1. If the wind does not serve, take to the oars.
2. You can't fall if you don't climb. But there is no joy in living your life on the ground.
3. Too many are not living their dreams because they are living their fears.
4. Challenges are what makes life interesting and overcoming them is what makes life meaningful.
5. The way to get started is to quit talking and start doing. Walt Disney.
6. Limitations live only in your mind. If you use your imagination your possibilities become limitless.
7. What's money? You are a success if you wake up in the morning and go to bed at night and in between do what you want to do.
8. In order to succeed, your desire for success must be greater than your fear of failure.
9. A person who never made a mistake never tried anything new. Albert Einstein.
10. The person who says it cannot be done should not interrupt the person who is doing it. Chinese Proverb.
11. There are no traffic jams on the extra mile. Roger Staubach.
12. You become what you believe. Oprah Winfrey.
13. Its not what you do for your children but what you have taught them to do for themselves that will make them successful human beings.
14. Education cost money. But then so does ignorance.
15. Remember that the happiest people are not those getting more, but giving more.
16. It doesn't matter how slowly you go as long as you do not stop.
17. Let the refining and improving of your own life keep you so busy that you have little time to criticize others.
18. You can't use up creativity. The more you use the more you have. Maya Angelou.
19. Our lives begin to end the day we become silent about things that matter.
20. It's your place in the world. It's your life. Go out and do all you can with it and make it the life you want to live.
21. Remember no one can make you feel inferior without your consent. Eleanor Roosevelt.
22. Change your thoughts and you change your world. Norman Vincent Peale.
23. The question isn't who is going to let me, it's who's going to stop me?
24. When everything seems to be going against you remember that the airplane takes off against the wind.
25. Life is what you make it, always has been, always will be.

Challenge:

The airplane goes through the turbulence in the clouds before breaking out on top into beautiful, clear and smooth air. Let these 25 thoughts be with you during your meditation today.

Tapping in Meditation:

My purpose today is to listen to my inner wisdom.

Journal Notes:

Day/Year	
Day/Year	
Day/Year	

September 10

Society Says There are Winners and Losers

Imagine that you are sitting across from someone about your same size. You lock your right hands together getting ready in the arm wrestling position. I explain that the object of the game is to get the back of your partners hand on the table as many times as possible in 30 seconds. Ready, set go!

I then ask the room how many times they were able to put the back of their partners hand on the table. I am careful not to use the word opponent. I usually hear 1, 0, 2, 3, 4, 2, 1 and then occasionally I'll hear 35. When I hear a number like that I know that they approached this not from a zero sum, win or lose perspective, but rather from a collaborative venture. There was no resistance. They simply went back and forth placing each other's hand on the table, back and forth, on and on until time was called.

Nowhere did I say that this was a win or lose structure. Economic development is not a zero sum game. The world does not need poor countries in order to have rich ones. We live in a world of abundance. Did you "get it?"

An extraordinary teacher, Annie Sullivan, had just come into a little girl's life She was teaching Helen Keller, who had up to this point been deemed unreachable. For months Sullivan had been spelling out the names of familiar objects into Helen's hand. Over and over again. Helen had not made the connection between finger spelling and the name of the object.

Finally there was a miraculous moment when Annie grasps Helen's 7 year old hand and puts it under the pump and spells out W-A-T-E-R. But this time Helen gets it. She makes the connection. She understands. This spells water and this is what it feels like. The mystery of language was revealed to her. At this point Helen Keller's intellect had a higher ground then her instincts, she finally "got it!"

Challenge:

Do you "get it?" Do you get the purpose of this program, the weighing and measuring of everything, the tools, the reading, the calls, the meditating, the service to others mindset, the unlimited faith? If you get it, today do one thing that helps someone else "get it."

Tapping in Meditation:

My purpose today is to get better day by day and I do. I am a magnet attracting everything I need to me for my own abundance. This allows me to be of service to others and I am of service to others.

Journal Notes:

Day/Year	
Day/Year	
Day/Year	
Day/Year	
Day/Year	

September 11

Promittere

Promittere is Latin for a word for promise. Alex Sheen lost his father to stage 4 lung cancer. One thing he remembered so well about his father is that he always did what he said he would do. So to honor his father he put up a Facebook page called "Because I said I would" and he promised to send out cards with that title printed on them. He sent those cards to over 150,000 to 48 countries around the world since September 2012.

What is it about a promise? It is elemental to humanity. What is it about writing down your promises that is so special? A clinical psychologist, Dr. Gail Mathews, did a study on written promises. She had one group that simply stated their promises and another group that wrote them down. Goal attainment rates increased 42% for the group with the written promises.

Alex received this letter; "Hi Alex. I've been keeping up with your blog 'Because I said I would' has really really helped me through a rough patch. There have been lots of times where I didn't think life was worth living and I almost took my life, almost. I am getting stronger everyday and a lot of that strength comes from a few promise cards I have written. I have lots of people who care about me. I am a very lucky person. It took a lot for me to realize that I should be alive. I'm not sure I would even be around if it wasn't for your organization. I DO have a purpose. So, thanks Mr. Sheen. I want to promise YOU that I will not give up."

On August 9th, 2013, a message was sent to him from a man named Matthew who made a bad decision. He got drunk, decided to drive anyway and at 3 am caused an accident resulting in a fatality. He has now made a promise to be on a crusade to persuade people not to drink and drive. Matthew decided to make a confession video. He knew the consequences. He released the video to Youtube and in 10 days it received over 2 million views across the world. Seven days later Matthew was arrested and sentenced to prison. He kept his promise, a promise to take responsibility for what he's done and to live a life of discouraging people from the senseless act of drinking and driving.

Is it the card that gives you strength to move on and do what's right or was that strength always in you? Alex has a quote that he thinks about every day, "You can pretend to care but you can't pretend to show up."

Challenge:
What does it mean to you to give your word? That is the core of this program. Do you do that casually? Do you allow yourself to negotiate out of your word and justify doing so? Today, make one promise that you will keep no matter what

Tapping in Meditation:
My purpose today is to live with integrity and I do. I do what I say I will do. Other people know that they can count on me. I live my word no matter what.

Journal Notes:

Day/Year	
Day/Year	
Day/Year	

September 12

Assumptions—The Cookie Thief

The Cookie Thief is a story by Valerie Cox. There are only two characters, a man and a lady. Put yourself in the situation. Be mindful, think about the situation and what you would do.

A woman was waiting at an airport one night several hours before her flight. She hunted for a book in the airport shop and brought a bag of cookies and found a place to drop.

She was engrossed in her book and happened to see that the man beside her as bold as could be, took a cookie or two from the bag in between which she tried to ignore to avoid a scene.

She read, munched cookies and watched the clock, as the gutsy cookie thief diminished her stock. She was getting more irritated as the minutes ticked by, thinking if I wasn't so nice I'd blacken his eye.

With each cookie she took, he took one too. When only one was left she wondered what he would do. With a smile on his face and a nervous laugh, he took the last cookie and he broke it in half. He offered her half as he ate the other. She grabbed the cookie and thought oh brother, this guy has some nerve and he's also so rude as he didn't even show any gratitude.

She never knew when she'd been so galled. She sighed with relief when her flight was called. She gathered her belongings and headed for the gate refusing to look back at the thieving ingrate.

She boarded the plane and sat in her seat, and then she sought her book which was almost complete. As she reached in her baggage she gasps with surprise, there was her bag of cookies in front of her eyes. If mine are here, she moaned in despair, then the others were his and he tried to share. Too late to apologize she realized with grief, that she was the rude one, the ingrate, the thief.

Challenge:
Where are you like the lady in your life? What assumptions do you make? Today take two steps. First, be aware of your assumptions. Second, challenge them. You have to guard against knowing that something is your true reality and having that as your internal world and not being open to other possibilities.

Tapping in Meditation:
My purpose today is to look at all things from multiple points of views. I see the world as being full of possibilities.

Journal Notes:

Day/Year	
Day/Year	
Day/Year	
Day/Year	
Day/Year	

September 13
From Homeless to Harvard Grad with the Serenity Prayer

God grant me the

Serenity to accept the things I cannot change

Courage to change the things I can and

Wisdom to know the difference.

Harvard grad and former homeless teen, author Liz Murray, reveals how the serenity prayer helped her through her toughest times. When she was 11 years old, her mother tried to sell her sisters coat to a drug dealer. She used to sell things around the house to get high. That night the drug dealer took some moral ground and saw that it was a child's coat and said I'm not buying that from you and he gave her a Narcotics Anonymous coin. On the back of the coin it had the serenity prayer, "God grant me the serenity to accept the things I cannot change, the courage to change the things I can, and the wisdom to know the difference.

Her mother came home frustrated that she couldn't get the coke and just slammed the coin down. Liz took that coin, not really knowing what those words meant. But there was something about the mystery and beauty of the coin and her mothers' connection to it that made her keep it. For years whenever she wanted to feel comforted she would hold this coin and rub it. When she was homeless she had that coin with her and she used to always read that prayer. She reflects;

"I remember being in this storm of a lifestyle. My mom had just died. I'm a high school dropout and chaos is around me. I'm sleeping on the streets and I have this coin.

I learned to separate the things I could and could not control. I could not bring my mother back and I loved her very much. I couldn't change the fact that my father was sleeping in a shelter and I was sleeping on the street. But if I could just pick the things that I had some control over and give the rest to something higher than myself, let it go, surrender to it, focus on what I could control, and for me that was education. I could show up at school every day. I could get there early and stay late. I could get not only a B but I could get an A. Being able to identify that in the eye of a storm you can't control so much of what happens, pick something. I love John Woodens' quote, don't let what you cannot do interfere with what you can do. If you try to control all of it all at once you'll give up. But if you identify the thing that you can do and you stick to that then by the grace of whatever else is around you and bigger than you in this world you'll see your life begin to take a different shape.

Challenge:
From a scientific perspective you do not have the capacity to understand the true reality. You are limited by your senses and time and space dimensions and you must rely on faith and believing what you cannot see. Have faith that the tools of this program will assist you in creating the best possible version of yourself and will lead you to performance excellence.

Tapping in Meditation:
Today accept the things you cannot change, change the things you can and have the wisdom to know the difference. Pick on thing to focus on and take action.

Journal Notes:

Day/Year	
Day/Year	
Day/Year	

September 14

You are Already Awesome Just Get Out of Your Own Way

Steve Mariucci and I coached together at Cal State Fullerton. The other day he was telling me how an athlete he coached, Brett Farve, was able to block out his sense of pain, the noise of the crowd and slow down the speed of the game and "know" the unplanned adjusted routes of the receivers during the critical moments of the big games. This was flow. Flow is a mental state when a person is fully immersed in the present in a feeling of energized focus.

GET OUT of YOUR OWN WAY

You have been in flow at some point in your life, maybe when playing sports, listening to music or even getting fully immersed in a project. If this is so great why don't you do this all the time? The answer, you get in your own way. Here's an example. Remember Lolo Jones? An American hurdler favored to win the 2008 Beijing Olympics. She was in the lead, in an amazing rhythm and at some point she knew she was winning the race. Then she started telling herself to make sure her legs were snapping out so she over tried. That's when she hit a hurdle. She finished 7th. Instead of letting herself do what she was trained to do she got in her own way. It wasn't that she was thinking, it was that she got caught up in her thinking. A Harvard study found that 50% of the time we get caught up in regretting things from the past or worrying about what we're going to do in the future. What about cravings and addictions? People get in their own way by getting caught up in resisting their own cravings. Flow is just being with all of this stuff.

Yale University researchers taught smokers mindfulness, how to just be with their cravings. The first thing that they learned was that these were just body sensations that were driving their lives. The next thing they learned is they could let these things come up, do their dance and go away. They didn't have to get hooked by them and resist them and they quit smoking. They brought in meditators to see what see what's going on in the brain when they meditate. An area of the brain called the Posterior Cingulate Cortex gets activated when you are anxious, when you're craving and getting in your own way, quiets down during meditation. There was a dramatic change in the feeling of the physical sensation of the feeling versus the thinking of the breath for a volunteer, that's flow. If you can track it, you can train it.

Challenge:

Pay attention to noticing thoughts versus resisting thoughts. Practice just being with sensations. Practice doesn't make perfect, perfect practice makes perfect. When you get out of your way you are happier and more engaged.

Tapping in Meditation:

My purpose today is to flow with whatever may happen today and let my mind be free. I stay centered by accepting whatever I am doing. This is the ultimate.

Journal Notes:

Day/Year	
Day/Year	
Day/Year	

September 15

Give it Up for the Down Side—Take a Nap

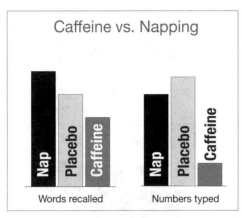

Caffeine vs. Napping

Nap Placebo Caffeine — Words recalled

Nap Placebo Caffeine — Numbers typed

We need to rest and we need to take more breaks. It's part of being productive. The earth is spinning on its axis, day and night—every plant and animal uses this cycle. Science shows us that sleep is very important for restoring our basic functions and they know this by looking at people who aren't sleeping. They have messed up metabolism; their insulin regulation is messed up. This makes you reach for more high fat, high sugar foods, and gain weight more quickly, even with just 5 nights of sleeping just 5 hours per night you start looking like you're pre-diabetic. So when we think about the epidemic of obesity and diabetes in this country we should also be thinking about how people sleep.

Along with these problems with metabolism, not sleeping enough also creates larger risks for cardiovascular diseases, depression and impaired cognition. Research shows that a nap during the day created a significant increases in memory, creativity and performance.. During waking on a moment to moment basis you need to interact with the world. When you sleep you go internal. You start to repair tissue, you promote growth. You start to protect and consolidate new memories into long term memory. Looking over a 7 day week, there is deterioration of performance over that time. We are not naturally supposed to be working this much. So what do we do to disregard the internal signals and keep ourselves to the grindstone? We self-medicate. 90% of North Americans drink caffeine on a daily basis. 75% of college kids say that they use Adderall.

A study was done by Dr. Sara Mednick at Cal State Riverside to compare the benefits of a nap to caffeine. Two types of tasks were tested, one was a vocabulary memory test and the other was a motor task where the subjects had to type a sequence of numbers with their non-dominant hand. The test is administered in the morning and then the subjects are split into 3 groups, they get either a nap, a dose of caffeine, or a placebo, which is no drug. Then in the evening they get retested. In each test caffeine did not perform as well as either the nap or the placebo in increasing performance.

Challenge:

Somewhere during the day and week you need a break. If you have to ability to take a 10-20 minute nap every day that would be one option. Another idea would be to take every Wednesday afternoon off. This is already happening all over the world. The average work week in France is down to 30 hours, in the Netherlands it's down to 25. Other than naps, switching activities and taking breaks also is beneficial. Americans get an average of 2 weeks' vacation per year. Europeans get 5 to 6 weeks. Today, decide what you can do on a daily/weekly basis for a break and do it.

Tapping in Meditation:

My purpose today is to nourish my soul by getting the proper rest and nutrition and I do. I take care of myself first so I can be of service to others

Journal Notes:

Day/Year	
Day/Year	
Day/Year	

September 16

The Secret to Happiness—4 Things

There have been 100s of studies about happiness. Americans when asked say that 31% are very happy, 56% pretty happy, 13% not so happy. That's not the most interesting question. That question is what brings happiness?

There are 3 things that cause happiness, genetics, big life events and choices. A few years ago social scientists from the Univ. of Min. constructed a data base that included 75 pairs of identical twins born between the mid 1930s and mid 1950s. They were separated at birth and adopted to separate families. At age 40 they were reunited and given a personality test. They found that 48% of their happiness was genetic. An important part of the 52% left is gender. Women are happier than men. The unhappiest age average for a man is 45.

Big life events. If you can only reach your goals you'll be happy. It's 40% of happiness. Unfortunately the big things never last. The big house only impacts you for 6 months. In 1978 quadriplegics were compared to people winning the lottery. Quads, 6 months after their accident reported their happiness had returned to almost their previous level. Lottery winners, 6 months the average winner is less happy than the day they won. Little things don't make them happy anymore. Hobbies are lost, friendships don't bring joy. The key is to develop the right habits. The last 12% left is under your control. If you do what you need to max out the 12% you'll also raise the 40%. There are 4 things:

1. Faith—not necessarily religious but something larger than yourself.
2. Family
3. Community—being charitable
4. Work—What % of Americans love their work? 89% are satisfied or completely satisfied with their jobs. It's the belief that you are creating value in your life and the lives of others, called earned success.

Challenge:
You have under your control the ability to give you the most happiness possible. Today pay attention to faith, family, community and work. You have the moral right to be happy and to work for happiness and to earn your success.

Tapping in Meditation:
My purpose today is to be happy by owning my own sunshine. I don't get happiness by getting something I don't have, but by recognizing and appreciating what I do have.

Journal Notes:

Day/Year	
Day/Year	
Day/Year	
Day/Year	
Day/Year	

September 17

The 12 Steps

When asked what surprised him most about humanity he answered, "Man, because he sacrifices his health in order to make money. Then he sacrifices money to recuperate his health. Then he is so anxious about the future that he does not enjoy the present; the result being that he does not live in the present or the future; he lives as if he is never going to die, and then dies having never really lived."

The 12 steps is an alcoholic recovery program that has been adapted to a variety of addiction recovery programs from food addictions to gambling to sexual and more. All of these programs have this in common; they have both psychological and physiological components.

The promise of these programs is that abstaining from the offending substance plus ongoing personal growth and development will produce and sustain the desired results. "If we are painstaking about this phase of our development we will be amazed before we are half way through. We are going to know a new freedom and a new happiness. We will not regret the past nor wish to shut the door on it. We will comprehend the word serenity and we will know peace. No matter how far down the scale we have gone we will see how our experience can benefit others. The feeling of uselessness and self-pity will disappear. We will lose interest in selfish things and gain interest in our fellows. Self-seeking will slip away. Our whole attitude and outlook upon life will change. Fear of people and economic insecurity will leave us. We will intuitively know how to handle situations which used to baffle us. We will suddenly realize that God is doing for us what we could not do for ourselves." By Bill Wilson, founder AA.

The twelve steps are:

1. I can't	5. Admit wrongs	9. Make amends
2. God can (good orderly design)	6. Ready self for change	10. Daily inventory
3. Let God	7. Seek God's help	11. Pray and meditate
4. Look within	8. Become willing	12. Give it away

Challenge:

Your participation in this program is out of a desire to reeducate your mind and think differently. It is not your circumstances that need altering so much as yourself. Take inventory of your faults and weaknesses and take one action to improve today.

Tapping in Meditation:

My purpose today is to design the better version of myself and live into that version and I do. I am a spiritual and mental magnet attracting all things which are good, bless and prosper me. I am good, blessed and prosperous.

Journal Notes:

Day/Year	
Day/Year	
Day/Year	

September 18

Is Stress Good or Bad?

A study tracked 30,000 adults in the US for 8 years. They were asked how much stress they experienced. They also asked do you believe that stress is harmful for your health. The experimenters then tracked deaths. People who experienced a lot of stress in the previous year had a 43% increased risk of dying. But that was only true for the people who also believed that stress is harmful for their health. People who experienced a lot of stress but viewed stress as healthy had the lowest chance of dying. Can changing how you think about stress make you healthier? Here the science says yes. When you change your mind about stress you can change your body's response to stress.

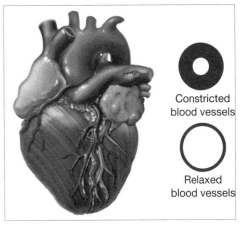

Constricted
blood vessels

Relaxed
blood vessels

In a Harvard study when subjects were trained to view their stress response as healthy their blood vessels rather than constricting under stress, remained open and relaxed. This is a much healthier response. In a life time of stress induced responses this one response could be the difference between a stress induced heart attack in your 50s and living well into your 90s. The new science reveals that how you think about stress matters.

The next time your heart is pounding with stress think to yourself, this is my body helping me rise to this challenge. My increased heart rate is bringing more blood to my brain for greater clarity. When you view stress in that way your body believes you.

An under appreciated result of stress is that stress makes your social. To understand this we need to talk about a hormone, oxytocin. It even has its own nick name, the cuddle hormone because it's released when you hug someone. This hormone makes you crave physical contact with your family, it increases empathy, it evens makes you more helpful and supportive. Under stress your pituitary gland pumps this out. It's as much a part of your stress response as the adrenalin that makes your heart pound. When oxytocin is released in the stress response it is motivating you to seek support. Your biological response is nudging your to tell someone how you feel instead of bottling it up and isolating. Oxytocin is also a natural anti-inflammatory; it helps your blood vessels stay relaxed. Your heart has receptors for this hormone. Oxytocin helps heart cells regenerate and heal from any stress induced damage. You can trust yourself to handle life challenges and you don't have to face them alone.

Challenge:
Reaching out to others in service and community is a evolutionary survival response. The opposite of this is isolation. Today, look to see if you can volunteer you time talent and resources to help another person or cause.

Tapping in Meditation:
My purpose today is to reach out to others. I include others in my life. I am outgoing. I nurture all of my relationships.

Journal Notes:

Day/Year	
Day/Year	
Day/Year	

September 19

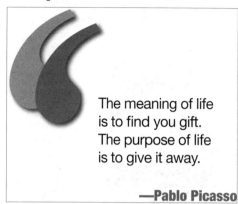

The meaning of life is to find you gift. The purpose of life is to give it away.

—Pablo Picasso

Your Life Purpose

A recent class reunion at Yale revealed that 80% of the attendees were not happy with the way their lives turned out. They had good jobs, power and money but were not fulfilled. The 20% who were, knew the answer to these 5 questions; who they were, what they did, who they did it for, what those people wanted and needed, and what they got out of it as a result. Amazon lists 151,928 books that refer to how you can learn your life purpose. Some people spend their entire life trying to learn their life purpose. We can all agree that the unexamined life is not worth living but if all you're doing is examining your life you're not living. Let's figure out your life's purpose.

Challenge:

- **Step one:** Who are you, right now, write your name now in this space: great, done with step one.
- **Step two:** What do you love to do? Do you love to write, cook, design, write code, crunch numbers, talk, teach, what do you love to do? And if there are a lot of things that come up for you focus it down by asking yourself this one question, what is the one thing that right now you feel supremely qualified to teach other people? Put it into one word and write it down here now.
- **Step three:** Think about who you do it for. Picture them in your mind. Now write who you do it for right here.
- **Step four:** What do those people want or need that they have come to you so you can give them this thing? In just one or two words write it down now.
- **Step five:** This is the best one. How do they change or transform as a result of what you give them? Write it down now.

Now put it together in one sentence, who are you_____, what do you do_____, who do you do it for _____what do they need _____how do they change as a result _____ _____. This is your life purpose. Only two of these are about yourself. The other 3 are about other people. This forces you to be outward oriented, to focus on whom you serve, what others think and how others change as a result of your service. Happier people make it a point to make other people happy and to have an outward orientation on how they can serve and benefit others, not themselves. When someone asks you what you do, just say the very last thing you just developed, how what you do changes the people you do it for. For example, "I give kids awesome dreams" if you're life purpose is "I write books for children so they can fall asleep at night so they can have awesome dreams." That becomes your personal elevator pitch. That will always start the conversation, "How do you give kids great dreams?"

Tapping in Meditation:

My purpose today is to know and live my life purpose and I do. I follow the tools of this program so I can be my best self and serve others.

Journal Notes:

Day/Year	
Day/Year	
Day/Year	

September 20

Sheri The Photographer's Story of Adversity

Sheri Geoffreys shares her story about her personal adversity. At age 30, days after my first child was born, I was diagnosed with Stage 2 Hodgkin's Lymphoma— the same disease my brother had succumbed to a few years before. I was devastated and heartsick but shortly, something clicked and I knew I would be a warrior and not a cancer victim. My first weapon was chemo which converted my long blonde tresses into an efficient buzz cut. After chemo I had a few weeks rest before starting radiation treatments on the tumor in my upper chest. I felt totally in charge as I breezed through the initial radiation. But after four days, I slammed into a wall of exhaustion, and the painful burns in my throat prevented me from even swallowing. After seven months of treatment, I was a fuzzy headed skeleton but victorious; my doctor announced I was cancer-

free. Then I was on fire! I started to look at my life to identify how I could make this second chance extraordinary. I continued to be in charge of my health by learning to EAT CLEAN and get fit. On a whim, I went back to school to study photography and discovered I had a natural talent for it, which catapulted me into my own very successful business specializing in corporate portraits.

My life had been hollow but pleasant before my illness. Now, at age 44, my life is radiant! I am firmly connected to my inner spirit, and I feel guided to live a healthier life, to be more engaged and to share the source of my boundless energy with everyone around me.

Challenge:

You don't have to wait for adversity to make a change but if you are challenged, whether it is your health, your work or your relationships here are five things you should consider. **Adversity is Opportunity**: The Universe is telling you to make a shift. What is it that you are not taking care of? Listen to your inner voice, and recognize that this challenge is a gift. **Adjust your Attitude**: You choose whether you suffer and succumb or plan and prevail. You are entitled to the initial shock and moment of despair, but then get going on your game plan. For motivation, identify others who are where you want to be, and visualize absorbing their positive energy. **Start Learning**: Educate yourself about your options. The more you know about your situation the better able you are to make the choices that benefit you. **Take Action**: Your plan and knowledge are only useful if you implement them. Have the confidence in yourself to jump in and wrestle your challenge into submission. **Prepare for Change**: Once you are on the other side of adversity, you'll be greeted by a stunning new you, beaming with joy; filled with confidence; and strong, healthy and powerful. And that is the real gift; embrace it.

Tapping in Meditation:

My purpose today is to compete with any adversity I am given realizing that all adversity makes me stronger. I welcome adversity and problems as opportunities to measure and observe my growth.

Journal Notes:

Day/Year	
Day/Year	
Day/Year	

September 21

Sam Berns Philosophy for a Happy Life

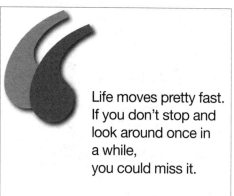

Life moves pretty fast.
If you don't stop and
look around once in
a while,
you could miss it.

—Ferris Bueller

Sam Berns was a junior at Foxboro High School in Ma. in 2013 where he has achieved the highest honors and was a percussion section leader in the high school marching band. He has achieved the rank of Eagle Scout in the Boy Scouts. Sam was diagnosed with Progeria, a rare rapid aging disease, at the age of 2. He was one of only 250 people worldwide with this disease. Sam reflects on his philosophy of life and gave these comments when interviewed at 17 years of age. Sam passed away in January of 2014.

"Life moves pretty fast. If you don't stop and look around once in a while you could miss it." Ferris Bueller

1. Be OK with what you ultimately can't do because there is so much you CAN do. He knows he can't go on a roller coaster ride or do other physical activities so he doesn't focus on them. He concentrates on what he can do like scouting. Sometimes he needs to find a different way of doing something by making adjustments to put those things in the "can do" category. He did that with his percussion drums by working with an engineer to design a harness that would allow him to carry the drums.
2. Surround yourself with people you want to be around. Sam feels that he is at his highest point when he is with the positive people who support him every day. This includes his family, his band members, and his friends.
3. Keep moving forward. "Around here…we don't look backwards for very long. We keep moving forward, opening up new doors and doing new things." Walt Disney. Sam always strives to have something to look forward to. It doesn't have to be big. It could be anything from looking forward to the next comic book to come out or to going on the next family vacation or hanging out with his friends etc. All of this helps him to focus on having a bright future ahead while he may be going through some current difficulty.

Sam doesn't waste energy feeling sorry for himself because when he does there is no room for any other emotion. It's not that he ignores when he's feeling badly, he accepts it. "I let it in, acknowledge it, and do what I need to do to move past it." This sounds like he's studied mindfulness. HBO filmed a documentary about Sam and his family titled *Life According to Sam* which aired in 2013.

Challenge:
Sam's philosophy is simple and filled with wisdom. Today take notice of where you might waste energy feeling sorry for yourself and who you surround yourself with. See if you are forward thinking. If not, today make any changes necessary.

Tapping in Meditation:
My purpose today is to keep on learning, growing, improving and serving and I do.

Journal Notes:

Day/Year	
Day/Year	
Day/Year	

September 22

The Effects of Humor

Other species have laughter. Rats when tickled have laughter. Apes have play. It looks like fighting but its play. Humor is social interaction. There is an emotion before laughter, the thing you feel. The laughter is the expression. Laughter has an impact on physiology. It increases respiration, our blood pressure is lowered, in the brain itself it's connected to pleasure just like food and sex and causes the release of endorphins and dopamine. Laughter reduces stress. Laughing is fun and makes us feel better. Research is verifying that humor has many of the positive effects that funny people have long suspected.

Researchers have found that you can even "act as if" you are feeling an emotion—say, happiness or irritation—by arranging your face in a smile or a frown, and you are likely to feel that emotion. In a classic study, participants were instructed to hold a felt-tip marker in their mouths in a way that caused their facial muscles to be formed into a smile or a frown. While holding the marker this way, they were asked to view comic strips and say how funny they found them. Those whose facial muscles were mimicking a smile found the same comics funnier than those whose facial muscles were set into a frown.

There are cognitive benefits of humor as well, including increased creativity, improved problem-solving ability, enhanced memory, increased ability to cope with stress, by providing an alternative, less serious perspective on one's problems. There is also an increase in hope, optimism and energy. Laughing also releases oxytocin, a hormone that leads to happier marriages and bonding in relationships.

Challenge:
My wife and I are regulars at the local comedy club. Look and see if there is a club near where you live. Go there at least once a month. If there aren't any clubs near you then watch comedy on T.V. at least once a month.

Tapping in Meditation:
My purpose today is to develop my sense of humor. A sense of humor is needed armor. Joy in my heart and some laughter on my lips is a sign that deep down I have a good grasp of life.

Journal Notes:

Day/Year	
Day/Year	
Day/Year	
Day/Year	
Day/Year	

September 23

No Time For Thoughts About Misfortune

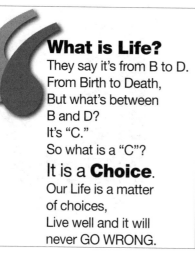

What is Life?
They say it's from B to D.
From Birth to Death,
But what's between
B and D?
It's "C."
So what is a "C"?
It is a Choice.
Our Life is a matter
of choices,
Live well and it will
never GO WRONG.

Once upon a time there was an unfortunate poor man. His home was also very poor, a small and empty house where mice made their nests and spiders made their webs. People tried to avoid coming into his house. Why should they stick their noses into those poor ruins? And the poor man thought that the poverty was the reason for his misfortunes and was his eternal destiny.

One day he met a wizard and complained to him about his poverty and miserable life. The wizard felt sorry for him and gave him a vase with this comment; "This is a magical vase that will save you from poverty."

The poor man took the vase and wanted to sell it at first and then spend the money on alcohol as usual, besides, why would he need such a beautiful thing? But then he started admiring the vase and couldn't take it to the market. He brought the vase home, put it on the table and started admiring it. It's not right for such a beautiful thing to be empty, so the poor man thought. So he picked some wildflowers and put them in the vase. It became more beautiful.

Not good, the poor man thought again, that such a beautiful thing stands next to a spider web. So the poor man started cleaning his house from spider webs, sweeping out cockroaches, mice and cleaning out the dust, washing the floor and walls, whitening the ceiling. It became clear that this house wasn't poor, but rather warm and cozy. And the poor man wasn't poor anymore, but a hard working host who had no time for thoughts about misfortune.

Challenge:

When you hear the word universe you think of space and the cosmos. You live on a tiny planet racing around a hot ball of gas at 67,000 mph with nothing significant around for millions of miles. If that wasn't fast enough, our solar system is located on an arm of the Milky Way Galaxy that is hurtling around it's center at close to 500,000 miles per hour. The scope and majesty of the universe out there is hard for you to imagine. Inside of you is a blueprint of that power of the cosmos, inside of each of us is the power that fuels great and magnificent change. Today, tap into it.

Tapping in Meditation:

My purpose today is to smile and let everyone know that today I'm a lot stronger than yesterday. I choose to be unstoppable. I am bigger than my concerns and worries. The strength of others inspires me daily. I focus on my goals; I trust my intuition and live a courageous life.

Journal Notes:

Day/Year	
Day/Year	
Day/Year	
Day/Year	
Day/Year	

September 24

Nelson Mandela Nelson Mandela Transcend Your Interpretations

Nelson Mandela spent 27 years in prison. He stated upon his release, "As I walked out the door toward the gate that would lead to my freedom, I knew if I didn't leave my bitterness and hatred behind, I'd still be in prison." Nelson Mandela was a South African anti-apartheid revolutionary, politician and philanthropist who served as President of South Africa from 1994 to 1999. He was South Africa's first black chief executive. The following is often attributed to Nelson Mandela but was actually originated in the 1992 work, "A Return to Love: Reflections on the Principles of a Course in Miracles" by author Marianne Williamson.

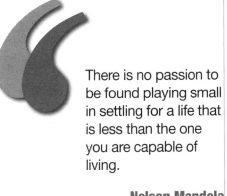

There is no passion to be found playing small in settling for a life that is less than the one you are capable of living.

—Nelson Mandela

"Our worst fear is not that we are inadequate. Our deepest fear is that we are powerful beyond measure. It is our light, not our darkness that most frightens us. We ask ourselves, who am I to be brilliant, gorgeous, talented, and fabulous? Actually, who are you not to be? You are a child of God; you're playing small doesn't serve the world. There is nothing enlightened about shrinking so that other people won't feel insecure around you. We were born to make manifest the glory of God within us. It is not just in some of us, it is in everyone and as we let our own light shine, we unconsciously give other people permission to do the same. As we are liberated from our own fear, our presence automatically liberates others."

Challenge:

Transcend the self-imposed limits of your interpretations. Today, notice when you are feeling uncomfortable about taking some action from getting up early for your workout to making a difficult call. Take that action anyway, regardless of how you are interpreting how you feel.

Tapping in Meditation:

My purpose today is to live life fully. I live George Bernard Shaw's words; I want to be thoroughly used up when I die, for the harder I work the more I live. I rejoice in life for its own sake. Life is no brief candle to me. It is a sort of splendid torch which I have got hold of for the moment, and I want to make it burn as brightly as possible before handing it on to future generations.

Journal Notes:

Day/Year	
Day/Year	
Day/Year	
Day/Year	
Day/Year	

September 25

The Gift of Giving—Pass it On Bryan Anderson

> Do good.
> And good will come to you.

A man was driving his car when he saw an old lady stranded on the side of the road. He saw that she needed help so he stopped his Pontiac near her Mercedes and got out. He smiled while he was approaching her; still she was worried as nobody had stopped for hours. Moreover, he did not look safe as his appearance was so poor and shabby. He could see how frightened she was so he tried to calm her, "I'm here to help you, don't worry. My name is Bryan Anderson."

The tire was flat so he had to crawl under the car. While changing the tire he got dirty and his hands were hurt. When the job was done she asked how much she owed him for his help. Bryan smiled and said, "If you really want to pay me back the next time you see someone who needs help, give that person the needed assistance and think of me!"

Later that same evening the lady stopped by a small café. The place looked dingy. Then she saw a waitress, nearly 8 months pregnant, wiping her wet head with a towel. The waitress had a sweet friendly smile although she had spent the entire day on her feet. The lady wondered how someone who has so little can be so kind and giving to a stranger. Then she remembered Bryan.

The lady had finished her meal and paid with $100 bill. The waitress went to get change and when she came back the lady was gone. She left a note on the napkin; "You don't owe me anything. Somebody once helped me, just like now I'm helping you. If you really want to pay me back do not let this chain of love end with you." The waitress found 4 more $100 bills under the napkin.

That night the waitress came home earlier than usual. She was thinking about the lady and the money she left. She was wondering how the lady could know how much she and her husband needed it. Especially now when the baby will arrive soon. She knew that her husband worried about that so she was glad to tell him the good news. Then she kissed him and whispered; "Now everything will be all right. I love you, Bryan Anderson."

Challenge:
Today practice one of the core principles of this program, being of service to others. This implies giving without expectations or conditions. Bryan Anderson didn't have conditions attached to his being of service but once you've tapped into the universe with a good deed it will come back to you.

Tapping in Meditation:
My purpose today is to tap into the spirit of the universal energy as I realize that as I help others I also help myself. We are all of the same source.

Journal Notes:

Day/Year	
Day/Year	
Day/Year	
Day/Year	
Day/Year	

September 26

Ashlyn Blocker—The Girl Who Can't Feel Pain

Ashlyn Blocker never has a stomach ache or cries about a scraped knee. But her rare condition also robs her of fear and caution and makes her world a strange and dangerous place. At first her parents thought that they were just lucky, a baby that never cries. But that all changed when Ashlyn developed a diaper rash so bad that it hurt just to look at it.

Her mom, Tara says, "We took her to the doctor and we were like, wow, we have the happiest baby in the world because she's not even affected by this."

It wasn't until a few months later when Ashlyn's left eye became bloodshot that the Blockers began to worry. Sure enough, an ophthalmologist discovered a massive corneal abrasion, a condition normally so painful that even an adult would be howling.

For most people, a diagnosis of congenital insensitivity to pain with anhidrosis (CIPA) is a death sentence, as the extremely rare disorder kills most while they are still toddlers. But this Georgia preteen Ashlyn Blocker, 12, has refused to let her condition ruin her life, competing in beauty pageants, playing in the school band and helping other children with her disease.

Challenge:
Pain is the body's warning system. There are so many lessons here, appreciation, gratitude, courage, refusal to be defined by limitations and more. When you notice any pain today take on an attitude of thankfulness. Thank your body for alerting you of the possible danger. Be appreciative that you have the ability to prevent further injury.

Tapping in Meditation:
My purpose today is to work hard, be kind and allow amazing things to happen and I do. I never wait for the perfect moment; I take each moment, one by one, and make it perfect.

Journal Notes:

Day/Year	
Day/Year	
Day/Year	
Day/Year	
Day/Year	

September 27

Rejection Can Kill You

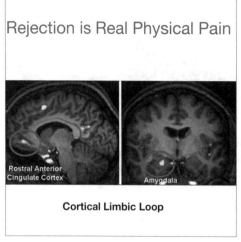

Rejection is Real Physical Pain

Rostral Anterior Cingulate Cortex

Amygdala

Cortical Limbic Loop

Ever get a paper cut? Hurts like crazy doesn't it? And it's real pain. I remember once I was reaching into the drawer to get a slicer to slice an apple so I could measure 6 ounces of fruit. I didn't realize that it was sharp side up and when I grabbed it I put a gash in my right forefinger. Ouch!

Instinctively there was an immediate shot of electrical activity to my anterior cingulate cortex in my brain with and instant projection to the amygdala, the emotional and arousal area of the brain. This resulted in a non-conscious instant command from the motor cortex to pull my hand away. A short time later there was communication with my outer cortex so I now knew what had just happen.

Now imagine this. You are making a prospecting call. You get your prospect on the phone and as you begin your discussion they yell, "You're interrupting me, I'm not interested, don't call again" and they slam the phone down!

Guess what the response is in the brain? It's exactly the same as I described above. Your brain doesn't distinguish between real pain, cutting your finger, and the mental pain of rejection. The same areas of the brain are fired on meaning that in both cases the pain is real. So if you ever hear a trainer or speaker tell you to say "thank you for the no every no is worth $50 because if you get enough no's you'll make a sale and a commission", you now know that they are not aware of the neurophysiology of rejection, but you are.

Challenge:

You need a different intervention for rejection than thank you for the no. The best intervention to rejection is to feel the pain, to be with the pain and not fight it. Use your mindset of constant energy and constant positive activity to fuel your consistent activity. Allow your purpose and commitment to serve to smooth over any rude and uncaring responses you may encounter. Also remember, keep your interpretations to what you experience at zero, they are empty and meaningless until you give it meaning. Remember quantum theory says that reality is in the mind of the observer so put the spin on any rejection that you receive that you are closer to finding the person who is also seeking you.

Tapping in Meditation:

My purpose today is to allow my commitment to serve others override and change my personal feelings and sensations. I exist to be of service to others. My value and compensation is directly related to my service to others.

Journal Notes:

Day/Year	
Day/Year	
Day/Year	
Day/Year	
Day/Year	

September 28

The Monty Hall Problem—Probability

Years ago there was a popular television show called *Let's Make a Deal*. The host of the show, Monty Hall, would show three doors with a wonderful prize such as a car behind one of the doors. After the contestant chose a door, Monty would open a different door revealing a joke prize like a live donkey that the contestant would be thrilled that they did not pick. You pick door 1. Monty then says, "Let's show you what's behind door number 3" and of course a beautiful woman is holding a rope on the donkey and Monty is quick to point out that the prize is the donkey, not the woman. That's what you didn't win. Next Monty gives you a choice. Do you want to keep to your original choice or change your mind and select door number 2 in the hopes of winning the new car? The audience cheers and shouts out their opinion as you are in agony. What would you do? What is the probability that you have correctly chosen the door that has the car? Most people think that you have a 50-50 chance of being right if you stay with your original choice. This is not correct.

This is a lesson in thinking and altering perspectives. Take this a step further to expand your thinking. Imagine there were 6 doors and you selected door number 1. After the choice is made Monty reveals the unwanted prizes behind 4 of the doors leaving only yours and one other. Do you still believe that there is an equal chance that the car is behind one of the remaining two doors or has your intuition about this changed? A method of thinking being used here is to exaggerate the potential outcomes. Suppose we exaggerate to 100 doors or even 1 billion and Monty opens all but two of them after you have made your choice. Should you switch or stay with your original choice? Switch of course. At this point you have a 1 over 1 billion chance of being correct.

Another way to view this is to take the opposite perspective. What is the chance that you would be correct if you changed your selection? It's almost certain that you were wrong on your first selection, 1/1,000,000,000 then the chance of being correct if you change is 999,999,999 in a billion. It's almost certain that you should change your pick. Returning to the original 3 doors, the chance that you were wrong with the first guess is 2/3. Therefore if you switch after the one prize is revealed you have a 2/3 chance of winning versus a 1/3 chance if you stay with your pick.

Challenge:

This problem has stumped mathematicians. It's an example of the law of large numbers used by exaggerating a problem to get a clearer view of solutions. Exaggeration enables you to see trends and make predictions. Pick a habit you want to change. Project out 30 years. What is the worst that could happen if you don't change? Make that change today

Tapping in Meditation:

My purpose today is to examine any habits that I may need to change to be the best version of myself and have performance excellence.

Journal Notes:

Day/Year	
Day/Year	
Day/Year	

September 29
What Can Be Measured Must Be Measured—Reminder

I came across an article in the sports section about a California Angel at the time, Mike Trout. It was addressing the question of whether he should be stealing more bases. The article said there was a case for both yes and no and started to list some metrics.

Through 55 games, Trout has 6 stolen bases on 6 tries. At this point in the previous season, (referring to 2013), he had 12 steals on 15 attempts. At this point in 2012, when he finished with 49 stolen bases, he had 22 steals on 25 tries. So his steals are down. Baseball wide runners have tried to steal once every 48 plate appearances and Trout's taken off once every 42.

The argument against goes like this. Albert Pujols, the guy almost always hitting behind Trout, is too much of a power threat to justify stealing. In 2014 Pujols has 30 singles, hits which would generally score Trout only after a steal, 29 doubles and homers, hits which would score Trout regardless of a steal. (Pujols has also taken Trout off the bases on a double play groundout seven times this year (2014).

Trout would need to be successful at a 78.1% rate to make stealing worth his while, compared to 67% for most big leaguers. The hitters behind the league's 25 most aggressive runners get 4.3% more first-pitch fastballs, and it goes on. Getting dizzy yet?

The conclusion by the way was that he should attempt to steal more often.

This is a reminder that the act of measurements changes what is being measured and what you can measure must be measured. This of course only matters if you are at stake about the results you create and are motivated for peak performance. Bill Gates said, "I've been struck again by how important measurement is to improving the human condition."

Challenge:
Take a look at what you currently measure in your health, business and personal life. At the end of this month you should be doing a tally and a year to date of your tracking. For today just ask yourself are you tracking what you should be tracking? If not, then start today.

Tapping in Meditation:
My purpose today is to take action on my dreams. I embrace tracking and measurement because I welcome accountability. The true measure of a man is not what he dreams, but what he aspires to be; a dream is nothing without action. Whether I fail or succeed is irrelevant; all that matters is that there is motion in my life. That alone affects the world.

Journal Notes:

Day/Year	
Day/Year	
Day/Year	
Day/Year	
Day/Year	

September 30

The End of the 3rd Quarter—Rabbit or Duck?

When you look at the picture what do you see a rabbit or a duck? It depends on which side you are paying attention to of course. If you look at it with the A side facing forward you see a duck, if your reference is the B side facing forward to the right then you see a rabbit. It's all a matter of perspective.

That's what measurement does for you. You are at the end of the 3rd quarter. It's important that you look at where you are versus where you had planned to be. It's important that you have that reference point as well. This data will be necessary for you to determine what level of intensity you will need to commit to for the last quarter of the year to reach your goals, or if you are going to adjust any of your commitments.

Rabbit or Duck?

Challenge:

Today do an analysis of what results you have created in the first 3 quarters of the year. Make any adjustments to the goals that you are committed to accomplishing by the end of the year. What level of activity are you committed to for the last 3 months? What does that mean for you today?

Tapping in Meditation:

My purpose today is to prioritize my goals and level of activities for the rest of the year in my health, business and personal life. I embrace the competitive spirit as I do compete and reach my goals. I love the process and have fun every day.

Journal Notes:

Day/Year	
Day/Year	
Day/Year	
Day/Year	
Day/Year	

OCTOBER

Davies Day Book

365 concepts for excellence

October 1

Declare Your Stand for Q4

Life is a competitive game. You better love this game because that's all there is to be engaged in between now and when you go into the ground. You have an opportunity to choose how you play this game. You already have the capacity to create the circumstances and events in your life to make the impossible happen.

The movie Rudy tells a story of a blue-collar youth growing up in a steel-mill town on the Great Lakes who creates a new life for himself. Rudy's dream is that someday he will play football for Notre Dame. That declaration, or STAND, establishes a context for his way of being throughout the rest of his life. Having made that declaration, Rudy had the power of the stand he took, to stay in action regardless of the circumstances to move the possibility he declared into a reality. With this kind of power, the kind that is not encumbered by the habitual ways of thinking of the past, he was now capable of handling everything life threw at him and despite all of the naysayers he stayed the path, kept on giving effort and eventually reached his dream.

You have complete authority over what you say is possible for your future. The Magna Carta was a declaration. Mahatma Gandi transformed himself from an attorney into a catalyst for his country's future by declaring the possibility of the British walking out of India. The Wright Brothers fulfilled the declaration of possibility that human beings can fly. Alexander Graham Bell declared that his new sound-transmitting device would be the cornerstone of a comprehensive communications network between all people who wanted to take part.

Challenge:
Look at the results you have created for the first 3 quarters this year and in your health, business and personal life. Adjust your goals and activities and make a commitment for what you want to accomplish by December 31st. Now create your STAND. Who do you need to be to accomplish this? What do you need to focus on? You don't need a sample, invent one. Make yours the example for others.

Tapping in Meditation:
My purpose today is to take a stand. I declare the possibility that what is possible is what I say is possible. From today until the end of this year I focus and execute my declared stand. I continue to act consistent with the possibility I have declared.

Journal Notes:

Day/Year	
Day/Year	
Day/Year	
Day/Year	
Day/Year	

October 2

The Power of Vulnerability—Expanding Perception

Brene Brown, PhD., University of Huston, researched human connection. These are notes from a variety of her talks and publications.

Brene's research was about connection. What's in the way is shame, is there something about you that if other people see then you won't be worthy of connection? I'm not good enough, etc. Excruciating vulnerability. In order for connection to happen you have to allow yourself to be seen. Shame boils down to a sense of a lack of worthiness. There is only one variable that separates the people who have connection and the ones who struggle is that the ones who have it believe that they are worthy of love and connection.

LOVING OURSELVES through the process of OWNING OUR STORY is the bravest thing WE'LL EVER DO.

—Brene Brown

Courage, compassion, connection. The key is to be able to tell the story of who you are with your whole heart. The courage to be imperfect. Compassion is to treat yourself well and others and the ability to let go of what you think you should be and to be vulnerable.

Those interviewed by Berne believed that what made them vulnerable made them beautiful. The willingness to say I love you first. The willingness to do something where there are no guarantees. Vulnerability is the core of shame, fear and struggle, but it's also the birth place of joy, creativity, belonging, of love. Why do you struggle so much?

As a society we numb vulnerability. There is evidence. We are the most in debt, obese, addicted, medicated adult population in US history. You can't numb your feelings without numbing all of your emotions. So when you numb grief, shame, guilt, you also numb joy, gratitude and happiness. Then you are miserable so you look for purpose and meaning. You make everything that is uncertain certain. I'm right, you're wrong. This is what politics looks like today. There's no discussion any more. There's no conversation. There's just blame. Blame is a way to discharge pain and discomfort. So you seek perfection.

Challenge:

There is a way. To let yourself be seen, deeply seen, vulnerably seen. Today love with your whole heart even though there's no guarantee. Today practice gratitude and lean into joy. Today believe that you are enough.

Tapping in Meditation:

My purpose today is to orient from a place that believes I am enough. I stop screaming and start listening. I am kinder and gentler to the people around me and to myself.

Journal Notes:

Day/Year	
Day/Year	
Day/Year	
Day/Year	
Day/Year	

October 3

Surrender—The Grace of Letting Go

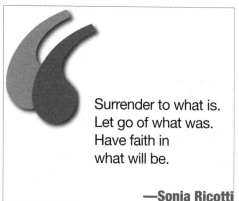

Surrender to what is.
Let go of what was.
Have faith in
what will be.

—Sonia Ricotti

No arguing, resisting, just letting go, this is the flow of surrender.. Surrender is the ability to give yourself wholly to something, to flow like water. To not force things, without self-doubt or over thinking, without holding back.

Do you recognize that you cannot control everything? Can you admit that you are not right or can you apologize, compromise and let go of the need to be right? Can you be spontaneous and not have to plan every single thing right down to the last detail? Can you stop long enough to enjoy life? That's the point of surrender because life goes by so quickly and you want to absorb every single moment and to do that you have to be able to let go.

What stands in the way of surrender? One thing is wanting something too much. Another thing is anxiety and fear. You need to surrender for so many things to happen that you take for granted. A good night's sleep requires surrender otherwise you're tossing and turning all night. You need to surrender for a good belly laugh or a good cry.

Judith Orloff, MD, author of Emotional Freedom, says there are 3 types of surrender. The **most common type** is the trial by fire kind of surrender. This is where everything is going so poorly, your relationships, your health, your business, a hitting rock bottom where you are forced to surrender. Crisis is an opportunity for change. **A second type** is learning to surrender to anxiety and fear. You can control your thoughts and focus on the positive images, the most probable positive outcomes. It's important to have an image that centers you, like a sunset over the ocean. **The third type** of surrender is accepting what is rather than trying to fit people or things into some preconceived notion of how you think things should be. Surrender is flowing with what is.

Workaholic? You can sabotage your success by pushing too hard. Surrender is the antidote to stress. Surrender boosts your brain's endorphins, euphoric opiate-like pain killers and serotonin, a natural antidepressant that allows you to relax, have more fun experience serenity. Life becomes easier and more joyful when you can let go.

Challenge:

Don't wait for the huge goals. The way to start is to realize the next time you drink a glass of water drink it slowly, feel the relaxation as you enjoy this sacred liquid. Let someone go in front of you in a very long line. Look at the expression on their face. People are so unaccustomed to small acts of kindness it will amaze you. You will notice that the line moves faster, your energy shifts. Small acts of kindness can change the world.

Tapping in Meditation:

My purpose today is to surrender to joy. I let go of my problems. I notice the simple things of life. I allow happiness to come in. I slow down. I quiet my mind.

Journal Notes:

Day/Year	
Day/Year	
Day/Year	

October 4

John Wooden—The Difference Between Winning and Succeeding

You should never try to be better than someone else. Never cease to strive to be better than you are and focus on what you can control. Wooden's definition of success: Peace of mind attained from self-satisfaction in knowing you made the effort to do the best at which you are capable. Character and perception—perception is what you are perceived to be and character is what you really are. He had 3 rules that he stuck with. 1. Never be late and be neat and clean. His practices started on time and ended on time. 2. No profanity. 3. Never criticize a team mate. Wooden developed a pyramid of success.

SUCCESS

Competitive Greatness

Poise   Confidence

Condition   Skill   Team Spirit

Self-Control   Alertness   Initiative   Intentness

Industriousness   Friendship   Loyalty   Cooperation   Enthusiasm

THE PYRAMID OF SUCCESS

The pyramid had blocks of traits stacked on each other. The base was industriousness, friendship, loyalty, cooperation and enthusiasm, which were followed by self-control, alertness, initiative, intentness, then condition, skill, team spirit, followed by poise, confidence, with competitive greatness at the very top. Wooden emphasizes patience, all change takes time, and faith, belief that things will work out as they should providing that you do what you should. You may have a tendency to hope that things will turn out the way that you want them to but you must do the things that are necessary to make those hopes become a reality. Wooden recites this poem; "The Road Ahead and the Road Behind"

"Sometimes I think the fates must grin as we denounce them and insist the only reason we can't win is the fates themselves have missed. Yet there lives on the ancient claim we win or lose within ourselves. The shining trophies on our shelves can never win tomorrow's game. You and I know deeper down there's always a chance to win the crown but when we fail to give our best we simply haven't met the test of giving all and saving none until the game is really won, of showing what is met by grit, of playing through another's quit, on playing through not letting up, it's bearing down that wins the cup. Dreaming there's a goal ahead, hoping when our dreams are dead, of praying when our hopes have fled, losing, not afraid to fall if bravely we have given our all. For who can ask more of a man than giving all within his span? Giving all it seems to me is not so far from victory. So the fates are seldom wrong, no matter how they twist and wind, it's you and I who make our fates, we open up or close the gates on the road ahead or the road behind."

Challenge:

Today don't whine, complain, or make excuses, just get out there and do what you're doing to the best of your ability. You can lose when you outscore someone in a game and you can win when you're outscored.

Tapping in Meditation:

My purpose today is to be all-in, all that I can be moment by moment in every activity I participate in and commit to today, all day long.

Journal Notes:

Day/Year	
Day/Year	
Day/Year	

October 5

Nick Saban, Alabama Football Coach on Success

There are three things we can't have.
We can't have complacency, we can't have selfishness, and we can't lose our accountability.

—**Nick Saban**

A man of vision answers the question, what makes you successful? The number one thing is consistency in performance in anything you choose to do. You've got to know what you want to do and it's got to be important to you. Whatever you choose to do, you make a commitment to it, you work at it, you invest your time in it. You reap what you sow. That's what farmers say about growing crops. It's the same thing in sports in being responsible and doing a great job. You work and you invest your time, you don't spend it. You work to improve. Mohamed Ali always said that when he won a championship fight he always won it somewhere far away from the ring, running off road, working in the gym, punching the bag, the preparation that you have is going to pay off for you in terms of getting the results that you want. It's the process of what you need to do to be successful. So many people want to succeed, but they're not willing to do the things that they have to do.

There's a difference between wanting something and committing yourself to something. Things that are worth having are not going to come easy. You will need to have a positive attitude about what you're doing and what you're going through. When you expect to have immediate gratification and results for whatever you're doing and it doesn't come what happens to you? You get frustrated. When you get frustrated you don't perform very well. Michael Jordan said he'd taken 26 game winning shots and missed, he's played in 384 games in the NBA and lost, he's taken 2962 shots and missed, and then he says because I failed that's why I succeed.

Be a relentless competitor. Always come back no matter what happened on the previous play. Character is an accumulation of your thoughts, habits and priorities. Discipline is doing what you're supposed to do, when you're supposed to do it and the way you're supposed to do it. You will either have the pain of discipline or the pain of disappointment

Challenge:

That's what is expected of you, to have the discipline to sustain and be a relentless competitor, and have pride in your performance and do everything that you can do the best that you can do it, because that becomes a habit and habits are what helps you be successful

Tapping in Meditation:

My purpose today is to compete. I give all that I can in blocks of time today. I sprint, break, sprint and during my sprints I am all out!

Journal Notes:

Day/Year	
Day/Year	
Day/Year	
Day/Year	
Day/Year	

October 6

Rick Elias—Seat 1D in the Hudson River

Imagine a big explosion as you climb through 3,000 feet. Imagine a plane full of smoke and an engine making a horrible clanking noise. Rick Elias had a unique seat that day, 1D. The flight attendant said, "No problem, we've probably hit some birds." The pilot had already turned the plane around and we weren't that far, you could still see Manhattan.

Two minutes later 3 things happened at the same time. The pilot lines up the plane with the Hudson River, turns off the engines, imagine being on a plane with no sound, and then he says 3 words, "Brace for impact."

Rick says he learned 3 things about himself that day. He learned that it all changes in an instant. Think about this, he thought he was going to die. He thought about all of the things he wanted to do, the people he wanted to reach out to that he didn't, all of the fences he wanted to mend, all the experiences he never had but wanted. He now had an urgency, a purpose, he no longer wants to postpone things.

The second thing he learned was about regrets. He allowed his ego to come forward too often. He regrets the time he wasted in things that did not matter with people that matter. He thought about his relationship with his wife, with friends. As he reflected on this he decided to eliminate negative energy from his life. He no longer tries to be right, he chooses to be happy.

The third thing he learned came to his on his mental countdown to what he thought were to be his last moments as the water came closer and closer. He had a sense of peace, "Dying is not scary." He had a sadness and one thought, "I only wish I could see my kids grow up." He was given the gift of a miracle of not dying that day. He was given another gift, to be able to see into the future and come back and live differently.

Challenge:
Imagine you are on your death bed. What regrets would you have? How would you change? What would you get done that you're waiting to get done because you think you'll be here forever? A will, estate planning, house remodel, vacation? How would you change your relationships and what you are committed to? Be that change today.

Tapping in Meditation:
My purpose today is to examine what is important to me and act on that with a sense of urgency, and I do. Today I take action and do the most loving next right thing.

Journal Notes:

Day/Year	
Day/Year	
Day/Year	
Day/Year	
Day/Year	

October 7

Instincts Always Drive Behavior

I was reading about how ants evacuate their nests and self-assemble into rafts that float to dry ground during a flood. This was observed in fire ants where scientists have discovered a peculiar design in living rafts where the ants use their babies as flotation devices. The queen ant lives for about 10-15 years and experiences flood conditions two to three times in her lifetime. During a flood the worker ants collect immobile larvae into a pile, then another 3 or 4 layers of workers climb on top and hold onto the eggs with their mandibles. The queen takes the protected middle of the raft. Surprisingly the ant babies did not appear to suffer at all. Their tremendous buoyancy, most likely a result of high fat content, prevents them from sinking. This is instinctual behavior. It is brought on by a set of conditions, (stimulus), the presence of water, and the response is automatic over the species.

This is the same with all species. Instincts drive behavior. You can't fight this. That's why diets don't work. First it's incorrect information. You don't count calories, it's not math, intake balanced against expenditure, it's not the deprivation of calorie restrictions. Your instincts won't let you do that. If you use starvation your instinct is to go from burning sugar, glycogen, for energy to breaking down protein. Of course there are waste products (lactic acid) from doing so but your body will not let you enter into a wasting strategy.

It's the same thing with other areas of performance. Your instincts will not let you execute activities that are perceived as threats like prospecting, talking with difficult people, and using large amounts of energy to accomplish a task. Regarding this type of performance, the instinct is to avoid the highest level of perceived pain for the comfort. If you try to fight through this with willpower you just can't sustain it. Fortunately, you have a solution. It's one of the tools of this program, behavioral contracting.

Don't you see what you're doing with a behavioral contract? You are tapping into your own compelling instinct of avoiding the highest level of perceived pain. You're taking away voluntary behavior and turning it into the instinct of avoiding the highest level of pain. Embrace your own instincts, don't fight them. You can't win that battle! That dog will never hunt!

Challenge:

Continue to use behavior contracts. Today, pick one challenging activity that you can accomplished with focused effort by the end of the day, place a painful penalty if you don't complete the activity, ask someone else to hold you accountable, report the result to them at the end of the day. I'll be that person if you don't have someone. Pick an activity and send it to me, info@bobdavies.com and its $100 if you don't complete it.

Tapping in Meditation:

My purpose today is to live my word. I make a plan and I do it because I said I would. I do what I say I will do on time or before.

Journal Notes:

Day/Year	
Day/Year	
Day/Year	

October 8

The Red/Black Game

This is an exercise that demonstrates that not all situations are best done in a competitive way. I divide the group into three (or, possibly, more) teams. The purpose of the game is to score as many points as possible. On each turn, each group decides whether to choose red or black and writes that on a sheet of paper. Scoring is as follows:

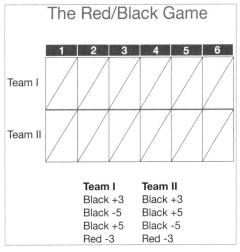

- If all choose black, each team scores 50.
- If exactly one team chooses red, that team scores 100 and all other teams score 0.
- If more than one team chooses red, all teams score 0.

Play about 5 or 6 rounds. What you should usually find is that at least one group will start using red almost immediately and others will join in so that by the end of the game, NO team will have as many points as they would have if everyone had "cooperated" and chosen black at each turn. You can also point out that you said "score as many points as possible" NOT "your team should score as many points as possible"—again emphasizing that the larger score by the whole group was a positive gain.

This is another example of being instinctively led to a zero sum game that in order for there to be a winner there must be a loser. No one said to compare how many points your team scored to the others yet we fall into the mindset that winning is only at the expense of someone else losing.

Also it's interesting to observe how people play the game. Do they disengage, do they lead, how do they handle conflict within the group? Does anyone ever think about talking with the other groups about co-operating? The rules never said you couldn't do that. Imagine how you would play this game.

Challenge:
Look for opportunities to collaborate not compete. You live in a world of abundance, not scarcity. There is enough prosperity for everyone. The competition is within yourself, your attitude, your ability to get yourself to take purposeful actions whether you feel like it or not.

Tapping in Meditation:
My purpose today is to collaborate with others. Rising tides lift all boats. I freely help others and by doing so I help myself. I live in abundance.

Journal Notes:

Day/Year	
Day/Year	
Day/Year	
Day/Year	
Day/Year	

October 9

Meditation Can Change Your Brain

Effects of Meditation

Frontal Lobe

Frontal Lobe

Baseline

Meditating

Neuroscientist Sara Lazar's amazing brain scans show mediation can actually change the size of key regions of your brain, improving your memory and making you more empathetic, compassionate and resilient under stress. There are scientifically validated benefits of mediation. Decreased stress, reduced symptoms associated with depression, anxiety disorders, pain, insomnia, enhanced ability to pay attention and increased quality of life. When you engage in a behavior over and over again this can cause physical changes in your brain. This is referred to as neuroplasticity. This means that the neurons can change how they talk to each other with experience. There are studies that show you can actually detect this using a MRI machine.

Sara Lazar's team recruited people to study if meditation can change areas of the brain. They recruited people, just average people with no prior experience in mediating. They scanned them and compared them to a similar group of people who did not meditate. What they found was that there were several areas of the brain that had more grey matter in the meditators than in the non-meditating group. One area in particular was the frontal lobe, necessary for working memory and executive decision making. As you age it is normal for the cortex to shrink in size. In this study, the 50 year old meditators had the same size cortex as the 25 year olds. This suggests that meditating may actually slow down the natural decline in cortical structure. They did a second study with people who had never meditated before. They scanned them and then taught them how to meditate and instructed them to meditate every day for 30-40 minutes. They scanned them again at the end of 8 weeks. The hippocampus, the area important in learning and memory and also for emotional regulation, there is less grey matter in this region in people who have depression and post-traumatic stress. There were several other areas that were changed. There was a decrease in the size of the amygdala for those who meditated. The more stress reduction people reported, the smaller the size of the amygdala. It wasn't the change in the environment but the individuals' reaction to the change that caused the amygdala to respond. There is a neurobiological reason why people felt less stress. Meditation can literally change your brain.

Challenge:

One of the tools of this program is daily meditation for 5-10 minutes.

Tapping in Meditation:

My purpose today is to tap into the intelligence of the universe through quite meditation and I do.

Journal Notes:

Day/Year	
Day/Year	
Day/Year	
Day/Year	
Day/Year	

October 10

Take Your Time—Don't Get Hijacked

What do you immediately recognize this picture as? A dog correct? This is an evolutionary adaptation that favors survival. I am talking about the ability for your brain to be able to fill in the blanks and to generate a non-conscious response long before you are aware of what you are responding to. The ability to recognize a pattern is an advantage. For example the ability to generate a retreat when you first glance at the left-bottom image, will save your life when you finally realize what you're looking at is the threat on the right-bottom image. Speed of response is essential and is an instinct.

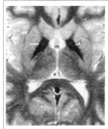

There is a direct connection between your 5 senses and the emotional, arousal limbic area of the brain. This bypasses the slower cortex. You've got to move fast and figure it out later to survive.

We are not being chased by lions today but we still have this fast primitive instinct of the recognition of perceived threats. Whether these threats are real or not doesn't matter, we are compelled to respond and we instantly get the "fight or flight" physiology as well.

The issue is where are you hijacked into an instant negative defensive response, one of anger perhaps, where you are instinctively being compelled to lash out? Is it your children, your spouse, colleagues? What triggers you?

I agreed to be a talent for another organization for no up-front pay and no guarantee in a revenue sharing joint venture. I was to produce the equivalent of 30 days of concepts for them. It turned out to be a huge effort much greater than I anticipated. When I sent them my scripts they edited them and sent them back to me to correct. Can you imagine the story I could have made up about that? I'm the talent, I'm the expert, I'm not getting paid, this is such a tremendous effort and you have the nerve to edit! I had a scathing email ready to go out to the principles telling them what I thought but I applied today's lesson of delay, delay, delay. The email I sent was "Thanks for the input. I appreciate the time you've invested in me. I'll work on these corrections this week." This protected our relationship and who knows what that bit of restraint will bring for the future.

Challenge:
Today identify a trigger for you to respond with anger or frustration, pause, delay, and then respond. Journal the difference that makes.

Tapping in Meditation:
My purpose today is to distance myself from being reactive and negative. I pause before responding emotionally. I am kind whenever possible. It is always possible to be kind and I am.

Journal Notes:

Day/Year	
Day/Year	
Day/Year	
Day/Year	
Day/Year	

October 11
The Power You Give to Authority—Tread with Caution

Obedience to Authority

Stanley Milgram (8.15.33–12.20.84) was an American social psychologist. He conducted various studies during his lifetime, with the most notable being his controversial study on obedience to authority, conducted in the 1960s during his professorship at Yale.

This was a study of obedience to authority figures particularly when you were "told" to do something against your moral code. The experiment consisted of the authority in the white coat, the leader, the learner and you, the teacher. The leader and the learner were both in on the experiment. You, the teacher would read pairs of words and ask the learner which phrase did not belong. The teacher thought that this was a test of the effect of pain on memory. Each time the learner answered incorrectly the teacher was told to administer a shock by flipping a switch on a board with the severity of the shocks escalating with each question missed. They ranged from mild to severe XXX. There never was any current delivered, the learner and the leader were actors but the teacher didn't know that.

As the shocks escalated in intensity (so the teacher thought) the learner screamed with pain and in many cases begged the teacher to let them out of the experiment, or complained that it was dangerous since he had a bad heart, etc. When the teacher asked the leader if he could stop the leader said one of 4 responses, 1. Please continue with the next higher shock level, 2. The experiment requires that you continue, 3. It is absolutely essential that you continue, 4. You have no other choice, you must continue. Several times the different teachers asked "Who's responsible for this persons health" to which the leader said "I am, please continue." They expected only about 4% of the subject teachers to continue to obey and even though they were morally objecting, apply the highest level of shock to the learner. However what they found was that 65% of the teachers continued to the very highest shock level.

This shows obedience to authority despite your own personal objections and deflection of personal responsibility.

Challenge:
Don't just blindly accept the claims of someone you hold as an authority. The next time a doctor or celebrity attempts to get you to buy a supplement or the next best, easiest and fastest way to lose weight run! Any program that allows you to eat flour and sugar, run! Stay on your program.

Tapping in Meditation:
My purpose today is to search for the truth rather than accepting what I hear. I inspect and verify. I research or reject outrageous too good to be true claims.

Journal Notes:

Day/Year	
Day/Year	
Day/Year	

October 12

The Power of Non Conformity

Imagine a mentality that can change the way you view the world and the way the world views you. A way of living that will make others stop and take note of you. This is the power of non-conformity. When faced with a problem or opportunity you approach it differently than someone else in your situation might do. When you do this you take on this problem and often times are led to a unique and unexpected resolution.

You may have heard of the antics of the Stanford University marching band. They have taken a traditional field and approached it differently that has created an effect that otherwise would not have been possible for them. People come to Stanford football games in part just to see the band. People are drawn to things that are unique, novel, so radically different.

Good
is the
enemy of
GREAT.

—John F. Kennedy

This is a concept that can be applied to other areas as well. A few years ago a moderately attractive young singer and piano player named Stefani Germanado was an unknown. She realized that her talent and average looks would not get her ahead in her industry. A couple of years later she put on a dress made out of raw meat and today you know her as Lady Gaga. To her credit she did something that no one had ever seen before in a music industry that is so packed with the "same old" style of entertainer and approach.

Good is the enemy of great! JFK said, "Conformity is the jailer of freedom and the enemy of growth." Albert Einstein realized that the traditional way of thinking about physics was not sufficient to solve the mysteries that he saw in the universe. So rather than continuing on with the same assumptions that were accepted as being true for the time, he reinvented the laws of physics.

Conventional wisdom specified that the central nervous system—the brain and spinal cord, cannot heal in adults. This "truth" no longer holds. Scientists discovered that a protein, oncomodulin, is secreted by immune cells and causes nerve regeneration. This was discovered in 2006 and is reinventing treatments for spinal cord injuries.

Challenge:
Think about the last time you were faced with a challenge that seemed impossible with the rules and expectations attached to it. What if you approached it like Einstein did that there is a solution out there but you need to see it from a different perspective. Do that today.

Tapping in Meditation:
My purpose today is to view situations form different points of view. I replace I can't with at my present mind set a solution does not exist and I change my approach.

Journal Notes:

Day/Year	
Day/Year	
Day/Year	
Day/Year	
Day/Year	

October 13

The Herd Senses Danger

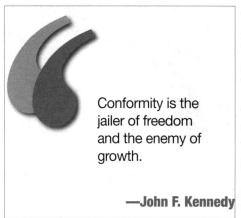

Conformity is the jailer of freedom and the enemy of growth.

—**John F. Kennedy**

We are social animals and what others think does matter. We have a genetic instinct of safety in numbers. This means that we are predisposed to go with the groups thinking, or conform to the mindset of the whole.

The University of California, Berkeley, did a study. Geometric shapes appear and you are asked to judge which is larger. At the beginning you are the first person directed to respond. Then you are asked to be the 2nd to answer which allows you to see the 1st persons' response before you give yours. You then move to the # 3 spot. Finally you are the last of the group to answer. A slide appears with 5 lines on it. Which line is longest? It's obvious the longest is # 4 but you have to wait before you can answer. The first person's answer pops up on your screen, #5. That's odd you think. You look carefully at the lines, #4 is obviously longer than #5. Then the second answer appears: #5. And the 3rd answer, #5, then the 4th answer, #5. Now it's your turn. What will you pick? You clearly see that everyone is wrong. You shouldn't hesitate to flip the switch for #4 yet there is a good chance that you won't. When this experiment was conducted by Richard Crutchfield and Solomon Ash in 1953, ¾ of the subjects ignored what they saw and went with the consensus of the group at least once during a series of trials. Only 1 person was the actual subject in the experiment. All the others were instructed to give answers that were clearly wrong.

From an evolutionary perspective the human tendency to conform is not so strange. Individual survival depended on the group working together, sharing common beliefs and agreeing. This is wired into us all.

However, it's going to take our ability to stand firm in your planning, in your beliefs, in your passion, your convictions, your willingness to fail forward and to be criticized for any innovation, progress and learning to occur.

Challenge:
Resist the temptation to have confirmation bias, to change your beliefs to conform to the group. Not everyone will approve of you but that price is worth it for the greater good of progress and learning. Today, resist the pull of the group.

Tapping in Meditation:
My purpose today is to allow my intuition to influence my perception. I look at things from different points of view. I slow down and consider the big picture in all of my doings today. I honor my stand, my beliefs and my gut reactions.

Journal Notes:

Day/Year	
Day/Year	
Day/Year	
Day/Year	
Day/Year	

October 14

Tell the Truth Faster or Conform to the Group? The Abilene Paradox

Groupthink is a psychological phenomenon that occurs within a group of people, in which the desire for harmony or conformity in the group results in an irrational or dysfunctional decision-making outcome. Group members try to minimize conflict and reach a consensus decision without critical evaluation of alternative viewpoints.

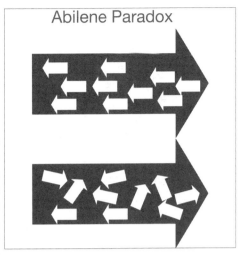

Abilene Paradox

The term was introduced by Jerry Harvey in his article *The Abilene Paradox: The Management of Agreement*. The name of the phenomenon comes from an anecdote in the article which Harvey uses to describe the paradox: On a hot afternoon visiting in Coleman, Texas, the family is comfortably playing dominoes on a porch, until the father-in-law suggests that they take a trip to Abilene [53 miles north] for dinner. The wife says, "Sounds like a great idea." The husband, despite having reservations because the drive is long and hot, thinks that his preferences must be out-of-step with the group and says, "Sounds good to me. I just hope your mother wants to go." The mother-in-law then says, "Of course I want to go. I haven't been to Abilene in a long time." The drive is hot, dusty, and long. When they arrive at the cafeteria, the food is as bad as the drive. They arrive back home four hours later, exhausted.

One of them dishonestly says, "It was a great trip, wasn't it?" The mother-in-law says that, actually, she would rather have stayed home, but went along since the other three were so enthusiastic. The husband says, "I wasn't delighted to be doing what we were doing. I only went to satisfy the rest of you." The wife says, "I just went along to keep you happy. I would have had to be crazy to want to go out in the heat like that." The father-in-law then says that he only suggested it because he thought the others might be bored. The group sits back, perplexed that they together decided to take a trip which none of them wanted.

Challenge:
What if your problems stem not from conflict but from agreement? The Abilene paradox exposes the fears that a lot of people have about voicing unpopular truths. This shows you how dangerous words are if you don't speak up. What about the courage of your convictions? Today notice and take opportunities to verbalize how you really feel.

Tapping in Meditation:
My purpose today is to realize that I am not responsible for how others feel. I tell the truth tastefully all day long. I am sincere, I am honest, and I am on purpose, focused and of service to others.

Journal Notes:

Day/Year	
Day/Year	
Day/Year	
Day/Year	
Day/Year	

October 15

The Lesson of the Lonely Tree

The lonely tree was growing among the hot sands of a dead desert. Prickly sands covered the wood. The sun mercilessly burned its bark. But the tree kept on living in spite of the harsh conditions.

Once a hawk flew over the desert. The hawk saw the tree and sat on its branch. He looked around the desert and said, "You are a strange tree. Why do you keep on living among these dead hot sands? Who needs it?"

"You", the tree answered. "Me", the hawk was surprised. "I don't need you." "But if not for me, you would have to sit on the hot sand instead of my branches. If not for me someone seeing you sitting on the tree alone would say that nobody needs you too. And they would ask what do you live for? Sitting on my branches you think that I need you?"

The hawk thought about it for a while and agreed with the tree. If there was no tree the hawk would feel himself alone and useless among this vast desert.

Challenge:

Who is counting on you? Who gives you unconditional love? Who do you least want to let down? Who can you keep in mind today to change how you feel and what you do particularly when you might lack energy and initiative? Think of that person now. Notice how you think, feel and act from that reference.

Tapping in Meditation:

My purpose today is to live with passion and love. I love what I do. I believe in what I do. I love my life and I live each moment with passion. I am significant. I am enough

Journal Notes:

Day/Year	
Day/Year	
Day/Year	
Day/Year	
Day/Year	

October 16

The Story of the Blind Girl

There was a blind girl who hated herself just because she was blind. She hated everyone, except her loving boyfriend. He was always there for her. She said that if she could only see the world, she would marry her boyfriend.

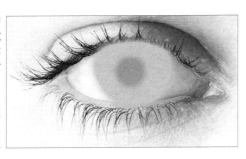

One day someone donated a pair of eyes to her and then she could see everything including her boyfriend. He asked her, "Now that you can see the world, will you marry me?"

The girl was shocked when she saw that her boyfriend was blind too and refused to marry him. Her boyfriend walked away in tears and later wrote a letter to her saying; "Just take care of my eyes dear."

It is easy to forget what life was like before and who's always been there even in the most painful situation. Life is a gift.

Challenge:
Today, before you think of saying an unkind word—think of someone who can't speak. Before you complain about the taste of your food think of someone who has nothing to eat. Before you complain about your husband or wife think of someone who is crying out for a companion. Before you complain about life think of someone who died too early. Before you complain about your children think of someone who desires children but they are barren. Before you argue about your dirty house think of someone who is living on the streets. When you are tired and complain about your job think of someone who is unemployed, disabled and those who wished they had your job.

Tapping in Meditation:
My purpose today is to live life, enjoy it, celebrate it and fulfill it and I do. I appreciate what I have and am grateful for my health, for those I love and who love me and for the freedom that I have.

Journal Notes:

Day/Year	
Day/Year	
Day/Year	
Day/Year	
Day/Year	

October 17

Tell the Truth Faster—a Meeting of the Minds

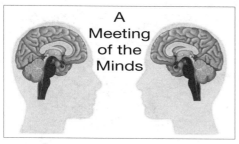

A Meeting of the Minds

Martin was returning to work in his London office after spending two weeks with his brother in New York. He was coming back with a heavy heart. It was not just that it was the end of a wonderful holiday; it was that Monday mornings always began with a team meeting and, he had grown to hate them. Martin was aware that colleagues approached these meetings with hidden agendas; they indulged in game-playing; and he knew that people were not being honest and open. The meetings themselves were bad enough—but then there was all the moaning afterwards.

As this morning's meeting began, Martin braced himself for the usual moroseness and monotony. But, as the meeting progressed, he became aware of a strange background noise. At first, he thought that he was still hearing the engine noise from the aircraft that had brought him back to London but as he concentrated on the noise it became a little clearer. He realized—to his amazement—that he could hear what his colleagues were thinking as well as what they were saying. What surprised him, even more than the acquisition of this strange power, was that he discovered that what people were saying was not really what they were thinking. They were not making clear their reservations. They were not supporting views which they thought might be unpopular. They were not contributing their new insights. They were not volunteering their new ideas.

Martin found it impossible not to respond to his new knowledge. So he started to make gentle interventions, based more on what he could hear his colleagues thinking than on what he could hear them saying. "So, John are you really saying ..." "Susan, Do you really think that ..." "Tom, have you got an idea on how we could take this forward?" He was aware that his colleagues were unsettled by how insightful were these interventions. They looked at him mystified. In truth, he felt rather proud of his newly-acquired talent.

As the meeting progressed, Martin became aware of changes to the tone and style of the event. It was clear to him now that, one by one, each member of the meeting was learning how to hear the thoughts of all the others and this was subtly changing how they inter-acted with one another. The game-playing started to fall away; people started to speak more directly; views became better understood; the atmosphere became more open and trusting. The meeting ended. As people left the room, Martin found that he could still hear what they were thinking. "That was the best meeting we've ever had." "All meetings should be like that." "In future, I'm going to say what I think."

Challenge:

Truth telling is the authentic way to communicate. Today notice saying what you really think. Notice the impact it has on your listeners.

Tapping in Meditation:

My purpose today is to tell others how I really feel. Opportunities can be lost in the blink of an eye but regret can last a life time.

Journal Notes:

Day/Year	
Day/Year	
Day/Year	

October 18

Nothing is Written—T.E. Lawrence

Lawrence of Arabia is a 1962 British drama film based on the life of T. E. Lawrence. The film stars Peter O'Toole in the title role. It is widely considered one of the most influential films in the history of cinema. The film depicts Lawrence's experiences in the Arabian Peninsula during World War I. Its themes include Lawrence's emotional struggles with the personal violence inherent in war, his own identity, and his divided allegiance between his native Britain and its army and his newfound comrades within the Arabian Desert tribes.

Having carried out the superhuman feat of enduring this desert furnace, it is discovered that one of the Arabs, Gasim, has fallen off his camel and is no doubt dying somewhere back in the desert. Lawrence is told that any idea of rescue is futile and, in any event, Gasim's death is "written." When Lawrence achieves the impossible and returns with Gasim still alive, Sherif Ali admits to him: "Truly, for some men nothing is written unless they write it."

Lawrence displays courage and unselfishness in going back into the hell of the Nefud to attempt to find a man he hardly knew among the vast expanse of this dangerous terrain. He has such a sense of purpose of a man who is determined to take nothing as "written" but to shape his own destiny.

T.E. Lawrence, popularly known as Lawrence of Arabia was a unique character and influential military leader. Winston Churchill described him as one of the greatest living people he knew. "The world looks with some awe upon a man who appears unconcernedly indifferent to home, money, comfort, rank, or even power and fame. The world feels not without certain apprehension that here is someone outside its jurisdiction, someone before whom its allurements may be spread in vain, someone strangely enfranchised, untamed, untrammeled by convention, moving independent of the ordinary currents of human action."

Yet for all his fame, T.E. Lawrence remained modest of his achievements. "I've been and am absurdly over estimated. There are no supermen and I am quite ordinary and will say so whatever the artistic results. I'm one of the few people who tell the truth about myself."

Challenge:
"All men dream: but not equally. Those who dream by night in the dusty recesses of their minds wake in the day to find that it was vanity: but the dreamers of the day are dangerous men, for they may act their dreams with open eyes, to make it possible. This I did." T.E. Lawrence. What unselfish action can you take today?

Tapping in Meditation:
My purpose today is to act on my dreams. I take action. I have a thought and then I act. I act out of service to others.

Journal Notes:

Day/Year	
Day/Year	
Day/Year	
Day/Year	

October 19
The Secret of Happiness—Don't Spill the Oil on the Spoon

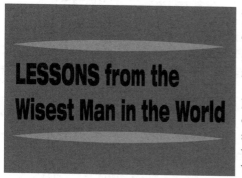

A certain shopkeeper sent his son to learn about the secret of happiness from the wisest man in the world. The lad wandered through the desert for 40 days, and finally came upon a beautiful castle, high atop a mountain. It was there that the wise man lived.

Rather than finding a saintly man, though, our hero, on entering the main room of the castle, saw a hive of activity: tradesmen came and went, a small orchestra was playing soft music, and there was a table covered with platters of the most delicious food in that part of the world. The wise man conversed with everyone, and the boy had to wait for two hours before it was his turn to be given the man's attention. The wise man listened attentively to the boy's explanation of why he had come, but told him that he didn't have time just then to explain the secret of happiness. He suggested that the boy look around the palace and return in two hours. "Meanwhile, I want to ask you to do something", said the wise man, handing the boy a teaspoon that held two drops of oil. "As you wander around, carry this spoon with you without allowing the oil to spill."

The boy began climbing the many stairways of the palace, keeping his eyes fixed on the spoon. After two hours, he returned to the room where the wise man was. "Well", asked the wise man, "Did you see the Persian tapestries that are hanging in my dining hall? Did you see the garden that it took the master gardener ten years to create? Did you notice the beautiful parchments in my library?" The boy was embarrassed, and confessed that he had observed nothing. His only concern had been not to spill the oil that the wise man had entrusted to him. "Then go back and observe the marvels of my world", said the wise man. "You cannot trust a man if you don't know his house."

Relieved, the boy picked up the spoon and returned to his exploration of the palace, this time observing all of the wonders and beauty in the palace. Upon returning to the wise man, he related in detail everything he had seen. "But where are the drops of oil I entrusted to you?" asked the wise man. Looking down at the spoon he held, the boy saw that the oil was gone. "Well, there is only one piece of advice I can give you", said the wisest of wise men. "The secret of happiness is to see all the marvels of the world and never to forget the drops of oil on the spoon."

Challenge:
Instead of being so focused on your task have a wider observation while still staying on purpose and executing your most productive activities. You have greater capacity for performance and awareness than you are aware of. You can take it all in and still be productive. Start today.

Tapping in Meditation:
My purpose today is to have a serene and calm mind and see spiritual things as my reality. Happiness is the by-product of living the right kind of life.

Journal Notes:

Day/Year	
Day/Year	
Day/Year	

October 20

Five Considerations to be Happy

1. First of all, be realistic. Nobody is happy all of the time and it is perfectly normal to have variations in moods and feelings from day to day, month to month, and even year to year. According to a study based on data from the British Household Panel Survey, overall levels of happiness decline from one's teens until one's 40s and then pick up until they peak in one's early 70s. So the chances are that your happiest days are yet to come. Doesn't that make you happier? At any time and at any age, though, it is possible to feel happier than you have been and here are some ideas for you to consider.

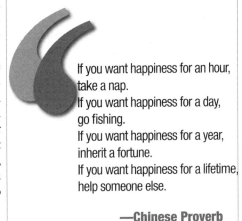

If you want happiness for an hour, take a nap.
If you want happiness for a day, go fishing.
If you want happiness for a year, inherit a fortune.
If you want happiness for a lifetime, help someone else.

—**Chinese Proverb**

2. Most fundamentally, recognize that happiness is a state of mind and not something which can be defined objectively. You can change your state of mind in many ways including these suggestions.

3. Perhaps above all, be as healthy as you can. Nothing is more valuable than your health and little is more likely to make you unhappy than ill-health.

4. More importantly than anything else, if you can live with a partner whom you love and respect and who feels the same about you. Kiss and cuddle and compliment often and regularly buy unexpected little gifts. Share your triumphs and your troubles. Evidence shows that a good relationship will not only make you happier; it will enable you to live longer.

5. When you're old enough and in a steady relationship, have a son or a daughter. Tell them often how much you love and admire him/her and do anything to help him/her. If you don't have a child, 'borrow' one—spend time with a nephew or niece or a friend's son or daughter or—when you're older—your grandson or granddaughter. Children really do bring joy.

Challenge:
Accept where you are in life and make every day count. This doesn't mean to live in resignation, it means to accept what is and do what you can to improve in every way, every day, starting today. Remember, if you want happiness for a lifetime help someone else

Tapping in Meditation:
My purpose today is to be happy. Nothing is perfect and I look beyond the imperfections. I surround myself with people who know my worth and appreciate me. I appreciate them.

Journal Notes:

Day/Year	
Day/Year	
Day/Year	
Day/Year	
Day/Year	

October 21

The Happiness Dozen

1. Have a cat or a dog. Stroke often.
2. Keep in close touch with relatives and a small circle of friends. You can't beat their love and support. Don't be afraid to admit when you're down and need a lift. Don't expect them to be mind readers—say how you feel and what you need.
3. Conversely, if there's a person in your life who is a negative influence and who is dragging you down in some way, don't be afraid to remove such a person from your life.
4. Be politely assertive. Say how you feel and explain what you want. Friends and colleagues can't be mind readers.
5. Don't procrastinate, do it now. Instead of worrying about a decision, make it. You'll immediately feel better. Most personal problems do not lend themselves to a simple right or wrong solution. The point is to decide and move on.
6. Give lots of compliments. You will make others feel good about themselves and find that this gives you pleasure too.
7. Give small gifts to your friends. To give is even more pleasurable than to receive. Or, as the social anthropologist Marshall Sahlins, puts it: "Gifts make friends and friends make gifts."
8. For a special thrill, perform acts of kindness anonymously so that the person benefiting does not know that you're responsible. If you don't understand this, watch the French film "Amélie"
9. Live below your means. The figures may have changed and the decimal system may have arrived, but the lesson is still the same as when, Charles Dickens in "David Copperfield" had Mr Micawber opine: "Annual income twenty pounds, annual expenditure nineteen, nineteen, six, result happiness. Annual income twenty pounds, annual expenditure twenty pounds, nought, and six, result misery."
10. Use your credit card as a convenient way to pay for your major expenditures on a monthly basis—not to obtain credit at an outrageous level of interest. Pay it off in full every month.
11. Give regularly to the charities of your choice. Make at least one of those charities an organization addressing world poverty. Regularly increase your contributions as your income rises.
12. Surround yourself with pleasant smells. Have flowers, pot-pourri, incense or scented candles in most rooms of the house and in your office.

Challenge:
Pick one to focus on today.

Tapping in Meditation:
My purpose today is to help those around me and I do. Helping others is the best way to help myself. I experience the presence of a higher power as I serve others.

Journal Notes:

Day/Year	
Day/Year	
Day/Year	
Day/Year	
Day/Year	

October 22

How to be Healthy in Ten Steps

1. Don't smoke. Cigarette smoke is a toxic cocktail of around 70 cancer-causing chemicals and hundreds of other poisons. Smoking is the single biggest cause of cancer in the world. Smoking kills five times more people than road accidents, overdoses, murder, suicide and HIV all put together.

2. Weigh and Measure your food. Use the Bob Davies food plan. It will give you your boundaries. You'll know when to start to eat, when to stop and how much to have. Have a purpose and a plan for your nutrition. Avoid flour, sugar and quantities. If it's not in the food plan then it's not your food. Only choose food with no sugar or flour in the first 5 ingredients.

3. Use the tools of this program. Read one page a day, meditate 5-10 minutes a day, use the food plan every day. Practice awareness and "being with what you feel" Before the food plan you would have a feeling and stuff your face. With the food plan you now face your stuff.

4. Walk or exercise every day. The aim should be to do around 10,000 steps which equates to around 60-90 minutes of walking. Using a pedometer on a belt is a good way to monitor this. On the way to or from work, shops, or meetings, leave the car or public transport a bit short of your destination. In the office, use stairs rather than the elevator. Exercise is for fitness and food management is for weight control. You'll see a difference in your blood fat level with exercise.

5. Don't sit around too long. Break up your sitting time by walking around at regular intervals. At home, do a chore. At work, visit a colleague.

6. Limit exposure to the sun. Between 11 am and 3 pm, it's better to be in the shade. When in the sun, wear sensible clothing and use appropriate sun factor lotion. Never burn.

7. Get enough sleep. The amount varies by individual and age, but most people need seven or eight hours a night. It's important to go to bed at a regular time and get up at a regular time. There is some evidence that people who take a short nap during the day lower the risk of heart disease.

8. Be happy. Happiness helps healthiness, especially mental health. Reality is in the mind of the observer, so choose happiness.

9. Be a reader. Constant learning helps the brain to stay healthy. Be passionate about learning.

10. Have an outward focus. Focus on the needs of others and have a service mindset regardless of your personal circumstances.

Challenge:
Which one of these do you need to focus on today?

Tapping in Meditation:
My purpose today is to be tuned into the universal energy. I receive my strength from my higher power. I strengthen my faith with my quiet time.

Journal Notes:

Day/Year	
Day/Year	
Day/Year	

October 23

Teamwork, The Sense of a Goose

Next autumn, when you see geese heading south for the winter, flying in a "V" formation, you might consider what science has discovered as to why they fly that way. As each bird flaps its wings, it creates uplift for the bird immediately following. By flying in a "V" formation, the whole flock adds at least 71 percent greater flying range than if each bird flew on its own. People who share a common direction and sense of community can get where they are going more quickly and easily, because they are traveling on the thrust of one another. When a goose falls out of formation, it suddenly feels the drag and resistance of trying to go it alone and quickly gets back into formation to take advantage of the lifting power of the bird in front.

If we have the sense of a goose, we will stay in formation with those people who are heading the same way we are. When the head goose gets tired, it rotates back in the wing and another goose flies point. It is sensible to take turns doing demanding jobs, whether with people or with geese flying south. Geese honk from behind to encourage those up front to keep up their speed. What message do we give when we honk from behind?

Finally—and this is important—when a goose gets sick or is wounded by gunshot, and falls out of the formation, two other geese fall out with that goose and follow it down to lend help and protection. They stay with the fallen goose until it is able to fly or until it dies; and only then do they launch out on their own, or with another formation to catch up with their own group. If we have the sense of a goose, we will stand by each other like that.

Challenge:

Take a moment today and look for ways you can collaborate with another to gain synergy and teamwork.

Tapping in Meditation:

My purpose today is to is to be in harmony with the energy and music of the universe. I live with a spirit of co-operation. I readily help others in need.

Journal Notes:

Day/Year	
Day/Year	
Day/Year	
Day/Year	
Day/Year	

October 24

The Seeker of Truth

After years of searching, the seeker was told to go to a cave, in which he would find a well. 'Ask the well what is truth', he was advised, 'and the well will reveal it to you'. Having found the well, the seeker asked that most fundamental question. And from the depths came the answer, 'Go to the village crossroad: there you shall find what you are seeking'.

Full of hope and anticipation the man ran to the crossroad to find only three rather uninteresting shops. One shop was selling pieces of metal, another sold wood, and thin wires were for sale in the third. Nothing and no one there seemed to have much to do with the revelation of truth.

Every Human Being Is a Seeker of Truth

Disappointed, the seeker returned to the well to demand an explanation, but he was told only, 'You will understand in the future.' When the man protested, all he got in return were the echoes of his own shouts. Indignant for having been made a fool of—or so he thought at the time—the seeker continued his wanderings in search of truth. As years went by, the memory of his experience at the well gradually faded until one night, while he was walking in the moonlight, the sound of sitar music caught his attention. It was wonderful music and it was played with great mastery and inspiration.

Profoundly moved, the truth seeker felt drawn towards the player. He looked at the fingers dancing over the strings. He became aware of the sitar itself. And then suddenly he exploded in a cry of joyous recognition: the sitar was made out of wires and pieces of metal and wood just like those he had once seen in the three stores and had thought it to be without any particular significance.

At last he understood the message of the well: we have already been given everything we need: our task is to assemble and use it in the appropriate way. Nothing is meaningful so long as we perceive only separate fragments. But as soon as the fragments come together into a synthesis, a new entity emerges, whose nature we could not have foreseen by considering the fragments alone.

Challenge:
Challenge: You already have everything you need to be happy and live a life of abundance. This program is a tool for getting access to that inherent talent and ability.

Tapping in Meditation:
My purpose today is to allow the universal intelligence to express itself through me. I have far more capacity to create the circumstances and events in my life than my intelligence allows me to comprehend. Therefore I have faith that by making right choices, abundance, health and happiness with follow, and I do make right choices.

Journal Notes:

Day/Year	
Day/Year	
Day/Year	

October 25

Collaboration Not Competition

We live in a world of abundance. This is the big sky theory, there is plenty of success for everyone so our competition is not against another person or company, its against our self.

"Collaboration is vital to every business," said Jay Bernstein, founder and CEO of B2B social networking platform WinWin. "There are so many opportunities out there for businesses to work together to exchange ideas and increase purchasing power."

Bernstein based WinWin on what he calls the "neighbor principle" — you go to your neighbor to borrow some milk because you're out. The next day, when it snows, you bring your snow blower down the hill to help him. When this idea is applied to small business, companies can leverage each other's strengths at little or no cost to grow both of their businesses.

There are plenty of ways that small business owners can use the neighbor principle and collaborate to bring about mutual growth. An independent Web development company can offer their website design services to other local businesses in exchange for a link back on the homepage. Small businesses with similar inventory needs can combine their orders to receive discounted wholesale prices. An entertainment company can host an event at a restaurant in town to bring in business while marketing its own services. These real-life examples prove that working for and with other small businesses can be more powerful than working against them.

"Collaboration saves time, saves money, and levels the playing field for American companies," Bernstein told Business News Daily. "[Instead of outsourcing], businesses who collaborate can keep money in the country and their local economies."

Challenge:

Make a list of businesses, entrepreneurs who serve the same marketplace yet offer a service different than yours. Identify 4 or 5 people you can approach for a collaborative effort.

Tapping in Meditation:

My purpose today is to be open to receiving help and collaboration with others. I act out of a commitment to serve others. Everyone I come into contact with today smiles because of my friendly attitude.

Journal Notes:

Day/Year	
Day/Year	
Day/Year	
Day/Year	
Day/Year	

Irrational Decision Making-The Trolley Car

When I present this weight management solution to groups of people who say they are motivated to find a solution you would think that every person in the room would come up to me and tell me that they want to join this program. That's not what happens. Why is that? They want to lose weight and improve their performances in their health, business and personal lives. So why don't they take the action? The answer is because people don't make logical rational decisions.

Imagine you're on a runaway trolley car. If the car continues straight it will kill 5 workers on the tracks. If you press a lever however you can cause the trolley to switch tracks and save the 5 but 1 worker will be killed. Would you do it? 93% of the responders responded that it was either morally mandatory or at least morally permitted to turn the trolley. Most pulled the lever.

Behavioral Decision Making

A) It is morally mandatory to turn the trolley
B) It is morally permitted but not mandatory to turn the trolley
C) It is morally prohibited to turn the trolley

Now make one small change. Imagine that you're standing on a bridge and you see a runaway trolley car. If you push the man in front of you off of the bridge you will stop the trolley car. Yes, you will kill that man but you will save the 5 remaining on the track straight ahead. Most people will not push the man off of the bridge. They will not sacrifice 1 to save 5. The numbers are the same so what's different?

A different area of the brain is being activated. In the first example of pulling the lever the orbital frontal cortex is active. This is the logical, reasoning part of the brain. In the second scenario the emotional limbic area of the brain is electrically active. This explains the lack of the proper action for most people.

Challenge:
You can't control that other people will do what is in their best interest. You can only control the choices you make. Make sure you slow down and consider other points of views before making decisions.

Tapping in Meditation:
My purpose today is to allow myself to slow down in my decision making today and I do. I consider other alternatives and perspectives before I decide on actions. I understand that others don't always act in their own best interests and I remain hopeful when they don't.

Journal Notes:

Day/Year	
Day/Year	
Day/Year	
Day/Year	
Day/Year	

October 27

Form a Strategic Alliance

The Alliance—Your All Star Team

Attorney
Real Estate
P&C
Payroll Company
Investment Advisor
Any other expert growth-oriented business with a database
Lender
Sports Agent
Dentist
Chiropractor
Funeral Home
Financial Advisor
Social Media Video Consultant
Accountant

The most successful performers in any field have developed a specialized group of experts and together they bring a full service orientation for the benefit of their clients. I teach this to financial advisors. The question is, "Who else solves the problems that a high net worth family would have?" They would have accounting issues, estate planning concerns, perhaps a real estate portfolio both commercial and residential, a web site, payroll etc. Of course they have home and auto insurance needs, medical needs, they go to a cleaners, they may even want to board their pets when they travel. The question becomes who else serves the needs of the same clients that you serve? Approach the owners of those businesses and determine if they have an interest in participating with you in being a part of a team that serves the client.

If you would vet one of each category, the one with the expertise and client profile that most matches what you are looking for, do your research, make your list, then get together and brainstorm with each other and continue to add to the "legs" of the star as an example, and finally get a group of like-minded, growth oriented individuals who all share a fiduciary responsibility to the high net worth family. Fiduciary means that not only are their recommendations suitable for the family, but they are also in the best interest of the family, not the provider.

This becomes an educational group and you would be a source of experts who are committed to educating your own individual data base as well as the public through quarterly events, workshops. This is how you would generate referrals as you present on a topic of interest to the invited attendees as the expert of choice in the alliance.

Challenge:

Make a decision today. Do you want to put in the effort to create a strategic alliance and then produce events for each other's data base and the public? If yes, then today make contact with one person on your list and explain the concept.

Tapping in Meditation:

My purpose today is to collaborate. Helen Keller said, "Alone we can do so little, together we can do so much." Unity is strength. Where there is teamwork and collaboration, wonderful things are achieved.

Journal Notes:

Day/Year	
Day/Year	
Day/Year	
Day/Year	
Day/Year	

October 28

The Blind Gurus

An Ancient Metaphor that Tells a Timeless Truth
Adapted from the book by Lillian Quigley.

There once was an Indian rajah who had a healthy skepticism about men who called themselves "gurus." So he decided to hold a contest to see which gurus really were as wise as they claimed. After many tests, just six gurus remained, and all were blind. The rajah asked each man to touch an elephant and to describe the nature of the beast. Here is what they said: The first blind man put out his hand and touched the elephant's side. "How smooth!" he said. "An elephant is like a wall." The second blind man touched the trunk. "How round! An elephant is like a snake. "The third blind man touched the tusk. "How sharp! An elephant is like a spear." The fourth blind man touched the leg. "How tall and straight! An elephant is like a tree." The fifth blind man touched the ear. "How wide! An elephant is like a fan." The sixth blind man touched the tail. "How thin! An elephant is like a rope."

An argument ensued, each blind guru thinking his perception of the elephant was correct. The rajah listened a few moments, and then said, "The elephant is large. Each man touched only one part. You must put all parts together to find out what an elephant is really like."

The fable teaches us to look at things from many different sides. In some ways, we are like the elephant in the story, with many aspects to our lives and dreams. Unfortunately, we are often surrounded by people who claim to know all about us. Yet they just know the part of us they touch. This is especially true in advisor and client relationships.

One author explains it this way: "The client is the elephant, a powerful, majestic being, capable of incredible achievement. Sadly, most clients are surrounded by a bunch of 'blind gurus' who don't know what they don't know."

Challenge:
This story is a wonderful reminder to you that wisdom comes from seeing the whole picture, from seeing the elephant and that you alone have one area of expertise. Today, share this concept with those you have invited to be a part of your strategic alliance.

Tapping in Meditation:
My purpose today is to make peace between my mind and my heart. I let go of attachments and selfishness. I let go of needing to be right. I move forward in the spirit of love and service.

Journal Notes:

Day/Year	
Day/Year	
Day/Year	
Day/Year	
Day/Year	

October 29

Confucius and Chinese Philosophy

You cannot consider Chinese philosophy without reference to this particular man, Confucius. He is one of China's greatest philosophers, born 551 BCE. He believed in education, hard work and the capacity for every human being to succeed. His world was filled with poverty and war. His fame spread and at 50 years old he became a governor. His policies included feeding the poor and elderly at the states expense. He developed a mission of what it meant to be human as concentric circles. You start with the person, then to the family, then the neighborhood, then the society, to the nation, to the country, to the world and beyond.

The warlords did not like his reforms and he was forced from his home into exile. For almost 14 years he walked eastern China spreading reform and peace with local leaders. Confucius was a man with a vision. The rulers at this time were not men of vision. Confusius died thinking he had been a failure, thinking that he did not have much influence over China. This is paradoxical because his philosophy has become a dominate philosophy for China and the surrounding regions for so many centuries. His social philosophy was based primarily on the principle of "ren" or "loving others" while exercising self-discipline. He believed that ren could be put into action using the Golden Rule, "What you do not wish for yourself, do not do to others."

Confucius' political beliefs were likewise based on the concept of self-discipline. He believed that a leader needed to exercise self-discipline in order to remain humble and treat his followers with compassion. In doing so, he would lead by positive example. According to Confucius, leaders could motivate their subjects to follow the law by teaching them virtue and the unifying force of ritual propriety. His philosophy of education focused on the "Six Arts": archery, calligraphy, computation, music, chariot-driving and ritual. To Confucius, the main objective of being an educator was to teach people to live with integrity. Through his teachings, he strove to resurrect the traditional values of benevolence, propriety and ritual in Chinese society.

Challenge:

One of the foundations of your program is to live with integrity. This means that you do what you say you will do and that you act in alignment with your stand, your purpose and your vision. So if you are committed to excellence then you would not eat flour and sugar, for example. Today, examine what you are truly committed to and ask yourself if your actions are proof of that commitment.

Tapping in Meditation:

My purpose today is to tap into the power of love. The day the power of love overrides the love of power our world will be at peace.

Journal Notes:

Day/Year	
Day/Year	
Day/Year	

October 30

Rick Warren: A Life of Purpose

Rick Warren, Pastor and author, uses his own story to explain the central tenet of his teaching that the antidote to spiritual emptiness is recognizing what we have been given, wealth, creativity, talent and using those gifts to make the world a better place. People are recognizing spiritual emptiness, get up, go to work, come home, watch television, and repeat. They are starting to think that there's got to be more to life than this. This is not living—it's just existing. Warren says that there are no accidents of birth that you matter. You matter to this universe. The difference between

the survival level of living, the success level of living and the significance level of living is that you figure what your purpose is. A lot of smart people can't figure out their problems. A lot of successful people feel so unfilled and fraudulent. These are not religious issues, they're human issues.

Leadership is stewardship. If you are a leader you don't own it. He believes that human beings have a responsibility to make the world a better place for the next generation. Most people never think this through in terms of their beliefs. Your world view determines everything else in your life.

His book, *The Purpose-Driven Life*, triggered his own crisis of purpose as two things happened that he wasn't expecting, money and fame. He made 5 decisions on what to do with the money. First, he didn't spend it on himself. He didn't buy anything bigger, better, or more. The second thing was he stopped taking a salary from the church that he pastors, Saddleback Church, Lake Forest, Ca. The third was that he added up all that the church had paid him over the last 25 years and he gave it back. He didn't want anyone thinking that he does what he does for money. Then he set up 3 foundations working on some of the world problems, illiteracy, poverty, diseases, particularly HIV-Aids, the last thing was giving it back through tithing. Every time he gives it breaks the grip of materialism in his life. It's all about getting and having more. The good life is not looking good and having the goods. It's about being good and doing good and giving it away. Significance in life doesn't come from status, it comes from serving. It is in giving our lives away we find meaning and significance.

Warren feels that the purpose of influence is to speak up for those who have no influence. The purpose of influence is not to build your ego or self-worth.

Challenge:
You value is not based on your valuables. What do you have that you've been given? Ideas, wealth, creativity? What are you doing with what you've been given? It's not about you; it's about making the world a better place.

Tapping in Meditation:
My purpose today is to be of service to others, to give to others less fortunate, to be the voice for others who don't have a voice. I see opportunities to serve all around me and I do serve.

Journal Notes:

Day/Year	
Day/Year	
Day/Year	

October 31

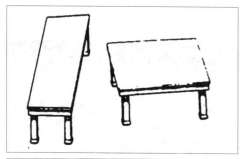

Simplify

Which table is longer? Everyone would agree that the vertical table looks longer but if you actually measure you will see that your eyes were deceiving you, they are the same size. Your intuition is consistently fooling you in a predictable way and there's almost nothing you can do about it. Vision is one of our most important senses. We rely on vision more hours of the day then we do any other sense.

We also have cognitive, decision making illusions in the same way.

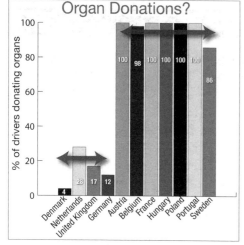

Organ Donations?

Why do some countries give a lot and some give a little in terms of organ donations? Usually people think it has to do with culture, how much do you care about people? But if you look at this chart, countries that you think as similar are actually very different. Sweden is all the way on the right and Denmark is all the way on the left. What are the countries on the right doing differently? It turns out that it has to do with the form at the DMV. The countries on the left have a form that is an opt in—check the box below if you **want** to participate in the organ donor program, while the countries on the right have a check the box if you **don't want** to participate in the organ donor program (opt out). Think about what this means. We wake up in the morning and we think that we are making decisions. It is very hard for us to accept the idea of the illusion of our making a decision rather than actually making a decision. It has to do with the complexity of the decision and we non-consciously select the easier path.

A study was done with physicians. They were told that everything that was tried with a hip replacement candidate was not working and that they had decided to refer the patient on to hip replacement surgery. Next the doctors were told that they had failed to try one drug, Ibuprofen. Would you recall the patient from surgery? Most of the doctors said yes. Next they were told that they had failed to try two medications, Ibuprofen and Piroxicam. Now most of the doctors would not pull the patient. The decision was too difficult. This is irrational decision making.

Challenge:

The most probable application of this research to you is to keep your life simple. Personally, get rid of clutter. In business, don't try to be all things to all people, niche to a smaller, simpler audience. What one action can you take today to simplify?

Tapping in Meditation:

My purpose today is to pause, become aware of my choices and deliberately make the right decisions, one at a time.

Journal Notes:

Day/Year	
Day/Year	
Day/Year	

NOVEMBER

Davies Day Book

365 concepts for excellence

November 1
Visual, Auditory, Kinesthetic—The Eyes Will Know

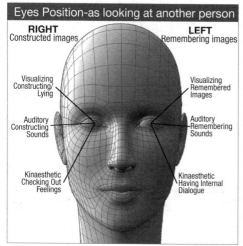

Eyes Position-as looking at another person

RIGHT Constructed images

LEFT Remembering images

Visualizing Constructing/ Lying

Visualizing Remembered Images

Auditory Constructing Sounds

Auditory Remembering Sounds

Kinaesthetic Checking Out Feelings

Kinaesthetic Having Internal Dialogue

I bring a volunteer up on stage. I ask them to spell the word G E O G R A P H Y. Their eyes will go up and to the left, visual memory. Next I ask them to spell the same word backwards. Now their eyes will go up right, visual construction. The first task what they did was remember the word and the second more difficult task they projected the word onto a metaphoric blackboard in the future and read it backwards.

These are both non-visual eye movement patterns. The volunteer didn't see the ceiling when they were looking up. The eye is connected to the brain through the optic nerve. They were electrically accessing areas of the brain to get the information they were seeking.

People have different wiring, different predispositions of their personality. Knowing how to recognize this can help you to match that persons preferred method of integrating data and communicating. When you match their preference system you then create rapport. You can then influence them in their decision making, for the good of course.

So just pay attention when you are communicating. If you keep seeing someone with their eyes constantly moving from side to side, auditory memory and construction, it's best for you to match that system by using phrases like, "How does this sound to you?" "Do you hear what I'm saying?" or "Does this resonate with you?" If you were to say to an auditory person, "Does this feel right to you?" That would be a mismatch.

Challenge:
Today, pay close attention both verbally and visually to the people you have conversations with today. They will have three preferences, Visual, Auditory, Kinesthetic. By watching how they move their eyes you will know which method they prefer. Match them and you will be amazed at how close they feel to you. That's rapport.

Tapping in Meditation:
My purpose today is to speak in such a way that others love to listen to me. I listen in such a way that others love to speak to me. The way that I listen inspires others to be more, to do more and to become more.

Journal Notes:

Day/Year	
Day/Year	
Day/Year	
Day/Year	
Day/Year	

November 2

The Cairn—Integrated Health

What's the most important part of your health? Eating properly? Exercise, getting enough sleep? What if I told you that caring for your body was the least important part of your health? The medical profession has it all backwards. The body doesn't shape the way you live your life. It's actually a mirror of how you live your life. The body speaks to you in whispers and if you ignore the whispers the body starts to yell. We are suffering from an epidemic that modern medicine has no idea of what to do. People are fatigued, anxious and depressed. They suffer from a whole variety of aches and pains. Many people are disillusioned; they don't know who they are so they cover themselves up with a series of masks of all of their roles.

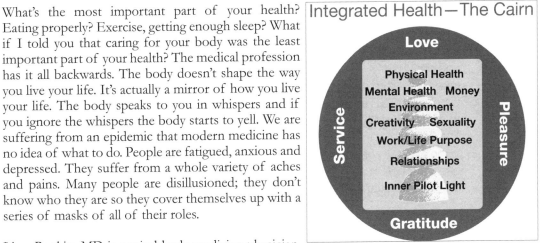

Integrated Health—The Cairn

Love
Service
Pleasure
Physical Health
Mental Health   Money
Environment
Creativity   Sexuality
Work/Life Purpose
Relationships
Inner Pilot Light
Gratitude

Lissa Rankin, MD is a mind-body medicine physician, founder of the Whole Health Medicine Institute, was tired of treating symptoms from the outside in. She uses the analogy of a cairn, rocks piled on top of each other. You can't remove one rock without upsetting the entire structure. She says what really matters is a life of love, pleasure, gratitude and service that allows what she calls your inner light and I call your authentic self, to shine through and be expressed.

All of what you think matters, yes, that you eat properly, that you exercise, but what really matters are healthy relationships, having a healthy professional life, expressing yourself creatively, being spiritually connected, having a healthy environment, being mentally healthy with physical health the manifestation of all of this and the top most rock. The most important part of health is caring for the mind, the heart, the soul.

Challenge:

If you have any physical symptoms, if you are suffering from the epidemic that plagues the developed world, ask yourself what's the real reason that you're sick and suffering? What's out of balance? What can you do about it? How can you be more transparent? How can you open yourself up to more possibilities? How can you be more honest with yourself about what you need? When you let your true self out then you heal from the inside out. What is it that you need to change?

Tapping in Meditation:

My purpose today is to be true to myself with awareness, authenticity, service, gratitude, love and pleasure, and I am.

Journal Notes:

Day/Year	
Day/Year	
Day/Year	
Day/Year	
Day/Year	

November 3

Man's Search For Meaning—Victor Frankl

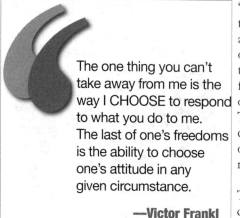

The one thing you can't take away from me is the way I CHOOSE to respond to what you do to me. The last of one's freedoms is the ability to choose one's attitude in any given circumstance.

—**Victor Frankl**

"Everything can be taken from a man but one thing, the last of the human freedom, to choose one's attitude in any given set of circumstances, to choose one's own way." All of the great teachers say the same thing. The idea is that we need to exercise that one freedom and not give it away, and choose a positive, optimistic response to anything that happens to us. This does go against human nature. We are genetically coded to see the negative, the threats, not the positive or the optimistic. We are wired to see what can kill us not opportunities to reach our goals.

This means that we can thank the scientists who have discovered brain plasticity. They have discovered that you can rewire your brain and grow new neurons, new connections, new habits. Positivity can be created into a preferred habitual way of responding through conscious repetition and intention. The Buddha talks about this in the context of emptiness. They like to say that everything that occurs is neutral, it just is, and you give it meaning. Steven Covey talked about this in his 7 Habits book with habit number 1, be proactive. You can be reactive and allow the instinct of the default of negativity to occur or you can take responsibility and make up a narrative of your own choosing.

The default approach is S-R, stimulus-response. You're stuck in traffic so you're upset. Or you can select a different approach, how peaceful it is to be aware of the beauty all-around of you as you listen to educational material in your car. Quantum physics reminds you that both types of realities are equally possible in a super imposed wave form until you choose, then all other wave forms collapse and the only thing that is left is your observed reality.

Another idea from Victor Frankl is that your potential is waiting. He says, "What man actually needs is not a tension free state, but rather the struggle and striving for some goal worthy of him. What he needs is not the discharge of tension at any cost, but the call of a potential meaning, waiting to be fulfilled by him." Frankl is essentially challenging you to be in the power of now and use the tension of what you can be to pull you forward into growth. Your objective is not a tension free state. He also emphasized to commit to and align your actions with something that is greater than you.

Challenge:

Tap into the dynamic tension between what you can be and where you are now by being uncomfortable every day. Today, do one activity that you are uncomfortable doing.

Tapping in Meditation:

My purpose today is to embrace the tension of growth and fulfillment. What gives light must endure the burning as I self-actualize and give of myself to my higher calling I endure the turbulence and discomfort and grow from it.

Journal Notes:

Day/Year	
Day/Year	
Day/Year	

November 4

The New Era of Positive Psychology—Martin Seligman

For every 100 articles written on negative psychology there was only one article written on positive stuff. Psychology was about finding out what's wrong with you. It was the disease model. The new trend in psychology is positive interventions, ways to make people better and self-actualize. Positive psychology has 3 aims. The first is that psychology should be just as concerned with strengths as with weakness, as interested in building the best things in life as in repairing the worst, and it should be as concerned with making the lives of normal people fulfilling and with nurturing high talent as with helping pathology.
In the last 10 years a measurable science has been developed. You can go to the website www.authentichappiness.org and take a variety of tests to see how you respond to positive emotions compared to thousands of other people. They started looking at how extremely happy people differ from the average and the one thing that they found was not about having more things, or more money, or less bad events, it was that they were extremely social. Seligman states that efficacy and effectiveness studies have been carried out to find out what actually makes people happier long term.

Positivity

Seligman defines happiness as having 3 categories. The first is the pleasant life. That is having as many pleasures as you can, as much positive emotion as you can and learning the skills of mindfulness that amplify them. The second is a sense of flow. Time stops, you have intense concentration. They take their highest strengths and craft their life around them. The third segment of happiness is meaning. This consists of knowing what your highest strengths are and using them in the service of something larger than you are.

An interesting result from Seligman's research is that it turns out that the pursuit of pleasure has almost no contribution to life satisfaction. The pursuit of meaning is the strongest. All of the great teachers have 6 core virtues in common.

Wisdom—Courage—Love—Justice—Temperance—Spirituality

Challenge:

This is a true testimonial to your program. All of these are a part of your journey towards being the best version of you that you can be. Today renew your commitment to learning and ongoing personal growth. Take one action today that verifies that commitment. Start a new book, watch a video, research something that is positive.

Tapping in Meditation:

My purpose today is to choose the way that I think. Habits of thinking are not forever, they are my choice. I make positive choices.

Journal Notes:

Day/Year

Day/Year

Day/Year

November 5

Think Disruptively

Do you need more ideas or do you have plenty? Are you "paralyzed by possibilities?" and you don't know what to do so you don't take any action? When is the last time you had disruptive thinking? Thinking about ways of doing things that are different then how you currently operate. This is what Clayton Christensen, Harvard University described as "disruptive technology." It's not about technology it's about how you think. The real challenge is to figure out how you can be the disruptive change in your category. In order for you to be this you'll have to give up the notion of being comfortable. You'll need to embrace your fears because taking disruptive risks is scary; you don't know where it's going to go. This is a turning point that is going to take your business in another direction. Steve Jobs is an example of a disruptive thinker. One board meeting he was about to present on the future direction of Apple Computers. The board members expected to hear the specs and technical requirements of about 7 products called Snow White but Jobs says simply, "I want Bob Dylan songs."

A disruptive hypothesis is an intentionally unreasonable statement that gets your thinking flowing in another direction quickly. You are most likely going to be wrong at the beginning and right at the end otherwise it's likely that someone else is already doing it. It's the difference between prediction and provocation.

Think of things in your everyday business and life that are not necessarily broken or problems. What assumptions do you make and take for granted every day? How about socks? Socks are always sold in matching pairs. What if you sold them in 3s and none of them matched? Someone actually did that, a company called Littlemissmatched. They discovered that these were wildly accepted by teenage girls as it allowed them to express themselves. The disruptive thinking came first then they had to find out who would have value with this. Look at the wildly popular soft drink soda. The present prevailing assumptions are that it's inexpensive, taste good and advertised appealing to the strong desires of the masses. The disruptive approach is that soda is expensive, taste bad and is advertised as functional. Red Bull did this. Red Bull gives you the functional boost when you need it, is expensive and tastes bad. When they launched Red Bull they placed no focus on taste and it was twice as expensive as soda. They went with it and successfully created a new market. The disruptive strategy leaves competitors scrambling to catch up. Ideas are the recipes that we use to rearrange things and create new value and insights.

Challenge:

Generate a steady stream of bold new ideas. How can you think differently today that could take your entire industry into the next generation? Too big a challenge? I think not.

Tapping in Meditation:

My purpose today is to be the potential for reinvention that is all around me. There has never been a better time for my giving back to the world in ways that create new value.

Journal Notes:

Day/Year	
Day/Year	
Day/Year	

November 6

The Top 10 Mistakes in Behavior Change

Stanford University researchers from their Persuasive Tech Lab, Fogg, Chanasyk, Nelson and others created research on the top 10 Mistakes in Behavior Change, along with my comments.

1. **Relying on willpower for long-term change.** Willpower happens in the prefrontal cortex. This is so energy intensive that you can only maintain a willpower deprived state for a short period of time. You've got to change your thinking, rewire your habits and change your physiology. Because you are on such a low glycemic high nutrient food plan you have a steady release of blood sugar and corresponding insulin so you will not need willpower because you won't have cravings to fight.

2. **Attempting big leaps instead of baby steps.** Though Dubai has the tallest building in the world, Chengdu in southwest China has the largest, the New Century Global Center. This building was built one brick, one concrete slab, one rivet at a time. Your success is a series of small steps, one after another. It's starting that stops most people.

3. **Ignoring how environment shapes behaviors.** The way that you spend your time, what you read, what you eat, who you associate with all influence your behavior. If you're doing what everyone else is doing then that's a clue that a change is needed.

4. **Trying to stop old behaviors instead of creating new ones.** The key here is to focus on the desired actions, not avoidance. Don't focus on what you don't want, focus on what your desired result is. A good exercise is to write down "why" you want the new behaviors? What benefits will they bring you?

5. **Blaming failures on lack of motivation.** There is no such thing as an unmotivated person. It's a lack of priorities and precise planning.

6. **Underestimating the power of triggers.** You have to change your daily routine, your habits and your environment. Don't walk around the inside isles of the grocery store. You will be bombarded by triggers. Shop on the outside. Go in, get what you need, get out, socialize somewhere else.

7. **Believing that information leads to action.** You never stop learning, it's a lifetime deal. However, it takes a 7 day commitment with accountability to guarantee action. If you don't declare your actions in a behavioral contract chances are you'll be distracted and pulled away from the implementation of your new knowledge rendering it useless.

8. **Focusing on abstract goals more than concrete behaviors.** The abstract goal might be to get in shape. The concrete behavior is to walk 15 minutes today.

9. **Seeking to change a behavior forever, not for a short time.** A fixed period works better than forever, particularly 7 days and "Just for Today."

10. **Assuming that behavior change is difficult.** Behavior change is not so hard when you have the right process and have identified the why. Use the tools of this program.

Challenge:

Lots of challenges in all 10. Pick one to implement today.

Tapping in Meditation:

My purpose today is to turn my dreams into reality through action.

Journal Notes:

Day/Year	
Day/Year	
Day/Year	

November 7

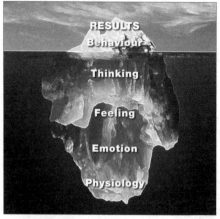

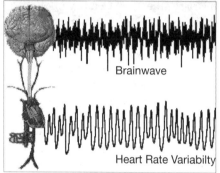

Brainwave

Heart Rate Variabilty

Be in the Zone Every Day

In order to change **results** you have to change **behavior**. You have to do things differently to get a different result. However, even though people know what to do sometimes they just don't do it. You have to get on the inside to what's really driving behavior and that's how you **think**. There is something even more fundamental that is driving behavior and that is how you **feel**. If you want to change what people do, you have to change their thinking and how they feel.

This is still not enough. There is something more fundamental driving how you feel and that is your raw **emotion**. Emotion is different than feeling. However, this is still not enough. There is something even more fundamental and that's your **physiology**. To be brilliant every day you need to have a grip on every single level. If a golfer is practicing his short game (behavior) and even this internal dialogue (thinking—I'm a champion golfer) he still has 3 levels he needs to pay attention to. What is physiology? Its streams of data. If you ate flour, you have signals to the brain indicating sugar. All of your senses, all of your organs send these electrical signals to your brain and all of these signals makes up your emotions. Emotion is Energy in Motion. Every second of every day there is an energetic state going through us. Feelings are the awareness of that energy.

Look at the signature of anxiety. The heart rate is fast. What else is happening? The mouth is dry, the palms of your hands are sweaty and your gut is churning. These are the specific physiological makeup of that thing you would know as anxiety. However, the problem may be that you're not noticing any of this you're just thinking away and doing what you're doing. To have your best day every day you need to tune in to what is happening on your physiological and emotional level and not only become aware of it but get control over it. So how do you get control of this? We'll start with the electrical signal of your heart. The distance between each heart beat varies over time. Doctors say your average is 70. What about the variance, that's the key. HRV—can tell you how much energy you have and it alters brain function. When you become stressed it shuts down your frontal lobes and you can't make decisions.

Challenge:

Tomorrow the concept will be a way to stay in the zone through your breathing. For today see if you can be aware of any sensations you feel during your meditation.

Tapping in Meditation:

My purpose today is to listen to my inner voice, my intuition that taps into the intelligence of the universe.

Journal Notes:

Day/Year	
Day/Year	
Day/Year	

November 8

Be in the Zone Every Day Part II

When the brain is inhibited by stress it also inhibits your perceptual awareness so you don't realize it's happening. The quality of your thoughts and creativity is influenced by your physiology. Thought is an emergent property in your system. You'll think differently if you're happy then if you're depressed. You have to change the context from which thoughts emerge, the emotional state, the physiology.

Breathing controls your physiology. There are 12 aspects of your breath that you can regulate. The single most important is rhythm. A fixed ratio of breaths in and out, 4 seconds in, 6 seconds out, repetitive. The second most important thing is smoothness. A fixed volume per second. The 3rd most important is the location of your attention while you're breathing. Breathe through the center of your chest. The heart generates more electrical power than any other area of your system. The heart generates 50x more electrical impulse than the brain. What's controlling what? We're so brain centered.

The big myth of performance is that it has to do with adrenalin. The debate, you've got to be either psyched up or relaxed. You get both types of advice, neither is true. You can ramp someone's system up negatively, anxiety, anger, frustration, or positively, passion, determination, focus which enhances performance. The only thing that matters is; are you on the left or right every day? There is a pull towards the right. Misery loves company. The zone, the state of flow is about being over to the left. Your breathing will get you to the center. The way you get to the left is to train yourself to regulate your emotions.

Your heart rate is the same but on the left side it's coherent.

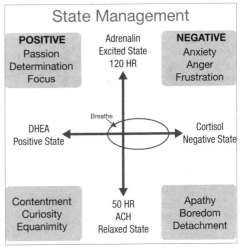

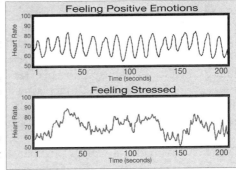

Challenge:

Notice your breathing in today's meditation.

B: Breathe R: Rhythmically E: Evenly A: And T: Through H: Heart E: Every day.

Breathe evenly in a rhythm and focus on your chest, your heart as you breath in and out.

Tapping in Meditation:

My purpose today is to be aware of my physiology, my emotions, my feelings, my thinking and my actions.

Journal Notes:

Day/Year	
Day/Year	
Day/Year	

November 9

The Top 5 End of Life Regrets Don't Mention Video Games

Reported by hospice workers, #1 I wish I hadn't worked so hard. #2 I wish I had stayed in touch with my friends. #3 I wish I had let myself be happier. #4 I wish I had the courage to express my true self. #5 I wish I'd lived a life true to my dreams instead of what others expected of me.

Jane McGonigal is an American game designer who advocates the use of games to channel positive attitudes and collaboration in the real world. She has gathered some interesting research. The end of life regrets are 5 deep human cravings that games fulfill. #1 for many people means that they wish they had spent more time with their family. A recent study from Brigham University reported that parents who spend more time playing video games with their kids have stronger real life relationships with them. #2 millions of people use social games like Words With Friends to stay in daily contact with their friends. A recent study from Michigan University showed that games are powerful relationship management tools #3 there have been ground breaking clinical trials recently conducted at East Carolina University that showed that on-line games can outperform pharmaceuticals in treating anxiety and depression. Just 30 minutes of game playing per day was enough to create long term increases in happiness. #4 Stanford University states that playing games with avatars has made the players more ambitious and courageous in real life. #5 game playing created freedom of expression and joy rather than fixed role playing to someone else's expectations.

Jane McGonigal had a concussion that didn't heal properly. She was bed ridden for 3 months and wanted to die. She had nonstop headaches, nausea, and memory loss. Her doctor told her that she in order to heal her brain she had to rest it. That meant no reading, no writing, no video games, no work or email, no running, no alcohol and no caffeine. She had thoughts of suicide. She decided that she was either going to kill herself or make it a game. She knew from the research that when you play a game you tackle tough challenges with more creativity, more optimism and determination. She created a role playing recovery game called Jane the Concussion Slayer. The game was to adopt a secret identity, recruit your allies, battle the bad guys and activate the positive power ups. She renamed the game to Super Better and started to hear from people all over the world who were getting better from cancer, chronic pain, depression and even terminal patients. The game was helping them the same way it had helped her. They talked about feeling stronger, braver, and better understood by their friends and family. They even talked about being happier even though they were in pain.

Challenge:

If you have children, today take 10 minutes and sit with them while they play their video games.

Tapping in Meditation:

My purpose today is to continue to challenge myself to grow, to learn, to appreciate, to love, to be of service to others and I do. I connect with people.

Journal Notes:

Day/Year	
Day/Year	
Day/Year	

November 10

Be the Change that you Seek

People intend to do the right things but it's their genetic coding that causes them not to. There is a guy in the gym who runs the water as he is shaving. We are in a drought in Southern California so why does he waste water like that? Doesn't he care? Is he not very smart? The answer is that he's on automatic.

Human behavior is driven by two systems, automatic and reflective. If you see a person with a certain type of emotion you easily and instinctively see the universal emotion of disgust. Your sense of vision bypasses all areas of the brain for analysis and goes directly to the limbic area and that immediately prevents you from

eating the poison berry that your cave mate just ate and became sick from. This is an automatic response. It is fast and energy efficient. However, if I ask you to take the square root of 9 and multiply it by 357 you have to pause. This is reflective. This type of thinking activates the prefrontal cortex, is slow and energy intensive. Biologically you are coded to conserve energy, so you are wired to avoid being reflective for too long. That's why there is candy near the check out lines at the grocery store. You've spent so much energy shopping that your willpower to resist is too low once you've made it to the front of the store.

Another consideration is your basic instincts. One of those is your pack mentality. This is one of the strongest instincts that you have. This means that you mirror the people around you. You have a tendency to do what you see other people do. If they stand in line you join behind them. If people start to whisper you lower your voice. This instinct is so strong that it overrides your good intentions or what you know is the right thing.

Sillie Krukow, a behavioral designer with The Wales Center for Behavior Change, designed a method to get compliance for recycling. She provided 3 easy to see and differentiate containers. Instead of telling people what not to do she made it very easy for people to clearly see what trash goes into each container. The behavior was changed.

Challenge:
The key is to keep things simple and to tap into the pack instinct and mirroring. Be the change you seek in others. Turn the water off while shaving or brushing your teeth in the gym, it matters. Others will notice.

Tapping in Meditation:
My purpose today is to model the behavior I want from others. I notice where I can "be the change I seek?" I take small actions today that are a model for others to mirror?

Journal Notes:

Day/Year	
Day/Year	
Day/Year	
Day/Year	
Day/Year	

November 11

Jerry Chooses to Live

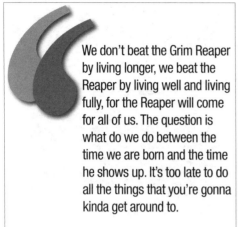

We don't beat the Grim Reaper by living longer, we beat the Reaper by living well and living fully, for the Reaper will come for all of us. The question is what do we do between the time we are born and the time he shows up. It's too late to do all the things that you're gonna kinda get around to.

—Randy Pausch

Jerry was one of the most positive people you'll ever meet. He was always in a good mood and always had something encouraging to say. He was a manager at a restaurant. If his employee had a bad day Jerry always helped them to look on the positive side of what they were experiencing.

Jerry's attitude was truly amazing. One day a customer asked "How can you be so positive all the time?" He replied; "You see, every morning I tell myself that I have two choices for that day—to be in a good or bad mood. If I choose the good mood then when something challenging happens I can be sad and angry or I can learn from it instead. I choose to learn. Thus I choose the positive side of life."

The customer replied, "It's not that easy." Jerry said, "Yes it is. Life is all about choices. You can choose how people or situations will affect your mood, your life."

One morning Jerry left the restaurant's back door open and he was held up at gunpoint by three armed robbers. He tried to open the safe but his hands trembled and he slipped off the combination. So the robbers shot him. Fortunately he was quickly found and brought to the nearest hospital. After many hours of surgery and long intensive care Jerry was discharged to go home.

When he came back to the restaurant that same customer asked him his thoughts during the robbery. He said, "I thought that I should have locked the back door. Then, when I lay on the floor I remembered the choices I have, to die or to live. I choose to live. The customer asked if he was scared. Jerry continued, "When they wheeled me into the emergency room and I looked at the faces of the doctors, then I got scared. I knew that I needed to do something. So when the nurse asked me if I was allergic to anything I replied yes. Everyone stopped working and waited for my answer. "I took a deep breath and yelled bullets." They started laughing and I said, "My choice is to live, operate on me as if I will live, not die."

Challenge:
Jerry is alive owing to the skills of his doctors. However, his amazing attitude played an important role too. Every day choose to live fully no matter what.

Tapping in Meditation:
My purpose today is to follow the tools of this program to live fully. The happiest people don't have the best of everything but they make the best of everything. I am divinely guided all day long.

Journal Notes:

Day/Year	
Day/Year	
Day/Year	
Day/Year	
Day/Year	

November 12

Learn a New Skill—It Only Takes 20 Hours

How long does it take to acquire a new skill? Research says it takes 10,000 hours. If you accept this then will you ever be able to learn anything new ever again? But it's not true! 10,000 hours is a full time job for 5 years. You've had the experience of learning something new and it didn't take 10,000 hours so something is going on between what the research says and what you have experienced. Josh Kaufman, author of *The Personal MBA: Master the Art of Business*, found that the 10,000 hour rule was for expert level performance. A psychology professor at Florida State named K Anders Ericsson is the originator of the 10,000 hour rule. He studied professional athletes, world class musicians, and ultra-competitive people. He found that the more time you practice the better you get and those at the very top of their field put in about 10,000 hours.

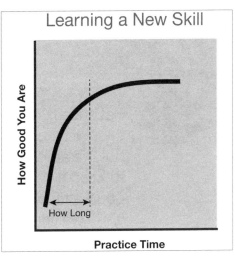

Learning a New Skill

Malcom Gladwell wrote a book in 2007 called *Outliers*. The center piece of that book was the 10,000 hour rule. The 10,000 rule was everywhere and became distorted and generalized. So the original message of it takes 10,000 hours to be the best in a narrow ultra-competitive field became it takes 10,000 hours to become an expert which became it takes 10,000 hours to become good, which became it takes 10,000 hours to learn. This last statement is not true. When you start you are very incompetent. But over time with practice you get very good really quick, then you reach a plateau and greater gains are tougher to get. How long does it take to go from terribly incompetent to being reasonably good? Josh's research says it takes 20 hours, that's it. This is very doable. It's about 45 minutes a day for about a month. There is a method to doing this. There is a way to practice intelligently that will make sure that you invest those 20 hours in the best way that you possibly can. This method applies to anything. The first step is to deconstruct the skill. Decide what you want to be able to do when you're done and break the skill down into small pieces. The second is to learn enough to self-correct. The third is to remove barriers to practice, distractions, TV, the internet. Forth, practice for at least 20 hours. There is the barrier of feeling incompetent. So by committing to 20 hours you will be able to overcome the frustration at the beginning of the task.

Challenge:

Test this theory. Decide what you want to learn. The major barrier to learning something new is not intellectual, it's emotional. You're scared. Feeling stupid doesn't feel good. You can put 20 hours into anything. What do you want to learn? What turns you on? What lights you up? Go out and do that thing.

Tapping in Meditation:

My purpose today is to go through fear and lean into my life. Whatever my future brings I will be brought again and again into contact with those who can be helped by my experience. Through these contacts I will be allowed to continue my own progress on this magnificent journey.

Journal Notes:

Day/Year	
Day/Year	
Day/Year	

November 13

Patience

Patience is not the ability to wait, but the ability to keep a good attitude while waiting.

A NYC taxi driver told the following story: I arrived at the address and honked the horn. After waiting a few minutes I honked again. Since this was going to be my last ride of my shift I thought about just driving away, but instead I put the car in park and walked up to the door and knocked. "Just a minute" answered a frail and elderly voice.

I could hear something being dragged across the floor. After a long pause, the door opened. A small woman in her 90s stood before me. By her side was a small nylon suitcase. "Would you carry my bag out to the car she said?" I took the suitcase to the cab, and then returned to assist the woman. She took my arm and we walked slowly toward the curb. She kept thanking me for my kindness. "It's nothing", I told her. "I just try to treat my passengers the way I would want my mother to be treated." "Oh, you're such a good boy," she said. When we got in the cab she gave me an address and then asked, "Could you drive through downtown?" "It's not the shortest way," I answered. "Oh, I don't mind," she said, "I'm in no hurry. I'm on my way to a hospice."

I looked in the rear view mirror. Her eyes were glistening. "I don't have any family left," she continued in a soft voice. "The doctor says I don't have very long." I quietly reached over and shut off the meter. "What route would you like me to take? I asked. For the next 2 hours we drove through the city. We drove through the neighborhood where she and her husband had lived when they were newlyweds. She had me pull up in front of a furniture warehouse that had once been a ballroom where she had gone dancing as a girl. Sometimes she'd ask me to slow in front of a particular building or corner and would sit staring into the darkness, saying nothing. As the sun began to set she finally said, "I'm tired, let's go now." We drove in silence to the address she had given me. It was a small convalescent home. I opened the trunk and took the small suitcase to the door. The woman was already seated in a wheelchair. "How much do I owe you?" She asked. Nothing I said. "You have to make a living," she answered. I said that there would be other passengers and almost without thinking I bent and gave her a hug. She held onto me tightly. "You gave an old woman a little moment of joy," she said, "Thank you."

I didn't pick up any more passengers that shift. I drove aimlessly lost in thought. What if that woman had gotten an angry driver, or one who was impatient to end his shift? On a quick review, I don't think that I have done anything more important in my life.

Challenge:
You are conditioned to think that your life revolves around great moments. But great moments often catch you unaware, wrapped in what others may consider a small one.

Tapping in Meditation:
My purpose today is to notice the moments, share myself and my kindness with others.

Journal Notes:

Day/Year	
Day/Year	
Day/Year	

November 14

Clay Balls

A man was exploring caves by the seashore. In one of the caves he found a canvas bag with a bunch of hardened clay balls. It was like someone had rolled clay balls and left them out in the sun to bake. They didn't look like much, but they intrigued the man, so he took the bag out of the cave with him. As he strolled along the beach, he would throw the clay balls one at a time out into the ocean as far as he could. He thought little about it, until he dropped one of the clay balls and it cracked open on a rock. Inside was a beautiful, precious stone!

Excited, the man started breaking open the remaining clay balls. Each contained a similar treasure. He found thousands of dollars' worth of jewels in the 20 or so clay balls he had left. Then it struck him. He had been on the beach a long time. He had thrown maybe 50 or 60 of the clay balls with their hidden treasure into the ocean waves. Instead of thousands of dollars in treasure, he could have taken home tens of thousands, but he had just thrown it away!

It's like that with people. We look at someone, maybe even ourselves, and we see the external clay vessel. It doesn't look like much from the outside. It isn't always beautiful or sparkling, so we discount it. We see that person as less important than someone more beautiful or stylish or well known or wealthy, but we have not taken the time to find the treasure hidden inside that person.

There is a treasure in each and every one of us. If you take the time to get to know that person, and if you ask your higher intuition to show you that person that way. May you not come to the end of your life and find out that you have thrown away a fortune in friendships because the gems were hidden in bits of clay.

Challenge:
May you see the people in your world for their goodness. You are so blessed by the gems of friendship you have. Today notice and be grateful for the wonderful moments you have all day long.

Tapping in Meditation:
My purpose today is to be willing to see the magic in everything around me and I do.

Journal Notes:

Day/Year	
Day/Year	
Day/Year	
Day/Year	
Day/Year	

November 15

Matt Woodrum—An Inspiration

(edited story that appeared July 2, 2014 in the Huffington Post)
Video: https://www.youtube.com/watch?v=rXwRWGoFtrO

I still can't watch the video of Matt Woodrum's run around the track with his entire class coming together behind him to cheer him on without getting teary-eyed. Matt has cerebral palsy. It's everything we want to teach our kids about courage and determination, of how an entire community of people came together to support one of their own. The link for the video is above. If it's not posted send me an email and I'll send it to you (info@bobdavies.com)

Beyond it just being an inspiring individual moment, his classmates rallying around Matt is a metaphor for what kind of country we should be. America should be a family where we rally behind our brothers and sisters who are having a tough time of it, where we lift each other up in the struggle to finish the race, where we treasure the slowest of our children just as much as the fastest. And the fact is that the people in this country who need that support and encouragement usually are the ones working harder than the rest of us in their effort to finish the race. Matt had to work far harder than anyone else in that race to finish and he still needed the rest of the class to help encourage him to make it home. Matt was inspired by his classmates, but they were inspired by him as well, and everyone has become a better person as a result. The story of Matt Woodrum's race and his entire class cheering him on is America at its best, America as it should be.

Challenge:
Today treat each person you come in contact with as a family, where you create a beautiful symphony of brotherhood, where you make others' conditions your own. Notice how the other person reacts to you and how it makes you feel. Journal below.

Tapping in Meditation:
My purpose today is to think serenity and love. My smile is a blessing to others and I pour it on. I have an unlimited supply.

Journal Notes:

Day/Year	
Day/Year	
Day/Year	
Day/Year	
Day/Year	

November 16

Sensory Goal Setting

If you want to be thin, you have to start seeing yourself thin in vivid detail. Run your hand over you smooth tight stomach. Smell the taste of the wonderful wholesome food you are eating. Hear your friends complementing you on how good you look. Stand in front of the mirror and visualize yourself thin. Do this all in your mind.

If you want to be financially independent, you have to see yourself dressed in nice clothes driving a nice car with the wind blowing in your hair, putting your hand down and feeling the leather seats. Now go to the car dealership and actually sit in one.

If you want to be a confident public speaker, you have to close your eyes and feel the feelings as they give you a standing ovation for the brilliant seminar you just gave. Hear them applauding. Feel the pride and joy of your accomplishment. Feel the feelings. Smell the perfume of the women who introduced you as she gives you a hug to congratulate you. Now go alone to an auditorium and just stand there visualizing the feelings.

If you want to have a new house, see the size of the yard, smell the flowers planted there, enjoy the color of the carpet, the smell of bread baking in the oven, look at the number of windows, feel the texture of the stones in the walk, hear the sound of the birds in the trees, admire the color of the house. Now go to Better Homes And Gardens and get a picture of it and hang it on your wall. Better yet, go to the home show and just stand there feeling it as yours.

Vivid Sensory Visualization includes all of the five senses: SEEING, HEARING, SMELLING, TASTING, and TOUCHING. Including your Vivid Sensory Visualizations as a part of your daily goal setting and your chances of success will increase by about 99%. May all your vivid sensory visualizations be positive, because both types work equally well.

Challenge:

One of the common traits of wildly successful people is their ability to visualize, seeing the image of what they want in great detail. As you do this and focus on all of your senses your eyes will naturally move to the position that they need to be in to access either memory or future construction of the experience. By using your senses you are recruiting neurons from the emotional area of the brain to connect with the outer prefrontal cortex and actually forming networks as if you have already achieved your goals. Add this to your meditation this morning.

Tapping in Meditation:

My purpose today is to know what I want, why I want it and then to be in action to create it.

Journal Notes:

Day/Year	
Day/Year	
Day/Year	
Day/Year	

November 17

Money is Not a Motivator

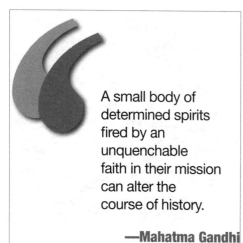

> A small body of determined spirits fired by an unquenchable faith in their mission can alter the course of history.
>
> —**Mahatma Gandhi**

I hypnotized a group of volunteers at a conference. This means that they were bypassing the prefrontal cortex and responding to my suggestions with the limbic area of the brain, also incorrectly referred to as the subconscious mind. The limbic brain accepts as being true whatever is vividly imagined or in this case suggested. I told a person that I would give them $100 if they could get up from the chair and come and take the money out of my hand. However, prior to that challenge I had given the command that she was stuck like glue to the chair. The result, she struggled and became frustrated and was unable to get up from the chair. Why? Because she had an overriding belief that she was stuck.

Traditional wisdom says if you offer people more money they'll work harder. Traditional wisdom is wrong. Motivation is one of the most misunderstood concepts in business. The mistake that most businesses make is assuming that people are motivated by money. They are not. Money is a stabilizer. Beyond food and shelter people have a need for connection and meaning. People want to know that what they are doing matters. They want close personal connections while they are on this planet and they want to make a contribution that outlasts their stay on it.

People will work to get money but you won't get their loyalty, you won't get their best effort and over time they'll feel entitled. If you over emphasize money people actually wind up less engaged. As a business owner you need to give people something to care about besides money. That something is a sense of purpose. The businesses that are most successful are those who have a larger purpose that goes beyond just profit.

Here is an example of two technology companies. Company A and B. The owner of company A tells the employees our goal is to sell computer systems. We sell back up services, hardware, software, the more you sell, the more money you make. They might have a good business but company B takes it a step further. Their owner tells the employees they are on a mission to make small businesses more successful. One is an internal focus, the other is an external focus, it's a purpose, a larger purpose and it makes a difference to the employees' engagement. Purpose ignites true passion.

Challenge:
Make sure you are clear about what your purpose is. Write it down in your journal today.

Tapping in Meditation:
My purpose today is to lean into my mission and fire it up with faith and action and through this I can create change.

Journal Notes:

Day/Year	
Day/Year	
Day/Year	

November 18

Add this to Your Goal Setting

There are 4 things that it actually takes to have a goal happen.

1. Make a mind connection—what you want to have happen.
2. Make a body connection—you need to write it down.
3. You need to say it—you need to declare what your outcome is. Saying it makes it real.
4. You need to anchor it. Anchor it in something that you can look at every day, a vision board. Identify your metrics. Put it into a visual.

In the long run
men hit
only what
they aim at.

—Henry David Thoreau

SANITY

S: Support—What support does your goal need in order to manifest? What financial support, what group support, what research does it need?

A: Action—What is the one next step that you have to take in order to have this happen?

N: No—You have to say no to something you already have to get something new. The space for what you want in your life is already being filled by what you are willing to settle for.

I: Integration—Are all of the parts working in the same way? Are your actions making progress towards the goals achievement?

T: Trust—Do you trust that it can actually happen? Do you believe it is possible? Do you trust the people that you're working with?

Y: Why—Why do you want it? If 2 or 3 agree on a common purpose, nothing is impossible.

Challenge:
Take any goal that you set and put the SANITY template over it. As soon as these 6 pieces are in place that goal will manifest.

Tapping in Meditation:
My purpose today is to become more than I am so I can have more than I've got. Success is something that I attract. I am a searcher for knowledge, awareness, learning and understanding.

Journal Notes:

Day/Year	
Day/Year	
Day/Year	
Day/Year	
Day/Year	

November 19

Jim Rohn's 10 Great Powers

International business philosopher, Jim Rohn, (1930-2009) prepares you to be more valuable tomorrow than you are today. Take Jim's words of wisdom along with my commentary to build your business and transform yourself. Jim Rohn's 10 great powers.

1. **Learn the power of purpose**. A person who has purpose in their lives has something to go for, some meaning. For some people it becomes a magnificent obsession. It has to be something that pulls you into the future.
2. **Self-confidence**. This comes from feeling good about you. One of the best ways to feel good about yourself is at the end of the day to know that you gave it your best effort.
3. **Enthusiasm**. 90% inside, 10% outside. The enthusiasm that affects people is that which is on the inside.
4. **Expertise**. Wanting to excel in all of the skills and settling for nothing less than an outstanding performance. Not accepting less than you can be.
5. **Preparation**. It takes time to prepare. The decisions you make in the preparation lasts a life time. Preparation means that you want to make the best contribution. Prepare yourself for your success. Life was designed not to give you what you want or need, but what you deserve. Every value in life must be paid for. Go search for good ideas.
6. **Self-reliance**. You simply look mostly to yourself. You are the person responsible. You will learn the necessary skills. Never complain.
7. **Image**. Other people need to see you as a leader to trust you and follow you. If you have the image of someone in control then that attracts other people. Also very important is your image of yourself. The way you dress, talk, your capacity for learning. Are you continually trying your best to be the best you can?
8. **Character**. Becoming a person of high value, principle, honesty, a person that's earned respect, that's character. Do people see you as honest, fair and willing to be helpful and doing the right thing?
9. **Self-discipline**. You may have a challenge with this because it's easy to let it go. If you will do the best job that you can that is self-discipline.
10. **Extraordinary performance**. Demanding of you excellent results. If you want to live extraordinary you must do extraordinary things. You earn your successes.

Challenge:

You must perform day after day, year after year. You have to ask this of yourself. You must demand this of yourself. Society doesn't demand that you take care of yourself and eat properly. That you must demand of yourself. Society doesn't demand that you constantly improve by reading that you must demand of yourself. Society doesn't demand that you use the tools of this program, it's not a law. But if you want the benefit of these tools you must demand it of yourself.

Tapping in Meditation:

My purpose today is to make the effort to rise above my circumstances and I do. I demand excellence of myself. I give everything I have to each moment.

Journal Notes:

Day/Year	
Day/Year	
Day/Year	
Day/Year	

November 20

The Story of the Golden Buddha

Over three hundred years ago, the Burmese army planned an attack to invade Thailand. The monks were in possession of the most amazing Buddha statue. The statue is over 10 feet tall and weighs in excess of 2 1/2 tons. It is made of solid gold and is valued today at $200 MILLION dollars. The monks were determined to protect the shrine that meant so much to them. They knew that the Burmese would stop at nothing to steal the statue because of its tremendous monetary value. They covered the Golden Buddha with 12 inches of clay knowing that the warriors would totally ignore it and think it worthless. Sadly, the monks were slaughtered in the invasion and the secret of the Golden Buddha stayed hidden for two centuries. The Buddha itself though, remained safe.

In the mid 50's, a monastery was to be relocated to make room for a new highway. The monks arranged for a crane to come and move the "Clay" Buddha to its new location. When the crane started to lift the statue, it was much heavier than expected and it began to crack. In the dark of night, the head monk took his flashlight and went out t examine the Buddha. When the light of the flashlight shone into the crack of the clay, he saw a reflection. He immediately started to carefully chisel away the clay. Hours later, and all the clay removed…he was in the presence of a Buddha made of solid gold.

The golden Buddha wasn't discovered, it was dis covered, finding something that was already there. Columbus didn't discover America, it was already there. That Buddha is a lot like you. You have this great creativity, this great talent, this great potential but it gets covered up with clay. The clay is your self-doubt, your fears, the wounds you experience, all that stuff you've accumulated growing up. You don't need to do anything to put "more" into you but you need to take away what's inhibiting your natural brilliance from coming out.

Challenge:
Imagine all your dreams coming true, imagine being free from irrational fears, and imagine realizing your true passion and living it. You may say I'm a dreamer……but I'm not the only one!! John Lennon was one, too.

Tapping in Meditation:
My purpose today is to remove what stops the expression of my true talents and I do. All of the people in the world are my teachers with each doing just the right things to help me to learn perfect patience, perfect wisdom and perfect compassion.

Journal Notes:

Day/Year	
Day/Year	
Day/Year	
Day/Year	
Day/Year	

November 21

The Great Illusion

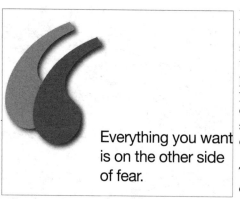

Everything you want is on the other side of fear.

It's an unreasoning terror, an irrational panic that clutches at your throat and offers no avenue of escape; a fear that alerts you to no real danger yet it causes the heart to pound, the blood pressure to rise and the palms to sweat. When it strikes your pupils will dilate, your hair will bristle, your muscles will tense. It will be difficult to swallow and you may feel nauseated and about to faint. Most of all, you will want to run to escape, to avoid.

The fear response is as old as mankind. When we encounter the perception of an emergency the sympathetic nervous system calls up the "flight or fight" response. Blood is transferred from internal organs to external muscles. Sugar is released by the liver to feed the active muscles and fat is broken down. Tiny structures in the lungs expand to take in more air. The heart beats faster to circulate blood more quickly. The blood becomes richer in oxygen. Digestion stops and diverts blood elsewhere. The adrenal glands release adrenaline and other hormones.

This is quite helpful if you are being chased by a bear. However, it's the same response if triggered by the illusion of fear, no real danger like being stuck in traffic. So how do you deal with your fears? There are 3 ways:

1. Ignore it. Pretend it doesn't exist. This is the lowest level, not the entrepreneur's response. Instead they have a story about why they don't get what they want.
2. Act in spite of it. When you live this way you become wealthy but you're miserable. Lots of anxiety.
3. Understand it and accept it. This is the best way to handle it. Live with positive emotions. Accept the fact that most of the fears that you feel are smoke screens for other fears. Two of them—on some level you're not enough. Next is if you don't measure up you won't be loved. As a baby you equated attention and love as the same thing. People know they'll get attention if they have problems. Others get their attention through achievement. We all have the strategies we run to get the connection back. It's the story, like a circuit breaker for the fear.

Challenge:

Eleanor Roosevelt said courage wasn't the absence of fear but being afraid and doing it anyway. Today, take that further, accept the fear, understand it, embrace it and step through it into action.

Tapping in Meditation:

My purpose today is to relax lovingly into my fear and accept that it is a part of my life but is no longer necessary, I thank the fear and continue on with my necessary actions. I keep my "Why" in front of me at all times.

Journal Notes:

Day/Year	
Day/Year	
Day/Year	

November 22

The Mystery of Change

Human behavior and decision making has always been a mystery to me. I'm committed to cracking the code regarding implementation. Mahatma Gandi says, "The difference between what we are doing and what we are capable of doing would solve most of the world's problems." Why don't you do what you know you should do—what you're capable of doing to solve your problems? There is a disconnect between the data input, everything you learn, and the behavioral output, what you implement and do. Fishermen were catching the Patagonian tooth fish but based on its looks they considered it to be a throw away. In 1977 a fish wholesaler named Lee Lance was first exposed to this menacing looking fish. Lance sensed that people would enjoy the mild taste but not its name so he began selling this cold water cod as Chilean sea bass. It wasn't even a bass! This is very important to understand because it tells you how human beings respond in the world and how they make decisions.

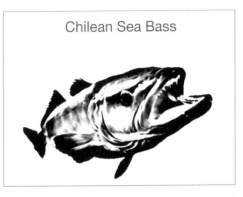

Chilean Sea Bass

Mark Twain said it best, "When we remember we are all mad, the mysteries disappear and life stands explained." We are not machines who make logical decisions based on the facts. We are mad human creatures who are being pushed and pulled by our previous experiences, our fears and our environment. The truth is that you are far more capable of creating the circumstances and events in your life than you are aware of. However, I follow that statement with "The truth is not relevant, it doesn't matter!"

Screenwriter Robert McKee writes, "What happens is fact, not truth. Truth is what we think about what happens." We make decisions based on facts but we only do that if those facts support your personal truths and primarily these 3, the look and feel of your future, how much control you think you have and your image—the evolving story of who you think you are and want to become. You are drawn to beautiful, fun and entertaining. You are drawn to the iPhone and the newest new technology. It's your nature. And it's the nature of the marketplace to keep on producing new enticing stimuli. New technology is moving in the direction to solve your need for control. Everything from calorie counting apps to GPS is aimed to give you the sense of control. Your mind thinks that the key to ongoing engagement and passion is to have more information. However, you already know that's not true. So what moves you? Desire moves you. Desire grows around your most potent personal truth, the stories you tell yourself about yourself. Who you think you are is why you do what you do.

Challenge:
Ask yourself, "Who am I." What story are you living?

Tapping in Meditation:
My purpose today is to embrace that I am lovable and develop and deepen relationships, inclusion and acceptance. I am capable, I develop new skills, learn and experience achieving success. I implement and take action.

Journal Notes:

Day/Year	
Day/Year	
Day/Year	

November 23

Some Thoughts From Coach Bob

To help as many people as possible, change their lives and become success stories.

I want to congratulate you for being a part of my vision to guide as many people who care to personal and performance excellence. Jesus said it best, "The road is narrow few will choose it." Notice he didn't say few are capable. He said few are willing. Everyone is capable.

My entire journey has been figuring out how to present concepts in a way that gets through the outer cortex, the logical part of the brain and into the feeling part, the limbic system. The science of change is well known. You make a decision of what you what, what you need to do to have it and what you are willing to do over a short period of time, 7 days, and then you add massive accountability to implementing over the next week.

I don't know how long you have been with this program. People are joining every day and they all plug into the same spot you are in right now. They use the tools of the program. They read one page a day, they have quiet time for 5 to 10 minutes every day, they pre plan their week and they are open to being the best version of themselves that they can be.

There are 3 pillars to personal excellence, health, business and personal development. It all starts with your physiology, what you put into your body so we have the weighed and measured food plan. That's where everyone starts. From there depending on your individual circumstances you will make adjustments to the recommended dosages. Then it's off to your mindset development. This is an ongoing program, supported by the conference calls.

If you've been with me for awhile you've already seen a dramatic and life changing transformation. Now it's ongoing learning and keeping the successes you've had. If you're just starting out keep at it. The principles you are being exposed to are not speculative. They will produce results in your life if you stay with them. Now it's time to start thinking about wrapping up your year. In 8 days you'll be in December. I'll be asking you to develop a "sprint-jog" approach to December and to begin the development of your business plan for next year. This will come in early December.

Challenge:

Start to take a look at what you have created this year. What successes have you had and where have you fallen short. It's not good or bad, it just is. Notice this. November is a month of looking back and giving thanks, and looking forward and preparing for greatness. Make sure you do both.

Tapping in Meditation:

My purpose today is to remain open to positive results in my life. Achievement always comes to me if I am looking for it, not waiting for it. I always remember that it's the giving that makes me what I am and I cannot give more then I get.

Journal Notes:

Day/Year	
Day/Year	
Day/Year	

November 24

Your Life Becomes the Story You Tell Yourself

It is urgent that you "get" the concept that all things that happen to you are void of any meaning and it is up to you to assign a story to the events of your life. It is your narrative about what you say that something means that matters. You must realize that you have to choice to give it whatever meaning you decide. This is the ultimate in personal responsibility. The illusion is that's it's easier to give this power away, to go victim and blame another person or the situation. This is so disempowering it's sad to see how prevalent it really is. Now I just made up a story about this being sad. It's not anything, it just is until I or you implant a meaning on it.

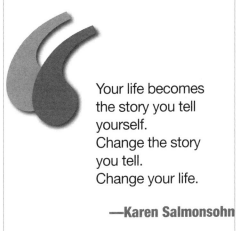

Your life becomes the story you tell yourself.
Change the story you tell.
Change your life.

—**Karen Salmonsohn**

Negative emotions, anger and frustration for example, creates increased disorder and incoherence in your heart's rhythms and the autonomic nervous system thereby affecting the rest of your body. In contrast, positive emotions such as love, care and appreciation create increased harmony and coherence in the hearts rhythms and improved balance in the nervous system. Disharmony of your heart rhythms leads to inefficiency and increased stress on the heart and other organs. If the sympathetic and parasympathetic are out of sync with each other it's like trying to drive your car with one foot on the accelerator and the other simultaneously on the brake.

When you have a disordered heart rhythm your blood vessels constrict, blood pressure rises and a lot of energy is wasted. If this happens consistently the result is hypertension (high blood pressure) which greatly increases the risk of heart disease and stroke. It is estimated that 1 in 4 Americans, approximately 50 million people are hypertensive and cardiovascular disease now claims more lives each year than the next 7 leading causes of death combined. The good news is that feelings of appreciation, love, compassion and care create the opposite effect. These positive heart feelings generate the smooth and harmonious heart rate variability rhythms that are considered to be indicators of cardiovascular efficiency and nervous system balance. When your body is in entrainment you feel better and you are at your optimal functioning capacity.

Challenge:

Just for today do not give away your power to give meaning to everything that happens to you. Today everything that happens to you is positive. Think of a challenging situation. Now write down 3 things about this situation to appreciate.

Tapping in Meditation:

My purpose today is to fix my thinking. My problems will fix themselves when my thinking is positive. I take full responsibility for the meaning I give to life. The highest form of human intelligence is to observe without evaluating and I do.

Journal Notes:

Day/Year	
Day/Year	
Day/Year	
Day/Year	

November 25

Lovely Logics

A GOOD LIFE is when you assume nothing, do more, heed less, smile often, dream big, laugh a lot and realize how blessed you are..

1. Make peace with your past so it doesn't spoil your present.

2. What others think of you is none of your business.

3. Time heals almost everything. Give the time some time.

4. No one is the reason for your happiness except for yourself.

5. Don't compare your life with others you have no idea what their journey is all about.

6. Stop thinking too much it's alright not to know the answers.

7. Smile, you don't own all the problems of the world.

Challenge:

"It's impossible said pride. It's risky, said experience, its pointless said reason. Give it a try whispered the heart." What would you do if you knew you could not fail? What does your heart tell you to do today?

Tapping in Meditation:

My purpose today is to sit quietly and bring my awareness to the divine guidance of the universe. Love makes my friends a little dearer. Joy makes my heart a little lighter. Faith makes my path a little clearer. Hope makes me a little brighter. Peace brings us all a little closer.

Journal Notes:

Day/Year	
Day/Year	
Day/Year	
Day/Year	
Day/Year	

November 26

Daniel Amen Says Change Your Brain

Your brain is involved in everything that you do, how you think, feel and act. At the Amen clinic Dr. Amen has looked at over 63,000 brain scans over the last 20 years. When your brain works right, you work right. His brain scans looks at blood flow and activity patterns. It basically shows 3 things, areas of the brain that work well, areas of the brain that are low in activity and areas in the brain that are high in activity. The brain on the left is smooth with evenly distributed activity. The brain on the right is the brain of an alcoholic. With a healthy brain you are happier, healthier, wealthier, wiser, more creative and more innovative. Your brain is the most complicated organ in the universe. It has over 100 billion nerve cells, more connections than stars, information travels at 268 mph, it is 2% of the body's weight but uses 20-30% of your daily calories. Your brain is the most expensive real estate in your body. You can accelerate the aging process with your behavior or you can decelerate it. So what hurts your brain? Brain injuries, drugs & alcohol, obesity, smoking,

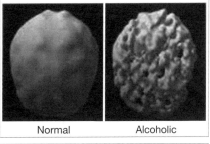

Normal   Alcoholic

Three 60 Year Old Brains

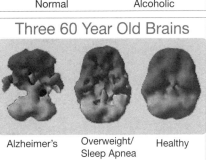

Alzheimer's   Overweight/   Healthy
          Sleep Apnea

high blood pressure, diabetes, diet, environmental toxins, lack of exercise, negative thoughts. As your weight goes up the actual physical size and function of your brain goes down. Smoking constricts blood flow to the brain. As your blood pressure goes up the blood flow to your brain goes down. Negative thoughts are the seeds of anxiety disorders and depression.

Here are things you can do to help your brain. Positive social connections, new learning, nutrient dense diet (your food plan), sleep, exercise, healthy anxiety, meditation, gratitude and guard your thoughts. The people you spend time with determine your longevity. You pick up their habits. When you learn you make new connections. When you eat you are consuming the nutrients that help you or the toxins that hurt you. Sleep is absolutely essential. In 1900 we got 9 hours of sleep in 2014 it was down to 6. This results in lower overall blood flow to the brain. As sleep goes down weight goes up because your cravings get out of control. The best medicine for depression is not Prozac its gratitude. Here are 3 60 year old brains. One that has Alzheimer's, one that is overweight with sleep apnea and one that is healthy. If you make good decisions today you can start to improve your brain within two months.

Challenge:
Be a student of this program. You have a chance to be a participant in a lifestyle that can change the world. This needs to happen in your family from the food you serve to the thoughts you support and model. There are 3 studies that show that if you eliminated the types of food that school kids eat and replaced it with high nutrient density food (your plan) then 75% would show a reduction in behavioral problems and attention symptoms.

Tapping in Meditation:
My purpose today is to change one habit, one action that will be healthy for my brain function.

Journal Notes:

Day/Year	
Day/Year	
Day/Year	

November 27

Brain Integration—It All Points to Meditation

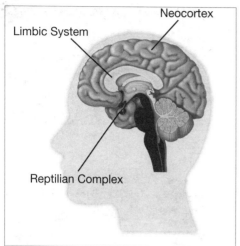

Neocortex

Limbic System

Reptilian Complex

Make a fist with both hands and put your knuckles together so that the heels of your hands are touching. Look at the top of your hands, that's the outer cortex. This is the part of your brain that enables you to critically think, to plan, to analyze. Open up your hands and notice your fingers mirrored on both sides and buried deep within the brain, that's the limbic system. This is your emotional area. Your wrist represents the brain stem, your autonomic system, breathing, heart rate.

There are 3 Rs that are important in brain development and life fulfillment. They are Reflection, Relationships and Resilience. This is the basis of emotional intelligence. When you understand your own feelings and learn to manage them you can understand others. Relationships, the number one factor in longevity and happiness is relationships, how you have positive connections with other people. If you are given $20 and asked to either gift it to someone else or to spend it on yourself, the reward center of the brain, driven by the neurotransmitter dopamine, gets active when you give to someone else. When you give in service to other people you are actually happier yourself.

What do relationships have to do with the brain? How is self-regulation related to the brain? The self is a part of your mind. This is the field of interpersonal neurobiology. The spinal cord and the vagus nerve all bring data from the body into the brain. You actually have a brain around your heart and a brain around your intestines as well. So the word brain means the whole body and how it processes information through the flow of energy. Deep in the brain is the oldest, over 3 million years old, called the reptilian brain. This is the brain stem. It will keep you awake, it has the fight or flight response. Next is the limbic area. This developed 2 million years ago. This limbic area works with the brain stem to create your emotions, it works with other areas to create memories, the outer cortex is the last part to grow and it's the part that is shaped by the experiences you have. The frontal cortex part of the brain is the part that allows you to mention and manage your emotions. Reflection develops the prefrontal cortex. This part of the brain lets you pick up on what's going on in someone else's nervous system, sad, happy. This area integrates all of your sensations. When you have reflection and you have relationships that are caring and connecting, you actually stimulate the growth of the integrative fibers in the brain. And these are the fibers that allow you to have resilience.

Challenge:
Make sure you get your 5-10 minutes of meditation every day.

Tapping in Meditation:
My purpose today is to quite my mind and listen to my soul.

Journal Notes:

Day/Year	
Day/Year	
Day/Year	

November 28

Breathe Deeply

Science has taught us that our brain makes us who we are. It filters our understanding of our world and our place in that world. However, not only does your brain shape you but you can actually shape your brain as well. One of the answers may very well be in your breathing and mediation.

Cancer cannot live in a high oxygen environment. Neither can depression or anxiety. If you learn to take deeper breaths you can actually re pattern and heal and move towards wholeness and fullness. The body has a profound connection to your breath. At the very end of each breath you take, just before the breath becomes an inhale, you have the capacity to learn something new. Most people think that meditation creates very peaceful calm states. However, what is created is very strong tension, radical integration, then you release. You become aware of your body.

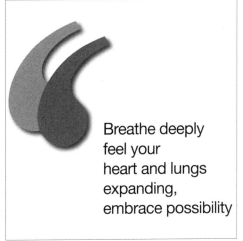

Breathe deeply
feel your
heart and lungs
expanding,
embrace possibility

Challenge:

Place your palms open and facing up. Take a deep breath and make a fist. As you exhale release the first. Right there you have the capacity to learn something. Inhale and squeeze. Exhale and release the tension and now think of someone you love. Once more inhale and squeeze, think of someone who loves you and then exhale and release your hands. When you thought of someone you loved you may have sat up a bit straighter. You breathed deeper. You were not in a cognitive state; you were in an embodied healing state. You have the capacity to line up with something absolutely awesome by the simple act of knowing where you are in your skin. So today, commit to notice how you breathe and commit to taking 5 deep breaths in the course of the day. Align yourself with the ability to respond rather than react.

Tapping in Meditation:

My purpose today is to breathe deeply, think positively, live simply, give generously, hug tightly, laugh loudly, speak kindly, love unconditionally, smile brightly, dream nightly and I do.

Journal Notes:

Day/Year	
Day/Year	
Day/Year	
Day/Year	
Day/Year	

November 29

Progressive Relaxation and Mindfullness

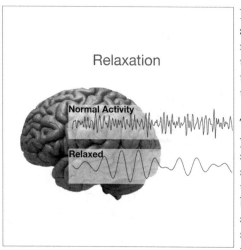

Relaxation

Normal Activity

Relaxed

Progressive Relaxation is simply directing your attention to one body part at a time and thinking relaxation. When you think relaxation your body has the wisdom of creating that effect. When I skydive I think of different maneuvers like turning a 360 and the body does what it needs to do to create the result.

The secret key to mindfulness is that you learn to direct your attention to your body and breath. Is mindfulness a mind focus or body focus? How might body focused attention produce specific benefits for the mind? It turns out that when you pay close attention to your body, your feet for example or your breathing, you're actually learning how to control the volume of the sensory input in your brain. There is a structure under the cortex called the thalamus. The thalamus is the gate keeper for the cortex. It creates a loop, a rhythmic loop that pulses 10 times per second called an alpha wave. It's editing sensations that are irrelevant. You can use your mind to regulate the height of the alpha wave.

Mindfulness practitioners learn to monitor their moment-by-moment experience so that they can "step back" from negative, distressing thoughts and feelings in order to view them as "mental events" rather than as unmediated reflections of reality.

Processing resources are biased towards the pain sensation. In chronic pain and depression the attention resources are consumed by negative preoccupation with thoughts and worries. With progressive relaxation practice you can influence the attention and perception of sensory inputs. It turns out that the early Buddhist 2500 years ago had the same theory with their 4 foundations of mindfulness. The first foundation is mindfulness of the body and breath. This is the first step in learning how to regulate emotion and repetitive negative thoughts. Aspects of sensations were viewed as continuous with aspects of thoughts. The sensory world and the thought world are related. You can develop a different level of consciousness about your environment and the sensory input that you are taking in. This mindfulness may be able to reset cognitive and emotional baselines. This is again another example that you have far more capacity to create the circumstances and events in your life then you are aware of.

Challenge:

The simple act of paying attention to the sensations at the bottom of your feet as you walk has great potential to give huge benefits for wellbeing. Do this today.

Tapping in Meditation:

My purpose today is to practice directing my body. I think relaxation in my feet, lower legs, upper legs, stomach, upper arms, back, shoulders, chest, lower arms, hands, neck, face and I do let go.

Journal Notes:

Day/Year	
Day/Year	
Day/Year	

November 30

Financial Literacy

Money is the #1 thing that young people worry about. 76% of people feel out of control when it comes to money. 61% of the country is living paycheck to paycheck. Look at the typical college graduate. Emily, age 22, graduates from college with $25k in student debt and $4k in credit card debt. She will end up if she is lucky with a $35k job right out of college. This means that she will take home approximately $2,300 in take home pay. Here are 5 decisions that she will make.

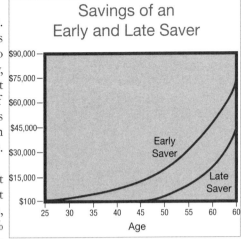

Savings of an Early and Late Saver

Decision 1: She won't have a budget. She doesn't know that good financial planning recommends that 50% of her money goes towards essential expenses, 20% to financial priorities, her future savings and 30% towards lifestyle choices. Her actual spending will be 63% for essential expenses, 11% for financial priorities and 26% lifestyle choices. She's going to get an apartment spending $1200 a month. This will put her in jeopardy for years to come.

Decision 2: she has a lot of debt but instead of aggressively paying it down she's only going to make her minimum payments.

Decision 3: she will miss a few of those payments because she doesn't understand what a credit score is or how it is critical to her future. After that she won't think about emergency savings.

Decision 4: she's not going to negotiate her salary. She's so thankful for having a job that she's not going to think about negotiating her salary. The result is that 3 years later she's still making $35k.

Decision 5: her final mistake is that she's not going to be thinking about retirement in her 20s. Because of that she doesn't take advantage of her employers' 401k match program and she doesn't open a Roth IRA.

Now fast forward 15 years. Emily gets married and has two children. She will be closer to $20k in debt, she still has about $10k in student loan debt, her credit score is 570. On a good note, she started thinking about retirement but she currently has less than $10k in retirement savings. She doesn't set up a 529 plan for her children. This is the story of millions of Americans. We are a country that has 2.5 trillion in consumer debt. The American dream of home ownership is not a reality and 25% of applications are denied. 31% of Americans today have no retirement savings. The #1 cause of fights in marriages is money and they are 30% more likely to divorce.

Challenge:

The solution is to teach the Emily's 5 principles, help them before they make mistakes. Teach them to #1 follow a budget, live beneath their means, #2, be debt free. pay cards in full. #3, have an emergency savings account, #4, negotiate salary and #5 save for retirement—now. The same amount of money saved grows compounded if started early in life.

Tapping in Meditation:

My purpose today is to learn about finances and live below my means. I make smart and conservative financial decisions.

Journal Notes:

Day/Year	
Day/Year	
Day/Year	

DECEMBER

Davies Day Book

365 concepts for excellence

December 1

The Myths of the Paleo Diet

Christina Warinner, Assistant Professor of Anthropology at the University of Oklahoma. The Paleo diet has no basis in archaeological history.

Myth 1: Humans are evolved to eat meat and Paleolithic people consumed large quantities of meat.
Debunk: Humans have no known anatomical, physiological or genetic adaptations to meat consumption. It's quite the opposite we have many adaptations to plant consumption. Take for example vitamin C. Carnivores can make their own vitamin C. Vitamin C is found in plants, if you don't eat plants you need to be able to make it yourself. We can't make it. We have to consume if from plants. We have a longer digestive track then carnivores. That's because our food needs to stay in our bodies longer so we'll have more time to digest plant matter, we need more surface area and more microbes. We have big molars that are there to shred fiber. We don't have the type of sharp teeth that carnivores have that are specialized to shred meat. We do have some genetic adaptations that are for animal consumption but it's for milk, not meat. Any meat that the Paleo would have eaten wouldn't be like the meat we eat today. It would have been leaner and smaller.

Myth 2: Paleolithic peoples did not eat whole grains or legumes.
Debunk: There is evidence of ancient tools that were used to grind up seeds and grains. Scientists can also analyze fossilized dental plaque where they can see evidence of massive consumption of grains and legumes.

Myth 3: Paleo diet foods are what our Paleolithic ancestors ate.
Debunk: That's just not true. Every food that is pictured in the advertisements for the Paleo diet are domesticated foods, a product of farming. There is no one Paleo diet. They are regionally variable based on the availability of food sources. They would eat meat but they would also eat the marrow and organs of their kill as well as plants, seeds, nuts, grains.

High food species diversity is the key. Today the food supply is in the wrong direction. No matter what processed food you get from the grocery store there are only 3 species of food, corn, soy and wheat. We evolved to eat whole foods in their complete package, with their fiber, their roughage, everything. It turns out that this is very important. Even the parts you can't digest are very important. The fiber that you eat regulates the speed at which the food passes through the intestines, it modulates metabolism and slows down the release of sugar and it feeds the good bacteria that live in your gut. Low fiber diets are creating microbial populations that cause obesity and diabetes.

Challenge:
You already have a sound food plan. The key is constant personal growth and the weighing and measuring of your food. Stay on your plan.

Tapping in Meditation:
My purpose today is to move forward with serenity and I do.

Journal Notes:

Day/Year	
Day/Year	
Day/Year	

December 2

The Year in Gear Questions 1-12

1. List 5-10 highlights from the past year.
2. How are you different now then you were in January?
3. What do you need to let go of or forgive yourself for, from the past year?
4. What do you want to celebrate about the year you're about to complete?
5. What do you want to be able to celebrate at the end of next year?
6. What lessons do you most want to take with you into the upcoming year?
7. How will you enrich your life and your family in the upcoming year? How can you make your relationships richer, more fun, more intimate and more loving?
8. What would you like to add, change or eliminate in your daily routine during the next 12 months?
9. What tolerations must go?
10. What joys and ordinary pleasure will you add to your schedule, starting today?
11. What financial goals do you have for the year ahead?
12. How can you save more and invest better?

Efforts and courage are not enough without purpose and direction.

—**John F. Kennedy**

Challenge:
It's the time of year to reflect back on what has worked, what hasn't worked and to recalibrate to finish out the year as productively as you can. Take your time for some preparation by using The Year in Gear questions.

Tapping in Meditation:
My purpose today is to tap into the higher divine power of the universe. My life is a constant reflection of who I am.

Journal Notes:

Day/Year	
Day/Year	
Day/Year	
Day/Year	
Day/Year	

December 3

The Year in Gear Questions 13-22

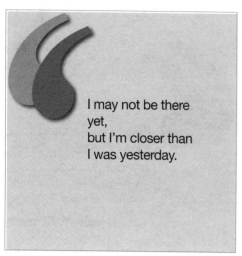

I may not be there yet,
but I'm closer than
I was yesterday.

Challenge:

13. What will you do to maintain your health? What are you committed to for fitness, vitality and wellness?

14. Intellectually, how will you grow? What will you read? What do you need to study? What skills do you need to master?

15. What is your theme for next year? (ex. "abundance in abundance" or "pay down debts)

16. What will you achieve in the future? Where are you headed in the next 5 years? 10, 20?

17. What are your major values and purposes for the next phase of your life?

18. What brings you the most fulfillment and gratification?

19. How can you use your greatest talents to benefit yourself and the world in the years ahead?

20. What is something you would do next year if you weren't worried about what other people thought?

21. If you could do only one big project in your lifetime, what would it be?

22. Picture yourself in the future—10 years from now, what would this future self-ask you now that would make life better in 10 years?

Tapping in Meditation:

My purpose today is to soar. I have a vision, I have skill, I have the drive to soar and to lift everyone I come into contact with and I do.

Journal Notes:

Day/Year	
Day/Year	
Day/Year	
Day/Year	
Day/Year	

December 4

Block Time and Reset Goals to Prevent Holiday Cruising

This is the time of the year where you and your staff need to guard against checking out and getting into the partying and celebration mind set too early. The way to do this is by reevaluating your year to date and making some decisions about what you want to accomplish this month to have a strong close to the quarter. Remind yourself and your staff that your focused efforts this month will bring revenues in the first quarter of next year. It is very important for you to finish strong and go into the New Year with the momentum gained by your collective best efforts this month. If you don't implement today's concept I can promise you that you and your team will check out very soon.

Challenge:

The first step is to physically take a calendar and block your time off. How many days do you plan to work this month? Christmas is in 21 days. When will you take off before and after? Get a block of time.

Now that you have your block of time, come up with agreed upon targets that you want to hit this month. Earn your time off. Earn your pleasures with a sprint effort from now until you're time off. I'll be visiting with you about your business plan for next year after Christmas but start to think about it now. The Year in Gear questions should be helpful to prime your thoughts. For now however, let's get a strong finish to this year.

Once you have your targets, plug in your normal plan of the 6 Ps, precise previous planning prevents poor performance and break down your remaining time into one week at a time. Identify the body of work to get accomplished. Make sure you are realistic but that you stretch just beyond your comfort zone. Now go and execute with passion and excitement.

Tapping in Meditation:

My purpose today is to lead myself and my staff to a highly focused and productive block of time this month and I do.

Journal Notes:

Day/Year	
Day/Year	
Day/Year	
Day/Year	
Day/Year	

December 5

The RAS and the Law of Attraction

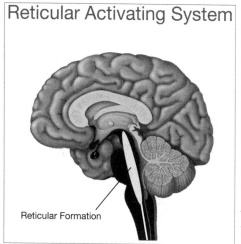

Reticular Activating System

Reticular Formation

The law of attraction would not work without this area of the brain, a dense bundle of nerve cells about the size of your pinky, located at the base of the brain called the reticular activating system or RAS. It has several functions but the one I'm focusing on now is the ability to filter out information. The human brain is bombarded with sensory stimuli. Of the 100 billion brain cells, with 100 Trillion synaptic connections handling 400 billion inputs per second you are only aware of about 7 inputs at a time. Everything else is either filtered out or sent to what is referred to as the subconscious mind.

You have witnessed the RAS at work. Remember back to the last time you purchased a new car. Do you remember how many of those same types of cars you saw? That's the RAS filtering. The numbers of those cars didn't change. What changed was what you were paying attention to, your observation changed. They were always there. Imagine that you are in a crowded room and there is a buzz of people speaking all around you. All the way across the room someone says your name and you hear it. It catches your attention out of all of the clutter of noise. That's because the RAS has tagged that sound as important.

You are probably familiar with the terms conscious and subconscious mind. This doesn't really exist. You can't point to the brain and say that this is the conscious mind although most of the time this is referring to the functions of the cortex and more specifically the left hemisphere of the brain. However, the brain is integrated and signals travel through the corpus callosum that connects both hemispheres. None the less, the conscious mind can handle 40 bits of data per second and the subconscious 40 million bits of data. The non-conscious mind, mostly the limbic area of the brain, is 400 times faster than the cortex. That's why it is important to set your gate keeper, the RAS, through precise planning over a short period of time, 7 days. You do this with the tool of behavioral contracting. When you have your goals, your vision planned, you are setting your RAS to allow in anything that is related to the accomplishing of those goals. Everything you need is already out there in the universe so you are dialing in, tapping in to a frequency to allow it to enter into your reality. That's what attraction is. That information is sent to your conscious mind where you can act on it or let it go. It's like having radar and any opportunity that comes into the path gets tagged and noticed as it relates to your plan.

Challenge:

Keep planning and take notice of what comes into your awareness because of your weekly precise plan. Using the tools of this program "sets" your RAS.

Tapping in Meditation:

My purpose today is to allow the universe to supply me with the resources, people, ideas and opportunities that I need to be of service to others and I do.

Journal Notes:

Day/Year	
Day/Year	
Day/Year	

December 6

The Limbic System and Regulating Emotion

The limbic system is a set of structures in the brain and many of them play an important role in regulating emotion. The 4 most important components of the limbic system when it comes to emotions are hypothalamus, amygdala, thalamus and hippocampus. The thalamus is a sensory relay station. The input from your senses ultimately ends up in the thalamus. The thalamus directs these inputs into the appropriate areas in the cortex. The amygdala is sometimes called the aggression center. If you stimulate the amygdala you can produce feelings of anger, violence, fear and anxiety. On the other hand if you destroy the amygdala it would cause a very mellowing effect. The hippocampus helps to convert your short term memory into long term. If your hippocampus is destroyed you can't form new memories but you still have your old memories intact. The hypothalamus is below the thalamus. It regulates the autonomic nervous system, flight or fight or rest and digest response. It controls your endocrine system, adrenalin for example.

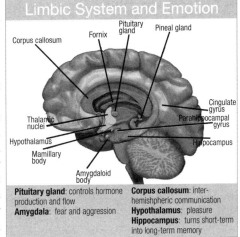

Limbic System and Emotion

Pituitary gland: controls hormone production and flow
Amygdala: fear and aggression
Corpus callosum: inter-hemishpheric communication
Hypothalamus: pleasure
Hippocampus: turns short-term into long-term memory

Challenge:

What this means to you is that you can influence the activity in these areas of your brain simply by planning and then visualizing the accomplishment of your goals. Take a moment in your quite time to use your senses to speed up the accomplishment of your dreams. Imagine what you will see, hear, feel and smell with the accomplishment of your goals. This will create an effect in the limbic system and that will send signals to your cortex that will impact what you do and how you think. You can have far more influence in your mood, your emotions, than you were ever aware of so simply use your senses to imagine your goals already completed in your meditation.

Tapping in Meditation:

My purpose today is to think success, fulfillment and abundance and I do. I think positive thoughts all day long.

Journal Notes:

Day/Year	
Day/Year	
Day/Year	
Day/Year	
Day/Year	

December 7

Self-Importance and Happiness

You imagine that you can control your life. With yourself as the center you may not feel important at all but haunted by negative commentary, judging yourself by the way you look, what you are capable of doing, comparing yourself to others in your health, wealth, smarts and you may come up lacking.

Polly Young-Eisendrath, psychologist at Middlebury College, defines happiness as that state of being where you're not restless, you're not distracted, and you are completely engaged in your own direct experience. When you are really happy that sense of self drops off, you are not comparing yourself to others, you don't have the experience or sense that you're controlling things instead your ideas come to you. They seem to flow to you. The Buddha teaches known self. This is a difficult concept to understand. Eisendrath states that we are all participating in a fabric of being that we don't understand and that there is no such thing and you and I. If you are not fascinated by that all of the time it's because you are collapsing back into a tiny self as center and you're worrying.

Psychologists have noticed that there are certain emotions that motivate human beings that don't motivate other animals. One of the major differences is our self conscious emotions. When our ego is aroused we are motivated to feel that we are separate and we are drawn into comparisons with others. Here are 4 self-conscious emotions:

1. **Shame**: the desire to hide, cover up, lie or die because you feel defective in your inferiority or superiority in relationship to others.
2. **Guilt**: the desire to repair wrong-doing or bad action because you feel responsible for what you've done.
3. **Envy**: the motivation to destroy attack or diminish an ability or resource or possession of another because you feel that you could never have that for yourself.
4. **Jealousy**: the desire to compete with or get what someone else has or is because you want it.

Pride, self-pity and embarrassment are also talked about but these 4 are the biggies that generate how you feel about yourself. These emotions operate in such a way that makes you feel like you control your life and that you should manage everything.

Challenge:
Experiment with these thoughts. You are tiny and the world is large. Anytime you feel restless, stop and be in contact with the world in a simple way. Feel the air on your face. Become engaged in your immediate world. Look at the environment that you are in moment to moment, when you walk through a door, when you look up and out look to see if someone needs help, or a smile or needs a door to be opened. If you do that you will find that the world is reaching out to you all of the time.

Tapping in Meditation:
My purpose today is to keep an empty mind. I am always ready and open to everything. In the beginners mind there are many possibilities and I see them.

Journal Notes:

Day/Year	
Day/Year	
Day/Year	

December 8

How To Incorporate 6 Human Needs to Make Behavior Addictive

Tony Robbins puts forth a theory that is backed by research that there are 6 basic human needs and any behavior that meets at least 3 of these will become an addiction. It's tough to test this in a scientific way but you can test it in your own life and see if it works for you. The first human need is for #1 significance. This is the desire to feel that you are important, that you matter. It's the ego.

Addiction Monitor

Crave It!

Need It

Want It

Like It

Another key driver of human behavior is #2. Certainty. The need for certainty is wrapped up in the need for security. We want to know that our expectations about the world are about to be met at least most of the time.

Paradoxically, the next human need is #3 Uncertainty. This is our need for a sense of variety, surprise and spice in life. If you are a rat and you press a lever for food, when it's unpredictable when you'll get food and how much you will press that lever like crazy. This is also why you buy lottery tickets. You know that your chances of winning are only slightly better if you buy a ticket than if you don't but you buy anyway.

The 4th human need is your need for connection. This is the need that ensures our survival as a species. The 5th human need is the need for growth. This is the need to feel that you are moving forward and becoming something. The most powerful predictor of employee engagement is a sense of progress. The 6th human need is the need for contribution. This need is necessary for fulfillment.

Wearing a motorcycle helmet—only meets one need which would be for certainty so you have to regulate it. You can contrast this list to Abraham Maslow's hierarchy of needs.

Challenge:
Use this as a way to make a behavior that you care about more addictive. List the behavior you want to do more of, say making phone calls. Next list the 6 human needs and across each one describe how you're doing that activity will fulfill that need. Put it on a card and read that card when you begin to waiver from the activity.

Tapping in Meditation:
My purpose today is to welcome the possibilities that I receive. Knowledge is learning something every day. Wisdom is letting go of something every day.

Journal Notes:

Day/Year	
Day/Year	
Day/Year	
Day/Year	
Day/Year	

December 9

Leadership and Fear

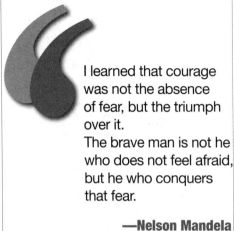

I learned that courage was not the absence of fear, but the triumph over it.
The brave man is not he who does not feel afraid, but he who conquers that fear.

—Nelson Mandela

I'd love to edit the quote from Nelson Mandela. I don't believe that it is neither necessary nor possible to conquer your fear. The rest of his quote is beautiful. Be afraid and do it anyway. I read the following anonymous story below about fear and an act of leadership. See if you can identify with it.

One evening my wife and I were reading in bed. Our 5 year old daughter appeared at the door. She was upset. "Honey, what's wrong?" we asked. "I'm afraid," she said. She explained that her two year old little brother was asleep on the couch and it was dark. She and her little brother were afraid of the dark. We tried to assure her it was okay. She left and didn't say a word.

We didn't think too much about it and went back to our reading. 10 or 15 minutes must have passed by. My wife decided to check on our little girl to make sure she was okay. She couldn't find her upstairs so she decided to check downstairs. As she came down the stairs she saw something she would never forget.

On our couch in that dark little room were our two little children sound asleep. Our daughter was by her brother's side laying over him. As she got closer she noticed our daughter had been crying. She had been protecting her little brother. She was able to overcome her fear because she cared more about him than what she was afraid of.

Challenge:

Leaders who care overcome their fears. Being courageous doesn't mean you aren't afraid; if just means you care more about something else than what you fear. As a courageous leader you do what is right, not what is easiest, because you care. George S. Patton said "Do not take counsel of your fears." What action might you avoid taking today that you can motivate yourself to take because you care? Identify and execute.

Tapping in Meditation:

My purpose today is to demonstrate what is possible through the actions I take and the thoughts I have. Most things are difficult before they are easy. I must go through turbulent air before I arrive at the smooth air on top. I embrace my difficulties as signs that I am closer to my purpose.

Journal Notes:

Day/Year	
Day/Year	
Day/Year	
Day/Year	
Day/Year	

December 10

Close Your Action Circles and OHIO

Do you begin activities and then not complete them? Do you start something and then move on to something else without completing what you just began? This causes tremendous incongruity and stress.

Draw 7 circles. Are all of them complete circles or are some of the tops open and not connected? For most people several of the circles will be incomplete. This is subconsciously indicative of a lot of overwhelm going on, a lot of starts and stops but not starts and completions.

If you start to do laundry then the completed circle is to fold it and put it away. It's 9:00 am PST and that makes it noon back east. If I say that I'm going to write a day of this book from 9:00 am my time on the west coast to 10:00 am then a completed circle would be to finish writing one day in the book. If I end early then don't start something that I won't be able to finish. It's so common to start to do an activity then get distracted by something else and something else again and again. This results in frustration, a feeling of emptiness, stress, lack of fulfillment and fatigue. So stop doing that! Only handle it once, OHIO. If you bring in the mail only open it if you are going to handle it to completion. Either toss it, delegate it, or handle it now. If it requires you to write a check then do it now. If it requires you to send a reply do it now.

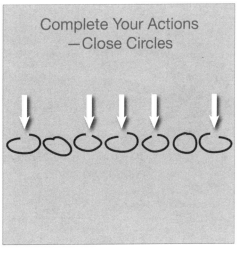

Complete Your Actions —Close Circles

Challenge:
How do your 7 circles look? What in your life is incomplete? Block your time. Pick a task and stay on that one task until completion. Then start your next task.

Tapping in Meditation:
My purpose today is to say no to the 100s of distracting good ideas that are out there. I pick carefully. I am as proud of the things I haven't done as I am of the things I have done. Innovation is saying no to 1000s of things and I stay on task, all day long.

Journal Notes:

Day/Year	
Day/Year	
Day/Year	
Day/Year	
Day/Year	

December 11

Mediocrity is Self-Induced So Tap In

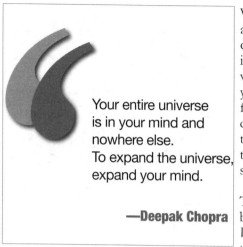

Your entire universe is in your mind and nowhere else.
To expand the universe, expand your mind.

—**Deepak Chopra**

We all have genius within us. Mediocrity is self-inflicted and genius is self-bestowed. Self-bestowed is connecting to the universe. When you are tapped into the divine you create an incredible amount of work, you have incredible energy and you start hitting your stride at 40 and experience constant growth and fulfillment where the average person's life steadily goes down. What is necessary is focused intention rather than being scattered by our distractions. It is important to trust in the universal intelligence. We are part of the same energy that has created the universe.

The difference between mediocrity and genius is small but according to Walter Russell, author of *The Man Who Tapped the Secrets of the Universe*, we can't bridge that gap until we tap in to that universal energy and intelligence. How do you do that? Russell says lock yourself in a room and create some stillness in your life.

All of the great teachers talk about this. Deepak Chopra in *The 7 Spiritual Laws of Success* talks about spiritual law #1, "Pure Potentiality", you have the divine universal intelligence within you. You are pure potential. Chopra says that the way that we connect to that spiritual potential is through stillness. We need to slow down long enough to find that stillness within.

Walter Russell also says that you need to love everything that you do. To not love it, to be bitter and resentful, creates life destroying toxins. The Buddha says if anything is worth doing do it with all of your heart. So that's your first decision. Stop doing the things that are not worth doing.

On failure, Russell refuses to recognize failure. He views defeats as stepping stones to success. Whatever is stressing you now see it as a step towards success.

Challenge:
Find more stillness in your life. Whether it is through meditation, exercise, or simply turning off the radio in your car and being with the silence, do it. Ask yourself what do I need to stop doing and what do I need to start doing?

Tapping in Meditation:
My purpose today is to tap into my wisdom. The wise person does nothing reluctantly. Everything I do I do with joy and mastery. I use every moment in my life to do my best. I bring conscious mastery to every moment. My life is a piece of art.

Journal Notes:

Day/Year	
Day/Year	
Day/Year	
Day/Year	
Day/Year	

December 12

How Your Brain Pays Attention

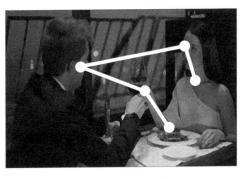

Attention is a limited resource that the brain allocates only to what it designates as the most important and relevant priorities. There are different subsystems in the brain that dictate what is or is not relevant. How did you look at the picture? Most likely you didn't look from the top left to the right as you would read a book. Instead you will scan with eye saccadics, short movements with eye fixations. This pattern is far from random. It will mostly target objects, items, faces and anything of interest. Your eyes are moving 3-4 times per second which means that every 1/3rd of a second our brain has to make a decision about where to look next. It does this because of the brains circuitry. In the back of the brain is the parietal lobe. This part of the brain is able to identify in a glance the presence of interesting items around you and direct your eyes. This generates what is called a priority map. There are 4 lessons about those maps.

Lesson #1: some items seem to be automatically included into the priority maps. For example, flashing lights. Also included are faces and text. The next time you are driving or at a crowded area you will notice the pulling of your attention to the ads on the walls

Lesson #2: if you look just a second longer your map will adjust to your current interest. So if you were interested in purchasing a necklace then your gaze would then focus on the woman's necklace.

Lesson #3: the map will take into account your likes and dislikes. This is because of the brain's reward system. This will encourage any behavioral approach to what is rewarding and it will encourage attention to it. That piece of cake or glass of wine will spike the reward system.

Lesson #4: you can move your attention. This is due to the opposition of a system that can resist the captivation of attention and that system is located in the prefrontal cortex and called the executive system.

So you have 3 systems trying to take control of your attention. The executive system is the main force in stabilizing attention. As long as the neurons in the prefrontal cortex are active your attention will be present. This will enable you to filter what fits with your intention and what doesn't, but it's very costly to keep those neurons firing for too long. The moment their activity weakens you get distracted.

Challenge:
Block off short periods of time so you can focus on one priority at a time. Use behavioral contracting to grab the attention of your prefrontal cortex. Use the novelty of a high fine as a penalty on your tougher items.

Tapping in Meditation:
My purpose today is to stay focused on one item at a time, all day long.

Journal Notes:

Day/Year	
Day/Year	
Day/Year	

December 13

Exercise for a New Brain

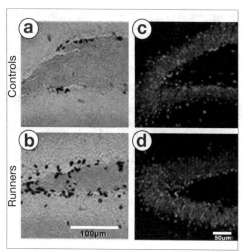

Brain plasticity is the process of how your brain changes based on what has happened to it. Neurons that fire together wire together. A memory is nothing more than your ability to reconstruct the whole from a degraded fragment. You make 1000s of new brain cells every day.

Physical exercise is most important in brain development. It's more important than having friends and more important than reading. What does exercise do? It increases levels of neurotrophic factors and specific glutamate subunits. As you get older your brain shrinks but if you exercise you brain doesn't shrink, it even gets bigger. Cardio and resistance training are both important.

This picture shows the neuron growth of an exerciser compared to a control that did not exercise. With neuro imaging techniques today scientists can see what neurons are firing, what their pathways are and how they change as a function of usage.

The great Canadian hockey player, Wayne Gretzky said, "Skate where the puck is going to be." Dr. Max Cynader is the director of the Brain Research Center in Vancouver Canada. He's been doing brain research for over 50 years. He says that there is tremendous challenge and opportunity today in understanding how the brain works. It has never been as exciting as it is today. We are right at the intersection of genetics, imaging, cell signaling, electrophysiology, and combining all of these methodologies will give unprecedented capabilities for changing the brain for the better.

Challenge:

Exercise is not necessary for weight management but it is essential for fitness and now you can see for brain health. Make sure you have a scheduled and routine fitness program where you are working your major muscle groups, front and back of the arms, legs, chest and back and aerobic exercise as well. The tools of this program are to read one page per day, meditate 5-10 minutes per day, follow the food plan, attend the conference calls and exercise. If you do that you are controlling that which you can control and setting the laws of attraction and abundance in place.

Tapping in Meditation:

My purpose today is to grow into my mastery. I have the power to create it, to own it, to shape it, to claim it and to live it and I do.

Journal Notes:

Day/Year	
Day/Year	
Day/Year	
Day/Year	
Day/Year	

December 14

Overcome Procrastination

Wikipedia defines procrastination as the practice of carrying out less urgent tasks in preference to more urgent ones, or doing more pleasurable things in place of less pleasurable ones, and thus putting off impending tasks to a later time, sometimes to the "last minute" before the deadline. Schraw, Wadkins, and Olafson in 2007 proposed three criteria for a behavior to be classified as academic procrastination: it must be counterproductive, needless, and delaying.

A sales manager asks one of his sales people, "What are you doing?" "Nothing" was the reply. "That's what you said yesterday." "I wasn't finished!"

The cure for procrastination is action. Acting despite the fear and resistance you have about not doing that thing. You need to break that cycle. Easier said than done? Procrastination is resistance. The resistance is your story, created within you. This is created when you make an activity a should, a must or a need. One of the strategies to overcome procrastination is to shift the framing of the activity from you have to do this to you could do this. You have a choice. You don't have to do the activity. Yes there will be consequences but you have a choice. Next, allow the feeling of resistance. Be aware of the tension. Instead of resisting this feeling allow yourself to feel it. Once you stop running away from this you start to think that it's not as bad as you think it is.

Here's another way to unblock resistance. The first question to ask yourself is "Can I allow myself to feel this?" Once you feel the resistance of whatever the action is that you're avoiding, and then ask yourself this question, "Could I let this go, in theory?" Answer yes or no. If your answer is yes then here is your next question, "Will I let this go?" Now you last question is "When will I let it go?"

Although this seems simplistic, it is a very effective method of dissipating emotions. Keep running this pattern on any action you are procrastinating on. Keep running this for as long as it takes to change the physiology associated with that action. This is the letting go of a negative emotion. Now I'm going to ask you to accept a positive emotion. Ask yourself this question, "Could I allow myself to get excited about this?" What is one small thing you can do that will make this exciting for you? Maybe it's listening to some nice music at the gym, or the excitement that comes with helping a client have a day better because you called, let yourself feel this positive emotion.

Challenge:
Use your meditation today to visualize yourself doing this activity. See yourself step by step doing this activity and being excited about it.

Tapping in Meditation:
My purpose today is to observe my procrastination in action without trying to change it. Instead of resisting the procrastination I just observe without judgment. When I feel myself procrastinating I step outside of myself and watch, I become an observer, I notice and allow myself to procrastinate. As I become the observer my procrastination dissipates and I find myself easily taking actions.

Journal Notes:

Day/Year	
Day/Year	
Day/Year	

December 15

Procrastination and Your Monkey Mind

Do you have a chronic addiction to procrastination. There actually is an argument going on in your brain between the limbic system and the prefrontal cortex. The cortex tells you that you should be working. However, the primitive part of your brain, the limbic system, wants to chat on Face Book just a little longer before you start prospecting.

Why is it that the limbic system always seems to win the argument? The answer lies in the part of the limbic system called the amygdala. This is the part of the brain that controls fear and anxiety and the fight or flight response to threats. When you get under stress, you see a wild lion in the jungle, you don't want a voice in your head reminding you what tasks you have to do today. You want to focus on what's going on in the world around you and respond to physiological needs. When you procrastinate you experience a mild anxiety response to a threatening stimulus, which just happens to be prospecting. Meet your monkey mind.

You might be taking on a big project and just not know where to start. You dread the displeasure of doing the task. Or you might have a fear of failure. Perfectionists use procrastination as a self handicapping tool to avoid personal failure. Your prefrontal cortex knows that failure is positive learning however your amygdala is about subconscious reactions. So how can you overcome procrastination if you have a monkey in your brain making decisions on your behalf?

The answer is something called meta cognition. This is thinking about thinking. You have to acknowledge that you are not going to be making the decision about prospecting tomorrow. You're going to have this monkey making the decision because it's linked to fear and threats.

Challenge:

There are a few steps you can take in order to overcome this. The first is to be well prepared. Identify the amount days you plan on working this month and set your targets. Today is the 15th so Christmas is just 11 days away counting today. Hanukkah is just two days. New Year's Eve is right around the corner. Identify your activities, then break them down into small bits. Research has shown that if you visualize the process needed to do something the task becomes easier to do. Plan for distractions. Make a commitment to stay in action. If you procrastinate when you come up to a road block then you'll never get around to solving the problem.

Tapping in Meditation:

My purpose today is to take action. Napoleon Hill said, "Don't wait. The time will never be just right." Get into the habit of planning, thinking about thinking and getting things done rapidly, then my future is very bright.

Journal Notes:

Day/Year	
Day/Year	
Day/Year	

December 16

The Wise Teacher and the Jar

One day as usual, many students began to gather in the teaching room. They came in and sat down very quietly, looking to the front with keen anticipation, ready to hear what the teacher had to say. The room was so quiet you could hear a pin drop. On one side of the teacher was a large glass jar. On the other side was a pile of dark grey rocks. Without saying a word, the teacher began to pick up the rocks one by one and place them very carefully in the glass jar. When all the rocks were in the jar, the teacher turned to the students and asked, 'Is the jar full?' 'Yes,' said the students.

Without saying a word, the teacher began to drop small round pink pebbles carefully into the large glass jar so that they fell down between the rocks. When all the pebbles were in the jar, the teacher turned to the students and asked, 'Is the jar now full?' The students started nodding and saying, 'Yes. Yes, teacher, the jar is now full. Yes'.

Without saying a word, the teacher took some fine silver sand and let it trickle into the large glass jar where it settled around the pink pebbles and the dark grey rocks. When all the sand was in the jar, the teacher turned to the students and asked, 'Is the jar now full?' The students were not so confident this time, but the sand had clearly filled all the space in the jar so a few still nodded and said, 'Yes, teacher, the jar is now full. Now it's full'.

Then the teacher took a jug of water and poured it carefully, without splashing a drop, into the large glass jar. When the water reached the brim, the teacher turned to the students and asked, 'Is the jar now full?' Most of the students were silent, but two or three ventured to answer, 'Yes, teacher, the jar is now full. Now it is'.

Without saying a word, the teacher took a handful of salt and sprinkled it slowly over the top of the water with a very quiet whishing sound. When all the salt had dissolved into the water, the teacher turned to the students and asked once more, 'Is the jar now full?' The students were totally silent. Eventually one brave student said, 'Yes, teacher. The jar is now full'. 'Yes,' said the teacher 'The jar is now full'.

Challenge:

What does it mean to you? With the holidays coming are you thinking that you're just too busy to get everything you need to do done with excellence? What else can you fit into your jar of life? Remember, you have far more capacity to create the circumstances and events in your life than you are aware of.

Tapping in Meditation:

My purpose today is to believe that I am tapped into a force for good in this universe. I am in the stream of goodness. I feel deeply secure no matter what happens.

Journal Notes:

Day/Year	
Day/Year	
Day/Year	

December 17

The Wise Teacher, the Jar and a Couple of Beers—Priorities

And another version of the same story ... A professor stood before his philosophy class and had some items in front of him. When the class began, wordlessly, he picked up a very large and empty jar and proceeded to fill it with golf balls. He then asked the students if the jar was full. They agreed that it was. So the professor then picked up a box of small pebbles and poured them into the jar. He shook the jar lightly. The pebbles rolled into the open areas between the golf balls. He then asked the students again if the jar was full. They agreed it was.

The professor next picked up a box of sand and poured it into the jar. Of course, the sand filled up everything else. He asked once more if the jar was full. The students responded with a unanimous "Yes." The professor then produced two cans of beer from under the table and poured the entire contents into the jar, effectively filling the empty space between the sand. The students laughed.

"Now", said the professor, as the laughter subsided, "I want you to recognize that this jar represents your life. The golf balls are the important things—your family, your children, your health, your friends, your favorite passions—things that, if everything else was lost and only they remained, your life would still be full. The pebbles are the other things that matter like your job, your house, your car.

The sand is everything else—the small stuff. If you put the sand into the jar first" he continued, "there is no room for the pebbles or the golf balls. The same goes for life. If you spend all your time and energy on the small stuff, you will never have room for the things that are important to you. Pay attention to the things that are critical to your happiness. Play with your children. Take time to get medical checkups. Take your partner out to dinner. There will always be time to clean the house, and fix the rubbish. Take care of the golf balls first, the things that really matter. Set your priorities. The rest is just sand."

One of the students raised her hand and inquired what the beer represented. The professor smiled. "I'm glad you asked. It just goes to show you that, no matter how full your life may seem, there's always room for a couple of beers."

Challenge:

Make sure you are not majoring in the minors. Don't sweat the small stuff and its all small stuff. Having serenity and peace of mind is a choice.

Tapping in Meditation:

My purpose today is to know that my weaknesses are imaginary. I delay action and reaction in my little daily situations in life until I am sure that I am doing the right thing at the right time.

Journal Notes:

Day/Year	
Day/Year	
Day/Year	

December 18

We are All One—In the Same Boat

Two men were out on the ocean in a boat. One of them began drilling in the bottom of the boat, and the other, aghast said "What are you doing? Stop drilling!" And the first man replied: "It's all right. I'm only drilling on my side."

Challenge:

What you do impacts everyone. There are no individuals, only the illusion of separateness. Everything and everyone is of the same source, energy. So as you treat others you are also treating yourself. Notice how you think, feel and act towards others today and do so with your heart open to giving and being of service. Ralph Waldo Emerson said "It is one of the most beautiful compensations in life that no man can sincerely try to help others without helping himself."

Tapping in Meditation:

My purpose today is to be of service to others. The heart that gives, gathers. I live four virtues, respect-sincerity-kindness and service. My ambition is transformed to purpose. My life is making a difference.

Journal Notes:

Day/Year	
Day/Year	
Day/Year	
Day/Year	
Day/Year	

December 19

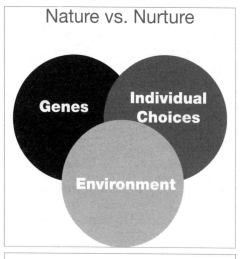

Nature vs. Nurture

Genes

Individual Choices

Environment

Approaches to Psychology

NATURE ←→ **NURTURE**

Biological Psychoanalysis Cognitive Psychology Humanism Behaviorism

The Eagle—Nature versus Nurture

A professor told his 8:00 am finance class the story of a farmer who found an abandoned eagle's nest and in it was an egg still warm. He took the egg back to his farm and laid it in the nest of one of his hens. The egg hatched and the baby eagle grew up along with the other chickens. It pecked about the farmyard, scrabbling for grain. It spent its life within the yard and rarely looked up. When it was very old, one day it lifted up its head and saw above it a wonderful sight—an eagle soaring high above in the sky. Looking at it, the old creature sighed and said to itself, "If only I'd been born an eagle."

The professor scanned the 60 faces in the lecture hall. Despite the early hour, no one seemed to be asleep. Somehow, his story had touched them. Or maybe it wasn't the story at all. In fact, it had all started with a student's observation that the professor was cheerful. A wise man once said: "Who you are speaks louder to me than anything you can say." I suppose it must be so.

There is a conversation amongst scientist today about nature versus nurture. There is a duration of extremes from nature to nurture. The nature camp believes in the biological approach for determinism of behavioral outcomes. The focus is on genetic hormonal and neuro chemical explanations. Next psychoanalysis believes that innate sex drives and aggression drives behavior. This is followed by the cognitive psychologist who attribute outcomes to innate mental structures such as schemas, perceptions and memory, constantly changed by the environment. The humanist view is Maslow's basic needs followed by behaviorism which believes that all behavior is learned from the environment through conditioning. My research supports that you have a genetic predisposition to behave a certain way, however twin studies clearly indicate that you are not locked into this predisposition that your environment can cause genes to be turned on or turned off and shape your behavior.

Challenge:

What does the eagle story mean to you? You get a pass on "it's empty and meaningless" so go ahead and project a meaning, interpretation and story that speaks to you.

Tapping in Meditation:

My purpose today is to surround myself with the dreamers and the dooers, the believers and thinkers, but most of all I surround myself with those who see greatness within me even when I don't see it myself.

Journal Notes:

Day/Year	
Day/Year	
Day/Year	
Day/Year	
Day/Year	

December 20

12 Things Successful People Do Differently

1. Create and pursue SMART Goals. Specific, Measurable, Attainable, Relevant and Timely.

2. Take decisive and immediate action. Knowledge and intelligence are both useless without action

3. Focus on being productive, not being busy. They work smarter, not harder.

4. Make logical, informed decisions. They think things through before making life changing decisions.

5. Progress not Perfection. They embrace failure as stepping stones and learning.

6. Work outside their comfort zone. They are committed to personal growth, success and understand that for weight training, the growth actually occurs after the damage to the muscle tissue.

7. Keep things simple. Rather than evaluating every last detail of every possible option, make a decision, pick one and then give it a shot. Don't be paralyzed by analysis.

8. Focus on Kaisen—making small continuous improvements. This creates inertia.

9. Embrace measurement. They track their progress and regularly assess.

10. Maintain a positive outlook. They manage their thinking. They are solution oriented and take responsibility.

11. Spend time with the right people. You are the sum of the choices you make and the people you spend time with.

12. Maintain excellence in all areas of their life. Health, business and personal fitness enables them to reach their full potential.

Challenge:
It's time to start to assess your year. Gather your data so you can evaluate your results for the year and set your goals for next year

Tapping in Meditation:
My purpose today is to celebrate what I have accomplished this year and those I have serviced. I raise the bar slightly higher for next year.

Journal Notes:

Day/Year	
Day/Year	
Day/Year	
Day/Year	
Day/Year	

December 21

The Worm Hole Exercise

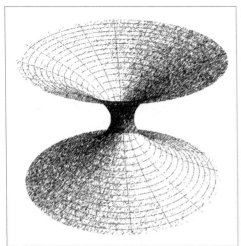

Imagine that there is a worm hole in the fabric of space time and you are able to project yourself to the end of next year. Look back and have a conversation with yourself from a place of wisdom, of confidence, of certainty and challenge. Take a stand for your own possibilities.

Challenge:

Declare where you need to be at the end of next year so you can celebrate a year of well-done accomplishments. Where do you need to be in your health, business and personal life to be satisfied with the year? Now what results do you need to create to be thrilled? Commit to those results, specifically.

I know you may be thinking that it's time to check out for the year and celebrate. Maintain a commitment to precise planning. Sometime between now and the new year start and complete your business-life plan for next year.

Tapping in Meditation:

My purpose today is to plan for my future. I bring the future into the present so I can do something about it now. I share with others what I have learned and the victories I have won over myself with this program. I pass on my strength to others.

Journal Notes:

Day/Year	
Day/Year	
Day/Year	
Day/Year	
Day/Year	

December 22

Transforming Yourself—Author Robert Greene's Story

Robert Greene is an American author and speaker known for his books on strategy, power and seduction. Robert had always known that he wanted to be a writer but he didn't know what kind. After he graduated he drifted into journalism as a way to make a living while writing. Then one day he was having lunch with a man told him that he should seriously consider a different career. You are not writer material. Your work is too undisciplined; your style is too bizarre, your ideas are just not relatable to the average reader.

In the months to come Robert realized that he had entered into a career that just didn't suit him and his work reflected this incompatibility. He then traveled all over the world and worked all types of jobs. While in Italy he met a man who was a packager and producer of books. This man asked Robert if he had any ideas for a book. Suddenly, seemingly out of nowhere an idea just gushed out of him. It was about power. This is what Robert had witnessed in all of his jobs, people want power. They manipulate while presenting a nice and friendly front. Robert would expose these games. Suddenly, in writing what would become "The 48 Laws of Power", everything in his disjointed past seemed to click into place (Seeding the Blue). All of his previous experiences had given him the skill to write this book. Those seemingly random jobs had exposed him to the rich layers of knowledge that altered him from the inside out.

The moral of his story is that humans tend to fixate on what they can see. What really allows for dramatic changes are the invisible things that happen on the inside. The slow accumulation of knowledge and skills, the incremental improvements in work habits and the ability to withstand criticism. Any change in a persons' fortune is the visible manifestation of all of that deep preparation over time.

Challenge:

Stop fixating on what other people are saying and doing on the money, the connections, the outward appearances. Instead, look inward. Focus on the smaller internal changes that lay the groundwork for a much larger change in fortune. It is the difference between grasping at an illusion and immersing yourself in reality. You are unique and out of your uniqueness you have been drawn to your area of interests. Your life task is to return to that uniqueness. You need to look at what you've been doing that inspires you. Keep moving on, welcoming mistakes and learning. The goal you are after is learning and the acquisition of skills. As you adopt this internally driven mindset you become immersed in the present and at some time a point is reached that you are prepared for what's next.

Tapping in Meditation:

My purpose today is to transform myself through my work. I attract opportunities to myself. I connect to who I am rather than run away. I am on a journey of self-discovery.

Journal Notes:

Day/Year

Day/Year

Day/Year

December 23
Chimps versus Humans—The Self Control Comparison

It's a competition you don't see every day: 19 chimpanzees versus 40 humans. Not just any humans, students from Harvard and the Max Planck Institute in Leipzig, Germany. The challenge: Delay the gratification of an immediate snack to win more food. The temptation: grapes for the chimps, and M&Ms for the humans. First the choice is between 2 and 6 of the rewards. This was an easy choice and both chimps and humans agreed 6 is better than 2. Then the researchers complicated the choice. Each competitor was given the opportunity to eat two treats immediately or wait 2 minutes for 6. The study was published in 2007. It was the first to directly compare the self-control of chimpanzees and humans. The results: Chimps chose to wait for the larger reward an impressive 72% of the time, the students only 19%.

Is this surprising? No. It has to do with the size of the human prefrontal cortex. This part of the human brain is significantly larger than the chimps and combined with language it allows you to rationalize bad decisions and promise that you'll be better tomorrow. Many of the problems you have with temptation have to do with the way that you think about the future. You have a genetic predisposition to favor the present over delay.

The chimps acted rationally despite having brains 1/3rd the size of humans. They maximized their gains with a very little personal cost of just 120 seconds delay. The humans' choice was irrational. Economists call this delay discounting. Ph.D. Kelly McGonigal, Stanford professor, states, "The longer you have to wait for a reward, the less it is worth to you. Even small delays can dramatically lower the perceived value." With just a mere 2 second delay 6 M&Ms became less worth then 2 immediately. Delay discounting is why you choose immediate satisfaction at the cost of future happiness. You take what you want when you want it and put off until tomorrow whatever you don't want to face today. The brain's reward system evolved to favor immediate rewards. When the genetic coding for dopamine was being wired in a reward that was far off was irrelevant to daily survival. The adaptation that you needed was one that ensured that you snapped up rewards when they were available. The immediate reward triggers the older limbic area of the brain, the primitive emotional area, and its dopamine induced desire. Future rewards don't stimulate this area of the brain.

Challenge:
Ask yourself what is the immediate payoff for giving in to your temptation? What is the long term cost? Is this a fair trade? Give yourself an automatic 10 second delay before giving in. Your brain will now view this as a future reward. This biological impulse to immediately gratify will be lessened. If after 10 seconds you still want to engage in the behavior allow yourself to do it.

Tapping in Meditation:
My purpose today is to control my choices and I do. Self-control is a key factor in achieving success. I can't control everything but I can control the choices I make.

Journal Notes:

Day/Year	
Day/Year	
Day/Year	
Day/Year	
Day/Year	

December 24

Listening at Christmas and Always

A bearded jolly man was invited to help out with his children's school's Christmas Fair and he decided to have a go at being Father Christmas. He had recently grown his first full beard and thought that he would enter into the role by rubbing flour into his growth. This added to the authenticity of his look and he sure did draw a lot of customers to his booth at the fair.

He was enjoying himself enormously, bringing a sense of magic to so many young children, but he was mystified by one young boy who paid for a second visit and then astonishingly for a third. The presents that were offered were really pretty pitiful, so he asked him why he was coming to back to visit him so often. He answered simply: "I just love talking to you."

It was then that he realized that, in many households, parents do not encourage their children to talk and really listen to them.

Challenge:
This is a lesson to take with you throughout your life. So, at home, at work, socially, always encourage family, friends, colleagues to talk about themselves and their feelings—and really listen. Happy Holidays.

Tapping in Meditation:
My purpose today is to allow the New Year to make my dreams come true. I celebrate and appreciate my family, friends and strangers alike. My life helps make this a world where people can thrive.

Journal Notes:

Day/Year	
Day/Year	
Day/Year	
Day/Year	
Day/Year	

December 25

The Doll and the Rose—Author Unknown

I was in a store and I saw a cashier hand a little boy his money back saying "I'm sorry, you don't have enough money to buy this doll." Then the little boy turned and said, "Granny, are you sure I don't have enough money?" The old lady replied: "You know that you don't have enough money to buy this doll, my dear." Then she asked him to stay there for 5 minutes while she went to look around. The little boy was still holding the doll in his hand. I walked toward him and I asked him who he wished to give this doll to. "It's the doll that my sister loved most and wanted for this Christmas. She was so sure that Santa Claus would bring it to her." I replied to him that maybe Santa Claus will bring it to her after all, and not to worry. But he replied to me sadly. "No, Santa Claus can't bring it to her where she is now. I have to give the doll to my mommy so that she can give it to my sister when she goes there. My sister has gone to be with God. Daddy says that Mommy is going to see God very soon too, so I thought that she could take the doll with her to give it to my sister."

My heart nearly stopped. The little boy looked up at me and said: "I told daddy to tell mommy not to go yet. I need her to wait until I come back from the mall." Then he showed me a photo of him where he was laughing. He then told me "I want mommy to take my picture with her so she won't forget me. I quickly reached for my wallet and said to the boy. "What if we checked again, just in case you do have enough money?" "OK" he said "I hope that I have enough." I added some of my money to his without him seeing. There was enough for the doll and even some spare money. The little boy said "I asked yesterday before I slept for God to make sure I have enough money to buy this, He heard me! I also wanted to have enough money to buy a white rose for my mommy, my mommy loves white roses." A few minutes later, the old lady came again and I left with my basket. I finished my shopping in a totally different state from when I started. I couldn't get the little boy out of my mind. Then I remembered a local newspaper article 2 days ago, which mentioned of a drunk man in a truck, who hit a car, where there was one young lady and a little girl. The little girl died right away, and the mother was left in a critical state. Was this the family of the little boy? Two days after this encounter, I read that the young lady had passed away. I bought a bunch of white roses and I went to the funeral home. She was there, in her coffin, holding a beautiful white rose in her hand with the photo of the little boy and the doll placed over her chest. I left the place, teary-eyed, feeling that my life had been changed forever.

Challenge:

There are many lessons in this story, love, appreciation, unselfishness, faith and giving. Notice how it was the giving that changed this man's life.

Tapping in Meditation:

My purpose today is to have awareness and appreciation of what I have and the freedom that I have to hope for an even better future.

Journal Notes:

Day/Year	
Day/Year	
Day/Year	

December 26

Values Clarification

If you're fortunate enough to have today off this is a perfect time to set aside some reflection time and do this values clarification exercise. This will be particularly helpful in the formation of your business plan for next year.

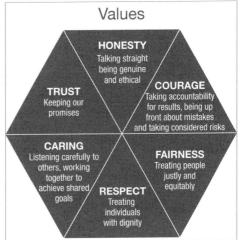

Values

HONESTY
Talking straight being genuine and ethical

TRUST
Keeping our promises

COURAGE
Taking accountability for results, being up front about mistakes and taking considered risks

CARING
Listening carefully to others, working together to achieve shared goals

RESPECT
Treating individuals with dignity

FAIRNESS
Treating people justly and equitably

Challenge:

Look at snapshots in time when life was really good. Those fond memories are times when a value was being honored.

Look at a time when you were particularly upset or angry. Look at feelings which caused the anger. Turn those feelings over and you will find a value that was being suppressed.

Use future self-visualization to find values. Attend your own 90th birthday party. What would people be saying about you? What would you want them to say about you?

1. Make a list of 12-20 values. Prioritize the top ten. This is just the first draft. Values show up over time, not simply in one sitting.
2. Next, evaluate how fully you are honoring those values by scoring them on a scale of zero to ten. Ask yourself what you would need to do to go to a score of ten.

Sample values include: Achievement, adventure, altruism, autonomy clarity, commitment, community, completion, connecting, creativity, emotional health, environment, freedom, fun, honesty, humor, independence, intimacy, joy, knowledge, money, morality, nature, prosperity, relationships, religion, responsibility, security, self-esteem, service, sex, space, spirituality, stability, support, thought, trust, truth, uniqueness, vision, wealth, wisdom.

My top 10 are:

1.	6.
2.	7.
3.	8.
4.	9.
5.	10.

Tapping in Meditation:

My purpose today is to keep my thoughts positive because they become my words. My words become my habits and they are driven by my values. My values drive my destiny.

Journal Notes:

Day/Year	
Day/Year	
Day/Year	
Day/Year	

December 27
Championship Skydiver Weighs in on Arrogance

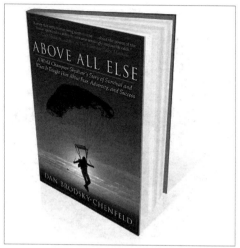

Dan Brodsky-Chenfeld, (Dan BC), is a world champion skydiver and author of "Above All Else". He has been an inspiration to many with his story of nearly dying in a skydiving aircraft accident and his comeback to with a world championship. Dan gives this bit of self reflection that may be helpful to you as you close out your year. In Dan's words, arrogance is an interesting trait. Few things are as annoying as arrogant people. After catching myself behaving arrogantly, and disliking it in myself even more than I did anyone else, I started thinking about it and tried to figure out where it was coming from. Here is what I learned.

Arrogance is not usually a display of true self confidence. It is more often a display of insecurity. It is a strategy we use, sometimes subconsciously, to convince ourselves that we are as self confident as we wish we were, as we want to be.

At times we all feel scared, nervous and not ready to perform. Allowing this fear to take over and dictate our behavior only weakens us. Rather than giving into fear some of us try to psych ourselves up by acting more confident than we actually are. Though this can sometimes result in obnoxious, arrogant behavior the intentions are good and it is far better for our performance than cowering in the corner in fear.

True self confidence is not something you have to display for others. It is something you hold within, something that calms and strengthens you, something you feel deep inside with certainty so there is no need to try and convince others around you. We may at times need to convince ourselves to have the self confidence we deserve (or may not deserve but still need). And I have no doubt that acting like the confident person we want to be helps us to actually become that confident person. But I think it's better to do it quietly in your own heart, in a calm, humble manner rather than in a public display. It will be much more convincing to yourself and those around you. And much less obnoxious."

Challenge:
Dan would be happy to know that he is correct, there is scientific evidence that proves that the thoughts you have do manifest into real matter. Today, notice having any less than powerful thoughts and immediately correct them to the best possible version of yourself.

Tapping in Meditation:
My purpose today is to acknowledge how powerful my thoughts are and guard them closely. My words have awesome power. In my thoughts and words I create my own strengths.

Journal Notes:

Day/Year	
Day/Year	
Day/Year	
Day/Year	
Day/Year	

December 28

Business-Life Planning

Before the end of the year make sure you have a business plan. There is a very high correlation between having a plan, setting goals, having metrics and overall success and fulfillment. Here are the questions that I use for business planning.

1. What product or service will you provide?
2. What unique benefits do you offer to differentiate from others?
3. Who is your ideal customer? How can you find them?
4. What will they want to buy from you?
5. Who are your competitors? What are their strengths and weaknesses? What are your opportunities?
6. How do you want to be known in the marketplace? What are the attributes of your product/service?
7. How will you get word out to your target market? What methods will you use?
8. How will you determine the best ways to use your limited dollars on marketing?
9. How will you develop your marketing mix?
10. What outcomes/goals do you have for marketing?

Evaluate Last Year.
1. Where are the numbers? How did you do versus plan to do?
2. What worked?
3. What did not work?
4. What will you measure specifically for next year? How will you know you had a great year?
5. Are there any strategic alliances or partnerships that you need to develop or enhance for next year?

Additional Considerations:
1. What keeps you up at night?
2. If you had to set your priorities now, what are your top three objectives?
3. What is the impact that you are seeking?
4. What market share increase do you want?
5. How are you to be evaluated in terms of the results of this intervention?
6. What would be the impact if you did nothing?
7. What does this mean to you personally?
8. What is the status quo now costing the company annually?
9. What is the status quo now costing you annually?

Challenge:

Did you deliver on your promises to your customers this year? How will you know if you do for next year? Complete your business plan by New Year's Eve!

Tapping in Meditation:

My purpose today is to precisely plan for my future. The best way to predict the future is to invent it. I am always well prepared.

Journal Notes:

Day/Year	
Day/Year	
Day/Year	

December 29

The 100 Year Plan

My friend and colleague Bruce Wright is a very sought after financial and estate planning expert. I credit Bruce with the 100 year plan concept. The most common definition of estate planning is, "when you're dead, how are we going to divide up your stuff?" That's level 1 estate planning. Level 2 is, "How do you generate maximum living benefits from your estate during your lifetime, and then how do you most effectively distribute your estate to your heirs after you pass away?" There is even a higher level, Level 3. Level 3 is the big picture. "What is your 100-year plan? What are you going to do while you are alive to fulfill your 100-year plan, and how is it going to be carried out after you are gone?" With the 100-year plan you are creating a legacy while you are alive and furthering that legacy after you are gone.

Challenge:

Step One: Gather and internalize information on true goal setting. In order to have any real power, your goals must be based on your deepest values, passions, dreams and desires. What are the really meaningful things you have or would like to have more of in your life? Imagine that you were given only one year to live. What would you do differently than you are doing now? Imagine yourself attending your own funeral. What would you want family and friends to say about you, your life, your contributions to family and community, the mark or legacy you left behind, the difference you made in the world? This is the type of thought process that must go into establishing true goals and a 100-year plan. As you begin to set goals, you should realize that goals fall into two very important categories—left brain and right brain.

Right Brain Questions: Do you spend your time doing what you really want to do? Are you spending your time and talents on the most important things possible? Is there a cause you would like to be involved in? Do you have any dreams you have not yet accomplished? If you could waive a magic wand and create the perfect situation during your lifetime and beyond, what would it look like? Put this into writing.

Left Brain Questions: How much of your estate do you want to pass on and to whom? Do you want your heirs to receive a lump sum or benefits over a period of time? When and how much? Are you afraid that a large inheritance will ruin your heirs? Do you want your heirs to receive any benefits while you are alive? Would you like to direct would be tax dollars away from the government and direct them instead to worthy causes?

Additional Consideration: What amount of assets do you need to accumulate before it is enough? How long will you wait before you make the transition from increasing your estate to enjoying your estate? How long do you intend to keep working?

Tapping in Meditation:

My purpose today is to leave a legacy of good deeds. I ensure that my life is an inspiration to others by the choices I make daily.

Journal Notes:

Day/Year	
Day/Year	
Day/Year	
Day/Year	

December 30

What If?

I love the phrase that has been made common by neuro linguistic practitioners, "what would happen if?" and "What causes or prevents?" Neuro linguistic is just like it sounds, nervous system and language. Actually language is the asset of the brain. It's the formation of neurons (neurogenesis) and the laying down of connected patterns or memories. These become attitudes and habits.

This is referred to as re-framing. It's a pattern interrupt. It's a way of disrupting neurological connections and rewiring the brain. Since your reality is in your own mind why not exercise your control over your thinking. Why not reinforce the desired reality rather than the undesirable difficulty? Re-framing is the basis of comedy. The reason that jokes are funny is because the frames are switched in the middle. A man walks into a pet store and sees a large angry dog. He asks the cashier, "Does your dog bite?" and the cashier says "No." The dog then bites the man. After several staff pull the dog off of the customer he says "I thought you said your dog doesn't bite!" and the cashier says; "That's not my dog!"

Re-framing with "what if" is a way to release creativity. Our shut down starts in the 1st grade by the way you are taught. What is 5+5? There is only one answer 10. What if you were asked the question differently, what two numbers add up to 10? Now you have many more answers. The way you ask the question determines the types of answers you get. The questions you ask contain the frame for which the answers will fall. The Copernican revolution came about by re-framing the question, what if the earth is not the center of the universe what if the sun was the center. This opened up the entire study of astronomy.

Challenge:

Today, every time you catch yourself or someone else thinking or saying "I can't do something", immediately interrupt that thought with one or both of these thoughts or statements, "What if you could?" Or "What stops or prevents you?" Then live into the new possibility. Make it real!

Tapping in Meditation:

My purpose today is to live my life to the fullest. I give my best in everything. I do what I love. I am thrilled with my spiritual and mental growth through this program and I continue to improve. I am looking forward to the New Year.

Journal Notes:

Day/Year	
Day/Year	
Day/Year	
Day/Year	
Day/Year	

December 31

Prescription for Living from the Good Doctors

The average person considers their life boring or uninspiring because they've made little or no attempt to gain personal growth that will inspire them. They are hypnotized by their environment—by television, though unattainable ideals of physical appearance, beauty and wealth that most struggle to become but cannot. So most people live their lives in resignation and mediocrity.

However, you know there is something more. You rise above the surface and seek your purpose in life. Why are you here? Dr. William Teller says that most people don't affect reality in a consistent substantial way because they don't believe that they can. He says, "They write their intention and then they erase it because they think that it's silly. I mean, I can't do that. It really comes down to the fact that they believe they can't do it."

Candace Pert, Ph.D., "Thought alone can completely change the body. Each cell is alive and each cell has a consciousness particularly if we define consciousness as the point of view of an observer." "You are living in a world where all you see is the tip of the iceberg. The immense tip of a quantum mechanical iceberg." John Hagelin, Ph.D.

You are much more than you think you are. You can influence the environment, the people, space itself. You can influence the future. You are responsible for all those things. You and your surroundings are not separate, you are connected to everything. You are not alone. It may be necessary for you to let go to get more. To let go of attachments, to let go of your will, of your selfishness, of doing it your way. Are you willing to do that?

Dr. Teller, "It's time for a course correction on your trajectory along the path of your adventure, and that course correction is the movement to a new paradigm."

Challenge:

I challenge you to pursue knowledge without any interference of your addictions. If you do that you will manifest knowledge in reality and your body will experience it in new ways. The way your brain is wired you only see what you believe is possible. You match patterns that already exist within yourself through conditioning. It's time to change patterns and possibilities. What is possible for you for next year?

Tapping in Meditation:

My purpose today is to be true to myself. Dr. Zeus, "Oh, the Places You'll Go!" I have brains in my head, feet in my shoes. I can steer myself any direction I choose. I'm on my own and I know what I know, and I am the guy who'll decide where to go! HAPPY NEW YEAR!

Journal Notes:

Day/Year	
Day/Year	
Day/Year	
Day/Year	
Day/Year	

About the Author

BOB DAVIES

America's Performance Coach

All of Bob's education has led him to where he is today. It all started in high school where his football coach told him that if he gained 30 pounds he could get a football scholarship. Bob did just that and did get a football scholarship to Rutgers University.

After graduating from Rutgers in 1975 Bob taught and coached at Cresskill High School in New Jersey for two years. From there he went on to graduate school at Springfield College where he received his masters degree in Psychology. He also was a graduate assistant coach in football and wrestling.

Bob was hired as the head football and wrestling coach at the California Institute of Technology in Pasadena in 1979 and has remained in California to this day. While at Cal Tech Bob had the opportunity to research and study Roger Sperry, who was awarded the Nobel Prize for his right and left brain research in 1982. After one year at Cal Tech, Bob was hired at Cal State Fullerton as an assistant football and strength and conditioning coach. Bob resigned from Cal State Fullerton in 1983 and has been helping entrepreneurs ever since.

While at Cal State Fullerton his performance techniques helped an average group of athletes win two conference championships. He was also the "mind coach" for the Women's gymnastics team where his techniques helped them to consistently rank in the top five nationally. He was invited to present to the Stanford Cardinal women's gymnastics team and helped them to have their highest national ranking ever.

Bob also is one of the leading and most innovative one-on-one personal and professional coaches. He had a hand in the creation of the industry of coaching and served on the original board of the International Coaches Federation. He was one of the first coaches to be certified as a Master Certified Coach, M.C.C. in September, 1998.

Bob is married to Jenifer, has three children, Danielle, Tyler, Emily, is an instrument rated pilot and a skydiver with over 2000 jumps.

There are always three pillars of Bob's coaching: health, business and personal.

Bob takes pride that his programs are based on a combination of the laws of science and the best practices of elite performers. Bob is constantly in research to stay on the leading edge of human potential and learning.

Bob with Dr. Larry Cahill, Department of Neurobiology, University of California, Irvine, California

It was from this ongoing research that Bob discovered that what he and every other "expert" was teaching for health excellence was WRONG!

There is so much misinformation and deception that is profit driven and you can't count on government to have a fiduciary outlook on your behalf. There is no money in healthy people or dead people. The money is in keeping you dependent on sugar and flour and buying those products.

Just look around and you will see unhealthy people who are examples of an inflammatory response to the way that they are eating. On top of that no one has taught them how to eat, until Bob's program. This is a program of learning how the body responds to the way that you eat. Most of what is currently being taught is, at best, ineffective and, at worst, fraudulent and dangerous. You do not count calories, you do not eliminate food groups, you do not fast, you do not avoid fat, you do not eat six meals throughout the day and you do not exercise for weight management.

Bob's program will teach people what to eat, how much to eat, when to eat and when to stop. For the first time in their lives people will have a planned system for eating that does not require willpower and deprivation. This is the way that humans were designed to nourish their bodies. The results will be immediate and sustainable. This has a chance to be life changing.

The Davies Day Book is the curriculum for excellence that is designed to examine one behavioral concept per day. It is only through personal growth that you are able to maintain the impact of this program. This is both a program for performance excellence and has a core of weight management.

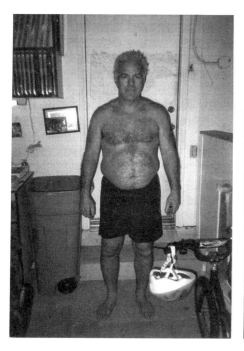 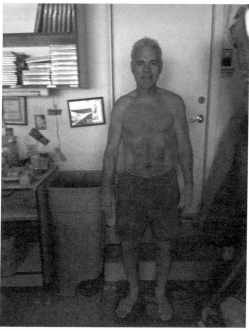

Before: 235 lbs

After: 175 lbs

Here is the formula, for the first 5 feet of height count 100 pounds. Each inch taller men add 7 pounds, women add 5 pounds and that's your normal range. If you're not in that range and you would like to be then this program is for you. Even if you do not have a weight management goal, this program will be of benefit to you. Your commitment to excellence starts today. It is the development of positive and healthy habits over time that will make the difference your quality of life!

Bob Davies

Bob Davies, M.Ed. Psychology, Springfield College
B.S. Health, Rutgers University
M.C.C. Master Certified Coach, ICF #1013

Index

Business Planning
Dec 3,4 The Year in Gear Questions 1-12, 13-22

C

Change
Jan 26 Small Changes—Large Results. The 1.2% Factor
May 23 Change—Metamorphosis or Gradual
May 24 Change, Easy Does It Or Else—The Wisdom of the Human Body
Nov 6 The Top 10 Mistakes of Behavior Change
Nov 10 Be the Change you Seek
Nov 22 The Mystery of Change

Coaching Commandments
Jan 8 What I can Control, I Must Control
Feb 19 What I can Control, I Must Control
Feb 7 Act as If Part I
Feb 8 Act as If Part II
Mar 31 What You Seek Also Seeks You
Apr 7 The Go-Givers-Core Principle I Service
Apr 8 Core Principle II—Synergy—Better as a Team
Apr 9 Core Principle III—I do What I say I Will Do
Apr 10 The Lesson of the Cart
Apr 23 The Power of the ANDS
Apr 26 Seed the Blue
May 8 The Lesson of the Landing Gear—Get Rid of Drag
May 9 Clean up Your Life—Get Rid of Clutter
May 16 Never Give Up
May 18 Inspect and Verify
May 19 Nick Saban and Aristotle—How You Do One Thing
May 25 Law of Accumulation—You've Got to Have Feedback—Blue Man
Jun 3 Take Responsibility and the 4 Core Principles
Jun 9 Always Give Great Effort—KOKO
Jun 22 Do Dogs Love Bones?
Jul 3 Who or What are You Tolerating?
Jul 12 Where Are You Being a Fraud—The Tell
Jul 16 Be Selfish—Put Yourself First
Jul 22 Be Uncomfortable Every Day
Jul 23 All the Way In or All the Way Out
Jul 24 All the Way In or All the Way Out—Holding Back
July 25 Dr. Seus—Oh The Places You'll Go—Progress Not Perfection

Communication
Jan 5 Be Precise with Precision Probing
Jan 6 Be Realistic Don't go from Zero to Hero
Jan 3 Making Commitments
Jul 19 Tell the Truth Faster!
Jul 20 Avoid Sloppy Communication
Jul 21 Effective Communication—3 Magic Phrases
Nov 1 Visual, Auditory, Kinesthetic—The Eyes Will Know
Dec 24 Listening at Christmas and Always

Competition
Sep 10 Society Says There are Winners and Losers
Oct 25 Collaboration Not Competition

Conformity
Oct 12 The Power of Non Conformity
Oct 13 The Herd Senses Danger

J

K

L

M

Measurement

Meditation

Mindset

Motivation

N

O

P

Peace of Mind

Perception

Personality

Personal Profiles

Philosophy

Q

R

Systems

Surrender

T

Time

U

V

Victim